# Madness and Distress in Music Education

*Madness and Distress in Music Education* offers an in-depth exploration of mental health and emotional distress in the context of music education, offering new ways of thinking about these experiences and constructing ways to support distress through affirming pedagogy, practices, and policies in music education. Centering the lived experiences of 15 people in a range of roles across music education who self-identify an issue with their mental health, the volume addresses impacts on both students and educators. The author draws on Mad Studies and disability studies to present new paradigms for thinking about Madness and distress in the music context. An essential resource for music educators, music education researchers, and preservice students seeking to understand the complexities of mental health in the music classroom, this book considers how people conceptualize their mental health, how distress impacts participation in music education, how music education may support or exacerbate distress, and what supports for distress can be implemented in music education.

**Juliet Hess** is Associate Professor of Music Education at Michigan State University. She is the author of *Music Education for Social Change* and co-editor of *Trauma and Resilience in Music Education*.

# Madness and Distress in Music Education
Toward a Mad-Affirming Approach

Juliet Hess

Designed cover image: © stellalevi / Getty Images

First published 2024
by Routledge
605 Third Avenue, New York, NY 10158

and by Routledge
4 Park Square, Milton Park, Abingdon, Oxon, OX14 4RN

Routledge is an imprint of the Taylor & Francis Group, an informa business

© 2024 Juliet Hess

The right of Juliet Hess to be identified as author of this work has been asserted in accordance with sections 77 and 78 of the Copyright, Designs and Patents Act 1988.

All rights reserved. No part of this book may be reprinted or reproduced or utilised in any form or by any electronic, mechanical, or other means, now known or hereafter invented, including photocopying and recording, or in any information storage or retrieval system, without permission in writing from the publishers.

*Trademark notice*: Product or corporate names may be trademarks or registered trademarks, and are used only for identification and explanation without intent to infringe.

ISBN: 978-1-032-66280-0 (hbk)
ISBN: 978-1-032-66278-7 (pbk)
ISBN: 978-1-032-66281-7 (ebk)

DOI: 10.4324/9781032662817

Typeset in Sabon
by Newgen Publishing UK

With deep gratitude to the 15 music educators who shared their experiences and ideas.

You make the world a better place.

# Contents

| | |
|---|---:|
| *Acknowledgments* | ix |
| Introduction: Madness and Distress in Music Education: Toward a Mad-Affirming Approach | 1 |
| 1 Just What Is Mad Studies and What Is It Doing in a "Nice" Field Like Music Education? | 24 |
| 2 Applying Models from Disability Studies to Experiences of Madness and Distress | 47 |
| 3 Conceptualizing and Discussing Mental Health Differences | 75 |
| 4 Benefits of Neurodivergence | 99 |
| 5 A Question of Visibility: Being "Out" in Music Education | 115 |
| 6 How Music (Education) Might Harm | 145 |
| 7 How Music (Education) Might Help | 179 |
| 8 Abolition and Distress | 213 |
| Conclusion: A Mad-Affirming Music Education | 248 |

| | |
|---|---|
| *Afterword* | *275* |
| *Appendix 1: A Note on Methods* | *277* |
| *Appendix 2: A Call for Activism* | *289* |
| *Notes on Sources* | *293* |
| *Index* | *294* |

# Acknowledgments

I am deeply grateful for the community that shaped this book. I would first like to offer immeasurable thanks and gratitude to the music educators who shared their ideas and experiences with me. You make the world a better place, and without you, this volume would not exist.

Numerous people contributed to this work by reading sections and providing feedback. First, I want to thank the participants for offering critique and suggestions on a draft that included their contributions. In addition, Deb Bradley, Christina DeJong, Teri Dobbs, Karin Hendricks, Michael Largey, Jesse Rathgeber, and Cara Stroud offered valuable insights that helped refine this work. I want to thank Julie Beauregard in particular for reading multiple versions of this book in its entirety and providing invaluable feedback and critique to push this project forward.

Since I began this project, being in conversation with many people has greatly informed my perspective. I appreciated the support I received in early thinking on this topic from Barbara Applebaum, Cara Bernard, Karin Hendricks, Jamie Magnusson, Jesse Rathgeber, Tawnya Smith, and Tanya Titchkosky. Lisa Laughman, Kelly Thomas and Joyce Weinberg also deeply influenced the way I approach this subject. In addition, I am grateful to Janet Barrett and one of the reviewers on my 2022 article on sanism in the *Bulletin of the Council for Research in Music Education* for asking me whether this work may, in fact, be a book. That review process planted the seed for this work.

I am also immeasurably grateful for my cheering section. In particular, I would like to thank Kristine Anderson, Laura Anderson, Barbara Applebaum, Julie Beauregard, Cara Bernard, Deb Bradley, Elizabeth Bucura, Mary Cohen, Elisa Dekaney, Rebecca DeWan, Teri Dobbs, Lori-Anne Dolloff, Alyssa Hadley Dunn, JoAnne Halpern, Karin Hendricks, Karen Howard, Michael Largey, Amy Lewis, Athena Madan, Jamie Magnusson, Nasim Niknafs, Jesse Rathgeber, Jen Shangraw, Tawnya Smith, Sandra Snow, Cara Stroud, Jennifer Thomas, Latasha Thomas-Durrell, Darrin Thornton, Linda Thornton, and Ruth Wright, as well as the Bravey Bunch. I have also appreciated the writing solidarity with Write Club, in particular Antía González Ben, Danielle Sirek, Jody Stark, Katie Tremblay, and Deanna Yerichuk. Your support has helped me see this project to fruition. I would also like to specifically thank the music education community at Michigan State University—both colleagues and graduate students—and the College of Music administration for supporting this project and facilitating a research leave in the spring of 2023.

Thank you to the entire Routledge team and Genevieve Aoki in particular for believing in this project from the beginning and supporting it through fruition. I would like to offer thanks as well to the two anonymous reviewers who provided immensely helpful feedback on the text.

On a personal note, love and thanks always to my family for the continual support and deep love and gratitude to my partner, Laura Anderson. I am immensely grateful for the community who helped to produce this work.

# Introduction
## Madness and Distress in Music Education: Toward a Mad-Affirming Approach

### Vignette 1

I receive an email from a music education major letting me know that they were just hospitalized for suicidality. They ask for grace on their assignments. I wish that this was the only time I had received such an email, but it is not. Grace is no problem. I wonder if they know that they did not have to disclose their situation to me—that grace is easy and never in short supply. I hope that they are okay and getting the care they need. I set a reminder to check on them weekly, as I have each time I have received such an email.

Another music education student struggles through a medication change. The meds were supposed to regulate but have actually *dys*regulated and left the student to deal with the fallout of an unfamiliar mind while somehow accomplishing their schoolwork. They are clearly receiving care, so there is really nothing additional for me to do. I know firsthand how unsettling medication changes can be. I again set a reminder to check in weekly.

### Vignette 2

I am bipolar. I am also a music teacher educator. In 2019, I was diagnosed with Bell's palsy—a palsy that affects one side of the face. The emergency room doctor prescribed the typical treatment—antivirals and high-dose steroids (prednisone) for 10 days. I knew steroids and bipolar do not mix and asked the doctor if I could go without. She understood the concern and suggested filling the prescription and seeing how I was the next day. (Bell's palsy often gets worse before it gets better.) She also said that steroids must be started in the first 48 hours to be of use. By the next day, it was clear to me from both the state of my face and from information online that I would have a better chance of recovery with the steroids if I started them, so I did. Steroids often wreak emotional havoc on sane people. When I took them, I started rapid cycling between mania and depression and fell into a series of mixed states. The experience was so severe that I wondered if I needed to take a leave of absence. It took 2 full months to find some stability, and I taught throughout.

**Vignette 3**

I was in my fourth year of teaching elementary and middle school music when Ryan entered my class. He was in fifth grade. At the beginning of the year, he was completely withdrawn. He did not talk much to other students and his affect was flat. I connected with his homeroom teacher to inquire about him. She had observed a similar flat affect and had been working to engage him and connect him with peers. I continued to pay attention to Ryan in class. A few weeks later, we began to study Ghanaian music. To provide historical context for the music, we were discussing colonialism in Ghana and movements toward independence in the mid-1900s across the African continent. That day, Ryan came into class a completely different person. He was bubbly and talking fast and contributed immensely to the discussion about the role of World War II in the overthrow of colonialism. He was knowledgeable, outgoing, and his affect was excited almost to the point of agitation. That day, Ryan presented so differently, I was startled. His affect felt manic and familiar to me as a bipolar teacher. I connected again with the homeroom teacher and this time also with the teacher responsible for convening school teams to support individual students. She asked me to observe and document Ryan's time in my classes.

**Vignette 4**

Sophomore music education students have a fieldwork component as part of a music education class that requires them to spend time in a kindergarten through 12th-grade (K–12) setting with students. During our regular fieldwork debrief time in class, one of the sophomore students is distraught. She has a high school placement and assists with the marching band. The previous day, she had encountered a student hiding in the changing room, upset about the short-sleeved band outfit. The sophomore student asked if she could help with anything. The girl showed her arms—full of fresh cuts—and asked the sophomore student to cover them with concealer so she could march. In our class, the student recounted that she had no idea what to do and that she had done as the girl requested. We followed up with the cooperating teacher, whom the sophomore student had already told, who then followed up with the principal and the high school student's parents (Hess, 2022, pp. 24–25).[1]

## Setting the Context

Madness and distress[2] thread through music education and are present, at times, in both students and teachers at all levels of education (Hess, 2022). Experiences of Madness and distress thus comprise an indelible part of music education. Researchers reported high levels of depression, burnout, anxiety, and stress among music students (Bernhard, 2005, 2007, 2010, 2021; Conway, Eros, Pellegrino, & West, 2010; Demirbatir, Bayram, & Bilgel, 2012; Koops & Kuebel, 2021; Kuebel, 2019; McConkey & Kuebel, 2022; Payne, Lewis, & McCaskill, 2020; Wristen, 2013). Demirbatir et al. (2012) observed in the Turkish context that when compared to medical students, music students reported higher levels of anxiety, depression, and stress. Research also shows that rates of mental health issues tended to be higher among musicians than in the general population (Kegelaers, Schuijer, & Oudejans, 2021). Given the pervasiveness of experiences of Madness and distress among people in music and music education, music educators must find ways to address these challenges.

Recently, the COVID-19 pandemic has exacerbated existing mental health issues and created new ones. Since the pandemic shutdowns began in the U.S. in March 2020, approximately one in four young adults has considered suicide, and 40.9% of people in the U.S. have reported at least one adverse symptom of mental health (Czeisler et al., 2020). In 2022, 49,000 people died by suicide in the U.S., an increase of 2.6% from 2021 (Singh, 2023). Forty percent of adults in the U.S. in June 2020 reported struggling with mental health or substance use (Czeisler et al., 2020). Indeed, Kola (2020) described the pandemic as a collective trauma. Moreover, the effects of this collective trauma have disproportionately impacted already minoritized and multiply minoritized communities (APM Research Lab Staff, 2020). President Biden highlighted mental health issues in the U.S. in his 2022 State of the Union address (Jacobson, 2022) because of their pervasiveness in both students (Radhakrishnan et al., 2022) and teachers (CDC Foundation, 2021).

During the pandemic, 24% of 1,325 music educators surveyed in a study of music teacher wellbeing reported severe levels of depression (Parkes, Russell, Bauer, & Miksza, 2021). At the preservice level, in a survey of 1,137 music education majors across the U.S., a substantial number of students reported moderate levels of depression and/or anxiety (Payne et al., 2020). In a smaller survey of music education majors, 23% of 226[3] students noted current treatment for a mental illness, and 36% of 225 students reported having been treated for a mental illness in the past (Koops & Kuebel, 2021). Experiences of Madness and distress profoundly and inevitably shape music education more so than historically recognized, particularly now and in the emergent future.

## A Note on Language Use

I have several priorities with my use of language throughout this book. Primarily, I use non-diagnostic language, except when participants themselves or the literature uses diagnostic language. I honor the different ways participants choose to identify their experiences of Madness and/or distress. I use the terms "Mad" and "Madness" throughout this book both to "claim disability" (Linton, 1998) and "reclaim madness" (Russo, 2001, 2016) as a politicized identity, rather than an individualized and pathologized identity. Following Cavar (2021), I "capitalize 'Mad' as a reclaimed identity and movement/field of study in order to distinguish it from the use of 'mad' as a common adjective." The use of this term further allows me to participate in Mad Studies—an "in/discipline" I explain briefly in this chapter, and thoroughly explicate in Chapter 1. The reclaiming of language that has previously been used pejoratively may serve as a means of empowerment (Clare, 1999). Russo (2001, 2016) wrote about the importance of reclaiming Mad identity from the psy- systems that shape it. I aim toward this work of reclaiming. I note that this move is contested, as varied degrees of privilege and oppression make reappropriation of this term differentially challenging and (im)possible for different people. As such, I honor participants' language choices throughout.

I also employ the word distress. Distress, as emotional suffering, constitutes part of the human experience (Beaupert & Brosnan, 2022, p. 122). Often pathologized as illness (Cantón, 2022; Fey & Mills, 2022; Sharma, 2022), distress is often deeply contextual, rooted in trauma and environmental factors (Cantón, 2022). In this book, distress does not mean illness, but rather an experience of suffering that ranges in severity and often emerges from environmental factors including trauma, oppression, poverty, and capitalism. Fey and Mills (2022) noted that in the U.K., distress differs across populations. They observed that people from Black and minority ethnic backgrounds, and people facing harsh economic conditions or living under austerity are more likely to experience emotional distress, receive a mental health diagnosis, and be harshly treated by mental health professionals (pp. 193–194). Such disparities are also true in North America (Meerai, Abdillahi, & Poole, 2016). Following Kadison and DiGeronimo (2004), emotional distress does not comprise "a personal weakness or character flaw" (p. 232). While the psy- professions often pathologize distress (Fey & Mills, 2022), I seek to normalize this common human experience and unsettle the artificially normalized and standardized way that society characterizes lived experience. Throughout, I do not pathologize. Instead, I take an affirming approach that recognizes strengths, resistance, endurance, resilience,[4] and survival in the context of a traumatic, toxic, and upsetting world (Maté & Maté, 2022). In centering so-called "marginal" experiences, I disrupt the very construct of "normal" or "typical" human experience.

Difference is often viewed as deficit in contrast with the so-called normative or dominant positionality. Indeed, dominant ideology often creates the perception of difference as lack. In his famous work *The Souls of Black Folk*, Du Bois (2007/1903) posed the question: "How does it feel to be a problem?" (p. 7). While the oppression that people with experiences of Madness and/or distress face (sanism) differs from racist oppression, this question nonetheless resonates in this sanist context and further points to the necessity of an intersectional analysis of sanist oppression. The medical model of disability facilitates a perception of disability as deficit, requiring medical intervention, management, and repair (Dobbs, 2012; Linton, 1998).[5] I do not align with this approach. I experience the language of "mental illness" as harmful, as it pathologizes and situates experiences of Madness and distress as problematic. Using non-medicalized language of Madness and distress, I situate these experiences apart from any notion of a functional deficit and instead, as part of the range of human responses to difficult experiences, contexts, systems, and circumstances. From this perspective, Madness and distress are social responses rather than individual pathologies, experiences to be understood as a social issue. Walker (2021) further distinguished between innate differences and differences that occur through brain-altering experiences such as trauma. I consider both possibilities in this book.

## A Music Education Conversation

This book centers the voices of people with experiences of Madness and/or distress to offer implications for music education regarding pedagogy and support. I also aim to build community and counter the isolation that can come with experiences of Madness and distress. Sharing the ideas, experiences, and philosophies of 15 music educators' experiences of Madness and/or distress lets others know they are not alone in their mental health experiences. As Brown (2021) argued, "we need to know we're not alone—especially when we're hurting" (p. 272). In this book I aim to facilitate a much-needed conversation in music education. In addition to their contributions to this book, many participants chose to be visible about their experiences in their communities and committed to leading conversations about this topic. As noted, mental health concerns have recently come to the forefront of societal consciousness (CDC Foundation, 2021; Radhakrishnan et al., 2022). People experience Madness and distress at all levels of music education—in K-12 schools, in preservice teacher education, among the music teacher population, during graduate study, and among higher education music faculty. The presence of these experiences across all levels of the field demands attention and discussion. Throughout, I use the term *musicking* following Small (1998) to describe the full range of possible musical engagements. These include but are not limited to creating, listening, performing, mixing, producing, and dancing. Like Small, I use musicking as a verb to note both the many facets of music-making and its relational nature.

**The Project**

As a music educator with both K-12 and higher education experience, I am deeply interested in finding ways to support individuals who experience Madness and/or distress, and believe that music education, when carefully facilitated, may serve to support emotional distress. In this project I spoke with 15 music educators (preservice students, in-service music educators, graduate students, music education professors, studio teachers—all adults) who self-identified an issue with their mental health. Literature illuminates the importance of listening to people with lived experiences of Madness and/or distress when making decisions about support and policy (Sweeney, 2016). I am interested in what practices music educators might put in place in our field and in classrooms to support individuals with experiences of Madness and/or distress. I am utilizing this project to create a mechanism for placing the knowledge(s) of individuals with lived experiences of Madness and distress at the center of the discussion. Through centering their contributions, I aim to construct ways to support Madness and distress through affirming pedagogy, practices, and policies in music education.

I specifically focus on several constructs: how people conceptualize their mental health; how distress may have impacted participation in music education; how music education currently addresses or fails to address experiences of Madness and distress; how people with experiences of Madness and/or distress navigate disclosure; how music and music education may have supported or exacerbated distress; what supports for distress may be useful to implement in music education; and how distress is surveilled. Four overarching questions oriented this research:

1. How do individuals in music education with experiences of Madness and/or distress describe their experiences with music and with mental health?
2. How do individuals in music education with experiences of Madness and/or distress conceptualize (their) mental health?

3. How might music education/music educators better support people with experiences of Madness and/or distress?
4. What aspects of music education might either ameliorate or exacerbate distress?

I ultimately develop implications for pedagogy and for institutions to better support students, teachers, and faculty/staff with experiences of Madness and/or distress.

At this juncture of collective trauma and emotional distress from the COVID-19 pandemic, I intend this project to support music teachers and professors as they support children, youth, and adults with experiences of Madness and distress through music. I also describe how music educators with experiences of Madness and/or distress across all levels might both support ourselves and be supported. Music can offer children, youth, and adults a profound tool for building resilience (Bradley & Hess, 2022; Hill, 2009; Rhodes & Schechter, 2014). Mapping the possible harm that music can create also becomes important for addressing mental health in music education. Music is uniquely positioned to support resilience (Bradley & Hess, 2022), and this project provides careful consideration of specific ways teachers and professors might enact pedagogy both to support their own needs and those of students.

Constructing a music education that accounts for Madness and distress is more imperative in this historical moment than ever. This project is geared toward preservice and in-service music educators as well as music teacher educators. Music educators need tools to understand and address emotional distress in the classroom, and I have shaped this project to provide those tools. While in this book I emphasize supporting individuals, I also situate discussion of resilience in the context of systems of oppression, and in relation to trauma. The implications I present for pedagogy, policy, and practice therefore address the effect of oppressive systems and contextual factors on people with experiences of Madness and/or distress. Following Andrzejewski (2023), I aim to find ways to make individual supports structural.

## Positionality

I identify as bipolar; I therefore come to this project as someone with lived experience of Madness and emotional distress. I thus situate myself as a member of the community with whom I am in conversation. I was diagnosed at age 18 after a tumultuous few years in high school. Over the last 28 years, I have experienced profound depressive periods lasting up to 13 months, mania and hypomania, and some particularly terrifying runs of mixed states.⁶ Something that has marked my journey has been my use of music. I use and have used music in equal measure to help and to harm myself when I am in emotional distress. My personal use of music in these ways has made me aware that music can work powerfully to soothe distress and can also serve to worsen it. Music's potential to both help and harm offered an impetus for this study. How might music educators help students find ways to use music to support themselves while resisting its harmful potential? Contemplating this question drove my work. In situating myself as bipolar, I also recognize my other intersections of identity. I am a white, middle-class, Jewish, queer, cis woman. While I am bipolar, my privilege in other identity categories and my longstanding ability to pass as "sane" means that I do not experience the discrimination and hate often targeted at BIPOC individuals with experiences of Madness and distress. Sanism disproportionately targets Mad people of color (see for example King, 2016; Meerai et al., 2016).

## Sanism and Stereotyping

Here I offer a brief introduction to the concept of sanism, which I elaborate in Chapter 1. Sanism involves "the systematic subjugation and oppression of people who have received 'mental health' diagnoses, or who are otherwise perceived to be 'mentally ill' (Perlin, 1992, 2003; Poole et al., 2012)" (LeBlanc & Kinsella, 2016, p. 62). Sanism heavily influences how people with experiences of Madness and distress perform themselves in society. It further intersects with other identity-based oppressions including racism, sexism, heterosexism, and ethnic bigotry, alongside other "isms" (Perlin, 2003, p. 536). Sanism is the context that people with experiences of Madness and distress navigate as we⁷ try to appear sane for the sake of bodily autonomy and livelihood (Hess, 2022).

Stereotypes of Madness also shape discourse surrounding mental health. I discuss stereotyping extensively in Chapter 1 but want to draw on two particular stereotypes in this introduction: the specter of the struggling artist and the "Mad musician." Much of the discourse about so-called "great" musicians and artists identified as "geniuses" involves struggles with Madness and distress. Sometimes the discourse goes so far as to suggest that the music/art is great *because* of the struggle, that struggling is an important part of the creative process. Chandler's (2013) article on Charles Mingus, for example, suggested that Mingus felt his music may have been richer because of his struggles with racial oppression and emotional distress. Jewel, too, credited her struggles with homelessness and anxiety as important facets of her success as an artist (Pelly, 2021; Pep Unlimited LLC, 2020). Black (2021) insisted that suffering, however, does not create art. Suffering does not necessarily beget art, nor is it desirable.

This stereotype is, in fact, dangerous. I am interested in finding ways for people to thrive while creating.

The second stereotype is that of the Mad genius musician. Rhodes (2015) described the "cliche of the reclusive composer who loses their mind over manuscript" as unhelpful. Yet these representations are pervasive in popular media and musician culture about musicianship. Many of the so-called "great" composers had experiences of Madness and/distress including Hector Berlioz, Edward Elgar, George Frideric Handel, and Robert Schumann (Redfield Jamison, 1993, p. 269), and these experiences of Madness are portrayed as central to the "greatness" of their creative output in public consciousness. Rhodes (2015) eschewed the myth of Madness and creativity. He argued instead that creativity can be supportive of Madness and distress, as opposed to the theory that Madness and distress provoke creativity. The image of the Mad genius musician portrays such musicians as almost divine or possessing a divine gift. Such representation is widespread (Rhodes, 2015). Following Rhodes, in this book I am compelled by how musicking (Small, 1998) may support people with experiences of Madness and/or distress.

## Grounding in Mad Studies

I situate this project in the "in/discipline" of Mad Studies, which emerged from longstanding activist movements that began in the latter half of the 20th century and continue today. Ingram coined the name Mad Studies in 2008, conceptualizing it as both a discipline and an "in/discipline" to preserve the unruliness and subversiveness of Madness—to not only "show the method in our madness" but also preserve "the madness in our method" (Ingram, 2016, p. 14). Mad activist movements centered people who self-identified as Mad and sought to center Mad experiences in discourse and praxis about Madness (Beresford & Russo, 2022; LeFrançois, Menzies, & Reaume, 2013; Russo & Sweeney, 2016). These movements aimed to reclaim Mad knowledge and experiences from psy- professionals (psychiatrists, psychologists, etc.) (LeFrançois et al., 2013; Menzies, LeFrançois, & Reaume, 2013) and, in doing so, refuse medicalized notions of Madness and distress. Situating this project in Mad Studies aids me in deliberately resisting sanist oppression and the stereotypes it produces and working toward understandings of experiences of Madness and distress that refuse constructions of illness, pathology, and deficit.

## Participants

This research features the experiences, perspectives, and philosophies of 15 music educators who held a range of identity positions. I interviewed

12 people who identified as white, two people who identified as Asian American, and one person who identified as mixed race (white and East Indian). Six women participated, one man, and seven people who identified as non-binary, trans, or gender expansive.[8] Participants occupied differing socioeconomic positions and had varied relationships to disability. Some participants identified their experiences of Madness and distress as a disability while others did not. Other participants disclosed physical disabilities; four identified as autistic, noting that they did not necessarily identify autism as disabling. While I did not ask about sexual orientation, seven people identified as LGBQ+ without prompting. Participants ranged in age from their 20s to 60s, including seven people in their 20s, two in their 30s, three in their 40s, one in their 50s, and two in their 60s. Participants were mostly based in the United States, with the exception of one participant from Canada, one from Western Europe currently living in the U.S., and one from New Zealand currently living in the U.S. Most participants chose to be identified in this book to receive credit for their ideas. One participant noted that she viewed being identified as a sign of solidarity with me and with others who are visible with their/our students about their/our experiences with Madness and distress. Five participants chose to use a pseudonym, and one participant chose to go by their first name only. I work to protect those participants' identities throughout this book by being deliberately vague about geography, specific achievements, and teaching positions. Appendix 1 offers further details and descriptions, and I more fully introduce each music educator at first mention in the book.

This group of participants is small and certainly skewed in relation to race, gender, age, geography, and disability. As such, it is not necessarily representative of a broader population, nor do I claim it to be. In conversations about Madness and distress, however, individuals' experiences and perspectives are extremely important. While mental health's relationship to music has been extensively discussed in the field of music therapy, these conversations occur far less frequently in music education. Moreover, much of the work to date has been quantitative and, as such, while providing a larger picture of the relationship of music to mental health, fails to capture the stories of individuals and their experiences of Madness and distress in music education. Attending to these stories here provides an entry point to wider discussions of Madness and distress in our field.

An important consideration that emerged from this research is the role of privilege in conversations about Madness and distress. Severe stigma shapes the ability to disclose experiences related to Madness and distress. Moreover, being able to "pass" as sane makes disclosure safer (Wolframe, 2013). Multiple participants noted that disclosure is easier when a person holds privilege across other sites of identity. In order for minoritized groups, and in particular racialized groups, to feel safe to disclose their experiences, significant work must take place toward destigmatization and normalization of experiences of Madness and distress.

Participants described a wide range of experiences of Madness and distress. These include, in their words: depression, anxiety, mania, panic, psychosis, suicidality, and intrusive thoughts. Participants also identified differences related to attention, eating, sleeping, self-control, perfectionism, and self-medicating. Individuals had differing views on the use of medication, and multiple participants had experiences of both voluntary and involuntary hospitalization for their Madness or distress. Many identified that their experiences of Madness and distress were impacted by social factors such as trauma or high stress levels. I purposefully generalize these to avoid attaching experiences that potentially hold stigma to specific individuals, particularly since many of the participants chose to be identified.

Importantly, all participants have backgrounds in music education. Beyond the larger discipline of music, the public widely perceives music as an unequivocal positive. Those of us in music and music education know, however, that trauma and harm are prevalent in the field (Bradley & Hess, 2022). Talking to people who are insiders in music education is thus important for understanding how music education both helps and harms emotional wellbeing. At the time I collected data for this study: four participants were in preservice music education programs; two were classroom music teachers; two were graduate students in music education; three taught music education at the postsecondary level; two were applied studio teachers; and three have music education backgrounds but are currently in social work or peer support careers. Of this last group, one is also a studio teacher, and another is a substitute music teacher. Participants' perspectives thus represent multiple relationships to music education.

I spoke with each participant in an individual interview lasting from one-and-a-half to three hours, and later conducted focus groups with multiple participants. I organized focus groups both by role in music education (e.g., preservice music teachers, studio teachers, higher education participants, social workers or peer support specialists with experience as music educators) and by identity (e.g., a non-binary, trans, and gender expansive individuals group). Because of the sensitive nature of this study's topic, most participants were either known to me personally or known to someone who knows me well. I shared my own bipolar diagnosis with all participants and was forthcoming, when relevant, about my experiences. I encouraged participants not to recount experiences that might upset them in an effort to avoid triggering any traumatic responses. In focus groups, we discussed the importance of confidentiality, as groups typically included a mix of people who chose to be identified in this book and those who chose to use a pseudonym. I discuss my methods and choices more extensively in Appendix 1.

## A Question of Systems

While I focus on the stories and experiences of individuals, I aim to do so in the context of the systems that shape these experiences. The interlocking structures of sexism, heterosexism, racism, cissexism, ableism, classism, ageism, and religious oppression among others enmesh with sanism to shape the possibilities for individuals with experiences of Madness and distress. Recognizing the role of oppressive systems in this work allows for emphasis on dismantling structures of oppression while attending to individuals. In putting forward the experiences, perspectives, and philosophies of these 15 individuals, I aim to simultaneously unsettle sanist structures and disrupt interlocking oppressive systems that silence stories of people with experiences of Madness and distress.

Resilience is often conceptualized at the individual level. Discourse about resilience is frequently steeped in neoliberalism (Evans & Reid, 2014; Hess, 2019; Saltman, 2015) and encourages individuals to "bounce back" from oppression and traumatic events. In invoking Mad Studies, I take an approach to resilience that acknowledges systemic oppression including sanism and works against these structures. Rather than calling upon individuals to be resilient despite the adversities they face, I advocate for collective resistance to, and abolition of, oppressive systems to give individuals the opportunity to thrive rather than urging self-sufficient "recovery." While agency can be important in discussions of Madness and distress, in my focus on systems, I prioritize implications for practice, pedagogy, and policy. In earlier work, I privileged a focus on dismantling systems of oppression over fostering individual resilience (Hess, 2019). I now view these ideas as a "both/and." As (music) educators, we need to work against societal systems and structures of oppression while also educating individuals on ways to be resilient. Attending to experiences of Madness and distress requires a dual effort that both cares for individuals and simultaneously dismantles oppressive systems. I take this dual approach to resilience throughout the book.

## An Interdisciplinary Approach

My approach to considering these issues is interdisciplinary. While I situate this project in Mad Studies within music education, I also draw on literature from disability studies, music therapy, anti-oppression theorizing across multiple sites of identity, sociology, education, and psychology. This rich base of literature allows for complexity in the theorizing of the lived experiences of these 15 individuals and draws connections between multiple bodies of literature that provide understanding of such experiences. Furthermore, participants' experiences complicate, ameliorate, and confound the literature.

## Music Educators, Not Therapists

I direct this book toward music educators with the full recognition that music educators do not have therapeutic training, nor should we act as therapists. Given the prevalence of music students and teachers with experiences of Madness and/or distress, however, music educators would do well to shape our pedagogy in ways that support people with such experiences. Drawing on the philosophies, ideas, and experiences of these 15 music educators, I offer possibilities for pedagogy, practice, and policy that fall firmly in the purview of music education and do not venture into the therapeutic realm. As music educators, we must "stay in our lane" and effect change and support in ways congruent with our skill set and education.

## A Contrapuntal Methodology

In this project, I engaged a contrapuntal methodology (Said, 1993) drawing on qualitative methods (see Appendix 1). I have elsewhere theorized Said's contrapuntal methodology extensively (see Hess, 2016), so will only briefly summarize the ideas here. A literature scholar, activist, and accomplished pianist, Said often wrote of music (for example Said, 2006, 2008). His contrapuntal methodology emerged explicitly from Western classical music counterpoint in all its intricacies. Said's text-based contrapuntal methodology compels reading canonic literature as a "polyphonic accompaniment to the expansion of Europe" (Said, 1993, p. 60).

> As we look back at the cultural archive, we begin to reread it not univocally but *contrapuntally*, with a simultaneous awareness both of the metropolitan history that is narrated and of other histories against which (and together with which) the dominating discourse acts. In the counterpoint of Western classical music, various themes play off one another, with only a provisional privilege being given to any particular one; yet in the resulting polyphony there is concert and order, an organized interplay that derives from the themes, not from a rigorous melodic or formal principle outside the work.
> 
> (Said, 1993, p. 51, emphasis in original)

Said committed to reading anti-colonial texts alongside the canon to provide a counterpoint to dominant colonial and hegemonic ways of knowing—to read Frantz Fanon alongside Jane Austen (p. 60) to situate hegemonic and colonial culture in juxtaposition with its counterhegemonic and anti-colonial counterpart.

> The point is that contrapuntal reading must take account of both processes, that of imperialism and that of resistance to it, which can be done by extending our reading of the texts to include what was once forcibly excluded—in *L'Etranger*, for example, the whole previous history of France's colonialism and its destruction of the Algerian state, and the later emergence of an independent Algeria (which Camus opposed).
> (Said, 1993, pp. 66–67)

The work I undertake in this book is distinctly contrapuntal. Sanism pervades music education practices as a dominant oppressive structure. While discussions of emotional wellbeing occur more frequently as a result of the COVID-19 pandemic, experiences of Madness and distress remain on the periphery. Recognizing these experiences as profound ways of knowing offers a powerful counterpoint to sanist practices. In this book, I center the voices of people with experiences of Madness and distress to trouble and resist sanism in music education. Said's (1993) call to read Fanon alongside Austen compels the reader to consider the anti-colonial alongside the colonial, thus situating the responsibility with the reader. The anti-colonial texts he elaborated make what he called the "voyage in" (p. 239) in opposition to imperialism. In employing a contrapuntal methodology, the responsibility rests with the reader/listener to attend to the voices of people with experiences of Madness and distress amidst the pervasive sanism of music education practices.

To return to counterpoint as a musical practice, I look to Dutch composer and musicologist de Groot (2005), who examined polyphony in Said's writings. De Groot emphasized the role of responsibility inherent in polyphony. For de Groot, polyphony constitutes the "simultaneous unfolding of two or more different voices, each with its own identity, and at the same time each with a 'responsibility' to the other and for the *ensemble* of voices" (de Groot, 2005, p. 221, emphasis in original). To elaborate this "responsibility," he drew on composer Boulez for whom contrapuntal voices "shape each other (e.g. in melodic and rhythmic complementarity), and contribute to the articulation of the overall texture and of overall processes (in particular, in the dimension of harmonic structure)" (Boulez, 1963/1971, p. 118, as cited in de Groot, 2005, p. 222). De Groot argued that both the responsibility and the ability to respond mean that the voices may be perceived as "transforming each other continuously" (p. 223). In proposing that music educators attend to those with experiences of Madness and distress, I propose a music education that offers a counterpoint to dominant practices. Moreover, my aim is transformation. Through centering participants' voices, I elucidate ways that such counterpoints to dominant practices make possible a transformation of practices that uphold pervasive sanism in music education. Ashcroft and Ahluwalia (2001) observed that:

> [a] Saidian strategy of resistance is the ability to make the "voyage in," to write back to imperialism. This is possible because of the potential for humans to negate their experiences, to imagine another world, a better world in which the colonisers and the colonised work towards liberation.
>
> (p. 113)

This study's participants made the voyage in to resist dominant music education practices toward a music education that better serves music educators, scholars, and students with experiences of Madness and distress. In writing back to sanism, I attend to people with experiences of Madness and distress to imagine another world—a better world.

To employ Said's (1993) contrapuntal methodology, I need to account for three important issues. First, Said situated his work in relation to imperialism and colonialism. To attend instead to sanism and sanist practices thus constitutes a significant change of context. Said attended to the hegemonic nature of imperialism and colonialism and worked against it through engaging with anti-colonial texts alongside the canon. His "voyage in" was thus explicitly counterhegemonic. In challenging sanism, I recognize its hegemonic dimensions and likewise position this work as counterhegemonic. This parallel is not sufficient, however, as it may create an erasure of colonial dynamics. Throughout this book I therefore attend to the multiple systems of oppression that intersect with sanism to create hegemonic dynamics for participants in music education.

I also recognize the dynamics of colonial psychiatry—the export and imposition of Western notions of Madness, distress, and "illness" to (formerly and presently) colonized countries (Fernando, 2014). Groups in these countries often conceptualize ideas of both health/illness and mind/body vastly differently from the West (Fernando, 2014). Carstairs and Kapur (1976) noted "What is odd or distressful or harmful to members of one cultural group may not be so regarded by members of another one" (pp. 11–12, as cited in Fernando, 2014, p. 51). Yet the West, and colonial forces specifically, impose conceptualizations of illness and distress on non-Western people(s). In employing Said's counterpoint to respond to sanism, I acknowledge the historical and present coloniality present in the psy- disciplines. Participants in this study predominantly reside in the U.S. Correspondingly, I do not aim to impose any U.S.-centric implications on other geographies or peoples. Implications from this work may provide insights globally but are not universal. I call for reader attention to the specificity of context in making decisions about implications. Given the colonial history of psychiatry, I do not aim to impose these ideas in contexts or cultures in which basic conceptualizations of Madness and distress do not align.

Second, Said made his case for contrapuntal methodology by relying on readers to engage with anti-colonial *texts* alongside the canon of literature, and not necessarily with lived experiences. His example of reading Fanon alongside Austen, however, engaged Fanon's lived experiences in counterpoint to the fictional worlds Austen created, rooted in her lived experiences. To make the leap from texts to lived experiences perhaps represents only a small step. The lived experiences of participants recounted in this book provide a textual representation of a verbal counterpoint to dominant music education practices. Engaging with them makes the "voyage in" in ways that align with Said's (1993) approach.

Finally, as I have argued elsewhere (Hess, 2016), the musical practice of counterpoint is itself embedded in colonial relations, yet Said (1993) employed it to do anti-colonial work. Several scholars have expressed their concerns with Said's overemphasis on Western works (Little, 1979; Sivan, 1985; Tibawi, 1979; Wahba, 1989; Wang, 1997). Radhakrishnan (1994) argued that Said is "partial to those theorists who use the master's tools to deconstruct the master's house" (Robbins et al., 1994, p. 17), alluding to Lorde's (2007/1984) famous work.[9] He further noted that Said does not claim total value for such strategies (p. 17). In 2016, I argued that enlisting the master's tools (counterpoint, in this case) alongside other anti-colonial strategies may allow for more robust resistance to domination (p. 53). Countering domination and oppression requires use of all available tools.

In employing Said's contrapuntal methodology for this project, I compel readers to accept the responsibility to engage with counterpoints offered by participants toward the transformation of music education. If voices in counterpoint transform each other continuously (de Groot, 2005, p. 223), I urge readers to stay open to the possibility of that transformation, particularly in regard to sanist practices in music education. Counterpoint, as a classical music form, is appropriate for the music educators who participated in this study, but they make it clear throughout the following chapters that transformation is essential. Using counterpoint to do subversive work both unsettles dominant sanist structures and "employs the master's tools to deconstruct the master's house" (Lorde, 2007/1984).[10] As a dominant oppressive structure, sanism readily pervades many music education practices in ways that affect music educators, scholars, and students, as will become evident. Attending to the counterpoint I offer here may allow readers to "encounter an other in such a way, in a *better* way, that allows something to give" (Ahmed, 2000, p. 154, emphasis in original).

## Book Outline

Following this introduction, in Chapter 1, I describe Mad Studies as the discursive framework for this book and situate the "in/discipline" (Ingram, 2016) in the context of music education. In Chapter 2, I describe different models of disability from disability studies that aligned with participants' ideas, to explore their use in considering experiences of Madness and distress. In so doing, I contemplate how disability studies models may be useful for thinking about Madness and distress. In Chapter 3, I draw on participants' own conceptualizations of (their) experiences of Madness and/or distress to engage with the wide range of conceptions possible to think about such experiences. Participants also identified several benefits to (their) neurodivergence. I describe their beliefs and experiences of these benefits in Chapter 4. In Chapter 5, I take up the question of visibility and disclosure—being "out" about experiences of Madness and/or distress in music education. The questions of visibility and disclosure are fraught for people with experiences of Madness and distress and bear significantly on music education. In Chapters 6 and 7, I consider ways that music can serve to exacerbate distress as well as ways that music can help to alleviate it. Participants also had strong views on police involvement in distress calls and the ways that they felt their experiences of Madness and/or distress were surveilled in (music) education contexts. Chapter 8 consequently takes up the question of (police and policing) abolition in relation to encounters with people who are experiencing Madness and/or distress. In the conclusion, I put forward what I call a Mad-affirming music education for both students and educators that draws together all the chapters of the book toward a neurocosmopolitan music education, following Walker (2021). Following the conclusion, I provide a brief afterword that shares some personal experiences of Madness and distress. I then offer two appendices. The first of these describes my research methods and includes a detailed table with descriptions of participants in their own words. The second situates this book in the current political context both in the U.S. and globally.

Ultimately, my intention for this project as a means of sharing the perspectives of 15 people with lived experiences of Madness and distress, is to facilitate consideration of how music educators might construct a Mad-affirming music education for their classrooms, research, and discourse. Acknowledging that contextual and personal factors influence implementation, I offer multiple possibilities of what might be helpful and what might be harmful when considering how a music education that attends to Madness and emotional distress might be enacted. In doing so I attend to multiple, interlocking systems of oppression, and work to destigmatize such experiences for the field. My hope is that more people will be comfortable disclosing such experiences and find community in doing so. The conversation about Madness and distress in music education is long overdue. This book offers necessary and timely implications for pedagogy, practice, and policy.

## Notes

1 Vignettes 1, 2, and 4 are excerpted from Hess (2022). The *Bulletin for the Council for Research in Music Education* granted permission for their use.
2 I explain my use of these words in the next section.
3 Researchers surveyed 252 people, but only 226 responded to this segment of the survey.
4 I take a critical approach to resilience that I discuss later in this introduction.
5 I discuss this idea extensively in Chapter 2.
6 Mixed states involve experiencing mania and depression simultaneously. The way mixed states manifest varies from person to person. For me, a mixed state results in experiencing suicidal thoughts at the speed of a mania. It is by far my most dangerous state. Redfield Jamison (1995) discussed mixed states.
7 Throughout this book, I use "we" and "our" to include myself among people with experiences of Madness and distress. I also use these words when I am discussing music educators, a group of which I am also a member.
8 As I discuss in Appendix 1, this gender composition likely reflects the pervasiveness of toxic masculinity, which can make it difficult for men to discuss emotions.
9 Lorde, however, argued that the master's tools *cannot* destroy the master's house.
10 See endnote 9.

## References

Ahmed, S. (2000). *Strange encounters: Embodied others in post-coloniality*. Routledge.
Andrzejewski, A. (2023, July 5). Academics don't talk about our mental ilnesses. We should. The Chronicle of Higher Education. Retrieved from www.chronicle.com/article/academics-dont-talk-about-our-mental-illnesses-we-should?cid=gen_sign_in&sra=true
APM Research Lab Staff. (2020, May 20). The color of Coronavirus: COVID-19 deaths by race and ethnicity in the U.S. APM Research Lab. Retrieved from www.apmresearchlab.org/covid/deaths-by-race?fbclid=IwAR2Y4IrKTkTzD_qsG5VC5_ckwhY8rPRkP2LKikOYBvXknBaOSg4VF7dRtPU

Ashcroft, B., & Ahluwalia, P. (2001). *Edward Said* (2nd ed.). Routledge.
Beaupert, F., & Brosnan, L. (2022). Weaponizing absent knowledges: Countering the violence of mental health law. In P. Beresford & J. Russo (Eds.), *The Routledge international handbook of Mad Studies* (pp. 119–131). Routledge.
Beresford, P., & Russo, J. (Eds.). (2022). *The Routledge international handbook of Mad Studies*. Routledge.
Bernhard, H. C. (2005). Burnout and the college music education major. *Journal of Music Teacher Education (JTME)*, *15*(1), 43–51. doi:10.1177/10570837050150010107
Bernhard, H. C. (2007). A survey of burnout among college music majors. *College Student Journal*, *41*(2), 392–401.
Bernhard, H. C. (2010). A survey of burnout among college music majors: A replication. *Music Performance Research*, *3*(1), 31–41.
Bernhard, H. C. (2021). *Managing stress in music education*. Routledge.
Black, E. R. (2021). *Frida Kahlo and my left leg*. Notting Hill Editions.
Boulez, P. (1963/1971). *Boulez on music today* (S. Bradshaw & R. R. Bennett, Trans.). Faber and Faber.
Bradley, D., & Hess, J. (Eds.). (2022). *Trauma and resilience in music education: Haunted melodies*. Routledge.
Brown, B. (2021). *Atlas of the heart: Mapping meaningful connection and the language of human experience*. Random House.
Cantón, M. I. (2022). Why we must talk about de-medicalization. In P. Beresford & J. Russo (Eds.), *The Routledge international handbook of Mad Studies* (pp. 205–216). Routledge.
Carstairs, G. M., & Kapur, R. L. (1976). *The great universe of Kota: Stress, change and mental disorder in an Indian village*. University of California Press.
Cavar, S. (2021). Blogging to counter epistemic injustice: Trans disabled digital micro-resistance. *Disability Studies Quarterly*, *41*(2). Retrieved from https://dsq-sds.org/article/view/7794/5954
CDC Foundation. (2021). *Mental health impact of the COVID-19 pandemic on teachers and parents of K-12 students*. Retrieved from www.cdcfoundation.org/mental-health-triangulated-report?inline
Chandler, S. J. (2013, March 21). The many moods of Charles Mingus. *Highbrow Magazine*. Retrieved from www.highbrowmagazine.com/2274-many-moods-charles-mingus
Clare, E. (1999). *Exile & pride: Disability, queerness, and liberation*. South End Press.
Conway, C. M., Eros, J., Pellegrino, K., & West, C. (2010). Instrumental music education students' perceptions of tensions experienced during their undergraduate degree. *Journal of Research in Music Education*, *58*(3), 260–275. doi:10.1177/0022429410377114
Czeisler, M. É., Lane, R. I., Petrosky, E., Wiley, J. F., Christensen, A., Njai, R., . . . Rajaratnam, S. M. W. (2020). Mental health, substance use, and suicidal ideation during the COVID-19 pandemic—United States, June 24–30, 2020. *Centers for Disease Control and Prevention*. Retrieved from www.cdc.gov/mmwr/volumes/69/wr/mm6932a1.htm?s_cid=mm6932a1_w

de Groot, R. (2005). Perspectives of the polyphony in Edward Said's writings. *Journal of Comparative Poetics, 25*, 219–240.

Demirbatir, E., Bayram, N., & Bilgel, N. (2012). Is the healing force of music far away from the undergraduate music education students? *International Journal of Academic Research in Business and Social Sciences, 2*(1), 341–354.

Dobbs, T. L. (2012). A critical analysis of disabilities discourse in the *Journal of Research in Music Education*, 1990-2011. *Bulletin of the Council for Research in Music Education, 194*, 7–30. doi:10.5406/bulcouresmusedu.194.0007

DuBois, W. E. B. (2007/1903). *The souls of black folk* (B. H. Edwards Ed.). Oxford University Press.

Evans, B., & Reid, J. (2014). *Resilient life: The art of living dangerously*. Polity Press.

Fernando, S. (2014). *Mental health worldwide: Culture, globalization and development*. Palgrave MacMillan.

Fey, J.-M., & Mills, C. (2022). The (global) rise of anti-stigma campaigns. In P. Beresford & J. Russo (Eds.), *The Routledge international handbook of Mad Studies* (pp. 190–201). Routledge.

Hess, J. (2016). Balancing the counterpoint: Exploring musical contexts and relations. *Action, Criticism & Theory for Music Education, 15*(2), 46–72. Retrieved from http://act.maydaygroup.org/articles/Hess15_2.pdf

Hess, J. (2019). Moving beyond resilience education: Musical counterstorytelling. *Music Education Research, 21*(5), 488–502. doi:10.1080/14613808.2019.1647153

Hess, J. (2022). Sanism and narrative research: Making room for Mad stories. *Bulletin of the Council for Research in Music Education, 234*, 24–44. doi:10.5406/21627223.234.02

Hill, M. L. (2009). Wounded healing: Forming a storytelling community in Hip-Hop Lit. *Teachers College Record, 111*(1), 248–293.

Ingram, R. A. (2016). Doing Mad Studies: Making (non)sense together. *Intersectionalities: A Global Journal of Social Work Analysis, Research, Polity, and Practice, 5*(3), 11–17.

Jacobson, L. (2022). State of the Union: Biden addresses student mental health, saying their 'lives and education have been turned upside-down'. *The 74 Million*. Retrieved from www.the74million.org/article/biden-to-declare-unprecedented-student-mental-health-crisis-during-tonights-state-of-the-union/

Kadison, R., & DiGeronimo, T. F. (2004). *College of the overwhelmed: The campus mental health crisis and what to do about it*. Jossey-Bass.

Kegelaers, J., Schuijer, M., & Oudejans, R. R. (2021). Resilience and mental health issues in classical musicians: A preliminary study. *Psychology of Music, 49*(5), 1273–1284. doi:10.1177/0305735620927789

King, C. (2016). Whiteness in psychiatry: The madness of European misdiagnoses. In J. Russo & A. Sweeney (Eds.), *Searching for a rose garden: Challenging psychiatry, fostering Mad Studies* (pp. 69–76). PCCS Books Ltd.

Kola, A. (2020, April 14). How collective is the trauma of COVID-19? *Psychology Today*. Retrieved from www.psychologytoday.com/us/blog/hyphenated/202004/how-collective-is-the-trauma-covid-19

Koops, L. H., & Kuebel, C. R. (2021). Self-reported mental health and mental illness among university music students in the United States. *Research Studies in Music Education*, *43*(2), 129–143. doi:10.1177/1321103X19863265

Kuebel, C. R. (2019). Health and wellness for in-service and future music teachers. *Music Educators Journal*, *105*(4), 52–58. doi:10.1177/0027432119846950

LeBlanc, S., & Kinsella, E. A. (2016). Toward epistemic justice: A critically reflexive examination of 'sanism' and implications for knowledge generation. *Studies in Social Justice*, *10*(1), 59–78.

LeFrançois, B. A., Menzies, R., & Reaume, G. (Eds.). (2013). *Mad matters: A critical reader in Canadian Mad Studies*. Canadian Scholars' Press, Inc.

Linton, S. (1998). *Claiming disability: Knowledge and identity*. New York University Press.

Little, D. P. (1979). Three Arabic critiques of Orientalism. *Muslim World*, *69*(2), 110–131.

Lorde, A. (2007/1984). *Sister outsider: Essays and speeches*. The Crossing Press.

Maté, G., & Maté, D. (2022). *The myth of normal: Trauma, illness and healing in a toxic culture*. Avery, an Imprint of Penguin Random House.

McConkey, M. S., & Kuebel, C. R. (2022). Emotional competence within the stress coping strategies of music education students. *Journal of Research in Music Education*, *70*(3), 321–338. doi:10.1177/00224294211061457

Meerai, S., Abdillahi, I., & Poole, J. (2016). An introduction to anti-black sanism. *Intersectionalities: A Global Journal of Social Work Analysis, Research, Polity, and Practice*, *5*(3), 18–35.

Menzies, R., LeFrançois, B. A., & Reaume, G. (2013). Introducing Mad Studies. In B. A. LeFrançois, R. Menzies, & G. Reaume (Eds.), *Mad matters: A critical reader in Canadian Mad Studies* (pp. 1–22). Canadian Scholars' Press, Inc.

Parkes, K. A., Russell, J. A., Bauer, W. I., & Miksza, P. (2021). The well-being and instructional experiences of K-12 music educators: Starting a year during a pandemic. *Frontiers in Psychology*, *12*(701189), 1–17. doi:10.3389/fpsyg.2021.701189

Payne, P. D., Lewis, W., & McCaskill, F. (2020). Looking within: An investigation of music education majors and mental health. *Journal of Music Teacher Education (JMTE)*, *29*(3), 50–61. doi:10.1177/1057083720927748

Pelly, J. (2021, September 1). Jewel reflects on surviving youth homelessness and influencing Taylor Swift. *Hemispheres*. Retrieved from www.hemispheresmag.com/people/hemi-q-and-a/jewel-interview/

Pep Unlimited LLC. (2020, October 22). The struggles of Jewel helped drive her success. Pep Unlimited LLC. Retrieved from https://pepunlimited.com/social/the-struggles-of-jewel-helped-drive-her-success/

Perlin, M. (1992). On 'sanism'. *SMU Law Review*, *46*, 373–407.

Perlin, M. (2003). You have discussed lepers and crooks: Sanism in clinical teaching. *Clinical Law Review*, *9*, 683–729.

Poole, J. M., Jivraj, T., Arslanian, A., Bellows, K., Chiasson, S., Hakimy, H., . . . Reid, J. (2012). Sanism, 'mental health', and social work/education: A review and call to action. *Intersectionalities: A Global Journal of Social Work Analysis, Research, Polity, and Practice*, *1*, 20–36.

Radhakrishnan, L., Leeb, R. T., Bitsko, R. H., Carey, K., Gates, A., Holland, K. M., . . . Anderson, K. N. (2022). Pediatric emergency department visits associated with mental health conditions before and during the COVID-19 pandemic—United States, January 2019–January 2022. *MMWR Morb Mortal Wkly Rep, 71*, 319–324. doi: http://dx.doi.org/10.15585/mmwr.mm7108e2

Redfield Jamison, K. (1993). *Touched with fire: Manic-depressive illness and the artistic temperament*. Simon & Schuster.

Redfield Jamison, K. (1995). *An unquiet mind: A memoir of moods and madness*. Vintage Books.

Rhodes, A. M., & Schechter, R. (2014). Fostering resilience among youth in inner city community arts centers: The case of the artists collective. *Education and Urban Society, 46*(7), 826–848. doi:10.1177/0013124512469816

Rhodes, J. (2015, September 19). Forget the mad genius composer myth: Music is good for the mind. *The Guardian*. Retrieved from www.theguardian.com/music/2015/sep/19/mad-composer-myth-music-good-for-mind-james-rhodes

Robbins, B., Pratt, M. L., Arac, J., Radhakrishnan, R., & Said, E. W. (1994). Edward Said's *Culture and Imperialism*: A symposium. *Social Text, 40*, 1–24.

Russo, J. (2001). Reclaiming madness. In J. Read (Ed.), *Something inside so strong: strategies for surviving mental distress* (pp. 36–39). Mental Health Foundation.

Russo, J. (2016). Towards our own framework, or reclaiming madness part two. In J. Russo & A. Sweeney (Eds.), *Searching for a rose garden: Challenging psychiatry, fostering Mad Studies* (pp. 59–68). PCCS Books Ltd.

Russo, J., & Sweeney, A. (Eds.). (2016). *Searching for a rose garden: Challenging psychiatry, fostering Mad Studies*. PCCS Books Ltd.

Said, E. W. (1993). *Culture and imperialism*. Vintage Books.

Said, E. W. (2006). *On late style: Music and literature against the grain*. Vintage Books.

Said, E. W. (2008). *Music at the limits: Three decades of essays and articles on music*. Bloomsbury Publishing.

Saltman, K. J. (2015). The austerity school: Grit, character, and the privatization of public education. *Symplokē, 22*(1/2), 41–57.

Sharma, P. (2022). Navigating voices, politics, positions amidst peers: Resonances and dissonances in India. In P. Beresford & J. Russo (Eds.), *The Routledge international handbook of Mad Studies* (pp. 340–350). New York, NY: Routledge.

Singh, K. (2023, August 10). US suicide deaths reached record high in 2022, CDC data shows. *Reuters*. Retrieved from www.reuters.com/world/us/us-suicide-deaths-reached-record-high-2022-cdc-data-shows-2023-08-11/

Sivan, E. (1985). *Interpretations of Islam: Past and present*. Darwin Press.

Small, C. (1998). *Musicking: The meanings of performing and listening*. Wesleyan University Press, University Press of New England.

Sweeney, A. (2016). The transformative potential of survivor research. In J. Russo & A. Sweeney (Eds.), *Searching for a rose garden: Challenging psychiatry, fostering Mad Studies* (pp. 49–58). PCCS Books Ltd.

Tibawi, A.-L. (1979). *Second critique of English-speaking Orientalists and their approach to Islam and to the Arabs*. Islamic Cultural Center.

Wahba, M. (1989). An anger observed. *Journal of Arabic Literature, 20*(2), 187–199.

Walker, N. (2021). *Neuroqueer heresies: Notes on the neurodiversity paradigm, autistic empowerment, and postnormal possibilities* (ePub ed.). Autonomous Press.

Wang, N. (1997). Orientalism versus Occidentalism? *New Literary History, 28*(1), 57–67.

Wolframe, P. M. (2013). The madwoman in the academy, or, revealing the invisible straightjacket: Theorizing and teaching saneism and sane privilege. *Disability Studies Quarterly, 33*(1). Retrieved from https://dsq-sds.org/article/view/3425/3200

Wristen, B. G. (2013). Depression and anxiety in university music students. *Update: Applications of Research in Music Education, 31*(2), 20–27. doi:10.1177/8755123312473613

# 1 Just What Is Mad Studies and What Is It Doing in a "Nice" Field Like Music Education?[1]

The "in/discipline" of Mad Studies emerged from longstanding activist movements[2] that began in the latter-20th century. These movements centered people who self-identified as Mad and sought to place Mad experiences at the center of discourse and praxis about Madness (Beresford & Russo, 2022; Costa, 2014; LeFrançois et al., 2013; Russo & Sweeney, 2016b). They also worked to reclaim Mad knowledge and experiences from psy- professionals (psychiatrists, psychologists, etc.) (LeFrançois et al., 2013; Menzies et al., 2013), and to refuse medicalized notions of Madness and distress. In 2008, Ingram coined the term "in/discipline" to describe Mad Studies in order to preserve the unruliness and subversiveness of Madness (Ingram, 2016).

As an international in/discipline (Beresford & Russo, 2022), Mad Studies has academic roots in Canada via the edited volume *Mad Matters: A Critical Reader in Canadian Mad Studies* (LeFrançois et al., 2013). In the introduction, Menzies et al. (2013) described Mad Studies as "a project of inquiry, knowledge production, and political action devoted to the critique and transcendence of psy-centred ways of thinking, behaving, relating, and being" (p. 13). Contributors to this publication centered the lived experiences of Mad-identified people and advocated for collaborative alternatives to medicalized models of Madness and distress. Proponents suggest working together to create possibilities for support, education, and research beyond the medical paradigm. Community, rooted in Mad activist movements, remains fundamental to Mad Studies; "Mad Studies, however, takes place within and without academia, but never without community" (LeFrançois, 2016, p. v). Moreover, with activism at its root, Mad Studies has liberatory aims (LeFrançois et al., 2013). Morgan (2022) described Mad Studies as a "praxis discipline" defined by its "commitment to practical action through and alongside more theoretical thinking" with an aim toward accessibility (p. 113).

I first discuss terminology in relation to Mad identity. I have chosen to use the words *Mad* and *Madness* as a way to both reclaim a stigmatized

DOI: 10.4324/9781032662817-2

identity (Russo, 2001, 2016) and to participate in Mad Studies, which I argue is a valuable in/discipline for music education. Reclaiming language that has been used in a derogatory way can serve as a mechanism of empowerment (Clare, 1999; Linton, 1998). This terminology, however, is quite contested and many do not wish to—or have the privilege to be able to—identify as Mad, given its negative connotations (Beresford, 2022; Gorman et al., 2013; Russo, 2022b; Sharma, 2022). Employing such politicized language may prove dangerous for people who also experience violence and oppression at the intersections of racism, sexism, heterosexism, classism, cissexism, and beyond, and thus have challenging and potentially coercive encounters with psy- systems that white Mad people may not experience (Gorman et al., 2013). Language used to describe Mad experiences include: *mental illness, survivor,*[3] *service user,*[4] *mental health, neurodiversity, people with experiences of mental and emotional distress* (Carver et al., 2017), or *individuals who experience mental disorder* (Sullivan, 2019). The participants in this research project used various descriptors for their experiences. I use their chosen language when describing them and situate this project using the terms *Mad, Madness,* distress, and emotional distress which I describe as experiences. In considering terminology, Spandler and Poursanidou (2019) observed:

> Mad Studies, like the Mad movements that preceded it, seeks to subvert negative connotations associated with the term "mad"—and reclaim & politicise it, like Queer, Fat, Crip, and so on. In societies where madness is usually seen as (only) negative and dangerous, the idea of reclaiming it "as part of our fabric" (Maglajilić, 2016, p. 210) is potentially challenging and unsettling (Church, 2013). It is worth emphasising that in Mad Studies, the use of the term "Mad" is usually not meant as an essentialised identity category (you are either mad or you're not) but as a reference to political categories of critique and resistance (signified by the use of upper-case Mad, like Queer, Deaf, Black, etc.).
>
> (p. 4)

Taking their cue, I use these terms not only as acts of reclaiming and to participate in Mad Studies but also as symbols of critique and resistance. I also do so while fully acknowledging that these words might remain legitimately uncomfortable or dangerous for some with experiences of Madness and distress.

I center Mad Studies as the orienting discursive framework of this book. In the remainder of this chapter, I discuss salient elements of Mad Studies. First, I explicate sanism—the type of discrimination that targets people with experiences of Madness and distress. I explore the effects of sanism on Mad individuals and communities which include, but are not limited to, epistemic injustice, stereotyping, and stigma. Subsequently, I examine what Mad Studies facilitates. This in/discipline foregrounds lived experiences and situates Madness as a way of knowing. Mad Studies rebukes sanism and resists stereotypes and stigma. It is inherently intersectional and problematizes the pervasiveness of whiteness in Mad research and activism. Rooted in activism, it thus shares some commonalities with Queer Theory and other critical movements. Mad Studies offers significant critiques of psy- frameworks while also recognizing that Mad experiences and responses to psy- frameworks are multiple and not monolithic. Furthermore, it critiques mental health laws. Ultimately, it accounts for context and considers possible factors that influence or cause Madness and distress. In centering the voices of people with experiences of Madness and/or distress in this work, I believe that these individuals can guide the discipline of music education. I thus conclude the chapter with a discussion of what Mad Studies might offer music education.

### Sanism and Its Effects

People with experiences of Madness and distress face a particular kind of discrimination—sanism—that manifests in various ways including enactment of epistemic injustice, promulgation of stereotypes, and widespread enactment of stigma. Drawing on Perlin (1992, 2003) and Poole et al. (2012), LeBlanc and Kinsella (2016) define sanism as "the systematic subjugation and oppression of people who have received 'mental health' diagnoses, or who are otherwise perceived to be 'mentally ill'" (p. 62). Coined by activist lawyer Birnbaum and feminist lawyer Kennedy in the 1960s (Fabris, 2011; LeBlanc & Kinsella, 2016), sanism occurs as an identity-based prejudice alongside other "isms" (Perlin, 2003, p. 536). Wolframe (2013) described sanism as:

> both discrimination against those who have been given a psychiatric diagnosis (who may or may not be perceived as "mentally ill" in some or all situations), as well as discrimination against people who are perceived to be "mentally ill," delusional, mad etc. (who may or may not have a psychiatric diagnosis, or be psychiatric users/consumers/survivors).
>
> (n.p.)

LeBlanc and Kinsella (2016) further contended that sanism "is arguably one of the last socially accepted, government-sanctioned forms of systemic discrimination against a large social group" (p. 63).[5] They observed that sanism is "self-perpetuating, socially acceptable, and practiced regularly"

(p. 63). Sanism resultantly remains pervasive as a systemically acceptable form of discrimination.

*Epistemic Injustice*

People with experiences of Madness and distress are often subject to epistemic injustice. Theorized by Miranda Fricker in 2007, epistemic injustice involves being wronged in one's capacity as a knower (p. 1). Fricker (2007) conceptualized two forms of epistemic injustice—*testimonial* and *hermeneutical*.

> Testimonial injustice occurs when prejudice causes a hearer to give a deflated level of credibility to a speaker's word; hermeneutical injustice occurs at a prior stage, when a gap in collective interpretive resources puts someone at an unfair disadvantage when it comes to making sense of their social experiences.
>
> (p. 1)

In cases of testimonial injustice, being wronged in one's capacity as a knower occurs as a result of how social identities (individual and group) are perceived by listeners. Fricker insisted that stereotypes significantly affect the "collective social imagination" (p. 15) and impact people's views of speaker credibility, typically deflating it (p. 17). Testimonial injustice thus occurs when listeners harbor what Fricker called a "negative identity prejudice" (p. 35), rendering prejudicial perception of a speaker as not credible. In doing so, the listener enacts a harm that is epistemic; any knowledge offered by the speaker is lost and they are wronged in their capacity as a knower. People with experiences of Madness and/or distress are often subject to testimonial injustice (Baylosis, 2019; Bueter, 2019; Carr, 2022; Carver et al., 2017; Crichton et al., 2017; Harcourt, 2021; LeBlanc & Kinsella, 2016; Liegghio, 2013; Russo, 2022b; Scrutton, 2017; Speed & Taggart, 2019; Sullivan, 2019; White, 2022). Speakers may be understood as unreliable or "voices of less eligibility" (Carver et al., 2017, p. 50). Indeed, the "failure to recognize the epistemic value of the perspectives of those living with madness is so entrenched in Western social practices and discourses" (LeBlanc & Kinsella, 2016, p. 61) that listeners may partially or entirely dismiss the knowledge and perspectives of Mad people (Scrutton, 2017).

Hermeneutical injustice is Fricker's (2007) second form of epistemic injustice, defined by "*having some significant area of one's social experience obscured from collective understanding owing to persistent and wideranging hermeneutical marginalization*" (p. 154, emphasis in original) or "*owing to a structural identity prejudice in the collective hermeneutical resource*" (p. 155, emphasis in original). While testimonial injustice involves agents, hermeneutical injustice is structural (p. 159) and involves lack of access to materials that may help a person to interpret their experience. Exemplifying the concept, Fricker described how coining the term "sexual harassment" filled a gap in hermeneutical resources in the 1970s. Before the naming of this phenomenon, (predominantly) women lacked a term to describe what they were experiencing. In such cases, not being able to name an experience impacts and potentially invalidates one's status as a knower. People with experiences of Madness and/or distress may similarly suffer from hermeneutical injustice, owing to a lack of collective resources about such experiences generated by the people who experience these phenomena (Speed & Taggart, 2019; White, 2022). White (2022), for example, observed that "[p]sychiatric patients and survivors have been traditionally excluded from creating knowledge about issues that affect us" (p. 78). Mad Studies aims to address this lacuna, though accessing the hermeneutical resources Mad Studies provides may prove difficult for people outside academia.

*Stereotypes*

Sanism also perpetuates stereotypes of Madness and distress. Fricker (2007) described stereotypes as "*widely held associations between a given social group and one or more attributes*" (p. 30, emphasis in original). Indeed, stereotypes dominate discourse, practice, and representations about mental illness and Madness (Bueter, 2019; Carver et al., 2017; Corrigan et al., 2010; Crichton et al., 2017; LeBlanc & Kinsella, 2016; Lee, 2021; Scrutton, 2017; Sullivan, 2019; Williams, 2014; Wolframe, 2013). Drawing on Fabris (2011), Perlin (2000, 2003, 2006, 2013), and Williams (2014), LeBlanc and Kinsella (2016) noted that "sanist stereotyping fosters a negative perception of Mad persons as delusional, emotionally unstable, unpredictable, untruthful, untrustworthy, lacking all capacity for 'rational' thought, and invariably dangerous to oneself or others" (p. 64). People with experiences of Madness and distress are often associated with risk, danger, unpredictability, and tendency toward violence (Carver et al., 2017; Mason & Mercer, 2014), as well as deemed potentially incompetent or unable to hold down a job (Corrigan et al., 2010, p. 260), or criminal (Carver et al., 2017).

The prevalence of stereotypes has strong links to epistemic injustice. What Fricker called "negative identity prejudices" (which are often shaped by stereotypes) significantly affect the credibility of people with experiences of Madness and/or distress (Bueter, 2019; Carver et al., 2017; Crichton et al., 2017; Scrutton, 2017; Sullivan, 2019), especially since people often fail to reconsider stereotypes even in the face of counter-evidence (Crichton et al., 2017). Sanism then not only facilitates the creation, sustaining, and circulating of stereotypes, but these stereotypes ultimately perpetuate epistemic injustice.

*Stigma (Discrimination)*

People with experiences of Madness and/or distress often experience stigma, which "is a process of stereotyping, prejudice, and discrimination and is very much a moral experience whereby the individual's identity is ear-marked or embodied as tainted, spoiled, or discounted" (Carver et al., 2017, p. 51). Public stigma—"the prejudice and discrimination that emerges when the general population endorses specific stereotypes" (Corrigan et al., 2010, p. 260)—and self-stigma or the "impact of internalizing stigma" (p. 260) are both relevant when considering how members of a particular group are perceived by society (Crichton et al., 2017).[6] Public "problems of knowledge (ignorance), attitudes (prejudice) and behaviour (discrimination)" (Fey & Mills, 2022, p. 197) require interventions in all three domains. Simultaneously, stigma significantly effects how people with experiences of Madness and/or distress are able to see ourselves, impacting how we move through the world and sometimes leading to social identity adjustment (Crichton et al., 2017, p. 68). Additionally troubling, Fey and Mills (2022) cautioned that stigmatization of mental illness is thought to be universal and to be worsening. Stigma is a form of power (Fey & Mills, 2022) enacted through discrimination and oppression, and deeply structured by sanism. Indeed, epistemic injustice, stereotyping, and stigma are interwoven and inextricably linked in the overarching landscape created by sanism.

## Putting Forward Mad Studies

Mad Studies offers a framework for understanding experiences of Madness and distress, and the people who have these experiences. It also deliberately works against and refuses sanism and sanist practices. I outline several tenets of Mad Studies salient to the present study, noting that this discussion is not exhaustive.

*Foregrounding Lived Experiences*

Centering first-person knowledge and perspectives is crucial in Mad Studies (Beresford, 2020, 2022; Campbell, 2022; Morgan, 2022; Russo, 2022b; Spandler & Poursanidou, 2019; Taggart, 2022; Webb, 2010). Beresford (2020) placed the histories, cultures, and politics of Mad people alongside our lived experiences and further called for us to bring the full complexity of our identities to bear (Beresford, 2022). Mad experiences are multifaceted and, as I have contended elsewhere, polyrhizovocal (Hess, 2022).[7] Campbell (2022) delineated three main aspects of first-hand Mad knowledge: "First, knowledge of living in, and receiving, mental health services. Secondly, living with mental distress in society. Finally, first-hand knowledge of the interior experience of distress (the 'madness' experience)" (p. 58). He thus considered experience not only of the mental health system but also context and epistemology.

Within the bio-medical paradigm (the psy- disciplines), there has been recent interest in including experiential knowledge of the system from those who have experiences with it (Costa et al., 2012; Joseph, 2019; Penney & Prescott, 2016; Taggart, 2022; Voronka, 2016). Costa et al. (2012), however, challenged the use of personal narratives by the psy- systems, particularly for attempts to capture funding, support, or media coverage for the bio-medical system in question.

Stories are often used to benefit the psy- disciplines rather than to serve the people most directly impacted by these systems, a dangerous process through which the co-opting and commodification of Mad stories emerges. Voronka (2016) further cautioned that "[u]niversalizing ourselves as 'experts by experience' belies the variances that our bodies carry, how we experience madness, and how mental health fields of power respond to us" (p. 197). The temptation toward a false universalizing of interior and exterior Mad experiences occurs within the imperative to share stories. The potential to elide complexities of identities also occurs. Centering the lived experiences of people with experiences of Madness and/or distress in this book challenges dominant and hegemonic understandings. I consider these stories to be a mechanism for resistance and a counterpoint to dominant normative paradigms rather than a capitulation to the desire for stories of the Other (hooks, 1992).

*Refusing Epistemic Injustice: Madness as a Way of Knowing*

As noted previously, people with experiences of Madness and/or distress are often subject to epistemic injustice (Baylosis, 2019; Bueter, 2019; Carr, 2022; Carver et al., 2017; Crichton et al., 2017; Harcourt, 2021; LeBlanc & Kinsella, 2016; Liegghio, 2013; Russo, 2022b; Scrutton, 2017; Speed & Taggart, 2019; Sullivan, 2019; White, 2022), invalidated in our capacities as knowers, and lacking in hermeneutical resources to make sense of our experiences (Fricker, 2007). Mad Studies emphasizes epistemic justice, compelling listeners to respect people with experiences of Madness and/or distress as knowers and making the compiling of hermeneutical resources possible.

Emergent scholarship aims to "embrace and extend new forms of Mad knowledge" (Spandler & Poursanidou, 2019, p. 9). Indeed, "[w]e need to imagine and create a world where mental distress is viewed primarily through the eyes of the people who experience it—as legitimate though challenging experience from which value and meaning can be derived" (O'Hagan, 2016, pp. 12–13). Shimrat (2022) affirmed:

> Our knowledge can help all of us relate to ourselves and to others. It can teach all of us, not just to cope with extremes of emotion and difference, but to learn from them—to find in them meaning, insight, and sometimes even joy—and consequently to live better, richer lives.
>
> (p. 53)

All individuals and groups have much to learn from those who possess Mad knowledge, particularly in regards to coping with distress and challenging emotions. To only look at Madness as a source of knowledge about difficulties, though, is to miss the meaning, insight, and joy Shimrat described.

Extending sources of knowledge to epistemology(ies), Liegghio (2013) argued "it is not enough to give voice but one must think of voice in different ways—in ways that recognize difference as legitimate rather than measuring differences against a standard of *normal* (Goldenberg, 2007)" (p. 127, emphasis in original). Madness offers novel ways of knowing the world. Fabris (2011) wrote:

> Madness is sound, but not because we live in a mad world (there is nothing mad about it either). We have identity *in* "mad" experience, in difference, not despite it. I would like to suggest that madness is not only excusable, interesting, or a version of rationality under pressure. Madness is an embodied way to know. It is intelligent, searching, and valuable. It is not regression, but a conscious reaching out, as is technical work, healing love, or creative feeling. Purpose is not impossible in "madness," but it is also not easily described in a non-normative relation to the world.
>
> (pp. 31–32, emphasis in original)

As an "embodied way to know," attending to people's experiences of Madness and distress involves honoring different/differing epistemologies that vary from a singular, normative model. Mad Studies scholars therefore treat Madness as a "potentially credible source of knowledge in its own right" (Spandler & Poursanidou, 2019, p. 11). Mad Studies ascribes credibility and immense value to Mad perspectives, and eschews neuronormativity (Walker, 2021). Recognizing the diversity of ways of knowing the world and honoring these varied epistemologies makes room for the full range of contributions people with experiences of Madness and/or distress may offer at the center of discourse and praxis, rather than on the margin. Further, Mad epistemologies may work to unsettle the "adultist, disableist, saneist, colonial and racist logics that often underpin the conventional academic imaginary" (Mills & LeFrançois, 2018, p. 506). Such epistemologies also resist the cooptation of Mad stories by the psy-system for the good of the system, rather for the people in the system (Costa et al., 2012). In looking to the perspectives of people in music education who have experiences of Madness and/or distress, I position them as sources of knowledge for music education. Their ideas illuminate often-silenced perspectives and offer constructive possibilities for the field.

*Resisting Sanism: Refusing Stereotypes and Stigma*

Since Mad Studies rebukes sanism, it provides a mechanism to resist embedded stereotypes and stigma as forms of discrimination and oppression. Morgan (2022) argued:

> At the heart of both Disability and Mad Studies is a responsibility to hear the concerns of those with lived experience as well as producing knowledge that is useful in challenging the discrimination and oppression they endure and promoting their rights and aspirations.
>
> (p. 113)

Resisting sanist oppression thus remains fundamental to Mad Studies as a "praxis discipline" (Morgan, 2022, p. 113). Importantly, Morgan highlighted the refusal of deficit framing of Madness and/or distress present in the stereotypes previously discussed. Mad Studies instead seeks to highlight the "intelligent, searching, and valuable" qualities of Madness that Fabris (2011, p. 32) identified.

Mad Studies scholars and activists work to decouple the negative associations society holds about those who experience Madness and/or distress (Crichton et al., 2017). Problematically, mainstream anti-stigma campaigns often "are constituted by and reproduce sanism" (Fey & Mills, 2022, p. 190). Remaining wary of attempts of psy- disciplines to combat stigmas is therefore crucial to working *against* those very stigmas. Fey and Mills specifically critiqued anti-stigma campaigns for their lack of intersectional analysis and accounting for structural discrimination. They argued instead that anti-stigma work must "make connections between personal narratives and social structures, power, racism, discrimination, and collective action (and that illustrate how narratives are themselves shaped by social and cultural context)" (p. 198). In order to make plain the structures of discrimination, anti-stigma work rooted in Mad Studies must situate stigma within systems of power.

*The Imperative of Intersectionality in Mad Studies*

Mad Studies has often privileged the perspectives of white people with experiences of Madness and/or distress; whiteness is thus pervasive in the in/discipline (Beaupert & Brosnan, 2022; Beresford, 2022; Eromosele, 2022; Fey & Mills, 2022; King, 2016, 2022; LeFrançois, 2016; Nabbali, 2022; Reaume, 2022; Russo, 2022a; Russo & Sweeney, 2016a; Spandler & Poursanidou, 2019). Change within Mad Scholarship has been rightfully compelled (Fey & Mills, 2022). LeFrançois (2016) noted:

> [W]e are asked to think about and confront racism within and outside of psychiatry, including systemic whiteness not just within psy-systems but also within the mad movement itself, the privileging of white survivor contributions and the erasure of cultural memory when it is not consistent with established white Western understandings.
>
> (p. vii)

King offered several explicit suggestions for Mad Studies scholars to "ensure that whiteness is not accepted as the 'professionalised norm'" (p. 358):

1) take "analytical responsibility to explore the role of whiteness amongst its white academics in relation to race and misdiagnosis" (p. 353),
2) "reflect on the way their whiteness influences their own position when truly working with black survivor researchers" (p. 353), and
3) "make [their] own whiteness explicit in the co-production process in order to produce new collaborative perspectives with black survivor researchers" (p. 357).

Mad Studies must become "attuned to potential exclusions" (Spandler & Poursanidou, 2019, p. 1) in order to appropriately consider perspectives of Mad scholars and others with experiences of Madness and/or distress. Russo cautioned, "social justice movements can become places of injustice that create their own 'others'" (Russo, 2022b, p. 22). Sanism intersects with heteropatriarchy, white supremacy, and classism (Gorman et al., 2013; Meerai et al., 2016), among other oppressive structures, and requires a complex understanding and accounting for privilege and positionality in opposition to sanism (Fey & Mills, 2022).

Sanism affects and harms different groups in different ways, as do Madness and distress:

> For example, in the UK, people from Black and minority ethnic backgrounds as well as those living under austerity or harsh economic conditions are much more likely to experience mental distress, to be diagnosed with a mental health condition, and to experience the hard end of mental health services (including force and coercion) (Legraien, 2018; Longhurst, 2017).
>
> (Fey & Mills, 2022, pp. 193–194)

Centering intersectionality facilitates understanding how structural oppression shapes a person's experience of Madness and/or distress, as well as the way society perceives them. Additionally, intersectionality clarifies the differential access people have to services. Speed and Taggart (2019) put forward a useful "social aetiology model":

> In contrast to the individual aetiology model, a social aetiology model emphasises the social, economic, cultural, political, and historical context in which the mental health problem occurs. Therefore, in this conceptualisation, the construct of "mental illness" is rejected as presenting an atomised, separate, and identity-based subject position. Instead, "mental health" is situated in relation to the multiple forms of intersectional disadvantage and structural discrimination that co-constitute it.
>
> (p. 8)

Intersectionality facilitates understanding of how different oppressive structures affect experiences. Given the whiteness of Mad Studies and the Mad movement (Gorman et al., 2013), accounting for ways one might receive privilege beyond one's Mad identity becomes important. Fabris (2016), for example, noticed the privilege stemming from his "maleness, whiteness, ablebodiedness, anglophony, and a host of other normalcies" including "'capable-mindedness' and 'voluntariness' under psychiatric care and control as models of sound societies" (pp. 100–101). He observed how "[t]he sanist society is indeed a place where the most 'sound' of us excel, while the less understood lag behind, get into trouble, get held back and get lost" (p. 101). The type and number of privileges one receives across a range of identity categories therefore amount to advantage in sanist systems.

Intersectionality is also important to understanding and addressing how society views people with experiences of Madness and/or distress. Racialized individuals and groups with such experiences are more likely to be seen as perpetrators of violence (Daley & Van Katwyk, 2022). Daley and Van Katwyk illuminated the "overrepresentation of Mad people as violent" in the perpetrator-victim binary (p. 255). "Dangerousness" sticks to some bodies more than others (Daley & Van Katwyk, 2022), with the stereotype of "black, dangerous, and mad" (p. 256) harming Black men in particular (see also King, 2016, 2022). Conversely, Mad individuals with the kinds of dominant group privileges Fabris (2016) identified are more likely to be seen as victims. "[I]ntersections between madness and social identities often determine which side of the binary Mad people are located—whether Mad people are more likely to be seen as perpetrators of violence or victims of violence" (Daley & Van Katwyk, 2022, p. 256). Rather than elide our Mad identities to address sanism over intersecting forms of oppression (Voronka, 2016), I support acknowledging that such collective identities "are never big or suitable enough to capture the many layers of social experience and therefore prove incapable of addressing them" (Russo, 2022b, p. 22). Intersectionality allows for differentiation and nuance and is fundamental to addressing of sanism and other systems of oppression in Mad Studies.

*Cross-Pollination with Critical Movements*

Mad Studies has much in common with other liberation movements and their associated scholarship (Russo, 2022b). Like other activist movements, the Mad movement and Mad Studies aim to reclaim and politicize a term—"Mad"—that has been used pejoratively. Other movements have reappropriated and reclaimed words such as "Queer," "Crip," "Fat," etc. (Spandler & Poursanidou, 2019, p. 4). Reclaiming the term "Mad" as a reference to political categories of critique and resistance constitutes a politicized move that may be seen as both challenging and unsettling (Spandler & Poursanidou, 2019, p. 4).

Spandler and Poursanidou (2019) further suggested that explicit cross-fertilization exists between critical projects that explicitly target "liberatory action, policy, and practice," notably queer, Black, and disability studies and movements (p. 2). Mad Studies also draws on disciplines that include sociology, anthropology, social work, cultural studies, and feminist studies (Beresford, 2022, p. 7), and "methods and approaches for research … from other educational fields such as women's studies, queer studies, critical race studies, legal studies, ethnography, auto-ethnography"[8] (Beresford, 2016, p. 32). Many of these disciplines have liberation as a core aim, while methodologies like ethnography and autoethnography allow for the expression of personal experiences. Part of the work of Mad Studies, then, involves building alliances with other movements and associated critical studies, learning from their triumphs and challenges (Beresford, 2020, p. 1341).

*The Relationship of Mad Studies to the Anti-Psychiatry Movement*

Mad Studies "rejects a bio-medical approach to the domain widely known as 'mental illness' or 'mental health' and substitutes instead a framework of 'madness'" (Beresford, 2020, p. 1337). The topic of psychiatry has been contentious within the in/discipline, with Burstow doing significant work calling for the abolition of psychiatry altogether (Burstow, 2015, 2016, 2019; Burstow et al., 2014). Burstow (2015) advocated for creating community supports under the supervision of people with experiences of Madness and/or distress and allies,[9] and adamantly opposed coercion and forced treatment in supporting people in crisis.

Spandler and Poursanidou (2019) cautioned against tying Mad Studies to an overtly anti-medical or anti-psychiatry position. They contended that doing so may exclude people who identify as service users who want support from psychiatry and/or medication (p. 7) and limit what Mad Studies can do as an area of knowledge production (p. 8), while also noting that psychiatry is not uniform (p. 7). They instead suggested "an ambivalent, non-binary approach to highly contested interventions such as psychiatric medication," recognizing such interventions as context-dependent based on the needs of each individual (p. 13).

> Criticising the dominance of bio-medical psychiatric models within mental health services and developing alternative Mad-centred frameworks is undoubtedly central to the Mad Studies project. However, it is also argued that Mad Studies should be pluralistic and not impose another monolithic theory or ideology on survivors (Beresford, 2016; Sweeney, 2016b).
>
> (Spandler & Poursanidou, 2019, p. 6)

As White (2022) observed, an intense anti-psychiatry focus may miss other important considerations:

> This hyper-focus on psychiatry and the mental health system has left the many sites of our oppression uncontested. And even in the arena that we do contest—the mental health system—our advocacy typically neither acknowledges nor challenges the root cause of the oppression and discrimination that effectively results in our erasure from society.
>
> (p. 77)

In this project, I reject dogma about psychiatry in favor of "pluralistic" and context-dependent considerations to reveal what else Mad Studies might make possible.

### Critiques of Mental Health Laws

Mad Studies also critiques mental health laws. These laws often strip away the rights of people experiencing Madness and/or distress in order to subject them to forced treatment (see for example Beaupert & Brosnan,

2022; Fabris, 2011, 2016; Karanikolas, 2022), assuming that "deprivation of liberty and violence are legitimate means of ensuring that people deemed dangerous and disordered due to 'mental illness' receive 'needed treatment'" (Beaupert & Brosnan, 2022, p. 123). Forced treatment might involve mandated medication, restraints, electroconvulsive therapy (ECT), battery, and beyond. In the context of community treatment orders wherein people with experiences of Madness and/or distress report for mandatory care while living in the community, Fabris (2011) described forced treatment as "chemical incarceration." Such acts produce epistemic and symbolic violence in addition to corporeal violence, denying people who have been psychiatrized the right to make meaning of our experiences and therefore effacing our ways of knowing and being (Beaupert & Brosnan, 2022, p. 120). This loss of rights and bodily autonomy is again not equally distributed; racialized groups are more likely to be treated with coercion (Joseph, 2019).

What Agamben (2005) theorized as a "state of exception" applies to mental health laws. Agamben examined the way that suspension of laws in a state of emergency may become prolonged, thus depriving individuals of their typical rights. He wrote that a "theory of the state of exception is the preliminary condition for any definition of the relation that binds and, at the same time, abandons the living being to law" (p. 1). He offered an example of the U.S. Patriot Act of 2001 which allowed the attorney general to "take into custody" any person suspected of endangering "the national security of the United States" and hold them for seven days without charges, thus erasing their legal status and making them temporarily "unclassifiable" (pp. 3–4). People with experiences of Madness and/or distress who find themselves subject to mental health laws similarly experience suspension of their rights, in a state of exception seemingly removed from any kind of judicial oversight, with violence and restraint as reasonable responses if not wishing to be "treated." Mad Studies challenges coerced treatment and critiques mental health laws, often drawing in particular upon the Convention on the Rights of Persons with Disabilities (CRPD) to counter the removal of rights (Beaupert & Brosnan, 2022; Eromosele, 2022; Karanikolas, 2022; Valdivia Quiroz, 2022). I likewise oppose any kind of coercion or forced treatment.

*Accounting for Contextual Factors*

Mad Studies strongly considers the role of contextual factors in any discussion of Madness and distress, shifting focus from the biomedical model to socially situated understandings of such experiences (Cantón, 2022; Eromosele, 2022; Filson, 2016; Maglajilić, 2022; Penney & Prescott, 2016; Speed & Taggart, 2019; Sweeney, 2016a; Tang, 2022). Individuals may experience distress based on a range of factors including, but not limited to, poverty, trauma, systemic violence, oppression, forced migration, war, persecution, climate disasters, loss, medical procedures, a global pandemic, and recovering from or witnessing an accident.[10] I return to Speed and Taggart's (2019) social aetiology model in which "the co-constitutive effects of poverty, inequality, and trauma can be held to be central to any emotional distress that a person may be experiencing" (p. 3). A social understanding of Madness and/or distress takes these contextual factors into account, which is crucial to understanding a person's experience holistically.

Failing to take contextual factors into account leads to a shortage of hermeneutical resources for individuals to make sense of their experiences of Madness and/or distress (Fricker, 2007; Tang, 2022). When the only explanation given is clinical and biomedical, the complex web of factors that may lead to experiences of Madness and/or distress go unacknowledged and/or discounted. Cantón (2022) explained:

> The biomedical approach to subjective suffering causes a person's experience in the world to be decontextualized and reduced to the "clinical picture" they present when they first encounter "mental health" services. All the possible causes for the person's diverse manifestations, like adverse childhood experiences, traumas, the experience of multiple oppressions, or just a different way of being in the world, are amputated at once and replaced by a supposed malfunction of fancy named neurotransmitters in the brain.
>
> (p. 211)

Mad Studies ensures consideration of contextual factors that may influence experiences of Madness and/or distress. Doing so enables contributions to hermeneutic resources that facilitate a holistic look at these experiences.

### *Summary: The Elements of Mad Studies*

As an in/discipline, Mad Studies foregrounds lived experiences and centers Mad and/or distressed people. It refuses epistemic injustice and values Madness as offering distinct ways of knowing. It resists sanism and its associated stereotypes and stigma. Mad Studies is also intersectional; it is self-conscious of its whiteness and seeks to address the centering of white voices in discourse about Madness and distress. It also draws on other critical theories and liberation movements. Furthermore, it takes a critical and nuanced stance on psychiatry and mental health laws and takes context into account when considering experiences of Madness and/or distress. Hence, Mad Studies offers a powerful counterpoint to normative paradigms for understanding experience.

## Mad Studies in Music Education

Given these elements of Mad Studies, this in/discipline has a great deal to offer to music education. In listening to the stories of individuals in music education who have experiences of Madness and/or distress, ways that music might contribute positively to wellbeing become apparent, alongside the ways that music might cause harm. Also, in centering the voices of this study's participants, I privilege the knowledge of a group that has often been denied epistemic justice. In the context of music education, I argue that room exists to honor a full range of epistemologies and ways of knowing the world, including Mad epistemologies.

In music education scholarship Mad voices are absent or, at the very least, underrepresented or unacknowledged as such. Indeed, people with experiences of Madness and/or distress are often relegated to the margin by mainstream music education discourse and practice—viewed, as I explored in the introduction, as a problem. Discussions of wellness in music education typically focus on social emotional learning (SEL) drawing on the Collaborative for Academic, Social, and Emotional Learning (CASEL) framework[11] (see for example Edgar, 2021; Edgar et al., 2017). The stated aims of SEL are to foster self-awareness, self-management, responsible decision-making, relationship skills, and social awareness in relation to emotions. It has also, however, been heavily critiqued for being neoliberal, racist, and more focused on compliance than vibrant emotional wellbeing (Richerme, 2022; Simmons, 2019, 2021). Simmons (2021) went so far as to call SEL "white supremacy with a hug." Music educators require a more robust discussion of the possibilities music offers for emotional wellbeing that centers the perspectives of people with experiences of Madness and/or distress. Mad Studies makes a holistic view of students and teachers possible, one that considers the full range of contextual factors influencing their distress with the aim to ameliorate it. In doing so, it also refuses the pathologization of students who do not conform to "classroom management" standards. Moreover, Mad Studies does not take the medicalized approach to distress so prevalent in the school system, instead seeking more social and structural solutions. As a music educator, I explicitly look for ways that Mad Studies might support the students and teachers with experiences of Madness and/or distress in ways that draw on the potential of our discipline.

As I will discuss at length in subsequent chapters, musicking clearly offers both ways to soothe distress and to worsen it. I suggest music educators might learn to harness the ability of musicking to help, and both respect and intentionally work against the ability of musicking to harm. Once music educators recognize these possibilities, we can explicitly teach students how to use and engage with musicking in ways that might help (through, for example, songwriting, listening practices, etc.) and also make them aware of how musicking might exacerbate distress. Finally, within music education we can create a model for responding to distress that is inherently abolitionist and does not rely on the police, or subject individuals to the potential harms mental health laws can cause. The following chapters draw on the voices of participants with experiences of Madness and/or distress to consider how we might work together to create a Mad-affirming music education in counterpoint with the dominant music education paradigm.

## Notes

1 My title riffs off of Ladson-Billings, G. (1998). "Just what is critical race theory and what's it doing in a *nice* field like education?" *Qualitative Studies in Education*, 11(1), 7–24. https://doi.org/10.1080/095183998236863
2 The activism related to people with experiences of Madness and/or distress includes multiple movements such as Mad Pride and anti-psychiatry organizing, among others.
3 A psychiatric survivor is someone who has suffered harm through the psy-system and survived. A survivor also often identifies as such.
4 A person who uses mental health services.
5 Government-sanctioned actions include police involvement in situations in which a person is experiencing distress (see for example Saleh et al., 2018).
6 Self-stigma occurs when individuals believe the stereotypes that circulate about their identities and apply them personally (Carver et al., 2017; Corrigan et al., 2010; Lee, 2021).
7 Polyrhizovocality combines polyvocality—or the presence of multiple voices—with rhizovocality, which moves beyond a plurality of voices to the *dimensions* of voice (Jackson, 2009; Powell, 2020). It considers both the multiplicity of voices (which may occur in a single person) alongside the rich textures of the dimensions of voice.
8 See http://madstudies2014.wordpress.com/.
9 Allies position themselves alongside anti-psychiatry activists to promote the abolition of psychiatry.
10 Adverse Childhood Experiences (ACEs) may also impact levels of distress. See for example Burke Harris (2018) and Waite and Ryan (2020).
11 See the CASEL website for information: https://casel.org.

## References

Agamben, G. (2005). *State of exception* (K. Attell, Trans.). The University of Chicago Press.

Baylosis, C. (2019). Mad Studies and an ethics of listening. *Journal of Ethics in Mental Health*, *10*(6), 1–18.

Beaupert, F., & Brosnan, L. (2022). Weaponizing absent knowledges: Countering the violence of mental health law. In P. Beresford & J. Russo (Eds.), *The Routledge international handbook of Mad Studies* (pp. 119–131). Routledge.

Beresford, P. (2016). The role of survivor knowledge in creating alternatives to psychiatry. In J. Russo & A. Sweeney (Eds.), *Searching for a rose garden: Challenging psychiatry, fostering Mad Studies* (pp. 25–34). PCCS Books Ltd.

Beresford, P. (2020). "Mad," Mad Studies and advancing inclusive resistance. *Disability & Society*, *35*(8), 1337–1342. https://doi.org/10.1080/09687599.2019.1692168

Beresford, P. (2022). Introduction. In P. Beresford & J. Russo (Eds.), *The Routledge international handbook of Mad Studies* (pp. 1–16). Routledge.

Beresford, P., & Russo, J. (Eds.). (2022). *The Routledge international handbook of Mad Studies*. Routledge.

Bueter, A. (2019). Epistemic injustice and psychiatric classification. *Philosophy of Science*, *86*, 1064–1074.

Burke Harris, N. (2018). *The deepest well: Healing the long-term effects of childhood adversity* (iBooks ed.). Houghton Mifflin Harcourt Publishing Company.

Burstow, B. (2015). *Psychiatry and the business of Madness: An ethical and epistemological accounting*. Palgrave Macmillan.

Burstow, B. (2019). *The revolt against psychiatry: A counterhegemonic dialogue*. Palgrave Macmillan.

Burstow, B. (Ed.). (2016). *Psychiatry interrogated: An institutional ethnography anthology*. Palgrave Macmillan.

Burstow, B., LeFrançois, B. A., & Diamond, S. (Eds.). (2014). *Psychiatry disrupted: Theorizing resistance and crafting the (r)evolution*. McGill-Queen's University Press.

Campbell, P. (2022). Speaking for ourselves: An early UK survivor activist's account. In P. Beresford & J. Russo (Eds.), *The Routledge international handbook of Mad Studies* (pp. 57–59). Routledge.

Cantón, M. I. (2022). Why we must talk about de-medicalization. In P. Beresford & J. Russo (Eds.), *The Routledge international handbook of Mad Studies* (pp. 205–216). Routledge.

Carr, S. (2022). Institutional ceremonies? The (im)possibilites of transformative co-production in mental health. In P. Beresford & J. Russo (Eds.), *The Routledge international handbook of Mad Studies* (pp. 142–153). Routledge.

Carver, L., Morley, S., & Taylor, P. (2017). Voices of deficit: Mental health, criminal victimization, and epistemic injustice. *Illness, Crisis, & Loss*, *25*(1), 43–62. https://doi.org/10.1177/1054137316675715

Church, K. (2013). Making Madness matter in academic practice. In B. A. LeFrançois, R. Menzies, & G. Reaume (Eds.), *Mad matters: A critical reader in Canadian Mad Studies* (pp. 181–190). Canadian Scholars' Press, Inc.

Clare, E. (1999). *Exile & pride: Disability, queerness, and liberation*. South End Press.

Corrigan, P. W., Morris, S., Larson, J., Rafacz, J., Wassel, A., Michaels, P., Wilkniss, S., Batia, K., & Rüsch, N. (2010). Self-stigma and coming out about one's mental illness. *Journal of Community Psychology, 38*(3), 259–275. https://doi.org/10.1002/jcop.20363

Costa, L. (2014). *Mad Studies—what it is and why you should care.* https://madstudies2014.wordpress.com/2014/10/15/mad-studies-what-it-is-and-why-you-should-care-2/

Costa, L., Voronka, J., Landry, D., Reid, J., McFarlane, B., Reville, D., & Church, K. (2012). Recovering our stories: A small act of resistance. *Studies in Social Justice, 6*(1), 85–101.

Crichton, P., Carel, H., & Kidd, I. J. (2017). Epistemic injustice in psychiatry. *BJPscych Bulletin, 41*(2), 65–70. https://doi.org/10.1192/pb.bp.115.050682

Daley, A., & Van Katwyk, T. (2022). De-coupling and re-coupling violence. In P. Beresford & J. Russo (Eds.), *The Routledge international handbook of Mad Studies* (pp. 253–265). Routledge.

Edgar, S. (Ed.). (2021). *Portraits of music education and social emotional learning: Teaching music with heart.* GIA Publications.

Edgar, S., Kelly-McHale, J., & Rawlings, J. (2017). *Music education and social emotional learning: The heart of teaching music.* GIA Publications.

Eromosele, F. (2022). Madness, decolonisation and mental health activism in Africa. In P. Beresford & J. Russo (Eds.), *The Routledge international handbook of Mad Studies* (pp. 327–339). Routledge.

Fabris, E. (2011). *Tranquil prisons: Chemical incarceration under community treatment orders.* University of Toronto Press.

Fabris, E. (2016). Community Treatment Orders: Once a rosy deinstitutional notion? In J. Russo & A. Sweeney (Eds.), *Searching for a rose garden: Challenging psychiatry, fostering Mad Studies* (pp. 97–105). PCCS Books Ltd.

Fey, J.-M., & Mills, C. (2022). The (global) rise of anti-stigma campaigns. In P. Beresford & J. Russo (Eds.), *The Routledge international handbook of Mad Studies* (pp. 190–201). Routledge.

Filson, B. (2016). The haunting can end: Trauma-informed approaches in healing from abuse and adversity. In J. Russo & A. Sweeney (Eds.), *Searching for a rose garden: Challenging psychiatry, fostering Mad Studies* (pp. 20–24). PCCS Books Ltd.

Fricker, M. (2007). *Epistemic injustice: Power and the ethics of knowing.* Oxford University Press.

Goldenberg, M. (2007). The problem of exclusion in feminist theory and politics: A metaphysical investigation into constructing a category of "woman" *Journal of Gender Studies, 16*(2), 139–153. https://doi.org/10.1080/09589230701324603

Gorman, R., Saini, A., Tam, L., Udegbe, O., & Usar, O. (2013). Mad people of colour: A manifesto. *Asylum, 20*(4). https://asylummagazine.org/2013/12/mad-people-of-color-a-manifesto-by-rachel-gorman-annu-saini-louise-tam-onyiny echukwu-udegbe-onar-usar/

Harcourt, E. (2021). Epistemic injustice, children and mental illness. *Journal of Medical Ethics, OnlineFirst,* 1–7. https://doi.org/10.1136/medethics-2021-107329

Hess, J. (2022). Sanism and narrative research: Making room for Mad stories. *Bulletin of the Council for Research in Music Education, 234*, 24–44. https://doi.org/10.5406/21627223.234.02

hooks, b. (1992). *Black looks: Race and representation*. South End Press.

Ingram, R. A. (2016). Doing Mad Studies: Making (non)sense together. *Intersectionalities: A Global Journal of Social Work Analysis, Research, Polity, and Practice, 5*(3), 11–17.

Jackson, A. Y. (2009). "What am I doing when I speak of this present?": Voice, power, and desire in truth-telling. In A. Y. Jackson & L. A. Mazzei (Eds.), *Voice in qualitative inquiry: Challenging conventional, interpretive, and critical conceptions in qualitative research* (pp. 165–174). Routledge.

Joseph, A. J. (2019). Constituting "lived experience" discourses in mental health: The Ethics of Racialized Identification/Representation and the erasure of intergeneration colonial violence. *Journal of Ethics in Mental Health, 10*(6), 1–23.

Karanikolas, P. (2022). Imagining non-carceral futures with(in) Mad Studies. In P. Beresford & J. Russo (Eds.), *The Routledge international handbook of Mad Studies* (pp. 217–222). Routledge.

King, C. (2016). Whiteness in psychiatry: The madness of European misdiagnoses. In J. Russo & A. Sweeney (Eds.), *Searching for a rose garden: Challenging psychiatry, fostering Mad Studies* (pp. 69–76). PCCS Books Ltd.

King, C. (2022). "Madness" as a term of division, or rejection. In P. Beresford & J. Russo (Eds.), *The Routledge international handbook of Mad Studies* (pp. 351–362). Routledge.

Ladson-Billings, G. (1998). Just what is critical race theory and what's it doing in a *nice* field like education? *Qualitative Studies in Education, 11*(1), 7–24. https://doi.org/10.1080/095183998236863

LeBlanc, S., & Kinsella, E. A. (2016). Toward epistemic justice: A critically reflexive examination of "sanism" and implications for knowledge generation. *Studies in Social Justice, 10*(1), 59–78.

Lee, J. Y. (2021). Anticipatory epistemic injustice. *Social Epistemology, 35*(6), 564–576. https://doi.org/10.1080/02691728.2021.1924306

LeFrançois, B. (2016). Foreword. In J. Russo & A. Sweeney (Eds.), *Searching for a rose garden: Challenging psychiatry, fostering Mad Studies* (pp. v–viii). PCCS Books Ltd.

LeFrançois, B. A., Menzies, R., & Reaume, G. (Eds.). (2013). *Mad matters: A critical reader in Canadian Mad Studies*. Canadian Scholars' Press, Inc.

Legraien, L. (2018). Mental health detentions four times higher for black or black British people. *Healthcare Leader*. https://healthcareleadernews.com/news/mental-health-detentions-four-times-higher-for-black-or-black-british-people/

Liegghio, M. (2013). A denial of being: Psychiatrization as epistemic violence. In B. LeFrancois, R. Menzies, & G. Reaume (Eds.), *Mad matters: A critical reader in Canadian Mad Studies* (pp. 122–129). Canadian Scholars' Press.

Linton, S. (1998). *Claiming disability: Knowledge and identity*. New York University Press.

Longhurst, C. (2017). Detention figures highlight "worrying" ethnic disparity. *Mental Health Practice, 21*(3), 6.

Maglajilić, R. A. (2016). Co-creating the ways we carry each other: Reflections on being an ally and a double agent. In J. Russo & A. Sweeney (Eds.), *Searching for a rose garden: Challenging psychiatry, fostering Mad Studies* (pp. 210–217). PCCS Books.

Maglajilić, R. A. (2022). Madness in a time of war: Post-war reflections on practice and research beyond the borders of psychiatry and development. In P. Beresford & J. Russo (Eds.), *The Routledge international handbook of Mad Studies* (pp. 223–234). Routledge.

Mason, T., & Mercer, D. (2014). *The sociology of the mentally disordered offender*. Routledge.

Meerai, S., Abdillahi, I., & Poole, J. (2016). An introduction to anti-black sanism. *Intersectionalities: A Global Journal of Social Work Analysis, Research, Polity, and Practice*, 5(3), 18–35.

Menzies, R., LeFrançois, B. A., & Reaume, G. (2013). Introducing Mad Studies. In B. A. LeFrançois, R. Menzies, & G. Reaume (Eds.), *Mad matters: A critical reader in Canadian Mad Studies* (pp. 1–22). Canadian Scholars' Press, Inc.

Mills, C., & LeFrançois, B. A. (2018). Child as metaphor: Colonialism, psygovernance, and epistemicide. *World Futures*, 74(7–8), 503–524. https://doi.org/10.1080/02604027.2018.1485438

Morgan, H. (2022). Mad Studies and disability studies. In P. Beresford & J. Russo (Eds.), *The Routledge international handbook of Mad Studies* (pp. 108–118). Routledge.

Nabbali, E. M. (2022). Bodies, boundaries, b/orders: A recent critical history of differentialism and structural adjustment. In P. Beresford & J. Russo (Eds.), *The Routledge international handbook of Mad Studies* (pp. 276–289). Routledge.

O'Hagan, M. (2016). Responses to a legacy of harm. In J. Russo & A. Sweeney (Eds.), *Searching for a rose garden: Challenging psychiatry, fostering Mad Studies* (pp. 9–13). PCCS Books Ltd.

Penney, D., & Prescott, L. (2016). The co-optation of survivor knowledge: The danger of substituted values and voice. In J. Russo & A. Sweeney (Eds.), *Searching for a rose garden: Challenging psychiatry, fostering Mad Studies* (pp. 35–45). PCCS Books Ltd.

Perlin, M. (1992). On "sanism." *SMU Law Review*, 46, 373–407.

Perlin, M. (2000). *The hidden prejudice: Mental disability on trial*. American Psychological Press.

Perlin, M. (2003). You have discussed lepers and crooks: Sanism in clinical teaching. *Clinical Law Review*, 9, 683–729.

Perlin, M. (2006). International human rights and comparative mental disability law: The role of institutional psychiatry in the suppression of political dissent. *Israel Law Review*, 39(3), 73–74.

Perlin, M. (2013). "There must be some way out of here": Why the convention on the right of persons with disabilities is potentially the best weapon in the fight against sanism. *Psychiatry, Psychology, and Law*, 20(3), 462–476.

Poole, J. M., Jivraj, T., Arslanian, A., Bellows, K., Chiasson, S., Hakimy, H., Pasini, J., & Reid, J. (2012). Sanism, "mental health," and social work/education: A review and call to action. *Intersectionalities: A Global Journal of Social Work Analysis, Research, Polity, and Practice*, 1, 20–36.

Powell, S. R. (2020). Whose story? (Re)presentation, rhizovocality, and friendship. In T. D. Smith & K. S. Hendricks (Eds.), *Narratives and reflections in music education: Listening to voices seldom heard*. Springer.

Reaume, G. (2022). How is Mad Studies different from anti-psychiatry and critical psychiatry? In P. Beresford & J. Russo (Eds.), *The Routledge international handbook of Mad Studies* (pp. 98–107). Routledge.

Richerme, L. K. (2022). The hidden neoliberalism of CASEL's social emotional learning framework: Concerns for equity. *Bulletin of the Council for Research in Music Education, 232*, 7–25. https://doi.org/10.5406/21627223.232.01

Russo, J. (2001). Reclaiming madness. In J. Read (Ed.), *Something inside so strong: strategies for surviving mental distress* (pp. 36–39). Mental Health Foundation.

Russo, J. (2016). Towards our own framework, or reclaiming madness part two. In J. Russo & A. Sweeney (Eds.), *Searching for a rose garden: Challenging psychiatry, fostering Mad Studies* (pp. 59–68). PCCS Books Ltd.

Russo, J. (2022a). Afterword: The ethics of making knowledge together. In P. Beresford & J. Russo (Eds.), *The Routledge international handbook of Mad Studies* (pp. 363–369). Routledge.

Russo, J. (2022b). The international foundation of Mad Studies: Knowledge generated in collective action. In P. Beresford & J. Russo (Eds.), *The Routledge international handbook of Mad Studies* (pp. 19–29). Routledge.

Russo, J., & Sweeney, A. (2016a). The search goes on. In J. Russo & A. Sweeney (Eds.), *Searching for a rose garden: Challenging psychiatry, fostering Mad Studies* (pp. 221–228). PCCS Books Ltd.

Russo, J., & Sweeney, A. (Eds.). (2016b). *Searching for a rose garden: Challenging psychiatry, fostering Mad Studies*. PCCS Books Ltd.

Saleh, A. Z., Appelbaum, P. S., Liu, X., Stroup, T. S., & Wall, M. (2018). Deaths of people with mental illness during interactions with law enforcement. *International Journal of Law and Psychiatry, 58*, 110–116. https://doi.org/10.1016/j.ijlp.2018.03.003

Scrutton, A. P. (2017). Epistemic injustice and mental illness. In I. J. Kidd, J. Medina, & G. Pohlhaus Jr. (Eds.), *The Routledge handbook of epistemic injustice* (pp. 347–355). Routledge.

Sharma, P. (2022). Navigating voices, politics, positions amidst peers: Resonances and dissonances in India. In P. Beresford & J. Russo (Eds.), *The Routledge international handbook of Mad Studies* (pp. 340–350). Routledge.

Shimrat, I. (2022). Reflections on survivor knowledge and Mad Studies. In P. Beresford & J. Russo (Eds.), *The Routledge international handbook of Mad Studies* (pp. 53–56). Routledge.

Simmons, D. (2019). Why we can't afford whitewashed social-emotional learning. *ASCD Education Update, 61*(4), 2–3. www.ascd.org/el/articles/why-we-cant-afford-whitewashed-social-emotional-learning

Simmons, D. (2021). Why SEL alone isn't enough. *ASCD, 78*(6). www.ascd.org/el/articles/why-sel-alone-isnt-enough

Spandler, H., & Poursanidou, K. D. (2019). Who is included in the Mad Studies project? *Journal of Ethics in Mental Health, 10*(6), 1–20.

Speed, E., & Taggart, D. (2019). Stigma and mental health: Exploring potential models to enhance opportunities for a parity of participation. *Journal of Ethics in Mental Health*, *10*(6), 1–19.

Sullivan, P. J. (2019). Epistemic injustice and self-injury: A concept with clinical implications. *Philosophy, Psychiatry, & Psychology*, *26*(4), 349–362. https://doi.org/10.1353/ppp.2019.0049

Sweeney, A. (2016a). The transformative potential of survivor research. In J. Russo & A. Sweeney (Eds.), *Searching for a rose garden: Challenging psychiatry, fostering Mad Studies* (pp. 49–58). PCCS Books Ltd.

Sweeney, A. (2016b). Why Mad Studies needs survivor research and survivor research needs Mad Studies. *Intersectionalities: A Global Journal of Social Work Analysis, Research, Polity, and Practice*, *5*(3), 36–61.

Taggart, D. (2022). "Are you experienced?" The use of experiential knowledge in mental health and its contribution to Mad Studies. In P. Beresford & J. Russo (Eds.), *The Routledge international handbook of Mad Studies* (pp. 154–165). Routledge.

Tang, L. (2022). Upcycling recovery: Potential alliances of recovery, inequality and Mad Studies. In P. Beresford & J. Russo (Eds.), *The Routledge international handbook of Mad Studies* (pp. 266–275). Routledge.

Valdivia Quiroz, B. D. R. (2022). A crazy, warrior and "respondona" Peruvian: All personal transformation is social and political. In P. Beresford & J. Russo (Eds.), *The Routledge international handbook of Mad Studies* (pp. 41–52). Routledge.

Voronka, J. (2016). The politics of "people with lived experience": Experiential authority and the risks of strategic essentialism. *Philosophy, Psychiatry & Psychology*, *23*(3–4), 189–201.

Waite, R., & Ryan, R. A. (2020). *Adverse childhood experiences: What students and health professionals need to know*. Routledge.

Walker, N. (2021). *Neuroqueer heresies: Notes on the neurodiversity paradigm, autistic empowerment, and postnormal possibilities* (ePub ed.). Autonomous Press.

Webb, D. (2010). *Thinking about suicide: Contemplating and comprehending the urge to die*. PCCS Books.

White, W. L. (2022). Re-writing the master narrative: A prerequisite for Mad liberation. In P. Beresford & J. Russo (Eds.), *The Routledge international handbook of Mad Studies* (pp. 76–89). Routledge.

Williams, V. (2014). *"Sanism," a socially acceptable prejudice: Addressing the prejudice associated with mental illness in the legal system* [Unpublished Doctoral Dissertation, University of Tasmania]. Australia.

Wolframe, P. M. (2013). The madwoman in the academy, or, revealing the invisible straightjacket: Theorizing and teaching saneism and sane privilege. *Disability Studies Quarterly*, *33*(1). https://dsq-sds.org/article/view/3425/3200

# 2 Applying Models from Disability Studies to Experiences of Madness and Distress

This chapter is the first of seven that foreground the perspectives, experiences, stories, and philosophies of 15 music educators. In centering their perspectives and ideas, I describe some of the possible ways one can think about experiences of Madness and/or distress. Some participants conceptualized their mental health differences as a disability. While Mad Studies offers a particularized framework to consider Madness and distress, participants also found disability studies concepts useful. I employ the concept of *bodyminds* (Baker, 2002; Price, 2015)—an idea that refuses Descartes' dualism of body and mind—to explore how participants and others who are similarly situated may benefit from thinking with disability studies. In this chapter, I discuss models that might be useful to conversations about Madness and distress. I assert that a blend of disability models may be helpful to considering such experiences. Following Mad Studies scholars (LeFrançois et al., 2013; Menzies et al., 2013), I move away from psy-based paradigms including the medical model (Dobbs, 2012; Linton, 1998) toward conceptualizations that include the social model (Oliver & Sapey, 1999; Shakespeare, 2017), complex embodiment (Siebers, 2008, 2017), the cultural model (Snyder & Mitchell, 2006), DisCrit (Annamma et al., 2022; Connor et al., 2016), a critical realist approach (Shakespeare, 2014), and the social confluence model (Lubet, 2013) for what they might offer people with experiences of Madness and distress.[1]

## Mental Health Differences as Disability

Multiple participants viewed (their) mental health differences as a disability, even as they recognized that doing so was at least somewhat contested.

*Rebecca:* I would love for [mental disabilities] to be societally recognized as being the same as a physical disability because it has affected

DOI: 10.4324/9781032662817-3

my life to the same extent, certainly. But it's always something I felt ashamed about, that I felt I had to cover up and make light of and put on a brave face about. I do see it now as a disability.

Rebecca (she/her) identified as a white female with "mental health problems in a number of areas." She previously taught high school music, and at the time of the interview she was teaching music education at a Canadian university. The stigma of mental health differences led to feelings of shame for Rebecca, which in turn led to silence, judgment, and secrecy—three vital elements of shame (Brown, 2021, p. 137).[2] Indeed, shame and secrecy comprise a key part of what makes framing experiences of Madness and/or distress as a disability contentious. Understanding mental health differences as disabilities, however, may work against some of the shame and stigma commonly encountered and internalized by people with experiences of Madness and/or distress.

Blaine Banghart-Broussard (they/them) described themself as white, non-binary, middle-class, and in their 20s. They also identified as trans. Blaine was from the southern U.S. They noted: "I'm bipolar with some depression and anxiety sprinkled in for zest." Blaine formerly taught elementary general music, and at the time of the interview, they had just begun teaching high school brass lesson groups. Blaine identified mental health differences as an invisible disability and felt that the invisibility prevented the receipt of accommodations on par with people who have visible disabilities.

Blaine: A lot of people don't consider mental illnesses disabilities. I definitely do. I feel like a disability is something that affects either how you interact with people or how you view yourself ... I feel like people, if they don't physically see something wrong with you, then it's not considered an actual disability. There's a lot of accommodations that can be made for people with mental illnesses that I think are just skipped over or not even considered, because it's not considered a real thing. But I do consider mental illnesses a disability.

Price (2015) contested invisibility and argued that "such disabilities are not exactly 'visible' or 'invisible,' but *intermittently* apparent" (p. 272, emphasis in original); these disabilities require accommodations in the same manner as those disabilities that are consistently apparent.

Cheryl (they/them) identified as white, queer, financially stable, able-bodied, and non-binary. They were from Western Europe. They had taught upper elementary school and middle school general music and some choir.

At the time of the interview, Cheryl was working on a master's degree in music education at a U.S. institution. They noted: "I would definitely agree that mental health issues or, in my case depression, is a disability to some extent." Understanding mental health differences as disabilities gives individuals with experiences of Madness and distress a different way to think about those experiences.

Laura resonated strongly with the word disability.

*Laura:* I like the word disability. I think it describes me, I think there's lots of other terms that we use sometimes in our profession like "exceptional" or other terms that I just really don't feel match me well or match other people. Disability. In our profession, I think we don't think of it as much as a marginalized population. I don't think it gets enough credit. And I don't think that when we think about marginalized populations, most people would not list disability ... as an umbrella term and things that are listed underneath that, I don't think that we have enough people in our profession listing disability as one of those areas. I think there's a lot of work to be done, first of all, in getting people to understand that disability is a part of marginalized populations.

Laura (she/her) identified as a white, middle-class female, with several mood disabilities. She had previously taught elementary music, beginning band, and multiple university classes as a graduate student and visiting assistant professor. She was working on completing her doctoral dissertation at the time of the interview. Not only did Laura see her differences as a disability, she also wanted recognition of the oppression disabled people experience as a "marginalized population." Noticing the oppression then situates accommodation, recognition, and equality as justice issues rather than charity or benevolence.[3] Ultimately, constructing these differences as disabilities makes looking to disability studies for what it might offer people with experiences of Madness and distress relevant.

## Bodyminds

Informed by trauma studies (specifically Rothschild, 2000), Price (2015) described her journey with the term *bodymind*, which she began to use to indicate that mental disability matters as a category of analysis. She argued that:

> mental and physical processes not only affect each other but also give rise to each other—that is, because they tend to act as one, even though

they are conventionally understood as two—it makes more sense to refer to them together, in a single term.

(p. 269)

Using the term operates as a marker that does not yet address the fact that body and mind are typically treated as rhetorically distinct. She further noted that non-Western philosophies conceptualized the bodymind before the trauma-informed approach she encountered (p. 280).

> Rooted in Buddhist philosophy, [Nagatomo's (1992)] attunement shares with Rothschild's trauma theory the notion that we can refer meaningfully, if tentatively, to "mind" and "body," but ultimately the two are so fully integrated that they should also be considered one.
> (Price, 2015, p. 280)

The bodymind is thus conceptualized as being in an integrated and mobile state of attunement (Nagatomo, 1992, as cited in Price, 2015).

Study participant Paulo also challenged the body/mind dichotomy.

*Paulo:* I wonder if the whole discussion of mental health versus general health roots back to that whole thing that Deleuze was trying to go against, right? Like the bodies without organs, separation (Deleuze & Guattari, 2005/1987). Maybe we separate this for some weird reason when we shouldn't, and it would be easier for us to navigate life identifying it as all one big kind of health.

Paulo (he/him) identified as a white, heterosexual, upper middle-class, cis man. He was a father and a musician and had previously taught elementary general music. At the time of data gathering, he was an assistant professor at a U.S. university. Paulo raised concerns that the failing U.S. healthcare system likely could not and does not handle the integration of mind and body well.

*Paulo:* Just talking through this makes me think about the way that we separate mental health and disability and ... I'm fine with saying that I'm disabled, right? That identity, that's something I feel. I also see it especially after every mass shooting, which is you know, unfortunately, way too common in our country. ... But it's also because of how we think of and how it feels like society has started to attend more to mental health as a thing that people care about even if they just pay lip service to it, but they desperately don't want to get lumped into disability. I'm guessing because of the negative stigma. I mean, there's already negative stigma around mental health. Anyway, it's weird to me because it almost separates ... It's almost like union busting in some respects. Like, we don't want these people to form a coalition, because God forbid, if all the people who've got mental health concerns realize that they're disabled and they form a voting block, "Oh, no! Then shit's gonna get real."

Understanding mental health differences as disabilities may foster important coalitions leading to political clout. Insightfully, Paulo acknowledged the stigma attached to both disability and mental health differences and suggested that not separating the two—the *body-and-mind* rhetoric that Price (2015) avoided with the *bodymind* construction—has potential to be quite powerful, both politically and socially.

## Models from Disability Studies

Disability Studies offers multiple models to consider. In this section, I share those models useful to the conversation about Madness and distress, and ultimately suggest a blend of disability models that may facilitate consideration of mental health differences from an intersectional perspective. In drawing on disability studies, I use the integrated *bodymind* (Baker, 2002; Price, 2015) as a foundation.

### The Medical Model

The medical model takes a distinctly biological approach to disability, situating disability in individual bodies and assuming they require medical intervention (Siebers, 2008, p. 25). In particular, therapeutic and rehabilitative professionals perceive disability as medicalized, related to function, and as deficit (Dobbs, 2012, p. 8). An individual with a disability who is unable to perform a particular function is subject to "management" or "repair" (Dobbs, 2012, p. 8). Linton (1998) observed:

> the medicalization of disability casts human variation as deviance from the norm, as pathological condition, as deficit, and significantly, as an individual burden and personal tragedy. Society, in agreeing to assign medical meaning to disability, colludes to keep the issue within the purview of the medical establishment, to keep it a personal matter and "treat" the condition and the person with the condition rather than "treating" the social processes and policies that constrict disabled people's lives.
> 
> (p. 11)

The individualizing and pathologizing of disability do not allow for the kind of coalition-building Paulo envisioned, nor for understanding of disabled people as an oppressed group like Laura suggested. Rather, the medical model locates the "problem" in the individual and limits connection to social practices, processes, and policies (Linton, 1998). This model's refusal to acknowledge the sociality of disability means that its individualizing approach often results in pathologizing people with disabilities. As such, the medical model encourages viewing disability as a personal issue to be "corrected" as opposed to human variation deeply informed by social structures.

Whereas disability studies scholars have offered significant critiques of the medical model (see for example Linton, 1998; Oliver & Sapey, 1999; UPIAS, 1976), most participants acknowledged its use value, at times, in their lives. Laura recognized the importance of pairing the medical model with the social model.

*Laura:* I think that they exist in tandem with one another. I think that the medical model is important for the actual diagnoses that we talk about within disability, but we can't go on that alone. Because the social model talks about disabilities within the social constructs, so we need that as well.

Some degree of balance between the medicalization of mental disabilities and the understanding of these disabilities in social context resonated with participants. Nine participants mentioned experiences with medication, so most made use of the medical possibilities available at some point(s).

*Paulo:* I think straight medical model doesn't work at all either, because it just considers things as fixable and treatable. And we know that's not the case, right? It's very complex from day to day. I think different aspects—like more of a social aspect, more of an individual aspect, more of a medicalized aspect—come into focus, right? On days when I have to take an anxiety med, the medicalized aspect of it really rears up ... When you take medicine every day, like I take my dosage of everything, it fades in the background because it's every day, just like brushing my teeth. I don't think about brushing my teeth. I just do it. But when you take something that's out of the order. If I take a Xanax just because I'm overly anxious about something, or when I have to take a pill to help me sleep a little bit better, those times, I think a lot more about the medicalized aspect of it.

The medical aspects of living with mental health differences became salient at times for Paulo, but he acknowledged that social and individual aspects sometimes took precedence.

Meena (she/her) identified as cis, female, and heterosexual. She was mixed race—"half white, Caucasian, and other half is East Indian. So Desi. So my mother has heritage of Italy, Hungary, and Slovakia. My father is from Nepal." Meena was a strings studio teacher with experience teaching elementary music at a Waldorf school. At the time of data gathering she was working as a social worker and writing articles about string pedagogy and mental health. Meena's language about adaptation aligns with the medical model.

*Meena:* When I think of somebody who is disabled, for example, somebody has an impairment, or a sort of barrier that occurs when their natural self is not able to fully ambulate or interact with the world seamlessly, that an adaptation has to be determined in order to access the world and to navigate through the world and to work in the world in a way that is fruitful. And at the equivalent level of a person who does not have a disability.

Dobbs (2012) noted that within the medical model, "the individual must be adapted to the environment, rather than the environment to the individual" (p. 10). Conversely, the social model, described in the next section, aims to modify the environment. I now look to models beyond the medical model which views disability as personal tragedy (Linton, 1998; Oliver & Sapey, 1999) and aims to diagnose, medicate, and correct. This pivot aligns with movement away from psy-based paradigms in Mad Studies (see for example LeFrançois et al., 2013; Menzies et al., 2013).

*The Social Model*

The social model originated in the United Kingdom. A radical departure from the medical model, the early disability rights organization Union of Physically Impaired Against Segregation (UPIAS) distinguished between *impairment* in the body, and *disability*, understood as the ways the physical and social environment make the impairment disabling (Oliver & Sapey, 1999; UPIAS, 1976).

[I]t is society which disables physically impaired people. Disability is something imposed on top of our impairments by the way we are unnecessarily isolated and excluded from full participation in society. To understand this it is necessary to grasp the distinction between the physical impairment and the social situation, called "disability," of people with such impairment.

(UPIAS, 1976, pp. 3–4)

"Disability is thus a relationship between individual impairments and the social restrictions imposed by social organization" (Oliver & Sapey, 1999, p. 63). The social model focuses on removing disabling barriers in the physical and social environment (Oliver & Sapey, 1999, p. 83).

Half of this study's participants appreciated and found value in the social model, including Chris Hansen, who worked on the *Convention on the Rights of Persons with Disabilities* (CRPD).

Chris:     We worked really hard in the CRPD to hone and refine and define the social model of disability. Definitely that's the lens that I take. I certainly acknowledge that some of us have an easier time navigating the world than others because of differences, and I do strongly align with the social model of disability.

As an international treaty, the CRPD offers a framework to create legislation and policies that support individuals with disabilities and ensure their rights and freedoms.[4] Chris (she/her) identified as a white, lesbian, married person with five children and a grandchild. She also identified as an educator, an activist, and a business owner, as well as a user and survivor of psychiatry. A citizen of New Zealand, she was living in the U.S. during this study. She had previously taught preschool and what she called "pre-instrumental" music, which she noted involved beginning music literacy, "making instruments, and introducing students to a range of instruments, musics, and sound-making." She worked as an itinerant music educator in a rural setting. She had been a private violin teacher and currently co-directed an international peer support education business.

Jillian Bowe (they/them) identified as white and middle-class, with mental health issues. In regard to gender, they noted: "Gender unknown, truly, I don't know. Who knows? I don't think gender is real." Jillian was completing their student teaching as the culmination of their undergraduate degree in music education during data gathering.

Jillian:     I think the social model change is a lot of people's first step. I think it's really eye-opening for a lot of people. ... Because, of course, you would look at a difference and pin it on the person who has the difference, not the people who are creating it. But once you realize how socially constructed everything is, it all falls apart pretty quickly.

Jillian recognized the value in the social model as a place to begin to consider disability. Because of its focus on removing disabling barriers, I find the social model pedagogically useful, as one can attend to any barriers that students and educators with impairments face in the classroom. I also see it as a first step, as Jillian described.

Laura saw the value in recognizing what barriers the physical and social environment create for a person with a disability. She also called attention to the imperative of considering stigma and its effects (Goffman, 1963).[5]

Laura: In the social [model] structure, disability is also a lot of what is put upon a person. So we can't just think about what's wrong with somebody, which often happens when we talk about disabilities. And often what I think about when I think about my disabilities, what's wrong with me. But also, we have to consider how we shape the environment and how much of the environment creates a disability for a person. ... When we think about the stigma that's associated with mental health, we really have to consider how that affects the person.

The social model is useful in considering barriers and other social constructs that negatively impact people with disabilities, as Laura expressed.

*The Need for More Complexity*

Both the literature and participants argued that the medical model and social model do not capture the complexity and nuance needed to describe experiences of disability. "Some scholars complain that the medical model pays too much attention to embodiment, while the social model leaves it out of the picture" (Siebers, 2008, p. 25). I therefore examine models that offer some explanatory power by speaking to both embodiment and societal barriers, and account for subtleties and multidimensionality. Dobbs (2012) identified the limits of the social model:

> Strict adherence to this model can be viewed as repudiating embodied impairments and their deleterious effects upon people's lives (Shakespeare, 2010, p. 269), failing to enfold the overlapping exigencies, complexities, and lived realities of disability when entwined with sexuality, race, gender, chronic pain, illness, multiple disabilities, and aging.
>
> (p. 11)

To consider disabilities in bodyminds, a model must capture both embodiment *and* social constructions. In a Mad Studies context, Morgan (2022) noted that survivors of psychiatry appreciated social models and their repudiation of medical models, but found the social model of disability too narrow. Survivors were similarly skeptical of Mad Studies (p. 113). Participants also sought nuance.

*Paulo:* I don't think a straight social model would ever fully work when attending to mental health. I also don't think a straight social model would work in anything except from a political standpoint. … But as an actual, active model for understanding complexities of life, it doesn't do a whole lot there. It does a whole lot if you're looking for barriers and you're looking for ways to build coalitions.

While identifying barriers and building coalitions remains important, other models may provide the nuances the social model lacks.

Emma Pilmer (she/her) described herself as a "proud Asian American who has been adopted. And female, she/her, and I identify as autistic." At the time of data collection she was in her final year of an undergraduate music education degree. Akin to Paulo, Emma talked about the need for a model to be less "basic" or "compartmentalized."

*Emma:* Kind of like what I was alluding to [with] the social model, one thing that I just find fascinating is these models all seem like they're so compartmentalized, it's almost a little too basic, because I feel like a lot of them could overlap. With our social perceptions of mental illness, that can impact how we treat them medically. … Maybe that's why I feel like I totally gravitate more towards the social [model], because the social one seems like it more so explains the relationships of how we socially view disorders and disabilities. In a way, I feel like the medical one almost can't truly exist without the social model coming first. As we perceive the social, we perceive disabilities socially through our interactions, then we research it, and then comes the medical. That's how I perceive it. It's not as neat and compartmentalized.

The models that follow capture greater subtlety, resonating with observations made by participants. Although models of disability exist beyond those that follow, my choices reflect participants' descriptions of theoretical components that best reflected their lived experiences.

*Complex Embodiment*

Siebers (2017) challenged what he called the "ideology of ability," which at its simplest is the "preference for ablebodiedness" (p. 312). At its extreme, the ideology of ability "defines the baseline by which humanness is determined" (Siebers, 2017, p. 312), thereby marking disabled people as less-than-human. The ideology of ability may also lead people with disabilities to camouflage them as possible (Churchill & Bernard, 2020, p. 40).[6] Siebers (2008) wrote that "[d]isability is not a pathological condition, only analyzable via individual psychology, but a social location *complexly embodied*" (p. 14, emphasis added). Complex embodiment frames disability as a form of human variation (p. 25). Following feminist philosophers, Siebers (2008) argued that knowledge is socially situated and embodied (p. 22). Marginality, for Siebers, comes with a distinct epistemic perspective to theorize society differently than those in dominant groups (p. 28). Like the social model, complex embodiment considers the effects of disabling environments on individuals' lived experiences and emphasizes factors that derive from the body (e.g., chronic pain). Siebers argued that there is no hierarchy between disabilities that derive from the body and those that derive from the environment. Both types of disabilities constitute human variation, both between individuals and across the lifespan (Siebers, 2008, p. 25). Importantly, complex embodiment takes an interactional approach:

> The theory of complex embodiment views the economy between social representations and the body not as unidirectional as in the social model, or nonexistent as in the medical model, but as reciprocal. Complex embodiment theorizes the body and its representations as mutually transformative.
>
> (Siebers, 2008, p. 25)

Siebers acknowledged that the body and the environment are mutually constitutive and thus deeply inform embodied perspectives. In his introduction to Siebers' (2017) chapter, Davis noted:

> The body and its representations mutually transform each other: what we think of a body is informed by the lived experience, and the experience of living with the body is informed by the social prejudices and ideologies that represent the body.
>
> (p. 311)

Mutuality and interaction remain crucial to theorizing complex embodiment. This argument also implies that identity-based prejudice, bias, discrimination, or oppression can potentially disable a person, or at least impede their access.

Complex embodiment contributes to arguments about intersectionality as well (Siebers, 2008). As an analytical tool, intersectionality facilitates understanding that racism, sexism, and classism do not function as mutually exclusive axes of power, but rather intersect in complex ways to enact oppression (Crenshaw, 2014/2000).[7] The intersections of these axes create burdens that constitute "dynamic or active aspects of disempowerment" (p. 17). Intersectionality, therefore, offers a way of "understanding and analyzing the complexity in the world, in people, and in human experiences" (Collins & Bilge, 2016, p. 22). Crucially, moving from single-axis thinking—that considers identities as sites of oppression in an additive way—to matrix thinking allows for a both/and approach that is inclusive of disability (Collins, 2000, 2019). Matrix thinking accounts for individuals' multiple subjectivities in a way that acknowledges both identity and context. Complex embodiment refuses to hierarchize identities and facilitates a way to understand the prejudices and oppressions a person faces based on their intersectional identities (Siebers, 2008, p. 28). It further acknowledges the variations that may occur between people who are similarly situated. Siebers emphasized:

> first, that intersectionality as a theory references the tendency of identities to construct one another reciprocally (Collins, 2003, p. 208); second, that identities are not merely standpoints where one may stand or try to stand but also complex embodiments; and, third, that the ideology of ability uses the language of pathology to justify labeling some identities as inferior to others.
>
> (Siebers, 2008, p. 28)

Ultimately Siebers' arguments rest on three ideas about social construction: (1) "knowledge is socially situated"; (2) "identities are socially constructed"; and (3) "some bodies are excluded by dominant social ideologies" (p. 33). Siebers' theory allows for complex understandings of variation in embodiment, and acknowledgment of the epistemic value of the liminality occupied by people with disabilities.

In recognizing liminality as an epistemic strength, complex embodiment accounts for disability and its intersections with other sites of identity. Moreover, Siebers (2008) called for people with disabilities to engage in identity politics (Churchill & Bernard, 2020, p. 32)—perhaps the kind of coalition-building Paulo described. Dobbs (2012) noted, however, that Siebers (2008) did not account for the ways that people with disabilities make meaning of their lived experiences, how some individuals resist stereotypes and create positive self-images while others resonate to and absorb *ableist* (Hehir, 2002) discourses and prejudices—preferring the so-called able body over that which is constructed as disabled.

(p. 11)

In other words, Dobbs was concerned with how people with disabilities may internalize Siebers' (2008) ideology of ability, or resist it.

Some participants appreciated the complex embodiment model or made observations that aligned with its tenets. When considering the usefulness of different models of disability, Paulo valued the interactional elements of complex embodiment, saying "I think anything that is more interactional, so complex embodiment works well-ish." Blaine appreciated the accounting for intersectionality this model provides.

*Blaine:* The intersections are obviously important. A really big part of my identity is my transness. Aside from my mental health, and a lot of things with that play into my mental health. Getting misgendered constantly does not have a good effect on my bipolar brain, so there's a lot of intersectionality there. There's also racial intersectionality that I don't experience as a white person, but I know that that's important. I know that there's a lot of stigma in other racial communities and around getting help for these things, so I think that definitely plays a big part.

Complex embodiment acknowledges the sites of intersecting oppressions and addresses the interactions, in this instance between getting misgendered and its effect on Blaine's "bipolar brain." It also recognizes the strength in Blaine's epistemic perspective.

Nicholas Prosini (they/them) identified as "white, trans non-binary, middle-class, disabled, 40 years old, queer, and Jewish." They previously taught band and orchestra, and at the time of data gathering were teaching general music and choir. Nicholas observed that some disabilities may be easier than others to view as human variation because of attached stigmas.

*Nicholas:* I'm partial to complex embodiment and cultural [models] in that human differentiation is a thing. It'd be great if people were able to view disability as that. That's all it is. I could see it being easier for people to conceptualize autism that way, and harder to conceptualize bipolar disorder that way.

The neurodiversity movement has certainly worked toward normalization (see for example Johnson & Olson, 2021; Walker, 2021). That may not extend, however, to some more stigmatized identities. Nicholas additionally sought a model that accounted for their Jewishness. Complex embodiment does aim to account for prejudice and oppression. In its embrace of intersectionality, complex embodiment recognizes religion as a facet of a socially situated identity *complexly embodied.*

*Cultural Model*

Like Siebers (2008, 2017), Snyder and Mitchell (2006) sought more complexity in theorizing disability. Whereas the social model conceptualizes impairment narrowly as a "neutral designator of biological difference" (Snyder & Mitchell, 2006, p. 6) and targets the social and physical environment as the site of disability, the cultural model views impairment as "both human variation encountering environmental obstacles *and* socially mediated difference that lends group identity and phenomenological perspective" (p. 10, emphasis in original). Following cultural and identity studies, *disability*

> is largely, but not strictly synonymous with sites of cultural oppression. It does not solely represent the social coordinates, as Liz Crow puts it, of restraints "that we must escape" (1996, p. 206). Instead, our use of this term is much closer to that offered by scholars such as Sally French (1994), Simi Linton (1998), and others who recognize disability as a site of phenomenological value that is not purely synonymous with the processes of social disablement.
> (Snyder & Mitchell, 2006, p. 6)

Snyder and Mitchell explained: "[t]he definition of disability must incorporate both the outer and inner reaches of culture and experience as a combination of profoundly social and biological forces" (p. 7). They acknowledged that both bodily variation (especially socially stigmatized differences) and the environment impinge on each other (pp. 6–7), with particular interest in how embodied differences influence people's experiences of both their bodies and the environment. Like complex embodiment, the cultural model accounts for interaction. Snyder and Mitchell examined this "interactional space between embodiment and social ideology" (p. 7). They did so by considering the cultural locations of disability, by which they meant the spaces of interaction that are "sites of violence, restriction, confinement, and absence of liberty for people with disabilities" (p. x). In examining cultural locations, Snyder and Mitchell elucidated how impairments are fraught with meaning. Indeed, embodiment potentially serves as a "meaningful materiality" (p. 10).

The cultural model is consequently political, "a politicized self-naming strategy that distances people with disabilities from dominant definitions of incapacity and dysfunction" (Snyder & Mitchell, 2006, p. 9). Their use of the term *disability* acknowledges the distance between dominant cultural perspectives of disability as tragedy and "a politically informed disability-subculture perspective that seeks to define itself against devaluing mainstream views of disability" (p. 9). In contrast with the social model's perspective of disability as defined by discriminatory encounters, Snyder and Mitchell argued that the cultural model prompts a politicized repositioning or renaming of disability as a site of both resistance and agency (p. 10). This self-naming strategy additionally "distances people with disabilities from dominant definitions of incapacity and dysfunction" (p. 9). Shakespeare (2014) cautioned, however, that most leading authors on the cultural model work in the humanities, making them more likely to interrogate representations than material conditions such as poverty or unemployment (p. 52).

Meghan Barrett (she/her) identified as a white, lower middle-class woman with severe ADHD and a "diagnosed but unnamed chronic illness." She recently completed student teaching in instrumental music education.

*Meghan:* I'm interested in the cultural model. That sounds very compelling. I liked the way that it blends the "yes, this is a legitimate diagnosis. Yes, this is an impairment," but it's more than just what this person is dealing with. It's the environment that they live in. It's also everything that's going on in the world and how that affects them and how that challenges them.

The intricacy that the cultural model facilitates in examining impairment and disability in their cultural locations, and its politicization as a self-naming strategy that refuses dominant definitions of disability while supporting both agency and resistance, makes the cultural model a useful analytical tool.

### DisCrit

DisCrit as a theoretical framework and methodological tool combines disability studies with critical race theory to "move past simplistic and unidimensional notions of identity" (Annamma et al., 2016a, p. 1) to understand how race and disability inform one another.

> [T]o recognize humanity in a richer, nuanced, and more accurate sense, we acknowledge how the works of those before us broke open existing boundaries allowing us to recognize the multiple dimensions of individuals and the systems of oppression and marginalization in which they survive, resist, and thrive.
>
> (Annamma et al., 2016a, pp. 1–2)

DisCrit, in alignment with other models, provides a tool to recognize human multidimensionality. It further considers the structural power of racism and ableism and their effects on people at their intersections (Annamma et al., 2022; Connor et al., 2016). Annamma et al. (2016b) put forward seven tenets of DisCrit:

1. DisCrit focuses on ways that the forces of racism and ableism circulate interdependently, often in neutralized and invisible ways, to uphold notions of normalcy.
2. DisCrit values multidimensional identities and troubles singular notions of identity such as race *or* dis/ability *or* class *or* gender *or* sexuality, and so on.
3. DisCrit emphasizes the social constructions of race and ability and yet recognizes the material and psychological impacts of being labeled as raced or dis/abled, which sets one outside of the western cultural norms.
4. DisCrit privileges voices of marginalized populations, traditionally not acknowledged within research.
5. DisCrit considers legal and historical aspects of dis/ability and race and how both have been used separately and together to deny the rights of some citizens.
6. DisCrit recognizes Whiteness and Ability as Property and that gains for people labeled with dis/abilities have largely been made as the result of interest convergence of White, middle-class citizens.
7. DisCrit requires activism and supports all forms of resistance. (p. 19)

DisCrit makes intersectionality fundamental to analysis and extends beyond additive accountings of difference—what Spelman (1988) called "the ampersand problem" (see Chapter 5)—that fail to capture complex intersections of different categories of identity. DisCrit makes accounting for and conceptualizing the ways that "multiple forms of inequality and identity are interrelated across different contexts and over time" possible (Annamma et al., 2016a, p. 2).

Most participants recognized the intersections of their identities and the degrees of oppression or privilege that resulted.

*QingYu:* What I really felt that helped me stand out as a teacher was because I experienced so much intersectionality being a person of color, being someone that experiences mental health problems, being a person that's disabled, being a person that is gay, I'm not cisgender, I am more prone to experiencing oppression. I'm prone to experiencing more trauma. It makes me a more compassionate, empathetic person. Being compassionate is not something that you can just outright learn. So it gives me an advantage.

QingYu Zhong (they/them) identified as non-binary. They noted: "I am Chinese, so I'm Asian. I'm Jewish. I identify as gay. I identify as a disabled person with a mobility disability, and I am part of the neurodivergent community. I have ADHD." They served as a substitute music teacher, and at the time of data gathering they were in the first year of a master's degree in social work. QingYu recognized that their intersecting identities made them more vulnerable to experiencing oppression, and how such experiences helped them be empathetic and compassionate in the classroom. Even though QingYu indicated positive outcomes from their experiences of oppression, doing so in no way validates oppression. Individuals make their own meaning about their experiences, and imposing positive meaning from external positions of privilege remains inappropriate and unethical. DisCrit facilitates recognition of ways that structures of oppression such as ableism and racism, alongside sexism, cissexism, religious oppression, sanism, and heterosexism, shape QingYu's experiences. It acknowledges the multidimensionality of their identity, and the material and psychological impacts of the labels externally imposed on them.

As a therapist and social worker, Meena wished that service provisions for people with experiences of Madness and/or distress accounted for culture. She noted: "People who are receiving services in a mental health capacity, you have the culture of the person, and then you have the culture of the service provider. I could say a lot about this." Accounting for race and other facets of culture such as religion and language in interpersonal interactions—in this case in relation to mental health differences—facilitates the consideration of the impact of different systems of oppression as they collide with ableism. In service provision relationships, an intersectional approach facilitates understanding the psychological impact(s) of systems of oppression on the individual. Applied in education contexts, recognition of students' cultures as strengths and consideration of culture in educator-student and student-student relationships is fundamental to culturally relevant pedagogy (Ladson-Billings, 1995, 2009, 2014), culturally responsive teaching (Gay, 2018; McKoy & Lind, 2023), and culturally sustaining pedagogy (Paris & Alim, 2014, 2017). Acknowledging the role of systems of oppression on educators and students remains crucial to the resistance so fundamental to DisCrit.

White participants noted their privilege and acknowledged the oppressions they did not experience because of their whiteness. In its recognition of whiteness and ability as property, DisCrit frames both whiteness and ability as social and economic capital that one might mobilize in various situations. In her argument on whiteness as property, Harris (1993) began with a story of her grandmother passing as white in order to receive particular advantages to which only white people had access. Her story illustrates that to possess whiteness is to possess something valuable that is generally unavailable to BIPOC individuals or groups. Erevelles et al. (2006) contended that the whiteness as property argument also applies to ability. They wrote that "in addition to Whiteness, ability (both cognitive and physical) was also an important property right that had to be safeguarded, protected, and defended in the attempt to decide who could or could not have access to public education" (pp. 93–94). Cognitive ability constitutes capital in education, which has offered justification for segregation alongside other sites of identity (p. 94). Whereas white participants did not necessarily have access to ability as property, they noticed how their whiteness likely made their experiences of Madness and distress easier than those of their BIPOC peers.

*Paulo:* Being a white male in the Midwest automatically grants me a whole lot of leeway that I did not earn, so I think that I usually don't experience a lot of stereotyping myself. I think also because I'm so proactive about being honest of who I am. ... I do think that I probably would have more negative, impactful stories if I didn't have other aspects of my identity that propped me up.

Paulo was acutely aware of his sites of privilege and the capital that comes with those privileges.

Lizabeth Desmet (they/them) identified as white, queer, and upper middle-class. They explained: "My gender, I identify as a non-binary woman. And I know that those terms are contrasting, but that's where I'm at. Non-binary woman. We can also call that gender non-conforming." They further observed how their ADHD, depression, and anxiety affected their life. Lizabeth completed student teaching in elementary general music for their music education degree shortly after the interview phase of data gathering. Lizabeth noticed the difference between the way they were treated and the way teachers responded to their peers, attributing it to their privilege.

*Lizabeth:* One thing about my ADHD, I think a lot about my privilege, just because of how supported I was, how many accommodations were made for me. I was able to advocate for myself. I think that's one reason why because my parents raised me to be really confident and to ask for what I need. I had so many privileges that I was listened to, and I think my whiteness has to do with that. I think growing up as a girl had to do with that. Whereas my classmates who experienced similar things, exhibited similar behaviors that I did, or possibly were struggling in the same ways that I was, were usually my male colleagues, the boys in my classes and particularly boys of color. They would be the ones that would be punished or reprimanded, given a pink slip or whatnot, whatever the punishment system was at the time for doing things that I either would do if I didn't have that accommodation I asked for, or things that I do but were just excused because it was me.

Lizabeth observed that educators punished their male peers of color for similar behaviors and recognized their privilege in avoiding such treatment. DisCrit problematizes and resists the school-to-prison pipeline that tracks racialized students for incarceration following carceral logics (Connor et al., 2016, see Part IV in particular). The tenets of DisCrit facilitate complex understandings of privilege and oppression and offer a tool for nuanced analyses of identities and structures of power.

*A Critical Realist Approach*

Shakespeare's (2014) *critical realist* approach offered an alternative to the social model that considers both impairment and disability. Shakespeare cautioned that a social model that cannot account for the effect of impairment will fail to fully capture the situations disabled people face (p. 32). He argued that unlike the social model's construction of impairment as a "neutral designator of biological difference" (Snyder & Mitchell, 2006, p. 6), impairments are not neutral—rather, they are often limiting or difficult (Shakespeare, 2014, p. 29). Moreover, impairment shapes the disability experience and has disparate effects (p. 32). He proposed an approach to disability that "suggests that disability is always an interaction between individual and structural factors" (p. 74) including "impairment, personality, individual attitudes, environment, policy, and culture" (p. 77). Critical realism resists theories that only address external barriers (such as the social model) or personal solutions (such as the medical model).

At the heart of the social model approach to disability is a kind of denial. Social model theory enables disabled people to deny the relevance of their impaired bodies or brains, and seek equality with non-disabled people on the basis of similarity. What divides disabled from non-disabled people, in this formulation, is the imposition of social oppression and social exclusion.

(p. 106)

A critical realist approach addresses both the personal and the systemic/structural (pp. 82–83).

Like complex embodiment, the cultural model, and DisCrit, Shakespeare's critical realist approach brings dimension to theorizing experiences of impairment and disability. He resisted affirmation approaches that challenge the notion of impairment as a problem, recognizing that many people with disabilities find impairment to be difficult (p. 108). Affirmation approaches, however, encourage scholars and activists to ensure balance in their representations of people's experiences of disabilities (p. 108). Shakespeare illuminated that a "model has to be complex enough to encompass the positive aspects of life with a health condition, and allow for the possibilities of adaptation and flourishing (Amundson, 2010)" (p. 108). A critical realist approach allows for recognition of the full disability and impairment experience while not precluding medical support. This model also situates these experiences in a wider social context that accounts for systemic factors, policies, and culture alongside personal experiences.

The only participant in the present study who directly referenced a critical realist approach was Paulo, who stated: "I'm a fan of the looseness of Shakespeare's critical realist kind of approach." As an approach to disability and impairment, a critical realist approach facilitates understanding the full range of factors that shape experiences of disability and impairment, including experiences of Madness and distress. As noted, a critical realist approach also addresses systemic factors. QingYu was acutely aware that these factors influenced experiences of Madness and distress.

QingYu: I definitely think that mental health needs to be more visible in general. I think if we're more open and visible about mental health, that a lot of issues that we have in society today will change. I have a very strong opinion that money is a very big issue. ... There are a lot of people that have a lot of money that could [effect] change. ... There's a lot of problems with homelessness, a lot of problems with people that depend on a lot of assistance programs in America, which cause people to be depressed, [have] anxiety. It causes mental health problems.

> Also, people can't access healthcare in general. There's millions of people that rely on like therapy that can't afford it. It frustrates me that there are millions of people that need health care that can't access it. I don't know how many people, but there are tons of millionaires and billionaires that sit there, and they will never be able to spend ... all that money. They don't do anything [to help. I'm] upset and angry. If I had that money I know exactly what I do with it. I would end poverty, I would end homelessness, I would end the hunger problem, I would end all the problems that America has. Obviously, there's a lot of issues behind all these issues, but a lot of it is because there's money problems.

Shakespeare perceived that "social and economic relations play a major role in disabling people, and it is not enough to address buildings and products without addressing money and power" (p. 34). A critical realist approach accounts for both the systemic and the personal, and the relationship between the two.

## Social Confluence

Lubet (2013), a composer, multi-instrumentalist, educator, and disability studies scholar, proposed a theory of *social confluence* to help to describe encounters between music and disability. Frustrated with the preponderance of writing about music by nonmusicians, Lubet theorized music as a musician through disability studies, and developed a theory of musicality as embodied (p. 6). He argued that the role in which an individual finds themself at any given time, including music contexts, is "subject to redefinition at a moment's notice, as soon as one proceeds to the next encounter" (p. 1). A person's experience may radically change from encounter to encounter. Unlike a nation-state, ethnic group, or nuclear or extended family, Lubet argued that disability is not a fundamentally stable category (p. 2). Lubet rooted this theory in his own experience of disability, a status he learned shifted moment-to-moment across social, cultural, and institutional contexts. He cited a day "when my disability identity morphed several times over, depending on with whom I was interacting" (p. 2) as the impetus for his theory of social confluence. Strikingly, each identity transformation occurred in a single workplace.

> Simply rendered, the theory of social confluence states that modern society does not consist of stable, intact units of identity known as individual human beings but rather of people whose identities morph constantly with changing circumstances or contexts. Such change and the

demand for flexibility it requires for both material and psychological survival are much in evidence in the lives of musicians.

(p. 10)

Social confluence thus accounts for the moment-to-moment experience of disability and impairment across the full range of encounters, including those in music contexts.

Some research participants noted ways their mental health differences refracted across different situations. They discussed how their experiences of Madness, distress, and/or disability shifted from encounter to encounter.

*Paulo:* The social confluence thing lately is, except for being home, a little bit different. ... In a space of a day I might realize that I see my disability differently, see my diagnosis differently based on the context of where we're at. If it's just the TV on, or I'm learning about another shooting, I hear something about mental illness, it's immediately something that makes you feel withdrawn and makes you feel in a spotlight almost. But then you can go into another space where that's not the case, we're not talking about that and that goes away. That spotlight kind of goes away on you.

Paulo's analysis of the way a mass shooting shines a spotlight on experiences of Madness and distress, and differing interactions through space and time, evidences how he experiences social confluence. His mention of the escape that home provides indicates that this theory accounts for public and professional as well as individual interpersonal encounters; social confluence perhaps offers a respite when with "safe people."[8]

While Jillian did not specifically name social confluence, their ideas aligned with that model as well.

*Jillian:* I notice differences in mental health most when I'm, obviously, of course, in academia, right? In any setting whose infrastructure requires compliance or order is when I most notice that. How do I conceptualize it? I don't know. I think it's very relative to where I am and what I'm doing.

For Jillian, their mental health differences felt dynamic and contextually interdependent. They looked for the kind of relativity across encounters the social confluence model offers. This model acknowledges that experiences of Madness and distress are not static, but rather dynamic and fluid from moment to moment and encounter to encounter.

Social confluence can account for rapid changes in individuals across different contexts, something Paulo sought.

*Paulo:* The instability of how I feel, conceptualized and experienced bipolar disorder, and all the related things is interesting. It's so not regular. It's not the same thing. It's not consistent. I don't think anything's consistent, but it's interesting to think about that, because you know we have this term for a specific disorder that's supposed to put parameters around [it]. Like, here's what this experience is like, and in any day, that circle of demarcation is really stretched and pushed on different ends and into different spaces. I think if we were to conceptualize a model that would work for me, it would have to be something that is broad enough, nuanced enough, and flexible enough to attend to rapid changes within me, rapid changes within other people. It would have to be a moving model. I think about those really cool models of the solar system that have each of the planets on a different orbit, how they actually are. You can move them around. That kind of a model is what I would need. Something that would allow me to think through things. Almost like a kaleidoscope. When you turn it, you see different facets of things. ... So many people would be like "Well, that's not really a model, then, because it changes so much." Yeah, but a kaleidoscope is a kaleidoscope. You know what a kaleidoscope is. It doesn't change the fact that it's a kaleidoscope because you turn it, right? We all know what that is, so we could call a model a model, even if it shifts.

Paulo was not convinced that the label *bipolar* offered any explanatory power in a way that attended to rapid individual and social changes. A kaleidoscope as a model would facilitate a way to acknowledge the kinds of intricate changes that occur in the day-to-day and moment-to-moment experiences of disability, Madness, and distress.

## Conclusion and Implications

Multiple participants viewed their experiences of Madness and/or distress as a disability. In this chapter, I looked to different models of disability to consider how they might explain or account for such experiences. Upon encountering explanations of the medical and social models of disability, participants sought more nuance and complexity to account for their lived experiences. I therefore offered an introduction to complex embodiment, the cultural model, DisCrit, a critical realist approach, and the social confluence model, then considered how each might support or offer explanatory power for people with experiences of Madness and distress. These models and theories make multidimensional and intersectional examination of identities and experiences possible, encompassing consideration of both representations and material conditions. They refuse the social model's neutral designation of impairment and instead acknowledge its significance in individual's realities. These models also allow for analyses across experiences that may vary widely from encounter to encounter. Participants found disability studies' models of some to moderate use in describing and explaining their experiences. Considering a blend of models, then, may be useful to the discourse about experiences of Madness and distress. Jillian and Paulo sought an even more expansive and flexible model than those discussed in this chapter, indicating further conceptualization and theorizing may be warranted.

Educators and administrators can employ concepts from disability studies when addressing experiences of Madness and/or distress. These models facilitate the kind of nuanced subtleties participants desired and may assist with pedagogical, praxis, and policy decisions. The social model helps educators and administrators identify barriers that might include a lack of diversity of music learning modalities, a classroom set-up not conducive for all bodyminds, or a program that privileges one particular mode of musicking. Once such barriers are identified, administrators and music educators can work collaboratively to address them through, for example, varying music learning modalities to include visual, aural, and kinesthetic approaches, creating an accessible classroom set-up that accounts for physical, learning, emotional, and contextual differences, and ensuring the inclusion of multiple modes of musicking such as listening and creating alongside performing.

Beyond the medical and social models, models discussed in the second half of this chapter demand intersectional analysis; these models offer critical perspectives on disability and material conditions that facilitate action, as well as a strong counterpoint to the medical model that pathologizes. Music learning spaces are often not conducive to the kind of flexibility employing these models requires. In order to genuinely address pathologization and exclusion in music education through disability studies, music educators and administrators must acknowledge and account for the subtleties and multidimensionality embedded in disability embodiment, including for people with experiences of Madness and/or distress. Doing so involves recognizing that how a student or educator feels about their ability in the music classroom may change moment-to-moment and encounter-to-encounter. Educators and administrators can work to improve encounters that do not feel inclusive by, for example, removing barriers to access and providing multiple mechanisms by which to express understanding[9] within pedagogical and administrative approaches. Accounting for complexity also requires realizing that people may require support that addresses material conditions such as poverty that intersect with identity in ways that can exacerbate Madness and distress. Acknowledging the degree of flexibility required to adequately support music students and educators with experiences of Madness and/or distress and working to check in regularly with them about their experiences in music education related to both access and satisfaction (at minimum) and joy (ideally) may increase the likelihood of positive encounters in music education.

## Notes

1 In this chapter, I offer an introduction to these models rather than a comprehensive presentation. I encourage readers to further pursue any models of interest.
2 I extend the discussion of shame in Chapter 5.
3 See Gebhard et al. (2022) for a discussion of benevolence related to race in the helping professions. Similar arguments could be made about benevolence toward disability.
4 See https://ncd.gov/policy/crpd.
5 Goffman (1963) offered foundational work on stigma and stigmatized identities.
6 Dobbs referred to these dynamics as the "tyranny of ableism" (June 19, 2023, personal correspondence).
7 Intersecting oppressions occur beyond the intersection of racism, sexism, and classism to also include cissexism, heterosexism, ableism, sanism, religious oppression, ageism, sizeism, and oppression rooted in national status, among other possibilities.
8 Nichols (2016) discussed safe people in an LGBTQ+ context. Safe people refers to the people who an LGBTQ+ person has identified as providing safety. A space often has too many factors at play to be deemed safe with any degree of consistency. People, conversely, may offer a consistent source of safety. Like with allyship, however, a person cannot deem themself to be a safe person; they must be identified as such by a member of a minoritized group.
9 Allowing for multiple means of expression is an important aspect of the Universal Design for Learning, an approach I explicate in Chapter 7.

## References

Amundson, R. (2010). Quality of life, disability, and hedonic psychology. *Journal for the Theory of Social Behaviour*, 40(4), 374–392. https://doi.org/10.1111/j.1468-5914.2010.00437.x

Annamma, S. A., Connor, D. J., & Ferri, B. A. (2016a). Introduction: A truncated genealogy of DisCrit. In D. J. Connor, B. A. Ferri, & S. A. Annamma (Eds.),

DisCrit: Disability studies and critical race theory in education (pp. 1–8). Teachers College Press.

Annamma, S. A., Connor, D. J., & Ferri, B. A. (2016b). Touchstone text—Dis/ability Critical Race Studies (DisCrit): Theorizing at the intersections of race and dis/ability. In D. J. Connor, B. A. Ferri, & S. A. Annamma (Eds.), *DisCrit: Disability studies and critical race theory in education* (pp. 9–32). Teachers College Press.

Annamma, S. A., Ferri, B. A., & Connor, D. J. (Eds.). (2022). *DisCrit expanded: Reverberations, ruptures, and inquiries.* Teachers College Press.

Baker, B. (2002). The hunt for disability: The new eugenics and the normalization of school children. *Teachers College Record, 104,* 663–703. https://doi.org/10.1111/1467-9620.00175

Brown, B. (2021). *Atlas of the heart: Mapping meaningful connection and the language of human experience.* Random House.

Churchill, W. N., & Bernard, C. F. (2020). Disability and ideology of ability: How might music educators respond? *Philosophy of Music Education Review, 28*(2), 24–46. https://doi.org/10.2979/philmusieducrevi.28.1.03

Collins, P. H. (2000). *Black feminist thought: Knowledge, consciousness, and the politics of empowerment* (2nd ed.). Routledge.

Collins, P. H. (2003). Some group matters: Intersectionality, situated standpoints, and Black feminist thought. In T. L. Lott & J. P. Pittman (Eds.), *A companion to African-American philosophy* (pp. 205–229). Blackwell.

Collins, P. H. (2019). *Intersectionality as critical social theory.* Duke University Press.

Collins, P. H., & Bilge, S. (2016). *Intersectionality* (iBooks ed.). Polity Press.

Connor, D. J., Ferri, B. A., & Annamma, S. A. (Eds.). (2016). *DisCrit: Disability studies and critical race theory in education.* Teachers College Press.

Crenshaw, K. (2014/2000). The structural and political dimensions of intersectional oppression. In P. R. Grzanka (Ed.), *Intersectionality: A foundations and frontiers reader* (pp. 16–22). Routledge.

Crow, L. (1996). Including all of our lives: Renewing the social model of disability. In J. Morris (Ed.), *Encounters with strangers: Feminism and disability* (pp. 206–226). Women's Press.

Deleuze, G., & Guattari, F. (2005/1987). *A thousand plateaus: Capitalism and schizophrenia* (B. Massumi, Trans.). University of Minnesota Press.

Dobbs, T. L. (2012). A critical analysis of disabilities discourse in the *Journal of Research in Music Education,* 1990–2011. *Bulletin of the Council for Research in Music Education, 194,* 7–30. https://doi.org/10.5406/bulcouresmusedu.194.0007

Erevelles, N., Kanga, A., & Middleton, R. (2006). How does it feel to be a problem?: Race, disability, and exclusion in educational policy. In E. A. Brantlinger (Ed.), *Who benefits from special education?: Remediating (fixing) other people's children* (pp. 77–99). Lawrence Erlbaum Associates.

French, S. (1994). What is disability? In S. French (Ed.), *On equal terms: Working with disabled people* (pp. 3–16). Butterworth Heinemann.

Gay, G. (2018). *Culturally responsive teaching: Theory, research, and practice* (3rd ed.). Teachers College Press.

Gebhard, A., McLean, S., & St. Denis, V. (Eds.). (2022). *White benevolence: Racism and colonial violence in the helping professions*. Fernwood.
Goffman, E. (1963). *Stigma: Notes on the management of spoiled identity*. Prentice-Hall, Inc.
Harris, C. I. (1993). Whiteness as property. *Harvard Law Review*, 106(8), 1707–1791.
Hehir, T. (2002). Eliminating ableism in education. *Harvard Educational Review*, 72(1), 1–32.
Johnson, M., & Olson, C. J. (Eds.). (2021). *Normalizing mental illness and neurodiversity in entertainment media: Quieting the madness*. Routledge.
Ladson-Billings, G. (1995). Toward a theory of culturally relevant pedagogy. *American Education Research Journal*, 32(3), 465–491. https://doi.org/10.3102/00028312032003465
Ladson-Billings, G. (2009). *The dream keepers: Successful teachers of African American children* (2nd ed.). Jossey-Bass.
Ladson-Billings, G. (2014). Culturally relevant pedagogy 2.0: A.k.a. the remix. *Harvard Educational Review*, 84(1), 74–84. https://doi.org/10.17763/haer.84.1.p2rj131485484751
LeFrançois, B. A., Menzies, R., & Reaume, G. (Eds.). (2013). *Mad matters: A critical reader in Canadian Mad Studies*. Canadian Scholars' Press, Inc.
Linton, S. (1998). *Claiming disability: Knowledge and identity*. New York University Press.
Lubet, A. (2013). *Music, disability, and society*. Temple University Press.
McKoy, C. L., & Lind, V. L. (2023). *Culturally responsive teaching in music education: From understanding to application*. Routledge.
Menzies, R., LeFrançois, B. A., & Reaume, G. (2013). Introducing Mad Studies. In B. A. LeFrançois, R. Menzies, & G. Reaume (Eds.), *Mad matters: A critical reader in Canadian Mad Studies* (pp. 1–22). Canadian Scholars' Press, Inc.
Morgan, H. (2022). Mad Studies and disability studies. In P. Beresford & J. Russo (Eds.), *The Routledge international handbook of Mad Studies* (pp. 108–118). Routledge.
Nagatomo, S. (1992). *Attunement through the body*. SUNY Press.
Nichols, J. (2016, September 26). Create safe people, not safe spaces. Maryland Political Review. http://web.archive.org/web/20161105122801/http://marylandpoliticalreview.org/create-safe-people-not-safe-spaces/
Oliver, M., & Sapey, B. (1999). *Social work with disabled people* (2nd ed.). Palgrave MacMillan.
Paris, D., & Alim, H. S. (2014). What are we seeking to sustain through culturally sustaining pedagogy? A loving critique forward. *Harvard Educational Review*, 84(1), 85–100. https://doi.org/10.17763/haer.84.1.982l873k2ht16m77
Paris, D., & Alim, H. S. (Eds.). (2017). *Culturally sustaining pedagogies: Teaching and learning for justice in a changing world*. Teachers College Press.
Price, M. (2015). The bodymind problem and the possibilities of pain. *Hypatia*, 30(1), 268–284. www.jstor.org/stable/24542071
Rothschild, B. (2000). *The body remembers: The psychophysiology of trauma and trauma treatment*. W.W. Norton & Co.

Shakespeare, T. (2010). The social model of disability. In L. J. Davis (Ed.), *The disability studies reader* (3rd ed., pp. 266–273). Routledge.
Shakespeare, T. (2014). *Disability rights and wrongs revisited* (2nd ed.). Routledge.
Shakespeare, T. (2017). The social model of disability. In L. J. Davis (Ed.), *The disability studies reader* (5th ed., pp. 190–199). Routledge.
Siebers, T. (2008). *Disability theory*. The University of Michigan Press.
Siebers, T. (2017). Disability and the theory of complex embodiment: For identity politics in a new register. In L. J. Davis (Ed.), *The disability studies reader* (5th ed., pp. 310–329). Routledge.
Snyder, S. L., & Mitchell, D. T. (2006). *Cultural locations of disability*. The University of Chicago Press.
Spelman, E. (1988). *Inessential woman: Problems of exclusion in feminist thought*. Beacon.
UPIAS. (1976). *Fundamental principles of disability*. Union of Physically Impaired Against Segregation.
Walker, N. (2021). *Neuroqueer heresies: Notes on the neurodiversity paradigm, autistic empowerment, and postnormal possibilities* (ePub ed.). Autonomous Press.

# 3 Conceptualizing and Discussing Mental Health Differences

Rather than capitulate to the sanist tendency toward wronging people with experiences of Madness and distress in our capacity as knowers (Baylosis, 2019; Bueter, 2019; Carr, 2022; Carver et al., 2017; Crichton et al., 2017; Harcourt, 2021; LeBlanc & Kinsella, 2016; Liegghio, 2013; Russo, 2022; Scrutton, 2017; Speed & Taggart, 2019; Sullivan, 2019; White, 2022), I center Madness as a *way of knowing*, following Fabris (2011); attending to participants' ideas, I also introduce neurodiversity. Rosqvist et al. (2020) elucidated the distinctly epistemological and ethical implications of considering neurodivergence and neurodiversity (p. 2). Chapman (2020a), too, viewed neurodiversity as an "epistemically useful concept" that helps us "access and generate new forms of knowledge" (p. 219). In this chapter, I therefore center participants' perspectives as a way to generate Mad-informed knowledges. I discuss how these 15 individuals conceptualized experiences of Madness and distress, then consider the language they used to describe those experiences. As noted in Chapter 2, privilege across different identities mediates experiences of Madness and distress. While sanist oppression affects people with experiences of Madness and distress, having privilege in other identity categories (i.e., being white, cisgender, heterosexual, etc.) may allow a person with these experiences to avoid harms they might otherwise experience.

## Conceptualizing Mental Health Differences

The 15 music educators who participated in this research conceptualized mental health differences and their own experiences in varied ways, using the neurodiversity paradigm, a spectrum of difference, an "ability profile," nonbinary thinking, and a whole body health model that attends holistically to the *bodymind* (Baker, 2002; Price, 2015). Broadening possibilities for conceptualizing experiences of Madness and distress makes it possible

DOI: 10.4324/9781032662817-4

to refuse to pathologize these experiences, while recognizing the kinds of knowledges they may produce (Chapman, 2020a).

*Neurodiversity*

Multiple participants preferred the paradigm of neurodiversity to frame their experiences of Madness and distress.

*Chris:* I like the term neurodiverse. That certainly works for me, I don't see that as a binary at all [between neurotypical and neurodivergent]. ... There's a great slide that I use in our presentation which shows a wide range of perspectives on mental health, depicting the window through which you can view it, whether it's ecological or spiritual or psychological. I just see myself as neurodiverse, and I see myself as having landed in a white, Western culture, where that diversity is often not acknowledged or valued or celebrated.

*Blaine:* I consider [bipolar] a neurodivergence because my brain does not function in a typical way. I guess I do view neurodivergence as opposed to neurotypicality, or however that would be worded. I do think it's a spectrum. I honestly don't know how many people in the world I would identify as neurotypical. I feel like most people have some kind of neurodivergency whether it's an easily identifiable one like autism or ADHD, or whether it's buried in bipolar disorder somewhere, or ... I think more people are neurodivergent than realize they're neurodivergent, and I think their lives would probably be a lot easier if they were able to identify their neurodivergence.[1]

Walker (2021) described neurodiversity as "the diversity of human minds, the infinite variation in neurocognitive functioning within our species" (p. 39). Neurodiversity thus describes differences in how people "think, perceive, know, and develop, how their minds process information and interact with the world" (p. 61). She outlined three principles of the neurodiversity paradigm:

1. Neurodiversity—the diversity among minds—is a natural, healthy, and valuable form of human diversity.
2. There is no "normal" or "right" style of human mind, any more than there is one "normal" or "right" ethnicity, gender, or culture.
3. The social dynamics that manifest in regard to neurodiversity are similar to the social dynamics that manifest in regard to other forms of human diversity (e.g., diversity of race, culture, gender, or sexual orientation).

These dynamics include the dynamics of social power relations—the dynamics of social inequality, privilege, and oppression—as well as the dynamics by which diversity, when embraced, acts as a source of creative potential within a group or society. (p. 20)

Chapman (2020b) described this paradigm as a "theoretical and ideological shift" that reframes people "who fall outside neurocognitive norms as 'neuro-minorities' marginalised by a 'neuronormative' organisation of society in favour of the 'neurotypical', rather than as a matter of individual medical pathology" (pp. 57–58).[2] The neurodiversity paradigm departs from what Walker (2021) called the pathology paradigm and refuses medicalized constructions of neurocognitive differences; it further positions neurocognitive diversity as the norm (Chapman, 2020b, p. 58). Indeed, neurodivergence encompasses a broad range of genetic and innate differences, as well as differences produced by brain-altering experiences. Walker (2021) cited autism and dyslexia as examples of innate neurodivergences, and trauma, meditation practice, and use of psychedelic drugs as examples of experience-based neurodivergences (p. 44). I consider both innate and experience-based neurodivergences in this book, following participants' definitions of their own experiences.

*Mental Health Differences as a Spectrum*

Chew (2013) explained, "[n]eurodiversity refers to the diversity, the spectrum of ways of thinking and perceiving the world" (p. 281). Lizabeth recognized this spectrum in relation to disability.

*Lizabeth:* I like to conceptualize dis/ability as a spectrum where our positions on the spectrum change throughout our lives. If you live long enough, you will become disabled, and some people's needs and levels of support necessary to thrive change daily. We also fail to consider temporary disability. It's more than likely that most folks will break a bone or suffer an injury in their lifetime leaving them disabled for some time. If we considered disability as fluid and as a spectrum, I think almost everyone would consider themselves disabled in one way or another.

They continued on to describe their height at 4'11 as disabling at moments when they needed to reach a high shelf at the grocery store or had to sit dangerously close to their car's steering wheel and airbags.

*Lizabeth:* I spent a lot of time kind of unlabeling myself. So yes, I have these labels, and they're helpful, but in terms of everything being on a

> spectrum, I feel like the label doesn't help because then it's just saying one thing, or it's opening up for assumptions. Whereas I feel like my anxiety or my depression or my ADHD sits somewhere on a spectrum, and even day to day it changes. I don't have any facts to back this up, but I feel like everyone has to be on every spectrum, right? That's what I think, at least. Maybe you don't have clinical or diagnosed depression, but you're somewhere there. I've been trying to think of things more holistically in that sense. I've also just realized how nuanced all of this is. I've really had to stop myself from wanting to just grab labels and then feel satisfied. Because just assigning something to myself doesn't help whatever is going on.

In her work on neurodiversity, Walker (2021) identified it as a spectrum as well.

> Humanity is neurodiverse, just as humanity is racially, ethnically, and culturally diverse. By definition, no human being falls outside of the spectrum of human neurodiversity, just as no human being falls outside of the spectrum of human racial, ethnic, and cultural diversity.
>
> (p. 50)

What Lizabeth added to this conceptualization is the idea that one's place on the spectrum changes based on context and expectations, but also internal differences that may occur day-to-day. They believed, like Walker (2021), that everyone falls somewhere on the spectrum, and that their place does not remain static but exists in flux. Lubet's (2013) social confluence model accounts for this flexibility (see Chapter 2), which resonated with QingYu who noted: "There's also completely different spectrums of neurodiversity. ... There's definitely a spectrum of both ADHD/ADD and autism in my opinion, because the different symptoms of either those things are very variable." Participants who appreciated a spectrum as a way to describe differences also thought of them as dynamic and contextual rather than stable across time.

### *Conceptualizing an Ability Profile: Relativity in Characteristics*

A few participants conceptualized an ability profile as a way to understand neurodiversity.

August: Neurodivergence is about how the pathways in your brain connect. It could either be something you're born with, like autism or ADHD or genetic predisposition to certain mental health conditions, or something you acquire through aversive conditions like depression because of an unfulfilling job, or PTSD because of active duty military service, for example. It results in a spiky ability profile. You have the quintessential platonic ideal of the neurotypical person, [that] would just be a very round circle. There's one category for social stuff, and another category for executive function. ... So all their ability categories would be very even. They're able to get a job and they're able to walk and they're able to cook meals and clean their house and all the rest, but they're not exceptional in anything. A neurodivergent person would have a spiky ability profile. Usually this would be pictured as average except for the areas they are deficient in, but also they could be average in a couple of things, exceptional in a couple of things, and very deficient in a few things. Depending on where the deficiencies lie they'd get labeled with different types of neurodivergence. Neurodiversity tends to be described in terms of deficiencies, but because it is a spiky profile, it often pairs with areas where someone is above average. It could be a spiky profile where a lot of things are average and then there are some deficits. But very, very commonly, it's a spiky profile where there are really strong areas. I've been starting to notice that sometimes what could be conceptualized as somebody's really weak area is a strong area in another setting or context.

August Knight (he/they) described themself as white. They noted: "Gender? Yes, probably. When I have to use words for it, I usually do stuff in the like, masculine-ish direction." August identified as autistic, which they consider a disability as understood through the social model (see Chapter 2). They were raised middle-class and at the time of data gathering noted: "I'm a broke musician in a large city. I don't know what class that is. I feel like I think I think private music teachers end up being like very high paid service class." They taught violin and viola, music theory, and composition privately.

August went on to describe how they get hyperfocused—a "phenomenon that reflects one's complete absorption in a task" (Ashinoff & Abu-Akel, 2021, p. 1)—on tasks in ways that can be alternately praise-worthy or problematic.

*August:* That's kind of a sore point for me in terms of neurodivergence being seen as, we need to get you to act more like other people. It's just like, if I acted more like "people" I wouldn't act like

> myself in the ways that are considered positive and acceptable, and I wouldn't BE myself. The things that are dislikable about me are the things that are also really cool about me. I can't amputate those parts; I don't want to amputate those parts of myself for the convenience of other people.

August offered insight into how different neurodivergent characteristics are contextual. For August, getting singularly focused on something proved a strength in some contexts and a liability in others. Chris commented along similar lines in specific relation to musicians.

*Chris:* I wonder what it would be like to have these kinds of conversations at conservatories, because I suspect that a very sizeable proportion of people who get into those places come with their neurodiversity, because that's actually partly what got them in there in the first place. It's often a two-sided coin, isn't it? You come out with your great strengths, and these often great Swiss cheese holes of things that disable, paralyze, or compel us as well. What would it be like to have these conversations and the opportunity to talk about it as a compulsory part of the training? The opportunity to think about what it is that's helped and encouraged and nurtured you. To listen to what other people have tried. To be offered the opportunity to not see that label or that diagnosis as a disability—to be able to see it as a superpower as well.

The notion of "strengths" and "Swiss cheese holes" engage imagery akin to the spiky ability profile August described. Chris continued on to discuss how certain neurocognitive characteristics that make good musicians often comprise the same characteristics that lead to diagnoses. Like August, Chris believed that different characteristics can be assets depending on context. She additionally wished for purposeful guidance about navigating the employing of these characteristics to help support neurodiversity among music students.

Asset pedagogies—culturally relevant pedagogy (Ladson-Billings, 1995, 2009, 2014), culturally responsive teaching (Gay, 2018; McKoy & Lind, 2023), and culturally sustaining pedagogy (Paris & Alim, 2014, 2017)—purposefully recognize the value and assets that students across all backgrounds bring to the classroom. Indeed, these are strengths-based pedagogies. However, thinking of certain characteristics as assets and strengths in particular contexts, but not necessarily in others, problematizes a narrow conceptualization of asset pedagogies and prompts educator recognition that characteristics' values are changeable.

With a broadened concept of asset pedagogy to include context-specific ability profiles, educators, including music educators, become responsible for helping students navigate their neurocognitive characteristics, recognize contexts in which these characteristics are assets or potential liabilities, and help students to cultivate or manage them in the relevant contexts. Understanding these variations may foster increased self-compassion[3] among students about their different characteristics, particularly if compassionate modeling is provided by teachers (see Hendricks, 2018 on compassionate music teaching).

*Contextual Factors*

Some participants conceptualized their experiences of Madness and/or distress in relation to contextual factors. Walker (2021) identified some neurodivergences as innate, and some as a result of experience (p. 44). Most participants wished to account for the role of experience in Madness and distress.

*August:* There's two more parts to that. There's ADHD and autism (the forms of purely congenital neurodiversity I'm qualified to speak to) as a component of mental health. They often get lumped in with mental health or result in mental health stuff. If you're constantly being told that your personality is wrong, you're probably going to end up being kind of depressed; there's a lot of other stuff that can happen. Which brings me to the second part of how I conceptualize mental health, which is environmental causes. Somebody could be doing extraordinarily well, be in a situation that's very positive for them, or just neutral enough that they can do stuff. Then all of a sudden, let's say they move to a new town where they don't have any friends, or they can't get a new job, or whatever. … Their presentation of mental health is going to decline. Traumatic events can cause mental health problems, as can changes in circumstances.

August felt that circumstances could significantly affect a person's emotional state and level of distress, describing the increased distress they had experienced while in poor housing situations. "Environmental causes" thus comprise a relevant contributor to experiences of Madness and distress. August's idea of a "spiky ability profile" further resonates here. In situations where a person might fail to thrive, their characteristics may not serve them well, as opposed to a situation in which those same characteristics may function as assets or value-neutral. For Lizabeth, the political climate heightened levels of distress.

*Lizabeth:* Recently I've been thinking about how my struggles would probably be less or diminished, reduced, if things in the world weren't so bad. So, yes, I have these mental illnesses regardless of the state of the world, but my struggles associated with my conditions are exacerbated by my experiences in the world. And not just my experiences, but witnessing others' experiences and being a part of the world causing those experiences.

They believed their differences fall in the "innate" category (Walker, 2021, p. 44), and also recognized the role that events and situations played in exacerbating distress.

Most participants had additionally experienced trauma and believed that was the root of some of their experiences of Madness and/or distress. They felt that considering traumatic experiences could be important to understanding any resulting Madness and/or distress. Recognizing how experiences such as trauma can change the brain (van der Kolk, 2014; Walker, 2021) makes accounting for contextual factors important to any conversation about Madness and distress.

*Cheryl:* Everyone growing up encounters experiences and events, and some are traumatic, and some are not. People have different experiences and are born with different biology, so we all have our blueprint of where we come from, and then our experiences … It feels normal that people have mental health issues. It's very unfortunate when people suffer, but, I guess maybe I tend to rationalize things. It makes sense in today's world and throughout history, that because of what happened, how much trauma there is in the world, that people develop these conditions.

Cheryl considered neurodivergence that is innate as well as neurodivergence that emerges from experience, specifically trauma (Walker, 2021, p. 44).

Nicholas' experiences of heteronormativity and cissexism impacted their levels of distress and denoted the way that structures of oppression exacerbate distress across all identity categories, particularly impacting levels of distress for people who are multiply minoritized. Nicholas also emphasized environmental factors that included sensitivities to the built environment (see for example Black et al., 2022) that negatively impacted wellbeing.

*Nicholas:* I am an emotionally sensitive person who is also sensitive to my environment. Sounds, other people's actions, even things that have nothing to do with me but are just happening in

> my environment can have an overwhelming impact on my executive functioning. I attribute the situational depression I've experienced to the fact that I lack an emotional shield and am very sensitive to sound. More specifically, I've had to hide queerness at work and have experienced very harmful events due to compulsory heterosexuality. Those two environmental factors plus my sensitivity to unorganized sound have resulted in pretty extreme situational depression and anxiety. Also, I think when I got my bipolar diagnosis, that was very depressing and hard to come to terms with. And the fact that I wasn't sleeping.

They also revealed experiencing distress as a result of receiving a medicalized label that might coincide with what Brown (2021) and Ferguson et al. (2000) called an "unwanted identity." Brown and Ferguson et al. further recognized the entanglement of shame when an unwanted identity is foisted on a person. Accounting for contextual factors including trauma, structures of oppression, and unwanted identities opens conversations about experiences of Madness and distress to recognize the role of the environment, personal history, dominant systems, and emotions such as shame on such experiences. Considering the factors that may well exacerbate distress thus becomes important to conceptualizing experiences of Madness and distress.

*Eschewing Binary Thinking*

In alignment with participants' ideas about a spectrum of neurodiversity (Walker, 2021), Lizabeth opposed binary thinking that places nondisabled and disabled people, and neurotypical and neurodivergent people, at opposite poles.

*Lizabeth:* I think that binary thinking can cause more harm than good. We like categorizing things, so of course we tend to label folks as abled or disabled, but I'd like to see us get away from that. I think it is important to acknowledge that many decisions around laws and the way people interact with the world are decided by folks who identify as able-bodied and neurotypical. This is important because disabled folks should be in control of laws and changes that affect them, but at the same time I think we need to be careful not to reinforce the binary between abled and disabled folks. I think this for a few reasons. If we approach the world in universally designed ways, adaptations or creations meant to serve disabled folks

> will serve everyone, whether they identify as having a disability or not. That's the basis of Universal Design—having a curb cut-out not only serves wheelchair users but also people with strollers or shopping carts. Additionally, I think "us vs. them" conversations are very divisive, and to truly make change we need to understand each other. I think conceptualizing disability as a spectrum that we all move around on throughout our lives, or from day to day, would help people who identify as neurotypical or able-bodied to understand the importance of meeting the needs of others, and the various ways that we can shape our world to be universally designed. It may also shift the thinking of those folks, to think that we all fall somewhere on the spectrum of dis/ability.

Lizabeth wanted to move away from binary thinking toward a spectrum that included both disability and neurodiversity, concurring with Walker's (2021) description of a spectrum of neurodiversity. Brune and Wilson (2013) explained: "As the field of disability studies has shown, minds and bodies are better understood in terms of variance than as deviation from a fixed norm" (p. 2). Human variation is therefore a more useful conceptualization than the binary of neurotypical and neurodivergent. Walker (2021) positioned someone who is neurotypical as a person who conforms easily to, and does not experience harm from, neuronormativity—that is, a set of norms that govern neurocognitive behavior (p. 66). Neuronormativity is the structure that organizes society in favor of the neurotypical (p. 58).

> When we say someone is neurotypical, what we mean is that they live, act, and experience the world in a way that consistently falls within the boundaries of neuronormativity—i.e., within the boundaries of what the prevailing culture imagines a person with a "normal mind" to be like. That's quite different from saying that a person actually has a normal mind or a normal brain.
>
> (p. 67)

Lizabeth did not find the constructs of neurotypical and neurodiverse useful when employed as binary constructions. They felt that refusing binary thinking would better serve everyone and also resist "us" and "them" conceptions. The concept of neuronormativity moreover acknowledges the socially constructed nature of neurotypical and neurodivergent brains and allows for the consideration of normative systems that shape people's experiences in ways that also resist the binary.

*Whole Body Health*

Several participants conceptualized their mental health differences in relation to facets of general health.

*Mary:* I conceptualize mental health as a large bubble, and within that large bubble are many other aspects of well-being that impact mental health, including: diet, sleep, social connections, generational health, how one navigates grief and trauma, and regular practices that impact health such as exercise, meditation, music-making, arts experiences. Each of these other life experiences might be different-sized bubbles (or nonexistent) depending on how one lives. If one has a crappy diet, that bubble would be moldy or look really gross.

Mary Cohen (she/her) identified as female, white, married, and heterosexual. Her ethnic background is second-generation Russian and German. She had previously taught elementary music and currently served as an Associate Professor at the University of Iowa. "I'm always coming back to Descartes," she mused, "and the problem of the separation of body and mind, which feels like it's still pretty prevalent in our society and the way people understand health and wellbeing." Like Price's (2015) conceptualization of the *bodymind* discussed in Chapter 2, Mary refused separation of the body and mind. In viewing the mind as an embodied phenomenon, Walker (2021) additionally recognized that "the diversity of minds must also be a diversity of embodiments" (p. 63). Full conceptualizations of a bodymind's experiences must include these numerous, coexisting factors.

*Metaphors*

Several participants drew on metaphors to conceptualize their experiences navigating Madness and distress. I share a few of these to illuminate how metaphors aid in conceptualization. Lakoff and Johnson (2003/1980) noted the pervasiveness of metaphors in everyday life and argued that these function far beyond language to actually shape thought and action. They asserted that a person's "ordinary conceptual system" is fundamentally metaphorical (p. 17). For Lakoff and Johnson, "[o]ur concepts structure what we perceive, how we get around in the world, and how we relate to other people. Our conceptual system thus plays a central role in defining our everyday realities" (p. 17). A person's conception of a construct or idea serves to partially characterize the concept, and their language use follows or aligns with the metaphor. The metaphors these research participants shared in relation to the way they conceptualized (their) experiences of Madness, distress, and/or neurodivergence therefore likely shape how they structured their ideas about such experiences and the language they use to discuss it.

Chris used a metaphor to describe her experience of navigating life as neurodivergent.

*Chris:* Sometimes I think about navigating life as being a supermarket cart with a wobbly wheel. How do I do that? How do other people do that? How can we support one another and talk about it and provide a language that is not shaming and say: "This is who I am, this is how I got here. This is what drives me to perfection. It has its downsides."

Importantly, she directed her comments toward supporting people to navigate life successfully. She further drew on her earlier remarks about the duality of neurodivergence—the way that it drives perfection and/or creativity in some circumstances and acts as a liability in others.

Emma used a metaphor as a way to describe an assortment of neurodivergences integrated together.

*Emma:* I compare [mental illness] to trail mix, ironically. If you think about it ... anxiety, depression, sometimes they tend to overlap. A way that I've conceptualized it is literally just comparing it to trail mix, and it just kind of normalizes it and humanizes the whole aspect of mental illness. With my close friends, I'm like, "What's your trail mix?" It even brings some joy and humor to it, because I will say, "Oh, my anxiety are M&Ms or my OCD are the raisins." I have all these things, but they kind of overlap over each other. That's kind of how I like to picture it.

She also drew on this metaphor as a way to start a conversation about experiences of Madness and distress with some lightheartedness in a way that might normalize and humanize these experiences, as well as decrease stigma.

A metaphor served Meghan well in describing the ups and downs she has had with mental health.

*Meghan:* I say my mental health journey has been pretty rocky. It started at a very young age. I don't think about it as this nice hiking trail that's beaten down by feet walking down it all the time that just goes up and down. It's like an off-road path that I got dropped in the middle of, and I've just been figuring out how to walk along it. I started therapy when I was in the second grade,

> which is very young. I got an official diagnosis for anxiety at that age.

She later acknowledged how past experiences of Madness and distress may bring some insight to what to expect in the near future: "I feel like I'm on an upswing, and every once in a while I have a few dips. But the view from the hike is in distance, I can see it coming up."

These metaphors, while radically different from each other, describe different facets of experiences of neurodivergence, Madness, and distress. They provide ways to think about such experiences and facilitate ways to think about support and beginning a conversation with others about these topics. Metaphors may not only help people describe experiences of Madness and/or distress, they may also assist in conceptualizing wellness, as evidenced by Meena's incorporation of metaphors into her clinical work.

*Meena:* I realize in my own work as a therapist, I use metaphors in conversation as a way to quickly describe and introduce wellness concepts and abstract ideas to clients. It seems to work really well, and it helps to bypass the tedium, boredom, and slowness of doing coping skills worksheets for CBT [cognitive behavioral therapy]. Instead, metaphors encourage movement, and also it humanizes the therapeutic process by being tailored to the conversation and the individual.

Participants thus found metaphors useful to conceptualizing a wide range of experiences.

## Words to Describe Mental Health

When discussing experiences of Madness and distress, participants had differing preferences regarding use of diagnostic language. They also used neutral language rooted in differences to account for context and neurodiversity. Foregrounding "whole body health," they nonetheless varied in preference for person-first vs. identity-first language, but more uniformly avoided pathologizing language. In broaching conversation on mental health differences, taking into account the language used by people with experiences of Madness and distress should inform subsequent language choices. This commitment is true in any setting, including in music education.

### Diagnostic Language

The majority of participants preferred using diagnostic language when discussing their experiences of Madness and/or distress. While this aligns with the medical model (Dobbs, 2012; Linton, 1998; Oliver & Sapey, 1999; Siebers, 2017) that many participants found problematic, most of these music educators found such labels useful in normalizing mental health differences. Meena, currently a social worker, described her language use as mostly that of a clinician.

*Meena:* For me, personally, I do use standard language that a clinician would use, it's just kind of the easiest way to communicate with clinicians. The nature of my experience, I know there's a lot of alternative language that people use. I myself [will] say, "I had a psychotic episode," or other times, if I don't want to be clinical, I'll say, "I had a descent into madness." This sort of thing.

She recounted the importance of using current clinical language for experiences of Madness and distress. Remaining up to date with the most recent research in the field was something Meena identified as an ethical responsibility for mental health providers, so clinicians' use of outdated terminology made her wary of their upholding of this important responsibility. She noted that she "straddle[s] both the worlds of clinical practice, but also transformative, non-clinical peer community building practices." She is thus well-versed in both clinical and community-based language for experiences of Madness and distress.

*Meena:* I'm curious, are there any differences between "distress" and "Madness?" For me personally, I guess I consider that "distress" is an *experience* that any person can have in reaction to hardship, abuse, or trauma. Whereas with "Madness," this is perhaps a *state of being* that is (or becomes) an integral part of the person which cannot be "corrected," which clashes with the world.

In this book, I discuss both Madness and distress as experiences, noting Price's (2015) observation that such experiences are "*intermittently* apparent" (p. 272, emphasis in original). At times in which they become apparent, these experiences may manifest more as a state of being, as Meena discussed. At other times, these experiences may remain as experiences that nonetheless influence ways of being and knowing in the world. Meena's use of scare quotes around the word "corrected" indicates her familiarity with the desire of the medical model (Linton, 1998) and pathology paradigm (Walker, 2021) to "fix," "medicate," and "correct" non-normative experiences and bodies. Her words, alternately, show the innate nature of such differences (see Walker, 2021).

While Meghan was specific with her language, she refused to allow any degree of pathologizing.

*Meghan:* I will talk about my diagnoses by name. Then when I'm discussing mental health in a broad topic, I will call it mental health. I try to avoid "mental illness" because it is an illness, but when you're talking to people who don't necessarily understand everything that comes along with it, when you say mental illness, they just think, "Oh, there's something wrong with you." That's not the verbiage that I believe in using because that pushes people down, it pushes them to the side and Others them. That's very hurtful.

Similarly, QingYu felt that using direct language helps destigmatize experiences with Madness and distress. They also found it important to use this language in discussions with young people.

*QingYu:* When I talk about my own mental health, I am very open. I do not skirt around the topic or use incorrect terms. If someone that I am comfortable with wants to discuss mental health I will be honest and share that I have depression, anxiety, and OCD. I believe it's important to use accurate terms to try to end the stigma associated with mental health. I would find this most crucial in situations discussing with children or younger teens. I think there is this idea that we need to protect young people from certain topics, but mental health affects many, and educating them on such [a] topic that affects all ages and all people is something that shouldn't be kept from this age group.

Nicholas found direct language most useful in promoting awareness.

*Nicholas:* Depending on the space, I will say outright that I have bipolar disorder, anxiety, and that I have suffered from depression. Sometimes, I name the difference between bipolar depression and major depressive disorder, as it's known by itself without bipolar disorder. Sometimes I tell people that I'm autistic and have ADHD, collectively (and perhaps affectionately) known as "AuDHD." It feels like those labels can be confining sometimes, but it does give people a general sense of what to expect from me. I think it's very important to spread awareness about these things, even if only by talking about them. I've noticed that not a lot of people initiate these conversations. The labels give me a direction to go in when seeking out resources. The cool thing is that the resources usually help.

In the U.S., both the Americans with Disabilities Act (ADA)[4] for teachers and students and the Individuals with Disabilities in Education Act (IDEA)[5] for students align with a medicalized paradigm of disability and rely on labels, which Nicholas ultimately found contributed to general understanding of specific neurodivergences and offered shared terminology. As Nicholas stated, having specific labels aids the process of seeking resources, making labels important to accessing supports.

*Non-Diagnostic Language*

A third of participants conversely preferred non-diagnostic language in describing their experiences.

*Jillian:* I'm realizing that I think I avoid using terminology in general. I avoid using things like "mentally ill" because I don't think anyone isn't. I just think it's a confluence of environmental factors that make me perceive the world the way I perceive it. That sometimes leads me to roadblocks, but I guess I don't really see it as necessarily illness. Just a state of being that we all have.

Jillian's thinking aligned with the idea of neurodiversity on a spectrum (Walker, 2021); everyone is somewhere on that spectrum. They also felt strongly that contextual or environmental factors shape one's experience and used language to account for that.

Lizabeth found that diagnostic language did not help them address what caused their struggle, and instead focused attention on what might be soothing. They noted: "I was using the word struggle before. What is causing a struggle and how I can soothe that thing rather than saying, 'Oh, it's my anxiety,' because that's not helpful. Or, 'Oh, it's my ADHD,' because that's not helpful." This more embodied approach focuses on reducing distress for a particular person at a particular time rather than a generalized approach based on responses to a named diagnosis.

As noted in this chapter's section on conceptualizations, multiple participants used neurodiversity language to describe their experiences of Madness and distress.

*Chris:* I choose not to do diagnosis. I've had well over a dozen in my time. Right now, I choose not to align myself with diagnoses and just say that I'm neurodiverse. Which means that

> I experience thinking, attention, focus, mood, and energy challenges and fluctuations.

Acknowledging the specifics of how neurodivergence relates to how one experiences the world moves away from diagnostic language toward neutral language that accounts for differences across varied contexts.

*Neutral Language Rooted in Difference*

Neutral language use rooted in differences corresponds with the notion of an ability profile presented above, in which characteristics may serve as strengths in some contexts and hindrances in others.

Chris: I think there's a strong correlation between the kind of neurodiversity that often acquires diagnoses, and what makes a really good musician. For example, at one stage, I decided that there's some obsessive compulsive qualities. I call them qualities rather than disorder, because there's order and beauty it brings, and that is almost required to be in the first violin section, for example. Yet, a lot of people sort of get caught and labeled by the mental health system and varying treatments. Some find this quite helpful, and for some it's really *not* helpful. Some of the other creative qualities that make really good jazz musicians, for example, often also acquire diagnoses. The ability to be able to practice for hours and hours and hours on end, and the ability to have music that comes from your heart and soul and lives in your head and won't shut up. Those are all qualities that actually make really good musicians and can also make us crazy (or lead others to label us as such). So being able to acknowledge the diversity of experiences without necessarily pathologizing them, I think, is really important, as is finding ways to work with them. To nurture and nourish some of them, rather than try and get rid of them, I think, is something that music education could work at. Acknowledging the different learning styles, seeing individual gifts. And rather than trying to get rid of something that's a part of people, finding ways to acknowledge and nurture and celebrate them and love them.

Chris made the linguistic choice to use "qualities" and, at other times, "characteristics"[6] as neutral, rather than "disordered" because they promote musicality, creativity, and a type of order. She further highlighted that some qualities or characteristics that make good musicians can also lead to diagnoses if considered through the medical model.

When another participant arrived late at a focus group due to the sedation effect of a medication, Chris called it "sleep diversity." These kinds of neutral descriptors make room for characteristics to be context-specific assets/liabilities. Chris felt strongly that this line of thinking should be built into education.

*Chris:* I just think it should be integral to music education and educating educators. It could perhaps be one of the first classes in the first year—thinking about what diversity looks like? What are some of our unique and diverse characteristics? I'm deliberately not using the words "strengths" or "weaknesses," because they're just characteristics. What has helped us? And what do we wish we'd had, if we could go back and sort of rejig things, what would have really helped? How can we support the people that we are teaching? What are some of the diverse ranges of characteristics that people might bring, and how can we work with them in ways that spark and inspire and fan the flames rather than the toxic stuff that many of us experience?

Reframing strengths and weaknesses as characteristics requires explicit support. Part of music education and music teacher education should therefore involve understanding and supporting the diverse characteristics students and teachers bring to the classroom, without any pathologizing.

*Whole Body Health*

Multiple participants discussed factors that influenced their emotional wellbeing—sleep, diet, exercise, etc. Mary referred to this as "whole body health" and used language to reflect that perspective: "I would describe [mental health] as much as possible using words like the 'whole body health,' 'whole self,' any words I can come up with to avoid the bifurcation of body and mind." She also suggested considering how someone responds to the people around them and a person's feelings about how others behave toward them, as well as having boundaries to delineate that others' responses are about them and not the person in question. Mary found these considerations to be particularly important when checking on someone else's emotional wellbeing:

*Mary:* "How is your sleep level? What types of things are you doing that help you find"—if I'm talking to a student, for example—"balance?" I go to the basics, "How's your diet? Are you finding time to balance work and rest? Exercise? What is your actual health environment?"

Inquiring about factors that influence emotional wellbeing aligns with the discussion of contextual factors presented in the section on conceptualizations; the language of whole body health, however, focuses on the personal.

*Empowering Language Choices*

Within disability studies there is some debate regarding person-first language (i.e., person with a disability) as opposed to identity-first language (i.e., a disabled person) (see for example Titchkosky, 2001). The language these participants used to describe themselves varied in this regard. QingYu observed: "When I talk about my own mental health, I always say I have experience with depression. I have experience with anxiety. I was diagnosed with XYZ." Nicholas, conversely, identified as disabled. Walker (2021) framed the medicalized paradigm as the "pathology paradigm" and placed it in opposition to the "neurodiversity paradigm" described earlier in this chapter. She argued that "the shift from the pathology paradigm to the neurodiversity paradigm calls for a radical shift in language, because the appropriate language for discussing medical problems is quite different from the appropriate language for discussing diversity" (pp. 22–23). She offered an example:

> If we use phrases like "person with autism," or "she has autism," or "families affected by autism," we're using the language of the pathology paradigm—language that implicitly accepts and reinforces the assumption that autism is intrinsically a problem, a Something-Wrong-With-You. In the language of the neurodiversity paradigm, on the other hand, we speak of neurodiversity in the same way we would speak of ethnic or sexual diversity, and we speak of autistics in the same way we would speak of any other social minority group: I am autistic. I am an autistic.
>
> (p. 23)

In this book, I largely follow QingYu's language choice of describing *experiences* of Madness and distress rather than using identity-first language. In my own life, I use identity-first language, identifying as bipolar, not as a person with bipolar disorder. Following Walker (2021), I support people using identity labels that they find meaningful and empowering for them (p. 218).

Participants mostly avoided pathologizing, deficit, or disempowering language. What they viewed as disempowering differed, however.

QingYu: I feel like there's a lot of stigma around talking about mental health. The one word I really refuse to use at any kind of dialogue is using the word *crazy*. I think that it's really harmful. Even just saying "wow, that sounds crazy." I will always use the word "that sounds wild." "I just think it's so wild." I think crazy is really harmful.

Unlike QingYu's refusal to use language of the pathology paradigm (Walker, 2021), Chris used "crazy" to self-describe, though not as a pathologizing term. Participants' support of empowering language and aversion to pathologization requires educators and students to be mindful of different language choices when describing oneself and others.

## Conclusion and Implications

These 15 individuals conceptualized (their) experiences of Madness and/or distress in vastly different ways. They found the construct of neurodiversity helpful, as well as the concept of a spectrum. Participants described an "ability profile" in which characteristics are viewed as context-specific assets or liabilities. These music educators further considered environmental factors that shape or exacerbate levels of distress, resisted binary thinking, conceptualized whole body health, and used metaphors to conceptualize their experiences. Conceptualizations varied widely and offer a strong counterpoint to sanist discourse about Madness and distress that is disempowering and deficit-oriented.

Understanding characteristics as assets or liabilities contextually illuminates a way to strengthen asset pedagogies. In music education contexts, certain characteristics such as hyperfocus (see Ashinoff & Abu-Akel, 2021) may be validated and rewarded. This same hyperfocus, however, may prove to be detrimental elsewhere and even potentially harmful. The task for music educators and administrators involves acknowledging these characteristics, but not coercing students to overuse or over-apply them, even when they do prove advantageous in music contexts. Acknowledging characteristics contextually as assets/liabilities requires educators to consider educating for balance rather than valorizing a characteristic that may ultimately prove harmful in other contexts or if overused. Doing so involves recognizing the needs of the whole person when weighing the cultivation both of musicianship and of future educators. Accepting that characteristics that seem detrimental in one context may be assets elsewhere may also encourage educators to refuse to pathologize a student who struggles in a music context. A "lack of talent," using this framework, becomes a social construct for music educators to eschew as they help students discover the contexts in which their characteristics are assets.

Participants' use of language varied widely. Most participants chose to use diagnostic language situationally, while others avoided it altogether.

Following the conceptualization of the ability profile, some participants worked to use neutral language rooted in difference—that is, the language of characteristics and qualities as opposed to strengths and weaknesses. Participants utilized the language of neurodiversity, also discussing whole body health factors' relationship to their emotional wellbeing. While they differed in choices of person-first vs. identity-first language, none used language they considered pathologizing or disempowering.

Music educators, administrators, and school boards can honor individuals' own conceptualizations of experiences of Madness and/or distress and notice how these can be widely variable. Listening to people with these experiences makes room for understanding our unique perspectives and epistemologies through which to perceive and engage with music education, education writ large, and society more broadly. Beyond listening, music educators, students, administrators, and school districts can mirror the language choices made by students and teachers with experiences of Madness and/or distress and reflect our own language decisions back to us.[7] In creating policies and practices, then, attending to people who have these experiences facilitates a multiplicity of ways to conceptualize and discuss Madness and distress. Grounding policy and practices in listening also makes tracing the implications of different conceptualizations easier and helps honor variety and multiplicity through acknowledging Mad epistemologies and the status of people with experiences of Madness and/or distress as knowers. Moreover, participants' comments on language use strongly suggest that educators, administrators, and policymakers discontinue using pathologizing language, instead employing language that affirms people with experiences of Madness and/or distress in ways that align with how we understand ourselves. Affirming language creates space for affirming and supportive policies and practices, all of which are conducive to effective teaching and learning.

## Notes

1 Blaine's final comment points to the potential use of psy- models in providing labels.
2 Chapman (2020b) drew on Walker's previous work, which Walker published as a compilation in 2021.
3 See Neff's (2003, 2011) work on self-compassion.
4 See www.ada.gov.
5 See https://sites.ed.gov/idea/.
6 I use both terms when discussing these ideas.
7 I note here that mirroring language choices applies to non-pathologizing language. If I self-identified as "crazy," I would likely be offended if others mirrored that language choice back to me.

## References

Ashinoff, B. K., & Abu-Akel, A. (2021). Hyperfocus: The forgotten frontier of attention. *Psychological Research*, *85*, 1–19. https://doi.org/10.1007/s00426-019-01245-8

Baker, B. (2002). The hunt for disability: The new eugenics and the normalization of school children. *Teachers College Record*, *104*, 663–703. https://doi.org/10.1111/1467-9620.00175

Baylosis, C. (2019). Mad Studies and an ethics of listening. *Journal of Ethics in Mental Health*, *10*(6), 1–18.

Black, M. H., McGarry, S., Churchill, L., D'Arcy, E., Dalgleish, J., Nash, I., Jones, A., Tse, T. Y., Gibson, J., Bölte, S., & Girdler, S. (2022). Considerations of the built environment for autistic individuals: A review of the literature. *Autism*, *26*(8), 1904–1915. https://doi.org/10.1177/13623613221102753

Brown, B. (2021). *Atlas of the heart: Mapping meaningful connection and the language of human experience*. Random House.

Brune, J. A., & Wilson, D. J. (2013). Introduction. In J. A. Brune & D. J. Wilson (Eds.), *Disability and passing: Blurring the lines of identity* (pp. 1–12). Temple University Press.

Bueter, A. (2019). Epistemic injustice and psychiatric classification. *Philosophy of Science*, *86*, 1064–1074.

Carr, S. (2022). Institutional ceremonies? The (im)possibilites of transformative co-production in mental health. In P. Beresford & J. Russo (Eds.), *The Routledge international handbook of Mad Studies* (pp. 142–153). Routledge.

Carver, L., Morley, S., & Taylor, P. (2017). Voices of deficit: Mental health, criminal victimization, and epistemic injustice. *Illness, Crisis, & Loss*, *25*(1), 43–62. https://doi.org/10.1177/1054137316675715

Chapman, R. (2020a). Defining neurodiversity for research and practice. In H. B. Rosqvist, N. Chown, & A. Stenning (Eds.), *Neurodiversity studies: A new critical paradigm* (pp. 218–220). Routledge.

Chapman, R. (2020b). Neurodiversity, disability, wellbeing. In H. B. Rosqvist, N. Chown, & A. Stenning (Eds.), *Neurodiversity studies: A new critical paradigm* (pp. 57–72). Routledge.

Chew, K. (2013). Odysseus and "The Fools": Applying concepts of neurodiversity to the ancient world. In C. D. Herrera & A. Perry (Eds.), *Ethics and neurodiversity* (pp. 276–285). Cambridge Scholars Publishing.

Crichton, P., Carel, H., & Kidd, I. J. (2017). Epistemic injustice in psychiatry. *BJPscych Bulletin*, *41*(2), 65–70. https://doi.org/10.1192/pb.bp.115.050682

Dobbs, T. L. (2012). A critical analysis of disabilities discourse in the *Journal of Research in Music Education*, 1990-2011. *Bulletin of the Council for Research in Music Education*, *194*, 7–30. https://doi.org/10.5406/bulcouresmusedu.194.0007

Fabris, E. (2011). *Tranquil prisons: Chemical incarceration under community treatment orders*. University of Toronto Press.

Ferguson, T. J., Eyre, H. L., & Ashbaker, M. (2000). Unwanted identities: A key variable in shame-anger links and gender differences in shame. *Sex Roles*, *42*(3–4), 133–157. https://doi.org/10.1023/A:1007061505251

Gay, G. (2018). *Culturally responsive teaching: Theory, research, and practice* (3rd ed.). Teachers College Press.
Harcourt, E. (2021). Epistemic injustice, children and mental illness. *Journal of Medical Ethics*, OnlineFirst, 1–7. https://doi.org/10.1136/medethics-2021-107329
Hendricks, K. S. (2018). *Compassionate music teaching: A framework for motivation and engagement in the 21st century*. Rowman & Littlefield.
Ladson-Billings, G. (1995). Toward a theory of culturally relevant pedagogy. *American Education Research Journal*, 32(3), 465–491. https://doi.org/10.3102/00028312032003465
Ladson-Billings, G. (2009). *The dream keepers: Successful teachers of African American children* (2nd ed.). Jossey-Bass.
Ladson-Billings, G. (2014). Culturally relevant pedagogy 2.0: A.k.a. the remix. *Harvard Educational Review*, 84(1), 74–84. https://doi.org/10.17763/haer.84.1.p2rj131485484751
Lakoff, G., & Johnson, M. (2003/1980). *Metaphors we live by* (iBooks ed.). The University of Chicago Press.
LeBlanc, S., & Kinsella, E. A. (2016). Toward epistemic justice: A critically reflexive examination of 'sanism' and implications for knowledge generation. *Studies in Social Justice*, 10(1), 59–78.
Liegghio, M. (2013). A denial of being: Psychiatrization as epistemic violence. In B. LeFrancois, R. Menzies, & G. Reaume (Eds.), *Mad matters: A critical reader in Canadian Mad Studies* (pp. 122–129). Canadian Scholars' Press.
Linton, S. (1998). *Claiming disability: Knowledge and identity*. New York University Press.
Lubet, A. (2013). *Music, disability, and society*. Temple University Press.
McKoy, C. L., & Lind, V. L. (2023). *Culturally responsive teaching in music education: From understanding to application*. Routledge.
Neff, K. (2003). Self-compassion: An alternative conceptualization of a healthy attitude toward oneself. *Self and Identity*, 2, 85–101.
Neff, K. (2011). *Self-compassion: The proven power of being kind to yourself*. HarperCollins.
Oliver, M., & Sapey, B. (1999). *Social work with disabled people* (2nd ed.). Palgrave MacMillan.
Paris, D., & Alim, H. S. (2014). What are we seeking to sustain through culturally sustaining pedagogy? A loving critique forward. *Harvard Educational Review*, 84(1), 85–100. https://doi.org/10.17763/haer.84.1.982l873k2ht16m77
Paris, D., & Alim, H. S. (Eds.). (2017). *Culturally sustaining pedagogies: Teaching and learning for justice in a changing world*. Teachers College Press.
Price, M. (2015). The bodymind problem and the possibilities of pain. *Hypatia*, 30(1), 268–284. www.jstor.org/stable/24542071
Rosqvist, H. B., Stenning, A., & Chown, N. (2020). Introduction. In H. B. Rosqvist, N. Chown, & A. Stenning (Eds.), *Neurodiversity studies: A new critical paradigm* (pp. 1–11). Routledge.
Russo, J. (2022). The international foundation of Mad Studies: Knowledge generated in collective action. In P. Beresford & J. Russo (Eds.), *The Routledge international handbook of Mad Studies* (pp. 19–29). Routledge.

Scrutton, A. P. (2017). Epistemic injustice and mental illness. In I. J. Kidd, J. Medina, & G. Pohlhaus Jr. (Eds.), *The Routledge handbook of epistemic injustice* (pp. 347–355). Routledge.

Siebers, T. (2017). Disability and the theory of complex embodiment: For identity politics in a new register. In L. J. Davis (Ed.), *The disability studies reader* (5th ed., pp. 310–329). Routledge.

Speed, E., & Taggart, D. (2019). Stigma and mental health: Exploring potential models to enhance opportunities for a parity of participation. *Journal of Ethics in Mental Health, 10*(6), 1–19.

Sullivan, P. J. (2019). Epistemic injustice and self-injury: A concept with clinical implications. *Philosophy, Psychiatry, & Psychology, 26*(4), 349–362. https://doi.org/10.1353/ppp.2019.0049

Titchkosky, T. (2001). Disability: A rose by any other name? "People-first" language in Canadian society. *The Canadian Review of Sociology and Anthropology, 38*(2), 125–140. https://doi.org/10.1111/j.1755-618X.2001.tb00967.x

van der Kolk, B. A. (2014). *The body keeps the score: Brain, mind, and body in the healing of trauma*. Viking (The Penguin Group).

Walker, N. (2021). *Neuroqueer heresies: Notes on the neurodiversity paradigm, autistic empowerment, and postnormal possibilities* (ePub ed.). Autonomous Press.

White, W. L. (2022). Re-writing the master narrative: A prerequisite for Mad liberation. In P. Beresford & J. Russo (Eds.), *The Routledge international handbook of Mad Studies* (pp. 76–89). Routledge.

# 4 Benefits of Neurodivergence

*Meena:* I've come to like my madness, actually. It requires being well-medicated, because I think for me a lot of my grief was that after developing the schizoaffective, I was on medication that didn't work for several years, which caused me to cycle in and out of the hospital. Then when they determined the right medication, I was dangerously over-medicated for eight years and I was sleeping 11-12 hours a day, for eight years. Now, finally, I'm at a good dose and I'm sleeping a normal amount. But getting to that medication sweet spot is required first, before you can start enjoying the fruits of having Madness. You have to know what medications to take, what works and what doesn't work, and what dosages are appropriate to reach the sweet spot. It can take decades to get to that point. I love it now. I like who I am.

In this chapter, I explore what participants identified as the benefits of neurodivergence. Aspects of their neurodivergence resulted in experiences they valued. Most identified as having high degrees of empathy and compassion. Some felt their experiences helped them cultivate relationality. Several participants found neurodivergent characteristics arising from experiences of Madness and/or distress to be helpful in their music teaching in a range of ways. Participants perceived having higher than typical levels of curiosity and one participant spoke to what he called his "overinclusiveness." These music educators also described the role of compassion and relationality in pedagogy, an awareness of others' needs, creative approaches to teaching, and the benefits of high energy.

In examining these participant-identified benefits of neurodivergence I do not seek to negate the difficulties, traumas, and harms experienced as a result of these same neurodivergences. Experiences of Madness and distress can constitute a significant struggle, and are often upsetting or traumatizing, sometimes to the point of being life-threatening.

DOI: 10.4324/9781032662817-5

*Lizabeth:* It's bad. The first word that I thought of was struggle. Which is really sad, but that's what came to mind. ... Unfortunately, having mental health issues, particularly like my anxiety and my depression, caused a lot of struggles for me, just day to day.

Participants described differences related to attention, behavior, eating, energy, and sleeping, as well as experiences of anxiety, depression, suicidality, paranoia, psychosis, mania, and self-injury.[1] Such experiences were common among participants. In exploring what they identified as benefits of neurodivergence, I do not aim to romanticize them, but rather recognize the full breadth of what such experiences entail. The utter strength of research participants and others who have created beauty out of realities that can be disturbing, terrifying, extremely dangerous, and isolating deserves attention not often included in discourse around Madness and distress. Fabris (2011) described Madness as a way of knowing as "intelligent, searching, and valuable" (p. 32); this chapter focuses on those kinds of characteristics.

In Chapter 3, I discussed how particular characteristics can act as assets or liabilities across different contexts following language used by Chris and August.

*Chris:* It really helps, I think, to be a really good violinist, if you have some obsessive compulsive characteristics. This is actually a positive characteristic for many, and what I will sometimes affectionately talk about as obsessive compulsive "order" rather than disorder. Because why put the "dis-" there when actually what it creates is often an order that is beautiful. It's a two-edged sword, and this doesn't work for everyone, but let's find ways to celebrate some of the positive it can bring.

Chris' refusal of obsessive compulsive characteristics as "disordered" indicates the ways such characteristics are considered assets in particular musical contexts (and likely contexts outside of music). Crucially, characteristics that are pathologized and diagnosed at times by psy-professions may at other times create profound "order that is beautiful." Chris wished to lean into the positive emergences of these characteristics, urging a focus on contexts in which they became assets and facilitated beauty. With a context-specific perspective shift of a characteristic into an asset, these qualities become some of the benefits and beauties of neurodivergence themselves. In this chapter, I explore the ways in which having had experiences of Madness and/or distress may cultivate characteristics that are assets both interpersonally and in music teaching contexts.

### Relationality

Almost all participants possessed what they viewed as heightened levels of compassion and empathy. These characteristics allowed them to engage in attunement and awareness of the needs of others, as well as cultivate self-awareness of their own needs. Participants also felt they built strong relationships and deep connections with others based on their ability to attune to people and consider others' needs.

*Empathy and Compassion*

Most participants identified as having high levels of empathy and compassion as a direct result of their experiences of Madness and distress. While empathy is far from an unequivocal good and can certainly be misappropriated or used to avoid owning complicity in oppression (Hess, 2019, 2023), these participants illuminated ways that their use of empathy and compassion provided insights into others' struggles.

*Rebecca:* I think for me, it's [benefits of neurodivergence] sensitivity and empathy. I can tell when people aren't well, mentally, and I can spot it in students in ways that I think maybe other people don't. And then I can empathize with where they are, in terms of what they can and can't do, realistically.

While Rebecca is not publicly "out" about her experiences of depression and anxiety, she sometimes shares these experiences in individual conversations with students with the aim of supporting them in their struggles. Cheryl felt similarly: "feeling like it helped—having the experience of depression myself—might help me empathize with students who struggle with depression." Both Rebecca and Cheryl believed their experiences aided understanding of students' needs while teaching. QingYu highlighted the importance of their intersectional identity in the empathy and compassion they were able to cultivate.

*QingYu:* Just being part of the community allows me to be more understanding about people that are different than us. I think it makes us more compassionate, empathetic people. I think that's really it. It allows us to have almost more tolerance really, not that we deserve to be more tolerant of other people. But the more intersectionality you have as a person, the more you have to experience oppression from other people, or barriers you are going to face. Something as simple as being neurodivergent is going to impact you in your experience with other people and how you behave and experience life, and just as simple as being in that community is going to affect your social life.

QingYu believed that experiencing oppressions, including sanism, may increase levels of compassion for others facing oppression across any and all identity categories.

Meena described a way the characteristics of empathy and compassion might be purposefully fostered.

*Meena:* Most recently I've practiced *Metta* meditation (a Buddhist practice), *compassion and loving-kindness towards the self and others*. It is immensely transformative and is a useful alternative to "mindfulness," which can be too intense for me with my history. So much work needs to be done integrating Eastern concepts into mainstream therapy as practiced in the West.

Practicing *Metta* cultivates compassion for self and others, and Meena felt it might be a useful practice for others with experiences of Madness and/or distress. Hendricks (2018) distinguished between cognitive empathy and affective empathy: "*cognitive empathy*, or the ability to consider in our minds what someone else might be experiencing, and *affective empathy*, or the ability to actually feel in our bodies and emotions what others are feeling" (p. 56). Hendricks' (2018) distinction between cognitive and affective empathy is useful in naming the dynamics participants identified. When faced with someone who is struggling with distress, a person who has had no such experiences themself may engage cognitive empathy. They may cognitively consider the distress this person is experiencing, but their lack of similar personal experiences makes affective empathy impossible. Conversely, people with experiences of Madness and distress may have access to affective empathy, wherein they can feel the pain of another.[2]

Brown (2018) noted that "[e]mpathy is not connecting to an experience, it's connecting to the emotions that underpin an experience" (p. 181). She wrote:

Empathy is a choice. And it's a vulnerable choice, because if I were to choose to connect with you through empathy, I would have to connect with something in myself that knows that feeling. In the face of a difficult conversation, when we see that someone's hurt or in pain, it's our instinct as human beings to try to make things better. We want to fix, we want to give advice. But empathy isn't about fixing, it's the brave choice to be with someone in their darkness—not to race to turn on the light so we feel better.

(p. 183)

The empathy Brown described requires drawing on, and deeply connecting with, a similar experience and emotion inside oneself to empathize with another. For participants, having experiences of Madness and distress allowed them to access that place in themselves toward affective empathy or *mitgefühl* in German—feeling with another. Razack (2007), however, cautioned against stealing the pain of others; she highlighted the danger that may allow people who hold dominant identities to feel good about themselves when employing empathy without acting to alter power relations and structures of oppression. Keeping this caveat in mind, participants found that their experiences helped them empathize with others. Participants who identified increased levels of empathy all valued this characteristic in themselves. Moreover, most had deep understandings and analysis of privilege and oppression, enabling them to actively work against reinscribing oppression through empathy.

Considerations of empathy also extend into music education discourse. Scholars have increasingly demonstrated music education's potential to foster empathy (Cho & Han, 2022; Hendricks, 2018; Hendricks et al., 2021; Laird, 2015; Silverman, 2015; Winter, 2013; Zhang, 2017). Participants in this study felt their experiences made them more empathetic and compassionate, particularly in relation to others who were experiencing distress. It follows that music education might help cultivate empathetic characteristics in students who may then better respond to distress. Music itself can also play a role in soothing distress. It can ameliorate depression and help people manage negative moods (Lonsdale & North, 2011; Thayer et al., 1994), aid in regulating sadness (Kahn et al., 2022), and provide consolation (ter Bogt et al., 2017). Music educators would be wise to honor the empathy that can emerge when a person has experienced distress, cultivate that empathy through musicking, and also be explicit in teaching students how music might soothe their distress.

*Awareness, Attunement, and Fostering Relationships*

Extending the idea that experiences of Madness and distress helped bring empathy and compassion to relationships, participants further described depth of connection, awareness of others' emotions, and other facets of emotional expression.

*Jillian:* My neurodivergency helps me to connect with people in a way that feels extremely deep and personal. I think that providing support to other people who are struggling is possible without being mentally ill, but only at a surface level. The support that has resonated the most with me has been from people who have survived the things I am afraid I will not. To be able to be that for someone else is really, really, special. You see the world differently because you understand that struggle exists and exists deeply. Otherwise, I'd say people who are not neurodivergent likely do not have access to as much empathy without making a conscious effort to do so.

Jillian described an experience of affective empathy, both giving and receiving, and highlighted the importance of shared emotions that underpin an experience when offering support following Brown (2018). They also elucidated the gap that occurs in cognitive empathy—one can provide support to someone experiencing distress without having had such experiences, but the level of support is superficial or "surface level."

Blaine specifically identified the ability to deeply attune to other's emotions.

*Blaine:* Being neurodivergent makes me very aware of other people's emotions, and other people's way that they communicate with me. I can tell when something's off. ... It helps me, I think, be compassionate to other people and try to understand where they're coming from. I try not to write off someone immediately. If we're not getting along, I try to understand why we're not getting along, or what might be underlying that is causing us to have a conflict. I try to see people through all of their different identities, understanding where they're coming from.

In a therapeutic context, Erskine (1998) defined attunement as:

a kinesthetic and emotional sensing of others—knowing their rhythm, affect and experience by metaphorically being in their skin, and going beyond empathy to create a two-person experience of unbroken feeling connectedness by providing a reciprocal affect and/or resonating response.

(p. 236)

While elsewhere I have challenged the impossibility of fully understanding another's perspective (Hess, 2023; Hess & Bradley, 2022), what Blaine described resonates with Erskine's definition of attunement. Moreover, Blaine used attunement deliberately to recognize the identities and experiences that shaped the emotions of another. Nicholas likewise pointed to ways that their neurodivergence created unique channels of communication, also describing how they amplified attunement by noticing physical cues.

*Nicholas:* I'm really great with relationships at this point. Now I can read people's body language, see their facial expressions, their eyes, and hear their tone of voice, which I couldn't really do until a few years ago. I'm still sensitive to how people are thinking and feeling but not completely overwhelmed and distressed by it. The gift is that I am able to build a relationship with almost anyone. I don't know if I could have done that or thought about it or realized how important it was if I wasn't neurodivergent.

Participants found that their personal experiences of Madness and distress assisted in attuning to others, helped them form strong and supportive relationships, and promoted empathy and compassion—particularly for others experiencing distress. Relationality and social connection may also be fostered through musicking (Lonsdale & North, 2011; McFerran & Saarikallio, 2014; Papinczak et al., 2015; Schäfer et al., 2013). Kahn et al. (2022) found that listening to music offers interpersonal benefits. Indeed, musicking offered as much interpersonal connection as talking to a friend or asking someone for advice (p. 1348). If musicking also fosters relationality, music educators can lean into these aspects of musicking to deepen relationships and community-building in classrooms, as well as honoring the attunement that can emerge from having experiences of Madness and distress.

*Self-Awareness of Needs*

Participants identified five broad categories of support they accessed: community, family, institutional, medical, and therapeutic support. Experiences of support, however, were mixed. Most (but not all) participants found community, family, and therapeutic support to be positive and helpful, while institutional and medical support skewed more negatively among participants. Due to these mixed experiences, most participants described awareness of their needs when experiencing distress and had learned through past experiences which supports they found most helpful.

*Cheryl:* I think it [experiences of depression] has sort of forced me to be a lot more aware of what it is that I need. How can I be healthier? ... I am happy that I feel like [coping mechanisms] have helped me when I am in depressive episodes, but also those help me when I am not depressed. So in a weird way, it has brought me good things, too.

Cheryl's experiences taught them what they needed in relation to support not just during depressive periods but also in times of stability.

### Effects on Music Teaching

Most of the characteristics identified in this chapter also prove supportive to pedagogy. Empathy, compassion, and the ability to cultivate relationships through attunement and awareness all assist in building a strong community in the classroom. Recognizing that characteristics can be assets or liabilities depending on the context provides a different perspective for teaching that disrupts conventional views of asset-based pedagogies, as discussed in Chapter 3. While some of the preceding discussion references teaching, in this section I include ways that characteristics that emerged from participants' neurodivergences specifically supported their music teaching praxis.

*Curiosity*

Some participants described how the heightened curiosity they experienced was useful in their interactions with students.

*Paulo:* I feel like I'm more curious about stuff and I can get drawn into being super excited about something. ... I've become very, very into wrestling recently, because that became the new thing that my mind was like, "I'm super curious about this." I've been able to catalyze that towards [being] super curious about students. I want to know more about them. ... I think that that inbuilt curiosity has been something that I've always leaned on. And now, knowing that it's part of literally the brain chemistry and brain structures makes me kind of excited. Because it feels like it's a perspective that not everyone is able to fully embrace as easily.

Paulo applied his curiosity in the classroom and found it helped him get to know different students, making it valuable to pedagogy. The way Paulo described it, curiosity may well serve as an extension of attunement when used in relationships. In this context, curiosity draws on empathy, compassion, and the relationship-building efforts participants identified as neurodivergent characteristics they considered assets. From a pedagogical perspective, music educators can also create projects that might pique students' curiosity. This tactic follows the approach of the Universal Design for Learning (UDL),[3] offering students the choice of how they can best express their learning to suit their skill set and interests.

*Overinclusiveness*

Paulo appreciated his ability to see connections between things that others might view as disparate or unrelated—what he called overinclusiveness—and considered it a benefit of neurodivergence.

*Paulo:* Overinclusiveness. That's a real common thing [in] bipolar disorder, [the] ability to see connections between things that other people wouldn't see. I didn't know that that was a thing, and I remember [professor] always giving me a hard time about, "well, they all can't be connected." Like yeah, "they are though." ... Ever since I found that there was a label for it, and that it was a common thing, it was definitely something that I'm very happy that I have at my disposal—the ability to do that.

Overinclusiveness in the context of Madness and distress is typically defined as the *inability* to preserve conceptual boundaries (Andreasen & Powers, 1974). Rather than construct overinclusiveness as a deficit or problem, Paulo embraced his ability to see beyond the limits of common conceptual boundaries and instead found it useful, particularly in his pedagogical praxis. Many current approaches to pedagogy aim to honor and validate what students bring to the classroom across the full range of human diversity (CAST, n.d.; Gay, 2018; Ladson-Billings, 2009, 2014; McKoy & Lind, 2023) but often fail to apply this same generosity to educators. Overinclusiveness in music education can extend beyond the focus on race, ethnicity, and disability to consider neurodiversity among students and educators. Both overinclusiveness and curiosity also help in building strong relationships with students across the full range of human diversity.

*Compassion and Relationality in Pedagogy*

Participants also identified ways that their compassion and emphasis on relationality proved useful to their pedagogy.

*QingYu:* I think a positive thing of experiencing mental health is being able to be compassionate and empathetic with my students. ... During my student teaching [the students] said, "You're really different than all of our other student teachers different because you actually care about us. You actually take the time to get to know us, and you actually really care about what's happening in our real lives. Everybody else that have been student teachers really just treat us like numbers. They don't really care and they don't take time to really care about our problems." ... I feel like I could be a more successful teacher, besides the skills I learned in music school, because I can understand my students, and just really be there for them. So there is a positive. I've been experiencing mental health, [which is obviously] very debilitating for many people. But I did see it as one positive aspect as a teacher because at the end of the day, your students are human beings.

QingYu's experiences informed their teaching and helped them to connect deeply with students and form relationships, as described in the section on relationality. As noted in Chapter 2, QingYu also felt that their intersectional identities helped them to relate to students.

Similarly, Emma found that her experiences with autism and distress fostered greater compassion and openmindedness toward the students she encountered.

*Emma:* It makes me a lot more open minded and compassionate towards students who are [struggling], honestly, because I feel I still sometimes struggle. Like when my co-op's like, oh, "that kid has ADHD and they haven't taken their meds." I still get annoyed by that student, don't get me wrong, but they're just having those experiences because they are autistic. I've already had to get a lot of help with making eye contact and communication, and have to work really, really hard at empathy. I think by workshopping some of those early on it helped me to be a lot more compassionate, open-minded towards my students, especially those who are going through stuff, because I get it. Versus if I have never experienced that, then being presented with this kid who's having a lot of behavioral issues. A lot of times teachers who have no experience whatsoever with mental illness, they just think that student's just being bad, and then they don't handle it the way that they probably could.

She observed that teachers often perceive students who act out because of neurodivergence as behaving "badly." In literature on trauma, pedagogues and psy- professionals have made a shift in language from "What is wrong with this child?" to "What has happened to this child?" (Hess, 2022; Ng'andu, 2015; Winfrey & Perry, 2021). The latter question refracts differently with neurodiversity, because while some neurodivergence occurs as a result of experiences such as trauma, other neurodivergence is innate (Walker, 2021). This question encourages looking for the source of the behavior rather than assuming that a student is acting out deliberately and maliciously. While Emma acknowledged she is sometimes still annoyed by the behavior, she remained interested in the underlying cause, and maintained compassion and openmindness when working with children and youth.

Meghan's personal experiences of distress led her to recognize and be intentional about ways to engage with students who she believed were struggling.

*Meghan:* It [My neurodivergence] has allowed me to see like, this student was really down yesterday. They're not here today. I'm

> going to check in with them tomorrow. The anxiety part of that has told me, don't pull that student aside and be like, "Are you doing okay, what's going on?" Because if a professor did that to me I would vomit, I would be so nervous. So it's taught me to be able to do these check-ins in passing and say, "What can I do to help you today? You want to go sit in the hallway, you want to put your noise cancelling headphones in today? Totally cool. Let's talk about it when you want to." That's not something that I learned in school, that was just part of my superpower.

She noted that she did not appreciate focused attention on her own distress which led her to conduct casual check-ins with students, something that her personal experiences of distress allowed her to do instinctively. She described an attunement with students and a willingness to help them to soothe their own distress.

### Applying Creativity to Pedagogy

Attuning to student needs and being a creative planner and instructor were positive characteristics Meghan shared as important to her teaching.

*Meghan:* From a teacher perspective, it [being neurodivergent] has definitely made me a lot more sensitive to how my students are, and it allows me to look out for them and to see this is a student who needs help. I recognize those things because of behaviors that I exhibit. Also from the standpoint of just being a student learning how to be a teacher, it really allows me to think outside of the box when it comes to thinking about how to teach certain things. Like when we're in classes and are told, "I need you to teach this thing to your peers." And we're all teaching the same thing. Having ADHD I'm sitting here and I'm like, well, "I could do it this way. Or I could do it this way. Or we could do it this way. Let's follow this thread and see where that goes." Then I'm doing something different and it's not getting boring.

Meghan observed when she taught peers that her attention differences allowed her to create lessons that were unique from those of her classmates. When we connected in a focus group, she had just finished student teaching and discussed the way she differentiated herself from her mentor teacher. She noted: "I don't want to do it the same way as her because I'm not her. We're two completely different teachers. So I sit there for like, three minutes [and think,] 'here's 18 different ways I can teach this.'" Meghan's neurodivergence and multidirectionality of thinking helped her to come up with abundant instructional possibilities and be pedagogically creative, strengthening her teaching. The Universal Design for Learning (UDL) calls on teachers to represent knowledge in multiple ways in the classroom (CAST, n.d.). Meghan knew instinctively how to do this, and thus offered students multiple points of access into each lesson she taught.

*High Energy in Teaching*

High levels of energy resulting from mania facilitated desirable outcomes in Laura's teaching.

*Laura:* It's really helped me when it comes to students and their needs. I think that part of my mania comes out when I'm teaching. I become very lively and very relatable, and just almost a whole different person. ... Not teaching for awhile now has been really hard on me because I don't have that outlet and I don't have that communication with students.
*Rebecca:* It's like a performance high, isn't it?
*Laura:* It is. That's a good way to put it.

Laura valued this aspect of her neurodivergence and appreciated what it brought to her work in the classroom, as numerous participants appreciated various ways in which neurodivergence brought dimension and depth to their teaching.

Participants drew on characteristics that they attributed to their neurodivergences in the music classroom. The proclivity toward curiosity and overinclusiveness supported their pedagogy, and tendencies toward compassion and relationality allowed them to cultivate strong relationships with students. They also described being highly creative with their planning and the benefits of having high energy in music teaching contexts. Not only, then, did participants identify characteristics they valued that they ascribed to their neurodivergences, they also found these characteristics useful in their teaching praxis.

## Conclusion and Implications

While acknowledging the immensity of distress they sometimes experienced, participants also identified several positive aspects of their neurodivergence as characteristics they appreciated, both personally and professionally. These characteristics acted as assets in various contexts. Participants believed that they cultivated high levels of empathy and compassion for people they encountered in their lives, especially students.

They felt able to attune deeply to others, particularly those in distress. This ability to attune supported them in fostering relationships in and out of the classroom. Their curiosity proved additionally useful in getting to know students and building relationships. Recognizing the contextual nature of characteristics as assets also supports pedagogy; teachers can lean into their characteristics in the contexts in which they present as assets, and support students in contexts where their characteristics are challenging. All participants identified having learned what kinds of support they found helpful in times of distress, and this self-awareness fostered awareness of others' potential needs as well. The concept of overinclusiveness—a term present in literature and described by Paulo as an ability to see connections between seemingly disparate ideas—also translates to the classroom via inclusive practice. Participants further drew on their creativity in their planning processes and valued high energy in the classroom. The positive characteristics participants observed in themselves provide an important counterpoint to discourse about people with experiences of Madness and/or distress that pathologizes and dismisses.

Educators and students with experiences of Madness and/or distress may be uniquely positioned to cultivate empathy and relationality in the classroom and engage in attunement with others. This finding is significant for teachers and administrators to recognize, especially when juxtaposed with current medically-based deficit perspectives so pervasive in schools. While these specific characteristics cannot be generalized among all people with experiences of Madness and/or distress, most of these research participants identified these qualities within themselves and as particularly useful to their teaching. In order to benefit from these characteristics, however, educators and students with experiences of Madness and/or distress must receive the accommodations and support needed for us to thrive in educational spaces. Lizabeth reminded readers at the beginning of this chapter that the first word that comes to mind in reflecting on experiences of Madness and/or distress is "struggle." The imperative for support is clear. Given the common difficulty of accommodation processes (see Chapter 8 for discussion), applying for accommodations must be streamlined and simplified for ease of accessibility. Without support, educators and students with experiences of Madness and/or distress are likely to experience a failure to thrive in (music) education spaces and become unable to use their gifts as the "superpowers"[4] they can be.

## Notes

1 I use the term "self-injury" following Price (2015), who argued that self-*harm* should be reserved for "occasions when negative outcome to the harmed subject is more certain" (p. 281).
2 See Hess (2019, 2023) for a discussion of the caveats involved.

3 I discuss UDL in Chapter 7 and in the conclusion. See www.cast.org for more information.
4 "Superpower" is deeply contested language in the disability/neurodiversity community (see for example NeuroClastic, 2019). The idea of disability or neurodiversity as superpower ventures into the territory of inspiration porn (Young, 2012, 2014) and the supercrip (Schalk, 2016), and valorizes the neurodivergent or disabled person for the benefit of non-neurodivergent, non-disabled communities. In this chapter, participants described positive attributes of their neurodivergence. It is up to individuals, however, to decide if they want to call one or more of these attributes "superpowers." Doing so requires recognizing that not all people feel this way, or even feel this way consistently about their own experience.

## References

Andreasen, N. J. C., & Powers, P. S. (1974). Overinclusive thinking in mania and schizophrenia. *The British Journal of Psychiatry, 125*(588), 452–456. https://doi.org/10.1192/bjp.125.5.452

Brown, B. (2018). *Dare to lead: Brave work. Tough conversations. Whole hearts* (iBooks ed.). Random House.

CAST. (n.d.). *CAST*. Retrieved March 6, 2023 from www.cast.org

Cho, E., & Han, J. Y. (2022). Small music ensemble and empathy: A replication study in a South Korean music student sample. *Psychology of Music, 50*(4), 1121–1135. https://doi.org/i.o0r.g1/107.711/0773/05370537536526121100 3311663

Erskine, R. G. (1998). Attunement and involvement: Therapeutic responses to relational needs. *International Journal of Psychotherapy, 3*(3), 235–244.

Fabris, E. (2011). *Tranquil prisons: Chemical incarceration under community treatment orders*. University of Toronto Press.

Gay, G. (2018). *Culturally responsive teaching: Theory, research, and practice* (3rd ed.). Teachers College Press.

Hendricks, K. S. (2018). *Compassionate music teaching: A framework for motivation and engagement in the 21st century*. Rowman & Littlefield.

Hendricks, K. S., Einarson, K. M., Mitchell, N., Guerriero, E. M., & D'Ercole, P. (2021). Caring for, about, and with: Exploring musical meaningfulness among Suzuki students and parents. *Frontiers in Education, 6*, 1–12. https://doi.org/10.3389/feduc.2021.648776

Hess, J. (2019). *Music education for social change: Constructing an activist music education*. Routledge.

Hess, J. (2022). Rethinking "bad behavior": A compassionate response to "acting out" in music education. In D. Bradley & J. Hess (Eds.), *Trauma and resilience in music education: Haunted melodies* (pp. 19–34). Routledge.

Hess, J. (2023). When the project is not understanding: Music education for the incomprehensible. *Studies in Philosophy and Education, 42*(3), 261–282. https://doi.org/10.1007/s11217-022-09861-5

Hess, J., & Bradley, D. (2022). Conclusion: On resilience. In D. Bradley & J. Hess (Eds.), *Trauma and resilience in music education: Haunted melodies* (pp. 199–213). Routledge.
Kahn, J. H., Ladd, K., Feltner-Williams, D. A., Martin, A. M., & White, B. L. (2022). Regulating sadness: Response-independent and response- dependent benefits of listening to music. *Psychology of Music, 50*(4), 1348–1361. https://doi.org/10.1177/03057356211048545
Ladson-Billings, G. (2009). *The dream keepers: Successful teachers of African American children* (2nd ed.). Jossey-Bass.
Ladson-Billings, G. (2014). Culturally relevant pedagogy 2.0: A.k.a. the remix. *Harvard Educational Review, 84*(1), 74–84. https://doi.org/10.17763/haer.84.1.p2rj131485484751
Laird, L. (2015). Empathy in the classroom: Can music bring us more in tune with one another? *Music Educators Journal, 101*(4), 56–61. https://doi.org/10.1177/0027432115572230
Lonsdale, A. J., & North, A. C. (2011). Why do we listen to music? A uses and gratifications analysis. *British Journal of Psychology, 102*(1), 108–134. https://doi.org/10.1348/000712610x506831
McFerran, K., & Saarikallio, S. (2014). Depending on music to feel better: Being conscious of responsibility when appropriating the power of music. *The Arts in Psychotherapy, 41*, 89–97. https://doi.org/10.1016/j.aip.2013.11.007
McKoy, C. L., & Lind, V. L. (2023). *Culturally responsive teaching in music education: From understanding to application*. Routledge.
NeuroClastic. (2019, September 7). Your disability is a tragedy vs your disability is your superpower. NeuroClastic. https://neuroclastic.com/disability-tragedy-or-superpower/?amp
Ng'andu, J. (2015, December 17, 2015). *"It's not what's wrong with the children, it's what's happened to them"*. www.edutopia.org/blog/not-whats-wrong-whats-happened-jennifer-ngandu
Papinczak, Z. E., Dingle, G. A., Stoyanov, S. R., Hides, L., & Zelenko, O. (2015). Young people's uses of music for well-being. *Journal of Youth Studies, 18*(9), 1119–1134. https://doi.org/10.1080/13676261.2015.1020935
Price, M. (2015). The bodymind problem and the possibilities of pain. *Hypatia, 30*(1), 268–284. www.jstor.org/stable/24542071
Razack, S. (2007). Stealing the pain of Others: Reflections on Canadian humanitarian responses. *The Review of Education Pedagogy, and Cultural Studies, 29*(4), 375–394.
Schäfer, T., Sedlmeier, P., Städtler, C., & Huron, D. (2013). The psychological functions of music listening. *Frontiers in Psychology, 4*. https://doi.org/10.3389/fpsyg.2013.00511
Schalk, S. (2016). Reevaluating the Supercrip. *Journal of Literary & Cultural Disability Studies, 10*(1), 71–86. https://doi.org/10.3828/jlcds.2016.5
Silverman, M. (2015). Listening-for social justice. In L. C. DeLorenzo (Ed.), *Giving voice to democracy in music education* (pp. 157–175). Routledge.
ter Bogt, T., Vieno, A., Doornwaard, S. M., Pastore, M., & Van den Eijnden, R. J. J. M. (2017). "You're not alone": Music as a source of consolation among

adolescents and young adults. *Psychology Of Music*, *45*(2), 155–171. https://doi.org/10.1177/0305735616650029

Thayer, R. E., Newman, J. R., & McClain, T. M. (1994). Self-regulation of mood: Strategies for changing a bad mood, raising energy, and reducing tension. *Journal of Personality and Social Psychology*, *67*(5), 910–925. https://doi.org/10.1037/0022-3514.67.5.910

Walker, N. (2021). *Neuroqueer heresies: Notes on the neurodiversity paradigm, autistic empowerment, and postnormal possibilities* (ePub ed.). Autonomous Press.

Winfrey, O., & Perry, B. D. (2021). *What happened to you?: Conversations on trauma, resilience, and healing*. Flatiron Books.

Winter, R. (2013). Language, empathy, archetype: Action-metaphors of the transcendental in musical experience. *Philosophy of Music Education Review*, *21*(2), 103–119.

Young, S. (2012, July 2). We're not here for your inspiration. *The Drum*. www.abc.net.au/news/2012-07-03/young-inspiration-porn/4107006

Young, S. (2014). *I'm not your inspiration, thank you very much*, TED. www.ted.com/talks/stella_young_i_m_not_your_inspiration_thank_you_very_much?language=en

Zhang, Y. (2017). Walking a mile in their shoes: Developing pre-service music teachers' empathy for ELL students. *International Journal of Music Education*, *35*(3), 425–434.

# 5 A Question of Visibility
## Being "Out" in Music Education

Navigating the decision of whether or not to disclose one's experiences of Madness or distress at work or school is extremely challenging. Stigma and discrimination as facets of sanism play a significant role. Stigma against people with experiences of Madness and distress leads to discrimination, which particularly affects employment (Elraz, 2018; Glover et al., 2010; Lettieri et al., 2021; Martin et al., 2000; Østerud, 2022; Russinovaa et al., 2011; Stuart, 2006). Martin et al. (2000) studied public attitudes toward people with mental illness and reported that 58.1% of those surveyed would prefer not to have someone with mental health differences as a coworker (p. 216). Half of U.S. employers show reluctance to hire someone with a past psychiatric history or current experiences of depression, and 70% hesitate to hire someone taking antipsychotic medication or with a history of substance abuse.[1] Almost 25% of employers would fire someone who had not disclosed a mental illness (Stuart, 2006, p. 523). While this research is not particularly current, Fey and Mills (2022) argued that stigma against mental illness is universal and actually worsening. Perceptions of dangerousness, unpredictability, unreliability, and instability are also intertwined (Lettieri et al., 2021; Martin et al., 2000; Østerud, 2022; Russinovaa et al., 2011; Sawaf, 2022). Discrimination and prejudice in employment manifest across both work performance and interpersonal collegial domains, and can range from subtle to overt (Russinovaa et al., 2011). Race and gender must also be factored into cases of discrimination across experiences of Madness and distress (Glover et al., 2010), as well as other sites of oppression. The degree of stigma and discrimination a particular individual endures weighs heavily on their decision of whether or not to disclose experiences of Madness or distress.

Amid well-founded fears of discrimination, disclosure often feels positive due to both supportive responses and ability to be one's authentic self (Barth & Wessel, 2022; Mayer et al., 2022; Taniguchi, 2022b; Toth et al., 2022). Østerud (2022) observed that disclosure of experiences of Madness

DOI: 10.4324/9781032662817-6

and distress resembles "coming out" as LGBTQ+. The ensuing openness about this stigmatized identity can help to challenge stigma (p. 104). Researchers found that the timing of disclosure (Kumble & Shen, 2022; Toth et al., 2022), as well as the approach to disclosure (i.e. direct, incremental, use of humor, etc.) (Taniguchi, 2022b), affect people's response to disclosure. Receiving positive and supportive responses bolstered well-being, self-acceptance, recovery, and self-esteem (Mayer et al., 2022; Taniguchi, 2022b; Taniguchi & Thompson, 2021; Toth et al., 2022). Such responses were extremely important to people who disclosed, while negative responses were highly detrimental (Barth & Wessel, 2022). Self-image goals (i.e. how individuals wished to be perceived by others) also influenced decisions about whether or not to disclose (Taniguchi, 2022a). Elraz (2018) observed that "public disclosure can thus be viewed as an act of generosity, which encourages others to discuss and be open about their mental health experiences" (p. 732). A number of participants in this study took that approach to visibility.

In this chapter, I describe the factors with which these 15 music educators grappled in considering whether or not to disclose experiences of Madness and/or distress, and the decisions they made. Many chose to be "out" about their experiences and worked to normalize them. Others chose not to disclose. Participants also readily discussed the importance of positive representation, and critiqued trendiness, romanticization, and fetishization within mental health discourse. They identified people who influenced them significantly, also observing instances when they saw themselves reflected in their encounters with various media, and conversely when they did not see reflections of themselves in the public sphere. In considering representation in music education, they argued that centering musicians with experiences of Madness and distress in music education may work to normalize such experiences and counter stigma.

## Factors Influencing Disclosure Decisions

Participants identified several factors in their decisions about disclosure. They worried about shame and stigma, which heavily impacted decisions to share this facet of their identities and experiences. They believed if the discourse about mental health differences became more normalized and silencing practices eased, it would become more possible to disclose.

### Stigma and Shame

On the topic of the sociology of deviance, Steinert (2005) discussed what he called normalizing and scandalizing movements; normalizing movements regularize behaviors or identities previously identified as deviant, and scandalizing movements mark certain behaviors formerly acceptable as deviant. He offered LGBTQ+ activism as an example of a normalizing movement in relation to a previously[2] stigmatized identity and asserted that violence against women has been scandalized.[3] Whereas people who identify as having experiences of Madness and distress have been labeled as having "concealable stigmatized identities" (Taniguchi, 2022b), a normalizing movement targeting mental health aims to remove the stigma and make concealment less necessary or appealing. Stigma, operationalized as discrimination (see Chapter 1), still pervades discourse on experiences of Madness and/or distress.

Brown (2021) identified silence, secrecy, and judgment as the three essential components that set the conditions for shame (Brown, 2021, p. 137). All three components permeate decisions to disclose mental health differences. Chris named the *culture* of shame that shapes people's disclosure decisions.

Chris: I think the more people can come out about their Madness (or whatever they choose to call it), the better. The more people are willing to talk about their own experiences, their own issues, their own struggles, their pathways through, the better for all of us. I think we just need to dismantle the culture of shame and make it something that we will all sort of talk about and be willing to have [be] part of everyday language. Because it's in the secrecy and the shame, it's like a vortex and it becomes much, much more intense.

The lack of supportive discourse in the popular sphere means that people with such experiences are met with silence when trying to make sense of their experiences, and then likely choose to silence themselves (Hess, in press; Lee, 2021). Self-imposed silence and secrecy often occur because of fear of judgment. Suppressing one's identity and related discussion both results from and leads to shame, compounding the intensity as Chris mentioned.

Meena actively worked against stigma and shame. She had been a mental health advocate since her time as a K-12 student. After experiencing a psychiatric hospitalization in 1999, she asked her English teacher if she could give a talk in case anyone had questions about mental health issues. Now in her 30s, she shared in a focus group that she was scheduled to present two upcoming, high-profile workshops on mental health to musicians— one on using cognitive behavioral therapy (CBT) wellness strategies in the practice room and the other about peer support for musicians. In response, Chris commented on how peer support and normalization are "really powerful" for someone with mental health differences, because that helps frame it "as one of the things that makes me who I am rather than something that is wrong and to hide." Meena's workshops reject secrecy and silence and therefore work to reduce shame and normalize conversations about experiences of Madness and/or distress among musicians.

August observed improvements in the mental health discourse over recent years, while simultaneously acknowledging that silencing is still pervasive. This idea aligns with the culture of shame that Chris identified.

*August:* I feel like current mental health discourse is very sanitized in terms of what people can talk about, which, if we are coming from a place where people couldn't talk about mental health at all is a step in the right direction. A sanitized discourse is miles better than absolute silence. However, I don't see us as starting from complete silence. To be fair, I can only really comment on how mental health discourse has shifted during the couple decades that I've been able to actively observe it. I don't know if we're actually making progress in bringing formerly closeted experiences into our metaphorical living rooms, or just certain things that have been quietly accepted are becoming more loud and more vocal. To argue against myself, I must iterate that speaking up can be a valid part of normalizing diverse mental health experiences. When people are open and out about anything that others are scared of or made uncomfortable [by], I recognize that there is a huge risk of personal and professional loss. I don't know how we'd get to a point where that risk is significantly diminished. It feels very stuck. I think if some celebrity was to come out as schizophrenic, that wouldn't normalize schizophrenia. Instead, I think culturally we would silence the celebrity. I don't know who has enough social clout to do that kind of normalizing ... with the less mainstreamed mental health conditions.

August believed that people with significantly stigmatized identities would be silenced rather than embraced upon disclosure regardless of their reputation or public stature. Setti et al. (2019) noted that different diagnostic categories are differentially stigmatized. They argued that schizophrenia is known as "one of the most severe and most stigmatized psychiatric illnesses" (p. 245), as the general population often attribute danger and unpredictability to people with schizophrenia, as opposed to people with depression or anxiety (p. 245). As such, stigma and the resulting discrimination differ across diagnoses. As August elucidated, destigmatizing highly stigmatized diagnoses remains significantly more difficult than those diagnoses considered more common and less "dangerous" or "unpredictable."

*Normalizing and Destigmatizing*

All participants strongly supported normalizing experiences of Madness and distress and creating opportunities for open discussion. Emma was willing to disclose even if she was the only one, with the goal of normalization and starting conversations.

*Emma:* No one wants to be the first person to raise their hand and be like, "I'm gonna talk about my mental illnesses." ... No one's gonna volunteer for that. So it's that mindset of, "Well, if you don't start that, who will?" That's one thing that's so frustrating. I feel like, as a teacher, I want to instill that it's okay to have mental illness, it's okay to not be feeling well. I think it'd be great if teachers and administration, adults, if we all started acknowledging when we're not feeling so good. ... Taking away this need to be perfect to create an actual dialogue of mental illness. My mom was at first hesitant about me being so open about my disabilities and mental illnesses. I flat out told her that honestly, I'm so open about it because someone needs to. Someone needs to start the conversation and to show that. [The] more people who are willing to start the conversation and are comfortable with who they are ... be more open towards talking about mental illness. ... Even addressing it overall in regards to amenities and certain services, the least we could do is start having a decent conversation about it.

Her comment about amenities and services implies that discussion also needs to lead to action.

Rather than leading in-depth conversations about mental health differences, Paulo worked toward dismantling stigma by integrating the subject into everyday routine classroom dialogue.

*Paulo:* I've been really honest with students about my diagnosis. I try to bring up little funny things, like we have renovations going on in the building and I get auditory hallucinations. It's one of my weird signs. I'm constantly asking, "Did that actually happen?" Which is a funny way of at least broaching the topic. I've been trying to find ways to allow myself in my teaching to swing, so [students] can see that it's not about stability. Stability is not stable, if that makes sense.

His choice to integrate his mental health differences into routine conversations casually works to normalize such differences. Paulo also emphasized the fluctuation possible under the umbrella term of *stability*—a term that may actually be an empty signifier given its vague, highly variable, and unspecific nature.

QingYu observed that today, discussion of mental health differences occurs much more frequently on social media than in direct conversations. Indeed, disclosures that occur via social media often result in community engagement and robust discussion, although diagnoses that are more stigmatized often receive less uptake (Griffith & Stein, 2021). Social media posts that involve disclosure may facilitate important conversations about experiences of Madness and distress.

*QingYu:* Teenagers … are doing a pretty decent job at talking about mental health more and more and more on platforms like TikTok, Instagram, Facebook. They are doing a pretty dang good job. But there are still people out there that believe that mental health is not a thing, and that it is not important until it affects their life or their family member.

They continued on to comment that people may not take mental health differences seriously until they have lost someone to suicide. QingYu wished current discussions would extend to an intersectional understanding of "hate, fear, racism, homophobia, the -isms" to work through stigma. Like Emma, they felt that action was needed, and suggested something similar to a first aid course that teachers take and recertify annually. Though encouraged by the normalizing discussions on social media, QingYu felt society had a long way to go. To return to Steinert (2005), normalizing movements entail complexity and likely resist a linear path. Most participants committed to engaging in normalizing and destigmatizing efforts regardless of these challenges.

**Disclosure Decisions**

Evans (2017) observed that people with invisible and intermittent impairments experience the widest range of possibilities for managing stigma, as they may more easily choose between disclosure, partial disclosure, or concealing their impairment. She named the process as *un/covering*. "Stigma management centers on individuals' ability to control their 'discredited identities.'" Passing as non-disabled has a long history in the disability community. Much of the disability studies literature on passing draws on Goffman's (1963) famous work on stigma, impression management, and "spoiled identities" (Brune & Wilson, 2013; Cureton, 2018; Evans, 2017; Michalko, 1998; Miller et al., 2019; Olney & Brockelman, 2003; Siebers, 2004). "Spoiled identities" are highly stigmatized identities; "impression management" describes how people with such identities manage perceptions of their identities and experiences (Goffman, 1963). Drawing on Goffman (1963) facilitates consideration of the way that people with experiences of Madness and/or distress engage in impression management to mask, conceal, or cover a disability or, conversely, to disclose or uncover. Indeed, people with disabilities and experiences of Madness and/or distress describe practical reasons for passing or concealing a disability. Participants in Olney and Brockelman's (2003) study elaborated multiple rationales for doing so:

1. those with invisible disabilities expressed concern that others would not believe that they had a bona fide disability;
2. participants felt that others would see them as less competent;
3. they wished to be viewed as consistent and trustworthy;
4. they worried that others would see them only as needing help rather than as a peer who can give and take in a relationship. (p. 48)

Disclosure decisions remain tricky to navigate, as these concerns elucidate. In the disability studies literature, many people with disabilities choose to conceal their impairment for a range of reasons such as fear of stigma (Boucher, 2017; Evans, 2017; Sierra-Zarella, 2005), concern that they will be accused of "faking it" (Cureton, 2018; Olney & Brockelman, 2003; Samuels, 2003; Sierra-Zarella, 2005), or fear of being met with low expectations (Cureton, 2018). In the context of Madness and distress, passing is successful when others do not perceive a person is distressed (Cox, 2013). In this section, I explore the disclosure decisions made by participants including choosing to conceal, mask, or disclose their experiences of Madness and/or distress.

*Not Disclosing*

While only six people chose not to be identified in this book, eight participants expressed some hesitancy about being "out" about their mental health differences. Toth et al. (2022) explained that disclosure "is not a single binary decision, but rather a continuum from complete concealment (fabrication) to complete openness (normalization) (Berkley et al., 2019) that occurs again and again in each new context and with each new person encountered (Toth & Dewa, 2014)" (p. 7791). Like the disclosure of LGBTQ+ identity, disclosure of mental health differences is an iterative process, one that must be repeated over and over. Navigating decisions to be "out" in music education settings requires careful consideration due to pervasive stigma.

*Jillian:* I've never thought about having that visibility for me as a teacher, but now I think it would be helpful because otherwise we're just going to ostracize it further. I mean, why aren't we talking about it if it's obviously so important to all of us? Everybody's mental state affects them all the time. It's the whole thing of being alive. I wish more people would talk about it. But I know it's scary, too, because I don't feel necessarily comfortable just disclosing to whoever.

Whereas Jillian felt that being out would work toward normalizing experiences of Madness and distress, they also recognized that their comfort level varied, and the decision seemed complex and multifaceted. A number of participants explicitly acknowledged the benefit of visibility while personally hesitating at the same time.

In a higher education focus group, the three professors and two graduate students participating in this research discussed disclosure decisions. While Paulo purposefully disclosed with students, I felt too precarious to do so until after obtaining tenure. Mary and Rebecca tended to disclose in individual situations with students when they thought their experience might be personally helpful. Laura felt that disclosure was not presently a possibility for her given her precarity as a graduate student having not yet secured a job, while Cheryl was comfortable disclosing to a supportive faculty during their master's degree in music education. These differing levels of (dis)comfort, hesitancy, and caution reveal the complexities of such decisions for music educators in academia.

*Juliet:* Have you noticed or been subjected to any stereotypes in relation to mental illness?
*Laura:* Yes, and it's very troubling to me. Because part of that's why I feel like I can't be out. I think even if I didn't feel uncomfortable with being out, outing myself gives those stigmas. But I guess if I were out with my mental disabilities, I would want to be able to follow that up with how I live that disability and what that means to me. Unless I had that voice to fully describe that and let people see my value in life.
*Juliet:* That you get to frame it.
*Laura:* Right, yeah, exactly. I think that's a really difficult place to be in.

To some extent, disclosure gives the power to make meaning of one's experiences away to outsiders. Laura wanted to ensure that she would be able to control the narrative about her experiences if she disclosed; recognizing the likelihood of stigmatization or stereotyping heavily contributed to her decision to remain silent.

Mary observed that future music educators appeared to be more successful when they brought their whole selves to their schoolwork, prompting her to wonder about the emotional energy she spent keeping her professional life and mental health separate.

*Mary:* The fact that part of my identity was something that I didn't outwardly share with others might have been kind of odd, you know? We are our whole person. We have so many students, for example, at [the university] that have a lot of different challenges in their life, and they're struggling with those. They've kind of separated that from what they're trying to do with getting their coursework done in their academic studies. Every time students separate that, it's always a problem. So we try to coach them to bring their whole selves to what they're doing at school. But I don't remember telling faculty members as an undergraduate, or even a graduate student, or as a faculty member to my own supervisors. I don't know. Maybe it's been fine to have that separation, but it kind of feels like that's bifurcating my own identity in some way, and that maybe people that don't have to do that might just have a lot less emotional energy they're having to work with, because they're separating this part of themselves from everything else they do.

Desire for authenticity motivates the decision to disclose (Toth et al., 2022) and such authenticity may improve worker (or student) wellbeing (van Beukering et al., 2022). In this case, refusing to bifurcate one's identity may increase feelings of authenticity and wellbeing. At the time of the interview, Mary had bifurcated her identity in her professional life. Shortly afterward, however, she disclosed this facet of her identity at work and explicitly discussed emotional wellbeing with the students. She was well-received, and disclosure proved to be a positive experience for her.

Paulo had disclosed his experiences of bipolar at work, but he was far less certain about whether first year music teachers would benefit from such candidness and outlined several related considerations.

*Paulo:* I'm lucky, as a professor, for many different reasons. I'm a professor and can say, "Hey, I'm bipolar." I do not think that I would have felt that way as a first year teacher. Actually, I've had students who have asked me. I had a student who ... has a couple different kind of mental health diagnoses [ask me] "What should I say? Should I tell my students? Should I tell them? Should I report it to the district?" I was like, "Well, legally, you're supposed to be able to report to the district so you can get accommodations if you need them. I can't promise you that they'll keep it in confidence. I'd love to say that they will, but I can't promise you. Should you say it in front of the kids? I don't know. That's the hard thing. I don't know. I don't know your school." I said, "I think you can feel okay about not saying it right away if you feel concerned." That also breaks my heart when I say that to a student … because I've talked to them for years about being their authentic selves. And then here they're asking, "Should I be my authentic self?" and I'm like, "I don't know. Maybe see for a year." I think that that's a tricky thing.

Disclosure makes it possible for a person to receive accommodations in the workplace, but as Paulo recognized, a guarantee of confidentiality is lacking. Discrimination in the workplace on the basis of "mental illness" is complex and multifaceted (Russinovaa et al., 2011), and being one's authentic self may not facilitate safety or ability to thrive because of potential ramifications of disclosure.

*Masking*

Masking involves hiding some characteristics of Madness and/or distress in order to pass as sane. Cox (2013) described multiple behaviors in which a person who experiences Madness and/or distress might engage in order to "get people to sit next to you on the bus." Such behaviors included not talking to oneself, avoiding eye movements that are too fast or too slow, limiting self-soothing or wringing of one's hands, among other behaviors, in order to pass as "sane" (p. 99). Some participants described masking signs of distress.

QingYu: I feel like I'm also masked. … Being able to allow myself to not mask in front of everybody allows me to really take care of myself and decide what situations I want to be in. For instance, for me, it's really hard to be in very heavily trafficked areas. I know that I can only stand being in them for maybe like an hour, and then I remove myself.

For QingYu, being around certain people (or not) helped them care for themself. In some cases then, non-disclosure may serve as a form of self-care. In LGBTQ+ discourse, the discussion moved from "safe spaces" to "safe people" in the 2010s (Nichols, 2016). While it remains difficult to ensure the safety of a space due to variables and inconsistencies in any space, people who hold "stigmatized identities" can identify people who do not require them to mask their true selves. Like QingYu, Blaine had safe people but felt the need to mask in professional environments due to pervasive misconceptions about bipolar disorder.

*Blaine:* There's definitely lots of misconceptions of what bipolar disorder is. So that also plays into [my decision]. And people not seeing me behind the scenes. Because whenever I'm out in public, especially at my job, I feel like I'm acting. I feel like I am masking who I really am. Because who I really am is not someone that people want to be around. So I try my hardest to not be myself a lot of times. When I get home is whenever I can finally be myself, and not a lot of people see me in that environment. So they think that I'm not really bipolar or it's not that bad, because you're pretty "normal" in our interactions, so I think it gets downplayed a little bit. If people do understand that I'm bipolar, they don't think it's as bad as it is. Because I mask so much around other people. There are very few people that I feel comfortable being my true self around.

Participants' need to keep a part of themselves hidden, to mask in order to hide their mental health experiences, demonstrates that there is still significant work to do to normalize mental health differences. These music educators elucidate the complexity of well-founded fears surrounding disclosure decisions, particularly in professional settings.

### *Being Visible*

Significantly, of the 15 music educators who participated in this research, nine chose to be identified in this book. They did so in order to be credited for their ideas, or as a sign of solidarity with other music educators with experiences of Madness and/or distress. They are open about their experiences, but also discussed the complexities and needs involved with being "out."

*Blaine:* I think [visibility] helps so much, and I wish that more people were comfortable being open about their mental illnesses. I'm very open. I'm very flamboyant with my diagnosis. At least on social media. It doesn't come up as much in person. [Visibility] benefits so many people. I've had so many people reach out to me … and thank me for being open about going to therapy and helping them find a therapist. … If more people were open about that, how much better would the world be … if there wasn't such a stigma around it not being normal, because you have an illness?

Blaine believed more visibility of people with experiences of Madness and distress would improve daily life for people with such experiences. Simultaneously, they recognized the stigma that influences people's decision to be open about such experiences.

Paulo observed that social structures do not permit the same authenticity around experiences of Madness and distress as they do physical ailments, which resonates with the literature on stigma and disclosure.

*Paulo:* It's so sad that there are social structures that don't allow us to share who we really are. If I was having a migraine I would be okay telling the students I had a migraine, but … there's a certain … bias related to a mental health specific diagnosis, that bringing that in is very, very different. The reason I have been so clear about saying it [disclosing], is just so that they know that there are teachers who've made it through it.

Paulo was explicit about having bipolar disorder and wanted students to know that it is possible to have experiences of Madness and distress *and* be a music educator. He was deliberately visible and open, and also took students' experiences seriously. Mary similarly felt that mental health comprised part of a holistic view of overall health.

*Mary:* Mental health is just part of health. Anybody trying to say that it's such a separate thing from the rest of what we do. … It's just part of being human. Just like someone might have issues with their teeth, someone might have issues with their heart. Our body is communicating different things to us all the time. So thank goodness, it feels like stigma for mental health … well, maybe I'm just hoping this is the case that the stigma's softening, and more people are comfortable talking about things.

She also perceived that stigma was decreasing, increasing the possibility for people to disclose. Like Mary and Paulo, Rebecca likened experiences of Madness and distress to issues with physical health.

*Rebecca:* [Visibility is] huge. Because I think so many youngsters think they're the only one who's feeling this or going through this, and it's so important that from the earliest days, people are aware that we can get mental health issues just like we can get flu or broken legs or whatever. And it's not the end of the world.

Moreover, she wanted people with such experiences to know that they are not alone. Neff (2003) described what she called "common humanity" as a key component of self-compassion—"seeing one's experiences as part of the larger human experience rather than seeing them as separating and isolating" (Neff, 2003, p. 89). Rebecca advocated for this shift toward a common humanity perspective, believing that doing so would reduce a sense of isolation among those with Madness and/or distress.

Laura wanted access to a community of people with experiences of Madness and/or distress that she felt was currently invisible.

*Laura:* I think we need more people [being visible], because I think that we have so many people struggling, but we haven't come out. There's so much that can happen when you have a community of people who can help each other and be there for each other and just be visible. But right now, we're missing that.

Increased visibility via disclosure may offer access to, and expand, the community that Laura craved. The present invisibility she observed, however, likely relates to the potential consequences of disclosure. Fear of discrimination rooted in stigma has a strong basis in reality and significantly affects employability (Elraz, 2018; Glover et al., 2010; Lettieri et al., 2021; Martin et al., 2000; Østerud, 2022; Russinovaa et al., 2011; Stuart, 2006). Discrimination needs to abate in order to enable our community to support each other openly.

*Meghan:* I think having visibility and presence across everything is really important, because it gives people of all ages someone to look to. It gives you that option to say, "Hey, me too." It makes you feel seen, it makes you feel heard. It gives you a place to look to when you're having those days where you're unsure.

Meghan curated her social media to help her followers realize that if they struggle with Madness and/or distress, they are not alone and are actually part of a community; this included re-posting from various mental health accounts she followed. Disclosure may generate authenticity in relationships (Corrigan et al., 2016; Østerud, 2022; Taniguchi & Thompson, 2021; Toth et al., 2022; van Beukering et al., 2022), something Meena sought as part of belonging to a community. Pushing aside any notion that experiences of Madness and distress are shameful, she cited "transparency" and "the right to be [my]self and disclose the flaws or setbacks" she experienced without "fear of being canceled or judged, or having people's opinions of me be diminished" as imperatives.

Nicholas felt that people started to talk about mental health experiences more frequently during the COVID-19 pandemic, which informed their decision to disclose. When I met Nicholas, they discussed pursuing an administrative degree in order to lead from their bipolar positionality. They discussed how much it might mean to future students who struggle with experiences of Madness and/or distress to have a principal who has also had such experiences. In instances of distress, Nicholas described their future self as being present with resources, prepared for parent consultations, with a strong team of professionals including, for example, a school psychologist.

*Nicholas:* When people are visible, it helps. It helps other people around us know that it's a disability and encourages everyone to break the silence, end the stigma, the taboo. It's not anything more than a disability. At the same time, it can be very, very hard professionally and personally to be open about it. But, if more people knew what bipolar disorder was and saw more narratives of it, perhaps bipolar disorder would be more routine. Maybe people would understand mood problems, and that bipolar people don't have the ability to filter out emotional information. Hopefully there will be more compassion. … I want to show people that we have gifts even though it's a disability. There's also good things that come with it. We can celebrate all of it.

As noted in Chapter 2, not all participants considered their experiences of Madness and/or distress a disability, so Nicholas' words may not resonate with participants who did not define their experiences in this way. Participants did, however, overwhelmingly support visibility, even when they themselves were not "out." Nicholas spoke to the importance of normalizing experiences of Madness and distress, a facet of this discussion that all participants desired.

## Representation

Participants sought authentic representations of experiences of Madness and/or distress alongside other identities. They critiqued and challenged representations of mental health differences as trendy, romanticized, and fetishized, and named influential people who constituted representatives of Madness and/or distress in their lives. They identified a need to feel seen and reflected in their encounters and considered issues of representation in music education. Ultimately, participants observed that the inclusion of musicians who are known to have personal experiences of Madness and/or distress provided a way to integrate these experiences into the classroom.

*Mental Health Differences as Trendy, Romanticized, and Fetishized*

Participants critiqued the representation of mental health differences as trendy, romanticized, and fetishized in popular culture, and opposed such portrayals. They instead sought a critical perspective on discussions about experiences of Madness and/or distress. While conversations about mental health have become more prevalent, particularly during and since the COVID-19 pandemic, Emma worried that these discussions were part of a trend and resultantly superficial. She used the musical *Dear Evan Hansen* as an example of something in public consciousness contributing to that problem.

*Emma:* Like what I was alluding to before with Dear Evan Hansen, with it being trendy. [Conversations are] getting somewhat better, because now we're at least using the [term] mental illness. Before I feel like we wouldn't even want to use that [term] because it's kind of taboo. However, I still feel like we're not—in general, not in music education … we're not going in deep enough. [We're] doing it to scratch the surface, to fill a checkmark and to be "inclusive" and to be trendy, to fit in with the trends. But we're not really talking about it. We're only talking about the good stuff about it, not talking about the ugly stuff about it. I see this tendency still now. One of the biggest things about people I've noticed is we absolutely do not like it to admit when we are wrong or to own up when we're not doing so good. We like to look like we have our life together.

Emma wanted the ugly side of experiences of Madness and distress to be part of the discourse—to be able to openly acknowledge when things are not okay instead of hiding distress or masking, as QingYu and Blaine described previously. Emma felt that superficial discussions of mental health fostered by engaging with materials like *Dear Evan Hansen* actually resulted in silencing youth who struggle with experiences of Madness and distress that do not match what she later called the "glamorized" versions presented in popular media. Emma was highly critical of superficial representations.

Lizabeth likewise craved authentic visibility, mapping their own initial encounter with what they deemed "romanticized" versions of experiences of Madness and distress on social media.

*Lizabeth:* Visibility is really important because if someone isn't exposed to [representations of experiences of distress], how do they know? My first exposure was on the internet, on Tumblr, to seeing what depression was. And it was kind of a negative. It was kind of a bad exposure because it romanticized mental health instead of being informative and helpful.

Lizabeth subsequently suggested that when people prefer not to be "out" about their own experiences they can instead highlight people who do share or are (historically) known to have had mental health differences. Doing so provides a way to access authentic experiences including the "ugly stuff" Emma mentioned.

*Emma:* I think there's both a good and bad part of visibility. If it's done in a way that's not meant to be educational, or if they're doing it for attention, or if it's for trendiness, [it] can be really dangerous because it sets up precedents. Like that movie by Sia, called *Music*. So inaccurate of autism. And yet, now that autism is becoming more "visible," now people want to cash out of it, are inspired by it and want to put their spin of visibility on it when it might not be actually correct. So there are good and bad. It's ... a sign that it's becoming more like, "Hey, these are people" more "inclusive," but it can be dangerous if the wrong people [who are] not quite as informed are the ones who are providing that visibility.

Emma wanted representation and visibility about neurodiversity to come from insiders to the experiences of Madness and distress as well as autism and felt that Sia's movie *Music* failed to authentically represent autism. She offered an important caveat about visibility that requires some degree of criticality—an awareness and critique of how people and experiences are represented, and the ideologies and discourses that circulate about and through these representations (Hess, 2019, Chapter 5).

Meena warned against what she called the fetishizing of Madness.

*Meena:* I am opposed to "fetishizing" Madness as something novel, quirky, humorous, fascinating, even sexy. (Think of the people who find Margo Robbie's Harley Quinn to be sexually attractive, and then comparing or projecting that image onto actual people they encounter who may have a diagnosis.) I'll also put out this caution: Writers must take care to preserve the integrity of the Mad person, and not try to pick apart how the Mad mind works for the prying curiosity of the reader.

Fetishization entails a process of transforming a subject into an object and also serves as a mechanism of dehumanization. Elsewhere, I have written about fetishization in the context of Buber's (2008/1937) *I-Thou* and *I-It* relationships (Hess, 2021). Briefly, *I-Thou* relationships are those that deeply honor the Other as a subject, whereas *I-It* relationships relate to the Other as an object. Here, Meena described an *I-It* relationship—that of subject to object. Fetishizing people who experience Madness and/or distress in the ways Meena described serves to dehumanize them and ascribe them "object" status, potentially leading to uncaring interactions that dismiss or disregard, and/or dangers including marginalization, stigmatization, bullying, and violence. Meena's analysis spoke to the dangers that can occur with fetishizing representations of Madness and/or distress. Visibility and representation involves the complexity and nuance discussed in Chapter 2 in relation to models from disability studies; assessing any encounter necessitates criticality of the individual as a fully realized and epistemically autonomous person in context.

*Influential Individuals*

Participants looked to a range of people as significant in influencing their thinking about experiences of Madness and distress—both positive and negative. They identified and appreciated the visibility of people in popular culture and on social media—comedians, movie stars, fashion icons, authors, TikTok content creators—who shared about experiences of Madness and distress and also held similar positionalities to their own. Participants also appreciated public figures who disclosed experiences of a range of disabilities including mental health user/survivor activists,[4] and people who provided public support for experiences of Madness and distress. Among people known to them personally, a number of participants identified doctors and mental health professionals who had been helpful, particularly when they shared common identities. They also appreciated teachers who shared some of their identities, and professors who openly shared their mental health differences.

Within their immediate social circles, participants appreciated peers and friends who publicly identified as neurodivergent and/or who had experiences of Madness and distress, and who openly shared about such experiences. This sharing was particularly meaningful when the peer sharing was done by someone they admired or considered knowledgeable. Alternately, time with friends who had experiences of Madness and distress felt negative to participants when they felt they could not provide the help or support their friend needed. Similarly ambivalent feelings were reflected among participants who found exemplars within their family. For some, family members served as role models of how to navigate such experiences, but for others, family modeled choices they did not wish to replicate. Among chosen family, multiple participants had partners who also had experiences of Madness and distress; these partners played a positive role in their own experiences. Other participants also viewed partners without such experiences as supportive.

### The Need to Feel Seen

Beyond influential individuals, most participants wanted to see themselves reflected in their encounters with various media including in schools. Style's (1996) theorization of curriculum as *window* and *mirror* illuminated the importance of children and youth seeing themselves reflected in school curriculum content (the mirror), while also offering different perspectives they may not otherwise encounter (the window). Music educators in this study found the mirror important in comprehending their experiences of Madness and distress.

*Paulo:* I had bought this [comic] book … called *Marbles* (Forney, 2012). It was about bipolar disorder and this person's life, this cartoonist's life. There is this one page that just struck me. … It's her pulling herself out of bed to go to a couch, and you never see her. You just see the blankets over her. There's commentary about just wishing you could disappear. Then on the next page there's this vibrant, her running around everywhere—things like that. It was the first time I saw myself in something like that. This was intentionally talking about bipolar disorder, so I couldn't take it as a metaphor, right? It's easy when songs use metaphors about bipolar disorder or about fluctuation, to brush it off as "Oh, everyone experiences this." But to see someone talking about their own life in a really artistic way. … It was just like a flashbulb moment for me. …I just remember looking at that page and seeing myself for the first time. I think I cried a little bit.

Paulo felt seen by and reflected in this graphic novel, which caused a powerful emotional response. This response is understandable given that representation comprises an important part of dismantling stigma and normalizing the full range of mental health differences, as well as finding words and images with which to personally identify.

*Paulo:* As for visibility, I think, unless people are visible and seen, the views and perspectives of other people are just not going to change. There have to be people willing to talk about it and there has to be a safety net for people to be able to talk about it.

Paulo viewed visibility related to experiences of Madness and/or distress as not only personally impactful but also crucial to raising these experiences in discussion.

Facets of representation beyond those with experiences of Madness and/or distress may also affect wellbeing.

*Cheryl:* Sometimes I wonder if being queer and growing up in a place where I didn't see anyone who was queer [affected me]. I think there was a lot of shame and loneliness in that that maybe I also still haven't processed really.

Style's (1996) mirror may be perceived as essential to wellbeing. When we see ourselves reflected, we learn powerfully that we have community and that our experiences are shared rather than unique—a crucial facet of self-compassion (Neff, 2003). This reflection via representation must include all facets of our intersectional identities.

Lizabeth concurred and connected the discussion specifically to music education.

*Lizabeth:* I think the lack of representation in music education fails to address mental health because it can be really isolating for students to not be able to relate to the people's music they're playing or the types of music they're playing, or whatever they're engaging in.
*Juliet:* So representation across all identities, not just mental health?
*Lizabeth:* Yeah, because I think not seeing representation in your other identities can negatively affect your mental health.

Lizabeth noted the commonplace lack of diversity among the composers, performers, and genres often encountered in music education. When considering Style's (1996) mirror, music educators should aim to not only reflect experiences of Madness and distress in curricula but also the full range of identities. Such reflection may become even more important when various identities carry stigma or typically comprise a site of oppression. This consideration pertains specifically to materials and practices encountered in educational contexts, as well as forms of musicking. Children and youth in K-12 music education need to see themselves mirrored as musickers, with gender, race, disability, sexual identity, socioeconomic class, religion, age, size, and national status, as well as mental health differences and other identities represented.

In music education, current discussions of representation mostly relate to gender and race (see for example Born & Hesmondhalgh, 2000; Bradley, 2006, 2007; Bull, 2019; Koza, 1993, 1994; McBride & Palkki, 2020; McKoy & Lind, 2023), with some discourse about how disability appears in music and music education (Bernabé-Villodre & Martínez-Bello, 2018; Darrow & Hairston, 2016; Hairston & Darrow, 2018). This study's participants made it clear that representations of people who have experiences of Madness and distress, alongside robust representation of the full range of identities, must become a part of the materials and resources encountered in music education spaces in order to offer children and youth the mirror they so vitally need. Such representations work toward the normalizing and destigmatizing efforts discussed earlier.

### Looking at Artists with Mental Health Struggles

Significantly, participants identified composers and musicians with mental health differences as important influences for themselves and students. Multiple people felt that including these musicians in tandem with discussion of their mental health differences in music education curricula would support student wellbeing, while also providing models to help students navigate personal experiences of Madness and distress. "Specifically in music education," Cheryl noted, "there might be an opportunity to look at artists who have shared about their mental struggles and work to destigmatize issues of mental health." Cheryl felt that inclusion of these artists might aid in normalization and destigmatization work. Lizabeth concurred:

*Lizabeth:* I'm thinking the best way to be informative and helpful [as music educators] is to share the experiences that we're comfortable sharing, and to highlight voices. Maybe if you're not comfortable sharing, highlight voices of people who are comfortable, who have put themselves out there.

Most participants cited teachers as significant influences on the way they navigated their experiences of Madness and/or distress. Cheryl and Lizabeth identified a way that teachers can offer support, through highlighting the voices of prominent musicians with such experiences.

In the Western classical music world, Redfield Jamison (1993) created a comprehensive list of composers with experiences of Madness and distress; in some cases these involved hospitalization or placement in an asylum (depending on the time period of the composer) and/or a suicide attempt or completion. These composers include Anton Arensky, Hector Berlioz, Anton Bruckner, Jeremiah Clarke, John Dowland, Edward Elgar,

Carlo Gesualdo, Mikhail Glinka, George Frideric Handel, Gustav Holst, Charles Ives, Orlando de Lassus, Gustav Mahler, Modest Mussorgsky, Sergei Rachmaninoff, Giocchino Rossini, Robert Schumann, Alexander Scriabin, Pyotr Tchaikovsky, Peter Warlock, Hugo Wolf, and Bernd Alois Zimmerman (p. 269). In keeping with much of the Western classical music historical canon, these composers primarily held white and male identities. While integration of their experiences of Madness and distress into the classroom might help to normalize and destigmatize these differences, accounting for their homogeneity across gender and racial identities must be part of the conversation as well.

Redfield Jamison (1993) also identified several other musicians with experiences of Madness and distress including Irving Berlin, Noel Coward, Charles Mingus, Charlie Parker, Cole Porter, and Bud Powell (p. 269). Many current musicians in popular genres have chosen to speak out about their mental health differences, and their widespread visibility may further help to normalize and destigmatize such struggles. These artists include Kendrick Lamar (MTV, 2015), Janet Jackson (Berger, 2018; Lockett, 2018), Big Sean (Aderoju, 2020), Camila Cabello (Aniftos, 2018), Halsey (Garvey, 2019; Miller, 2019), Sam Smith (Krol, 2020), Katy Perry (Boboltz, 2017; Cassidy, 2018), Lady Gaga (Blackford, 2019), Billie Eilish (Foy, 2020), Selena Gomez (Ledbetter, 2022), Suga (Mamo, 2021), Pete Wentz (Leon, 2020), and David Draiman (Enis, 2023), among others.[5] These artists further represent a diverse range of gender, racial, ethnic, and sexual identities, as well as different musical genres.

Such discussions may also engage with recent completed suicides among white, male rock stars in the 2010s including *Linkin Park*'s Chester Bennington, *Soundgarden*'s Chris Cornell, *Stone Temple Pilots*' Scott Weiland (Enis, 2023), and Keith Flint of *The Prodigy* (Blistein, 2019). Men are much less likely to seek mental health support than women, and depression and suicide are a leading cause of death for men (Chatmon, 2020, p. 1). Men successfully complete suicide at four times the rate of women (79% of 38,364 in 2020 in the U.S.) (Chatmon, 2020, p. 1). The norms of masculinity and the presence of toxic masculinity[6] in combination with sanism in the wider culture increase the stigma around seeking help for some individuals more than others (Chatmon, 2020; Lindsey & Marcell, 2012; Nadeem et al., 2007; Woodward et al., 2010).[7] Indeed, in this research, only one participant identified as a man, while seven identified as women and seven as trans, non-binary, or gender expansive. The lack of men participants in this work bolsters the argument that this subject is more taboo among men, likely due to the presence of patriarchy and toxic masculinity, which involves the suppression of emotions among men (Chatmon, 2020). Given the recent completion of suicide among high-profile white, male artists, engaging with musicians who have experiences of Madness and/or distress in music classes also requires resisting patriarchy and toxic masculinity to normalize the process of men seeking help, and discussing distress and emotions. Approaching these topics pedagogically must be done mindfully with an option for students to opt out of the discussion. Focusing discussion on normalizing the presence and expression of difficult emotions and explicit education about patriarchy and toxic masculinity may encourage students with experiences of Madness and/or distress to seek support. Such discussions must also then include the provision of affirming resources based in the local community or broadly accessible.

The fact that participants were also predominantly white points to the increased stigma surrounding the disclosure of experiences of Madness and/or distress for racialized groups. Scholars have recognized the challenges that Black men, Black women, and Latina women face in disclosing these experiences to receive support (Lindsey & Marcell, 2012; Nadeem et al., 2007; Woodward et al., 2010) and this challenge likely extends to other racialized groups. The stigma surrounding disclosure in racialized groups requires normalization work alongside explicitly addressing the racism that increases the stigma for individuals who are minoritized and multiply minoritized. Indeed, the call for representation in the music classroom demands both the representation of BIPOC musicians with experiences of Madness and/or distress as well as discussion of the ways that race can complicate disclosure and visibility. Music educators can once again provide affirming resources and encourage students to seek support.

Experiences of Madness and distress can, and should, be a part of music education, and not via the culture of shame discussed previously. Including a diverse range of artists with mental health differences in curricula gives music teachers conduits to having explicit conversations about Madness and distress, something most participants in this research valued as a helpful practice (see Chapter 7). Having these examples enables educators to address such experiences in all of their diversity through exemplars, while simultaneously offering helpful models to students who struggle with mood, distress, and identity. While some participants understood that music educators with mental health differences could not always appropriately or comfortably disclose because of stigma, Lizabeth and Cheryl urged them to provide examples of musicians who do openly share or are (historically) known to have had these experiences as a way to normalize and destigmatize Madness and distress.

### Conclusion and Implications

Participants identified the visibility of experiences of Madness and distress as a crucial facet of normalizing and destigmatizing such experiences but also varied in how visible and open they felt they could be in their own professional and personal lives. They discussed the question of disclosing mental health differences and the complexities embedded in doing so and problematized the romanticization, fetishization and perceived "trendiness" of experiences of Madness and distress in today's popular culture and social media. All participants appreciated having their experiences of Madness and distress reflected in the content and media they encountered, and they identified a wide range of people who influenced their sense of identity and decisions regarding disclosure. While some participants felt they could not disclose their experiences, they suggested normalizing and destigmatizing experiences of Madness and distress through centering people including musicians who have publicly disclosed or are historically known to have struggled with mental health differences in curricula. For participants, having people they respected who shared various identities including mental health differences helped them in their own lived experiences of Madness and distress, and they believed this would extend to students as well. Educators and administrators without experiences of Madness and/or distress can position themselves as allies—"neurotypical" people who align themselves with people who have experiences of Madness and/or distress[8]—through engaging in stigma-free discussions, centering representations of experiences of Madness and/or distress in the classroom, as well as normalizing support and accommodations for educators and students so they can be more readily and thoroughly involved. In seeking to offer allyship, it is important to remember that it is members of the minoritized group in question who determine whether a person is, in fact, an ally.

Participants identified visibility as essential to destigmatizing and normalizing experiences of Madness and distress. The stigma associated with such experiences, however, led eight participants to express some hesitancy about their own disclosure, which speaks to their current perceptions of the climate and culture surrounding these experiences. Representation of experiences of Madness and distress is important in and outside of music education spaces, as it increases visibility and may make disclosure a safe possibility for more individuals, including individuals in one or more minoritized groups who must grapple with compounded stigma. Participants sought to dismantle the culture of shame they so often encountered in regard to mental health differences.

Visibility and representation provide a counterpoint that unsettles dominant deficit and pathologizing discourses about Madness and distress in schools and society. This counterpoint to dominant discourse offers a window into what authentic representation and visibility might mean for people with experiences of Madness and/or distress. Participants appreciated seeing themselves reflected across their varied identities in the public sphere, including among musickers. As educators, the efforts we make toward representation of diverse identities in our curricula, repertoire, materials, and pedagogy must include people with experiences of Madness and distress. Moreover, when educators or students choose to disclose, either publicly or privately, facilitating institutional support via work and study modifications and accommodations remains crucial so that these educators and students can fully participate in the learning environment. Though participants valued visibility and seeing themselves reflected, disclosure requires institutional, alongside emotional, supports. Educators and students with experiences of Madness and/or distress may require accommodations or services to facilitate effective music teaching and learning and, ideally, to thrive in music education. Administrators and school boards across all levels of education are obligated to foster and maintain the material and cultural conditions necessary for music educators and learners to flourish, regardless of—and with respect to—mental health status.

**Notes**

1 Substance abuse is a different but related issue. Martin et al. (2000) examined use of both antipsychotic medication and substances. Many people with experiences of Madness and/or distress self-medicate with substances (see for example McHugh & McBride, 2020).
2 Recent anti-trans and anti-LGBTQ+ legislation in the U.S. brings the "previous" status of LGBTQ+ identity as stigmatized into question, alongside the prevalence of hate crimes (Alfonseca, 2023). See Appendix 2 for more extensive discussion.
3 This assertion is also questionable following the repeal of Roe v. Wade in the U.S. The World Health Organization (2021) reported that violence against women remains "devastatingly pervasive." One in three women across their lifetime are subject to physical or sexual violence by their intimate partner or sexual violence from a non-partner.
4 Chris pointed specifically to mental health user/survivor activists she found inspiring. Mental health users are people who use and access the psy- system, while survivor activists identify as having survived the coercive elements of the psy- system.
5 See Arbour (2021) for a list of country artists, for example.
6 Chatmon (2020) noted: "Traditional masculinity or hegemonic masculinity is a subset of masculine norms that accentuate certain expressions of masculinity and invoke some men's power, dominance, and privilege over women and some men. Toxic masculinity closely aligns with certain expressions of hegemonic masculinity. Toxic masculinity is the demonstration of masculinities that are enforced by restriction in behaviors (e.g., crying, fear) based on gender roles that amplify existing power structures that favor the dominance of men. Toxic

masculinity may lead to difficulty in expressing emotions, which is seen often" (p. 2).
7  These sources indicate that men and people in racialized groups and new immigrants are less likely to seek help.
8  The term "ally" is used across identities and typically denotes a person from a dominant group aligning with the goals and causes of a minoritized group.

## References

Aderoju, D. (2020, December 17). How Big Sean overcame his mental health struggles—"Take a break before you need a break". *People.* https://people.com/music/how-big-sean-overcame-his-mental-health-struggles/

Alfonseca, K. (2023, June 22). Rise in anti-LGBTQ hate and extremism captured in new reports. *ABC News.* https://abcnews.go.com/US/rise-anti-lgbtq-hate-extremism-captured-new-reports/story?id=100304706

Aniftos, R. (2018, May 1). Camila Cabello opens up about living with Obsessive-Compulsive Disorder: 'I'll start to have the same thought over and over again". *Billboard.* www.billboard.com/music/music-news/camila-cabello-opens-up-about-living-with-obsessive-compulsive-disorder-8428210/

Arbour, M. (2021, May 26). Country artists open up about their mental health struggles. *Countrytown.* https://countrytown.com/news/country-artists-open-up-about-their-mental-health-struggles/vPKkrtHQ09I/26-05-21

Barth, S. E., & Wessel, J. L. (2022). Mental illness disclosure in organizations: Defining and predicting (un) supportive responses. *Journal of Business and Psychology, 37,* 407–428. https://doi.org/10.1007/s10869-021-09753-4

Berger, M. (2018, July 11). Janet Jackson's honesty reveals how depression can strike anyone. *Healthline: Health News.* www.healthline.com/health-news/janet-jacksons-honesty-depression

Berkley, R. A., Beard, R., & Daus, C. S. (2019). The emotional context of disclosing a concealable stigmatized identity: A conceptual model. *Human Resource Management Review, 29*(3), 428–445. https://doi.org/10.1016/j.hrmr.2018.09.001

Bernabé-Villodre, M. d. M., & Martínez-Bello, V. (2018). Analysis of gender, age and disability representation in music education textbooks: A research update. *International Journal of Music Education, 36*(4), 494–508. https://doi.org/10.1177/0255761418763900

Blackford, M. (2019, September 5). Lady Gaga: Mental health and advocacy. *The Florida House Experience Health.* https://fherehab.com/learning/lady-gaga-mental-health/

Blistein, J. (2019, March 11). Death of Prodigy's Keith Flint ruled suicide. *Rolling Stone.* www.rollingstone.com/music/music-news/prodigy-keith-flint-cause-death-suicide-hanging-803020/

Boboltz, S. (2017, June 12). Katy Perry opens up about addiction and suicidal thoughts in emotional livestream. *Huffington Post.* www.huffpost.com/entry/katy-perry-opens-up-about-addiction-and-suicidal-thoughts-livestream_n_593ee535e4b0c5a35ca22e58

Born, G., & Hesmondhalgh, D. (2000). Introduction: On difference, representation, and appropriation in music. In G. Born & D. Hesmondhalgh (Eds.), *Western Music and its others: Difference, representation, and appropriation in music* (pp. 1–58). University of California Press.

Boucher, C. (2017). The roles of power, passing, and surface acting in the workplace relationships of female leaders with disability. *Business & Society*, 56(7), 1004–1032. https://doi.org/10.1177/0007650315610610

Bradley, D. (2006). Education, multiculturalism, and anti-racism — Can we talk? Action, *Criticism & Theory for Music Education*, 5(2), 1–30.

Bradley, D. (2007). The sounds of silence: Talking race in music education. *Action, Criticism & Theory for Music Education*, 6(4), 132–162.

Brown, B. (2021). *Atlas of the heart: Mapping meaningful connection and the language of human experience*. Random House.

Brune, J. A., & Wilson, D. J. (2013). Introduction. In J. A. Brune & D. J. Wilson (Eds.), *Disability and passing: Blurring the lines of identity* (pp. 1–12). Temple University Press.

Buber, M. (2008/1937). *I and Thou* (R. G. Smith, Trans.). Hesperides Press.

Bull, A. (2019). *Class, control, and classical music*. Oxford University Press.

Cassidy, E. (2018, July 18). Katy Perry's metaphor for coping with situational depression is one you'll want to hear. *The Mighty*. https://themighty.com/topic/mental-health/katy-perry-situational-depression-witness/

Chatmon, B. N. (2020). Males and mental health stigma. *American Journal of Men's Health*, 14(4), 1–3. https://doi.org/10.1177/1557988320949322

Corrigan, P. W., Kosyluk, K. A., Markowitz, F., Brown, R. L., Conlon, B., Rees, J., Rosenberg, J., Ellefson, S., & Al-Khouja, M. (2016). Mental illness stigma and disclosure in college students. *Journal of Mental Health*, 25(3), 224–230. https://doi.org/10.3109/09638237.2015.1101056

Cox, P. (2013). Passing as sane, or how to get people to sit next to you on the bus. In J. A. Brune & D. J. Wilson (Eds.), *Disability and passing: Blurring the lines of identity* (pp. 99–110). Temple University Press.

Cureton, A. (2018). Hiding a disability and passing as non-disabled. In A. Cureton & T. E. Hill Jr. (Eds.), *Disability in practice: Attitudes, policies, and relationships* (pp. 15–32). Oxford University Press.

Darrow, A.-A., & Hairston, M. (2016, July 20-23, 2016). *Inspiration porn: A qualitative analysis of comments on musicians with disabilities found on international YouTube posts*. The 21st International Seminar of the ISME Commission on Special Music Education and Music Therapy, Drake Music Scotland and University of Edinburgh, Edinburgh, Scotland.

Elraz, H. (2018). Identity, mental health and work: How employees with mental health conditions recount stigma and the pejorative discourse of mental illness. *Human Relations*, 71(5), 722–741. https://doi.org/10.1177/0018726617716752

Enis, E. (2023, May 10). Disturbed's David Draiman: I almost died during recent depression battle. *Revolver*. www.revolvermag.com/music/disturbeds-david-draiman-i-almost-died-during-recent-depression-battle

Evans, H. D. (2017). Un/covering: Making disability identity legible. *Disability Studies Quarterly*, 37(1). https://dsq-sds.org/index.php/dsq/article/view/5556/4550

Fey, J.-M., & Mills, C. (2022). The (global) rise of anti-stigma campaigns. In P. Beresford & J. Russo (Eds.), *The Routledge international handbook of Mad Studies* (pp. 190–201). Routledge.

Forney, E. (2012). *Marbles—Mania, depression, Michelangelo, and me: A graphic memoir*. Gothan Books.

Foy, C. (2020, January 23). Billie Eilish gets transparent about her depression and mental health struggles. *The Florida House Experience Health*. https://fherehab.com/learning/billie-eilish-her-depression-mental-health-struggles/

Garvey, M. (2019, June 24). Halsey opens up about her mental health. *CNN Entertainment*. www.cnn.com/2019/06/24/entertainment/halsey-mental-illness/index.html

Glover, C. M., Corrigan, P. W., & Wilkniss, S. (2010). The effects of multiple categorization on perceptions of discrimination, life domains, and stress for individuals with severe mental illness. *Journal of Vocational Rehabilitation, 33*(2), 113–121. https://doi.org/10.3233/JVR-2010-0520

Goffman, E. (1963). *Stigma: Notes on the management of spoiled identity*. Prentice-Hall, Inc.

Griffith, F. J., & Stein, C. H. (2021). Behind the hashtag: Online disclosure of mental illness and community response on Tumblr. *American Journal of Community Psychology, 67*(3/4). https://doi.org/10.1002/ajcp.12483

Hairston, M., & Darrow, A.-A. (2018, July 12-14, 2018). *Inspiration porn — Part II: An analysis of music education and music therapy majors' descriptors of musicians with disabilities profiled on the internet*. The 22nd International Seminar of the ISME Commission on Special Music Education and Music Therapy, The Orff Institute, Mozarteum University, Salzburg, Austria.

Hess, J. (2019). *Music education for social change: Constructing an activist music education*. Routledge.

Hess, J. (2021). "Putting a face on it": The trouble with storytelling for social justice in music education. *Philosophy of Music Education Review, 29*(1), 67–87. https://doi.org/10.2979/philmusieducrevi.29.1.05

Hess, J. (in press). Bipolar in the academy: A case of testimonial smothering. *Disability Studies Quarterly*.

Koza, J. E. (1993). The "missing males" and other gender issues in music education: Evidence from the "Music Supervisors' Journal," 1914–1924. *Journal of Research in Music Education, 41*(3), 212–232.

Koza, J. E. (1994). Females in 1988 middle school music textbooks: An analysis of illustrations. *Journal of Research in Music Education, 42*(2), 145–171.

Krol, C. (2020, October 18). Sam Smith opens up about mental health issues: "I think it was PTSD". *New Musical Express*. www.nme.com/news/music/sam-smith-opens-up-about-mental-health-issues-i-think-it-was-ptsd-2789995

Kumble, S., & Shen, F. (2022). The effects of narratives and disclosure timings on reducing stigma and implicit bias against people suffering from mental illness *International Journal of Communication, 16*, 5297–5317.

Ledbetter, C. (2022, April 5). Selena Gomez reveals how her mental health diagnosis changed her life. *Huffington Post*. www.huffpost.com/entry/selena-gomez-bipolar-disorder-diagnosis_n_6249f477e4b0587dee6ada77

Lee, J. Y. (2021). Anticipatory epistemic injustice. *Social Epistemology*, *Online First*, 1–13. https://doi.org/10.1080/02691728.2021.1924306

Leon, A. (2020, December 1). Pete Wentz on being bipolar, his split from Ashlee Simpson. *People*. https://people.com/celebrity/pete-wentz-on-bipolar-disorder-split-from-ashlee-simpson/

Lettieri, A., Soto-Pérez, F., Franco-Martín, M. A., de Urríes, F. d. B. J., Shiells, K. R., & D'íez, E. (2021). Employability with mental illness: The perspectives of employers and mental health workers. *Rehabilitation Counseling Bulletin*, *64*(4), 195–207. https://doi.org/10.1177/0034355220922607

Lindsey, M. A., & Marcell, A. V. (2012). "We're going through a lot of struggles that people don't even know about": The need to understand African American male's help-seeking for mental health on multiple levels. *American Journal of Men's Health*, *6*(5), 354–364. https://doi.org/10.1177/1557988312441520

Lockett, D. (2018, June 20). Janet Jackson opens up about overcoming 'intense' struggle with depression. *Vulture*. www.vulture.com/2018/06/janet-jackson-details-intense-struggle-with-depression.html

Mamo, H. (2021, May 19). Here's why BTS' Suga doesn't shy away from singing about depression. *Billboard*. www.billboard.com/music/music-news/bts-suga-opens-up-depression-struggles-lyrics-9575036/

Martin, J. K., Pescosolido, B. A., & Tuch, S. (2000). Of fear and loathing: The role of "disturbing behavior," labels, and casual attributions in shaping public attitudes toward people with mental illness. *Journal of Health and Social Behavior*, *41*(2), 208–223. https://doi.org/10.2307/2676306

Mayer, L., Corrigan, P. W., Eisheuer, D., Oexle, N., & Rüsch, N. (2022). Attitudes towards disclosing a mental illness: Impact on quality of life and recovery. *Social Psychiatry and Psychiatric Epidemiology*, *57*, 363–374. https://doi.org/10.1007/s00127-021-02081-1

McBride, N. R., & Palkki, J. (2020). Big boys don't cry (or sing) ... still?: A modern exploration of gender, misogyny, and homophobia in college choral methods texts. *Music Education Research*, *22*(4), 408–420. https://doi.org/10.1080/14613808.2020.1784862

McHugh, R., & McBride, O. (2020). Self-medicating low mood with alcohol use: Examining the role of frequency of alcohol use, quantity consumed and context of drinking. *Addictive Behaviors*, *111*, 1–7. https://doi.org/10.1016/j.addbeh.2020.106557

McKoy, C. L., & Lind, V. L. (2023). *Culturally responsive teaching in music education: From understanding to application*. Routledge.

Michalko, R. (1998). *The mystery of the eye and the shadow of blindness*. University of Toronto Press.

Miller, K. (2019, June 25). Halsey opens up about living with Bipolar Disorder: "You are controlled by impulses". *Prevention*. www.prevention.com/health/mental-health/a28182863/halsey-bipolar-disorder-rolling-stone-cover/

Miller, R. A., Wynn, R. D., & Webb, K. W. (2019). "This really interesting juggling act": How university students manage disability/queer identity disclosure and visibility. *Journal of Diversity in Higher Education*, *12*(4), 307–318. https://doi.org/10.1037/dhe0000083

MTV. (2015, April 1). *Kendrick Lamar talks about 'U,' his depression & suicidal thoughts (Pt. 2) | MTV News*. www.youtube.com/watch?v=Hu4Pz9PjolI

Nadeem, E., Lange, J. M., Edge, D., Fongwa, M., Belin, T., & Miranda, J. (2007). Does stigma keep poor young immigrant and U.S.-born Black and Latina women from seeking mental health care? *Psychiatric Services, 58*(12), 1547–1554.

Neff, K. (2003). Self-compassion: An alternative conceptualization of a healthy attitude toward oneself. *Self and Identity, 2*, 85–101.

Nichols, J. (2016, September 26). Create safe people, not safe spaces. *Maryland Political Review*. http://web.archive.org/web/20161105122801/http://maryland politicalreview.org/create-safe-people-not-safe-spaces/

Olney, M. F., & Brockelman, K. F. (2003). Out of the disability closet: Strategic use of perception management by select university students with disabilities. *Disability & Society, 18*(1), 35–50. https://doi.org/10.1080/713662200

Østerud, K. L. (2022). Mental illness stigma and employer evaluation in hiring: Stereotypes, discrimination and the role of experience. *Sociology of Health & Illness, 45*(1), 90–108. https://doi.org/10.1111/1467-9566.13544

Redfield Jamison, K. (1993). *Touched with fire: Manic-depressive illness and the artistic temperament*. Simon & Schuster.

Russinovaa, Z., Griffinb, S., Blocha, P., Wewiorskic, N. J., & Rosoklijad, I. (2011). Workplace prejudice and discrimination toward individuals with mental illnesses. *Journal of Vocational Rehabilitation, 35*(3), 227–241. https://doi.org/10.3233/JVR-2011-0574

Samuels, E. J. (2003). My body, my closet: Invisible disability and the limits of coming-out discourse. *GLQ: A Journal of Lesbian and Gay Studies, 9*(1-2), 233–255. www.muse.jhu.edu/article/40803

Sawaf, S. (2022). Applying theoretical perspectives and activism to understand and combat mental health stigma *Journal of Recovery in Mental Health, 5*(2), 42–46. https://doi.org/10.33137/jrmh.v5i2.37860

Setti, V. P. C., Loch, A. A., Modelli, A., de Almeida Rocca, C. C., Hungerbuehler, I., van de Bilt, M. T., Gattaz, W. F., & Wulf, R. (2019). Disclosing the diagnosis of schizophrenia: A pilot study of the 'Coming Out Proud' intervention. *International Journal of Social Psychiatry, 65*(3), 244–251. https://doi.org/10.1177/0020764019840057

Siebers, T. (2004). Disability as masquerade. *Literature and Medicine, 23*(1), 1–22. https://doi.org/10.1353/lm.2004.0010

Sierra-Zarella, E. (2005). Adapting and "passing": My experiences as a graduate student with multiple invisible disabilities. In L. Ben-Moshe, R. C. Cory, M. Feldbaum, & K. Sagendorf (Eds.), *Building pedagogical curb cuts: Incorporating disability in the university classroom and curriculum* (pp. 139–146). The Graduate School, Syracuse University.

Steinert, H. (2005). Sociology of deviance: The disciplines of social exclusion. In C. Calhoun, C. Rojek, & B. Turner (Eds.), *The Sage Handbook of Sociology* (pp. 471–491). SAGE Publications.

Stuart, H. (2006). Mental illness and employment discrimination. *Current Opinion in Psychiatry, 19*(5), 522–526. https://doi.org/10.1097/01.yco.0000238482.27270.5d

Style, E. (1996). Curriculum as window and mirror. *Social Science Record, Fall 1996*, 35–42.

Taniguchi, E. (2022a). College students' mental illness disclosure and self-esteem: A moderating role of self-image goals. *Journal of American College Health*, 70(8), 2416–2422. https://doi.org/10.1080/07448481.2020.1865973

Taniguchi, E. (2022b). The roles of mental illness disclosure and disclosure strategies on well-being among college students. *Journal of American College Health*, 70(3), 929–939. https://doi.org/10.1080/07448481.2020.1781868

Taniguchi, E., & Thompson, C. M. (2021). Mental illness self-disclosure among college students: A pre-requisite of social support or a booster of social support benefits? *Journal of Mental Health*, 30(3), 323–332. https://doi.org/10.1080/09638237.2021.1922626

Toth, K. E., & Dewa, C. S. (2014). Employee decision-making about disclosure of a mental disorder at work. *Journal of Occupational Rehabilitation*, 24(4), 732–746. https://doi.org/10.1007/s10926-014-9504-y

Toth, K. E., Yvon, F., Villotti, P., Lecomte, T., Lachance, J.-P., Kirsh, B., Stuart, H., Berbiche, D., & Corbière, M. (2022). Disclosure dilemmas: How people with a mental health condition perceive and manage disclosure at work. *Disability and Rehabilitation*, 44(25), 7791–7801. https://doi.org/10.1080/09638288.2021.1998667

van Beukering, I. E., Bakker, M., Corrigan, P. W., Gürbüz, S., Bogaers, R. I., Janssens, K. M. E., Joosen, M. C. W., & Brouwers, E. P. M. (2022). Expectations of mental illness disclosure outcomes in the work context: A cross-sectional study among Dutch workers *Journal of Occupational Rehabilitation*, 32, 652–663. https://doi.org/10.1007/s10926-022-10026-x

Woodward, A. T., Taylor, R. J., & Chatters, L. M. (2010). Use of professional and informal support by Black men with mental disorders. *Research on Social Work Practice*, 21(3), 328–336. https://doi.org/10.1177/1049731510388668

World Health Organization. (2021, March 9). *Devastatingly pervasive: 1 in 3 women globally experience violence*. Retrieved September 30, 2023 from www.who.int/news/item/09-03-2021-devastatingly-pervasive-1-in-3-women-globally-experience-violence

# 6 How Music (Education) Might Harm[1]

*Rebecca:* Every time I played, I just thought about all the things that I was doing wrong, not the things I was doing right.

*Rebecca:* I came to the conclusion that the purpose of that three years [in the conservatory] was to show [students] that they weren't as good as their professor. That seemed to be the attitude that all of them had. It was the "I am not worthy." That's what they'd learned during those three years.

*Chris:* Feeling ashamed that I wasn't good enough, that I wasn't perfect enough, I wasn't going to be in the National Symphony Orchestra back in New Zealand. That fed a really deep sort of sense of despair.

Both the potential for help and harm inherently exist in the act of musicking (Ansdell, 2014; Bradley & Hess, 2022). As a field, music education consistently emphasizes the "good" of music—its transformative potential, its connective power, its affirming possibilities. Music educators map the goodness that music possesses onto the field of music education. As a school subject, music is often under threat from budget cuts.[2] Music educators frequently feel the need to advocate for curricular inclusion, placing significant pressure on how we portray music to public stakeholders. Stories told about music often become intertwined in advocacy arguments, typically portraying it as an unequivocal good. The National Association for Music Education (NAfME) claims they "are changing the national conversation about music's role in delivering an outstanding well-rounded education to all students."[3] In making this argument, they position music as "good for students." The role of musicking, however, is not that straightforward. Musicking can also cause harm (Ansdell, 2014; Bradley & Hess, 2022). As Ansdell (2014) observed:

> my title [*How Music Helps*] could suggest that music always helps. This is clearly untrue, as a growing list of its uses in torture and warfare

DOI: 10.4324/9781032662817-7

demonstrates (Pieslak, 2009). I think the simple point is that music is morally neutral. It can harm in the same way that it can help. But its harmful potential detracts nothing from how it can help—this simply alerts us to the intentions and actions of the people who use it. Its potency to work for "both sides" rather shows up its essential power as a medium. We must be mindful of our uses of it.

(p. xvii)

Ansdell reminded readers that music is not a "straightforward panacea for personal and social problems" (p. xvii). Music is thus paradoxical. In the context of Madness and distress in music education, I define harm as a facet of musicking, pedagogy, curriculum, or practice that exacerbates or increases emotional (and sometimes physical) distress.

Acknowledging the potential for harm, coupled with the knowledge that some musickers may in fact crave harm, complicates normative narratives about music education. I seek to highlight the contradictions, paradoxes, and antimonies in music education. Musicking is messy. In putting forward musicking, Small (1998) theorized how musickers participate in musicking in ways that impact how we[4] explore, affirm, and celebrate our sense of ideal relationships, our values, and reflect our experiences. Yet music can be used to inscribe a full range of values and experiences, not simply the ones deemed socially acceptable. I aim to make room for the messiness of what music can do and explicate some of the lesser-acknowledged possibilities. Despite the perpetual threat of cuts to music education, I believe we must bravely assert the harm that musicking might cause and describe how harm may also be a part of musicking and music education. Music educators must make room for the complexity of what musicking does—for different people, and in classrooms, studios, rehearsal and performance spaces, and in the world.

While musicking helps to support Madness and distress in many ways, noticing the ways in which musicking may also cause harm is important. In my own life, and particularly in relation to being bipolar, I have used musicking both as a means of helping or further hurting myself in times of Madness and distress. Remembering that musicking can do both is essential to how we approach music education. Most people involved in music experience the harms I describe in this chapter to some extent (Bernhard, 2007a, 2007b, 2010; Bradley & Hess, 2022; Bull, 2019; Conway et al., 2010; McGrath et al., 2017; Powell, 2023; Stoeber & Eismann, 2007). Harm is prevalent in the culture of music education; it is a common experience. Participants with experiences of Madness and/or distress explicated how the harms described exacerbated their distress and negatively impacted their emotional wellbeing. Ameliorating distress requires addressing the toxic culture in music education and the harm that can occur through musicking. Experiences of Madness and/or distress are challenging on their own. Because musicking and music education can worsen these experiences, music educators must work against the harm-inducing elements of the culture and musicking to avoid causing or exacerbating distress. In this chapter, I explicate the harm that participants experienced in relation to their musicking in educational settings. This discussion has two facets—an examination of the toxic culture of music education that many participants identified, and harm that emerged through musicking itself. In conclusion, I offer implications based on participants' observations.

## Culture of Music Education

In this section, I describe facets of the toxic culture of music education that participants identified as harmful to their wellbeing. These include: an emphasis on competition, perfectionism, distress from a failure to meet unrealistic expectations, high levels of pressure and stress, invalidations, and relationships with abusive teachers.

### *Competition*

Most participants experienced competition in music education as harmful to their emotional wellbeing. While the bulk of their comments pertained to undergraduate experiences, competition shapes K-12 school music experiences as well. Powell (2021) elucidated the ideology of competition in music education—it "operates in the unconscious background, constraining agency in a largely unnoticed manner" (p. 20). Powell argued:

> the ideology of competition [presents] itself as a natural evolution—as "just the way things are"—and obscures the fact that these competitive structures are the *constructions* of human agents which are historically *contingent*. Because many can mistake these material conditions for a natural state of affairs, it is easier for many music educators to imagine losing their music programs altogether than it is for them to conceive of coherent alternatives to the current system.
> 
> (p. 26, emphasis in original)

The ideology of competition pervades music education contexts, "limit[ing] possibilities, creat[ing] and exacerbat[ing] inequities, and reinforc[ing] the harmful fantasy of the neoliberal meritocracy" (Powell, 2021, p. 36). Powell posed the question "why complain?" when music competition offers bragging rights, school support, and material awards (p. 27). In a subsequent complex and compelling argument against competition he cited, among other issues, constraints on teacher agency. Moreover, he cautioned that everything can be co-opted into "a standardized, competitive accountability regime, replete with preset methods, practices, and institutionally authorized tools of evaluation" (Powell, 2021, p. 37). Powell (2023) revealed those who may be harmed by this regime:

> Everyone struggles under competition—the losers who work and work but can never seem to win, those who do not participate at all, those whose music-making is not validated by the hegemonic system, and even those who win consistently but feel the pressure to maintain this one-dimensional focus.
>
> (p. 109)

Participants' perspectives reflected this view of struggle and dehumanization in a competitive climate.

A competition-based music education also fails to acknowledge how students are differentially situated in relation to privilege and access. Socioeconomic privilege or lack thereof, for example, greatly affects one's standing in a competitive climate. Social locations across all identity categories inherently affect students' ability to succeed at a competition (Hendricks, 2018, p. 129). Indeed, the ideology of competition is harmful to emotional wellbeing in any context, and certainly music education is one such example. In her study of depression and anxiety among university music students, Wristen (2013) observed:

> Music is a highly competitive professional field, with many applicants auditioning for a limited number of positions. This competitiveness can be quite pervasive throughout the musician's career, from the audition process to gain admission to elite precollege programs, university, or conservatory of choice, to competing for a limited number of professional positions.
>
> (p. 21)

She argued that this climate of competitiveness negatively impacts the mental health and wellbeing of music students.

While Jillian did not feel mental health impacted their music learning experience, musicking in an educational context with its inherently competitive structure and embedded pressure did affect their emotional wellbeing.

*Jillian:* I think there's a competitive aspect of music that worsens all things mental health for a lot of people. There's a lot of pressure. So I guess it's more like, how has music impacted my mental health? But how has mental health impacted music? Maybe not so much. I think the other way around, though.

Though Lizabeth felt they benefited from the competitive environment at the time, upon reflection they did not feel it served them well.

*Lizabeth:* Eliminating competition would have been really supportive [to my mental health] because all of high school and band was very competitive. I think I was really convinced that I liked it, mostly because I usually benefited from it. But ultimately, I don't think that was good for me. I think having opportunities to collaborate with my peers, and to construct things together rather than only being in competition as individuals would have been very supportive.

Lizabeth identified a collaborative approach and the opportunity to focus on constructive musical processes rather than only products as potentially beneficial. In encouraging a move away from competition to prioritizing emotional wellbeing alongside other compelling arguments against competition (Abramo, 2017; Allsup, 2012; Kohn, 1986/1992; Powell, 2023; Tucker, 2020), music educators must be mindful not to allow standardization and an accountability regime to shape curricula and pedagogy.

Mary mentioned stress in relation to All-State ensembles—a U.S. practice of highly competitive, auditioned ensembles comprised of the "top" high school music students from around the state.

*Mary:* The quantity of students who express so much stress related to All-State was crazy.[5] The fact that we have these traditions that involve certain people [who] have the level of quality to be able to participate and others don't just doesn't make any sense. It just sets up for all those people that didn't make All-State to feel like they're not musicians or they're not good enough. Just the competition, depending on how the teacher facilitates with their students, that competition can be so problematic.

Mary cited a collaborative festival in Australia rooted in cooperation instead of competition. De Quadros and Amrein's (2023) *empowering song* approach, which I discuss in the Conclusion chapter, also offers possibilities. Given the widespread and significant impact on emotional wellbeing, rethinking ensembles with highly competitive entrance requirements in lieu of more creative and collaborative options becomes important.

Participants expressed feelings of not belonging and not being good enough within competitive musicking contexts. These feelings also occurred in high school, structurally fostered through career pressure.

Blaine: Now, kids' focus is not on making music to experience joy. It's "I have a college audition coming up and I need help with my etude." It just makes me sad that I know that they enjoy making beats ... and that's not something that they focus on because they're so focused on what this college professor is going to think about their playing. There's already that culture of stress before they're even in a college program, just because of how it is set up and how high school directors talk about college auditions. I think that's part of it, too. I don't know the language that we use in regards to what a college education will be like in a music program. They basically just try to intimidate the kids or make them feel like they're not good enough.

For students for whom music education is a career interest, experiencing stress instead of joy while musicking in high school does not bode well for finding joy in musicking later, or being an effective music educator who will refuse perpetuation of competitive disciplinary norms.

*Perfectionism*

Perfectionism pervades music education through a shared standard of "excellence" and a disdain for mistakes. Brown (2021) contrasted perfectionism—which is externally motivated—with healthy striving—which is internally driven (p. 142). She noted that perfectionism gets in the way of mastery:

> [A]chieving mastery requires curiosity and viewing mistakes and failures as opportunities for learning. Perfectionism kills curiosity by telling us that we have to know everything or we risk looking "less than." Perfectionism tells us that our mistakes and failures are personal defects, so we either avoid trying new things or we barely recover every time we inevitably fall short.
>
> (p. 142)

Most participants identified perfectionism as part of the culture of music education both in tertiary music schools (Bernhard, 2010; Dews & Williams, 1989; Kuebel, 2019; McGrath et al., 2017; Wristen, 2013) and in K-12 contexts (McGrath et al., 2017; Stoeber & Eismann, 2007).

Musical study requires intensive perfectionism often to the detriment of music students' emotional wellbeing (Dews & Williams, 1989; McGrath et al., 2017; Stoeber & Eismann, 2007). In fact, a high degree of perfectionism "can lead to anxiety, depression, and suicide risk if a failure to uphold flawless standards is observed—and critiqued—by others" (McGrath et al., 2017, p. 20). Among young musicians, perfectionism can cause distress (Stoeber & Eismann, 2007).

*August:* I've seen a fair bit of classical music being presented pedagogically as if there's no margin for error. Maybe if one is operating at a truly elite, world-class level, there really isn't, but I suspect it's rhetorical. At this point I suspect it's a rhetorical technique, and I just took it very literally.

McGrath et al. (2017) described this unrealistic pedagogical expectation as a "fantastical illusion that even the slightest error indicates technical incompetence" (p. 22). Without a margin for error, mistakes cannot serve as learning opportunities. They become devastations revealing musicians' worst self-criticisms as potential truths.

*Chris:* I felt there was a high standard of perfection, particularly for violinists actually, and that if I didn't achieve it, I wasn't good enough; I was a second class citizen. The system of orchestral rankings play into all of that. I actually still have dreams about going to perform somewhere and realizing I haven't practiced enough.

As co-director of an Intentional Peer Support training organization and a "recovering social worker," Chris began her career in music education. That she still experiences dreams about not measuring up to a model of perfection belies the harm of this kind of climate and its lasting effect on the subconscious—if not also conscious—mind.

Meghan identified the standard of excellence and perfectionist climate set early in music students' lives, with demands for professional level focus put on children and youth.

*Meghan:* I don't think music education addresses [mental health] at all until you get to college. I think coming from that standpoint of, "we need it to be perfection for the concert." That just totally dismisses students where they're at. Saying that and having the standard of excellence in music classrooms, while [it] can be great, totally destroys mental wellbeing. I think at high school and lower level classrooms, we fail to understand that students are doing other things. They're in musicals, they're in sports, they're doing all of these other things that they also enjoy just as much as music. And we just dismiss that. We expect all their time to be put into music, and that isn't going to help them at all.

The naturalization of excellence in music education requires unsettling. Bucura (2020) argued:

> [Excellence] is a term that conjures up notions of distinction, success, and superior advantage—competition, that is—the achievement of becoming the best. According to Saunders (2015), one of the problems involving excellence in education is that it is so widely accepted. They stated, "Because excellence appears neutral, natural, universal, and a legitimate educational goal, it obfuscates the embedded assumptions that undergird the material practices associated with performances of excellence (pp. 393–394)."
>
> (Bucura, 2020, p. 3)

For Bucura, excellence can be used to enforce certain values (p. 3) and to reinscribe social inequalities (p. 4). She urged us to rethink excellence and move away from competitive and standardized traditions (p. 6), instead embracing positive expectations and goal-setting. The shift she promoted aligns with Brown's (2021) point that perfectionism is externally motivated. Conversely, healthy striving occurs with internal motivation, which correlates with positive expectations and goal-setting.

Emma experienced pressure to be perfect and to perform at an extremely high level across all of her classes as a student and noticed that same climate across all levels of education now in her role as a future educator.

*Emma:* I think that [perfectionism] still applies to school with the competitive nature, the need to be the best, the need for things to be perfect. I see that in some of my students and for preschoolers, for arts and crafts where they're like, "Oh, no, my craft doesn't look exactly like the model one" or "Oh, she did hers better than me." Why do we need to make everything look perfect and shiny when it's not? Why can't we just enjoy things because we want to enjoy them? That's one thing that's so frustrating about schools is, it's this fear of not being perfect and this need to consistently ace everything. ... This need for perfection prevents us from feeling comfortable enough with talking about when we're not so perfect, when things aren't so great.

Her last point speaks to the impact on wellbeing, as a perfectionist climate might also foster shame—indeed Brown (2021) called shame the "birthplace of perfectionism" (p. 142)—and thus an unwillingness to disclose any performance that does not measure up. Unwillingness to share likely leads to isolation and also fails to make space for the kind of curiosity Brown (2021) described as fundamental to growth and mastery (p. 142).

Chris also had an interesting theory about Western classical music and perfectionism.

*Chris:* There was quite a lot of trauma ... I think particularly [in] the classical music teaching world. It would be interesting to think about the correlation between great beauty and great pain. It's almost like it's this two-edged sword. It's the same with dance (and with ballet in particular). It's so beautiful and it's so brutal. ... Sometimes I think the drive for perfection is what makes it so compelling to the rest of the world, but it's almost like self-sacrifice. How do we nurture the beauty and the uniqueness and yet nurture one another?

If the drive for perfection is indeed what makes Western classical music and other arts compelling, we must go beyond resisting perfectionism within music education, extending to a rethinking of values for the public—a task beyond the scope of this book. Challenging standards of "excellence" must also be a part of this reimagining. Like competition, perfectionism negatively impacted participants' wellbeing. In rethinking constructs such as excellence and the drive to perfection, we might consider moving toward practices that may encourage emotional wellbeing and the kind of curiosity and playfulness that Brown (2021) identified as crucial to growth. From that perspective, embracing mistakes becomes a part of that growth process, and of learning (Brown, 2021).

*Failure to Meet Expectations*

The benchmarks of excellence and high standards discussed in the previous section often led participants to feel they fell short of expectations. Multiple participants shared a fear of failure or making mistakes that Cheryl most specifically noted felt culturally normalized. While Cheryl did not recall having bad experiences in musical study, they identified a "mild fear of failure" associated with performing. For August, shame played a significant role in how they felt about musicking.

*August:* I tend to get down on myself a lot. I get expectations of how I should be able to play and when I cannot keep up with those expectations I feel a lot of shame. These tend to be a lot of my negative experiences with music. When you're feeling shame you tend to pull away from things, and then you keep feeling shame, [so] you keep pulling away. So I have a very hard time practicing. Whether or not I practice is either correspondent to outside pressure like a symphony gig or to how I'm generally doing with life.

In shame, the "focus is on self, not behavior. The result is feeling flawed and unworthy of love, belonging, and connection. Shame is not a driver of positive change" (Brown, 2021, p. 134). Shame prompts individuals to internalize their negative self-talk as truth about the self. Brown wrote that shame arises from the "fear of disconnection" (p. 137) and feelings of unworthiness. Musicking can result in feeling shame, and many participants identified the feelings Brown discussed arising as a result of experiencing failure as a music student.

The internalized feeling of "not being good enough" emerged as a theme among participants.

*Meghan:* Coming in [as a music school student], way below the skill level of my peers as a freshman and not realizing that until my first band rehearsal, until our first studio class, and then it hit me like that. I was very behind my peers. That came across as a big discouragement to me. It wasn't a "work harder," it was a, "you're not good enough to be here."

Rebecca recalled her own experience as an undergraduate student:

*Rebecca:* I got accepted to all the major music colleges in [city name removed]. But when I got there, I realized that I just was not in the same ballpark as the other people there. The administration there were really focused on producing the next two or three big stars, and everybody else, we were just bringing in the tuition to support these Wunderkinds and there was no pastoral system, no counseling, no help. I just started sinking very quickly. … After I left there I didn't play the piano for seven years. It just killed it for me. I've spoken to so many of my students now and they say that when they finish a music degree, all they've learned is they're not good enough, and that they'll never be as good as their professor. And I so empathize with that, because [studying music in university] killed my love for music. Every time I played I just thought about all the things that I was doing wrong, not the things I was doing right.

While their undergraduate experiences were over 30 years apart, the atmosphere of competitiveness and the feeling of not being good enough were consistent. Rebecca observed a benchmark wherein faculty valued only the next "Wunderkind," resulting in an impossible standard that made other students feel unworthy of praise, attention, or guidance.

When comparing themself to peers in undergraduate study, QingYu felt deficient.

*QingYu:* Talking about the competitiveness of music education in general. I felt that with the program at [school removed], the way they structured the program itself, it was fine. You have to pass such courses, and you have to get specific grades in the course to progress. I didn't get correct grades for such courses like music theory and ear training, so I had to retake them a lot. … I'd retake freshman theory and ear training, and I was so behind, and it was so defeating because a lot of the problems I was having was that my ADHD held me back, especially in ear training, because I just couldn't figure it out in my head. I don't know if it was my ADHD. … I can't sing back the solfege when you play me the notes, and I had to sing it back. I just completely failed so many of those lessons and quizzes. There's so much competition in that program already. Watching my other peers advance and just be completely fine or like, "I'm doing great. I'm not having any problems with this." And I'm like, "Is something wrong with me?"

QingYu's attention differences, in particular, impacted success in their program. They felt they did not measure up to a standard that seemed unachievable but were under the impression that peers excelled effortlessly. This impression led them to internalize their perceived lack of success and pathologize it as "something wrong" with them.

While Cheryl identified a mild fear of failure as the background to their musicking experiences, multiple participants described experiences of failure as more significant, negatively impacting their emotional wellbeing and sense of self.[6] Failing the barrier jury required of students before being permitted to enroll in upper level courses prompted Meghan to question herself and her skills.

*Meghan:* My sophomore year I failed my barrier jury. That kind of made me take a step back and think, "Am I in the right place? Is this the major I should be studying? Is this the right place for me? I'm not even good enough on my instrument? How can I teach other people about it?" So that was a big moment of "What the fuck am I gonna do now?" That was a lot of reflection for me of trying to figure out whether I was in the right place or not.

She identified this experience as one of her worst musical experiences, influencing how she felt about herself well beyond musical capabilities. Similar to Meghan, failing an undergraduate degree entrance audition caused Paulo emotional turmoil.[7]

*Paulo:* Failing my audition is probably one of the biggest [negative experiences]. However, I would actually call it probably the most defining features of me as a music teacher, important moments. Because failing at that immediately made me an outsider, and I kept that outsider status throughout. I still have it. I feel like I have a chip on my shoulder about how music education works. I'm so glad I'm here at a school where if you want to be in music ed, you show up. ... You don't really have to audition. We have to teach you. I love that. ... [That audition outcome] caused the most amount of kind of emotional turmoil because it made me think about, "Is this really who I am anymore?" Which every 18-year-old needs in their life.

He contrasted his experience with audition requirements and program norms at the small liberal arts college where he taught at the time of data gathering. This kind of policy likely circumvents the emotional distress embedded in a significant failure experience. Such policies are also conducive to lower levels of competition across the program, and encourage faculty commitment to help all students acquire needed skills.

Failing her first-year piano examination also caused Rebecca to question herself, negatively impacting her self-esteem and feeling of belonging in her undergraduate degree music program.

*Rebecca:* The most negative [musicking event was] my first-year piano examination at the college, which I failed. The reason they gave me for failing it was that I played too many right notes. ... I was cripplingly nervous and I remember thinking, "I'm just going to disconnect my mind from my body and let my body do this because it knows what to do." I probably played a bit, I don't know, unemotionally, maybe. I played a Mozart sonata, and there was a cadenza in it. They said, "if it had all been like the cadenza, you would have been fine." I think in the cadenza I sort of invested a bit more, but to be failed? I really needed to pass that exam because I was struggling with the feeling that I didn't belong there. I'd done a Tuesday recital, which everybody had to do ... and they told me it was the best one they'd heard that year. Then to go into this exam and fail it. I don't think I've ever failed an exam before in my life, so I had no training in resilience or coping with that. That just completely destroyed any self-confidence or self-esteem I had. ... I started the second year, but I was dying. So I think it was a good part of the reason why I didn't play for seven years after that.

Rebecca purposefully dissociated in order to play her first-year piano examination. This response speaks to the extreme degree of distress this kind of assessment created for Rebecca. Dissociating is common for people who have experienced trauma (Van der Kolk & Van der Hart, 1995) and also, as Rebecca's experience demonstrated, can be useful in mediating performance anxiety.[8] A person should not feel compelled to disconnect their mind from their body, however, to succeed at a musical examination. Judging dissociation to be a necessary mechanism by which to endure a performance indicates that the benchmark for excellence is too high.

Participants consistently reported these failure experiences as their most negative musicking memories. Failure experiences prompted self-doubt and feelings of not belonging. The fact that these kinds of auditions and examinations remain typical in music schools, and also sometimes in K-12 music, aligns with the ideology of competition explored previously in tandem with the perfectionist culture and unreasonably high expectations. Moreover, the shame August described and the fear of interpersonal disconnection that shame prompts (Brown, 2021, p. 137) are likely also at play during such experiences. Rebecca's need to dissociate also demonstrates the possibility for intrapersonal disconnection. The liberal arts college where Paulo teaches offers a glimpse of other possibilities.

*Pressure and Stress*

Participants noted that the constant pressure and stress present in music education negatively impacted their emotional wellbeing and caused distress. Scholars have observed high levels of stress in postsecondary music students in addition to burnout, depression, and anxiety (Bernhard, 2005, 2007a, 2010, 2021; Conway et al., 2010; Demirbatir et al., 2012; Kuebel, 2019; Payne et al., 2020; Sternbach, 2008). These issues filter down to K-12 music education contexts given similar practices and norms.

Jillian recognized how self-worth can become entangled with productivity, musical output, and achievement, and the way that entanglement can seriously impact emotional wellbeing.

*Jillian:* We know music is inherently more than just the musical experience. Obviously, we've talked about it being social. I also think that there is the competitive aspect, not just because of wanting to play the part, but there's the approval of your friends and of other people in the school. Especially in college music ... everybody knows what group [ensemble] you're in. The directors all know you. There's a pressure to just be better. That makes you really not want to do it. It also makes you tie your personal worth to your musical output, and productivity, and achievement. And that's enough to keep you down for a few days if you do poorly.

Most participants experienced an especially marked degree of pressure and stress during their undergraduate studies in music.

*Jillian:* Playing my primary instrument ... doesn't make me feel anything except for stress most of the time. I listen to a lot, but not classical music. I don't listen to that as much as I used to. [I] have to get creative with the ways [I] find music to listen to even.

Because of the degree of stress felt in relation to their instrument and to Western classical music during undergraduate study, playing and listening to music no longer elicited a sense of joy or satisfaction unless Jillian creatively and intentionally worked to avoid a negative musicking experience.

Pressure can result from academic or discussion-based classes as well as performance-based spaces.

*QingYu:* Group conversations can be hard for people with different types of mental health diagnoses or ADHD. I've always found it really hard to be able to process things quickly, and then decide what I want to say and then say them. So I had to sit here and process every single thing that all of you have said, then decide, "Okay, I think [this] is what I'm going to say to this." But by the time that I get there we've already moved on. ... What I have also struggled with when I was in school a lot was that I hated when our teachers are like, "You will get participation points if you talk two times. If you don't talk two times, you don't get points." I hated that because I was like, how can you expect students that have challenges with such things that I already said? You're forcing them to have to speak a specific enough number of times. It just adds these barriers and stresses your students out even more.

QingYu's point shows that forced participation—in whatever form—creates unnecessary pressure on students, which is likely true across educational levels. Alleviating pressure in discussion-based classes would likely require forgoing policies incentivizing verbal contributions concomitant with classmates; educators could instead allow students to share their preferred modes of participation and make space for these different modes in and between music class sessions, with grading equal among these options.

Articulating the need for a systemic change, Emma expressed how the constant pressure of an undergraduate music education program became exhausting.

*Emma:* I'm so tired. That's one thing I'm absolutely so sick of … I'm so tired of having to act like I have all my shit together. Can we please stop that? Can we just be honest, because that's just one thing that's really, really tough.

In order for a culture shift, everyone needs to be more authentic about their experiences rather than masking them.[9] As noted in Chapter 5, masking in the context of Madness and distress involves concealing one's level of distress so that it remains unapparent to others. Undertaking a widespread culture shift as Emma suggested, bringing our authentic selves to musicking and music education specifically, may prompt a healthy increase in discussion about the kind of pressure and stresses embedded in current practices in our field.

Meghan articulated the challenges of a schedule that kept her in music classes from 8:00 a.m. until 4:00 p.m., with general education classes after that. She did not have time to eat, which was extremely detrimental to her wellbeing as she was recovering from an eating disorder. On a larger scale, Meghan voiced concerns about music education degrees in the U.S. requiring more credits than should reasonably be expected of students in a 4-year program.

*Meghan:* First of all, blanket statement, music ed should be a 5.5-year program, or at least 4.5. There is no reason for it to be displayed as a 4-year program. That's insane. But because it is marketed as either a 4 or a 4.5-year program, we're expected to be taking all of these credits. I took 21 credits every single semester until the second semester of my junior year and I still ended up graduating in 5.5 years. That expectation should be taken away. We shouldn't be told, "Oh, you can do it in 4.5" because then we're pulling our hair out and clawing our way to the end. We're mentally drained. We don't have any physical energy left by the end. We don't have the time to make friends. We don't have the time to network. We don't have time to make these connections. But we're expected to do those things for our career. We're also expected to go to all of our classes and maintain all of our classwork.

This kind of required course load is untenable for any student and is a recognized concern in music teacher preparation.[10] Rather than a revision to the credit count, which Bernhard (2010) suggested to decrease burnout, Meghan sought transparency about how long a degree would actually take. Payne et al. (2020) observed that a higher credit load is associated with higher levels of depression and anxiety (p. 57), further illuminating the levels of stress, burnout, depression, and anxiety other scholars identified among music students (Bernhard, 2005, 2007a, 2010, 2021; Conway et al., 2010; Demirbatir et al., 2012; Kuebel, 2019; Sternbach, 2008). With undergraduate students chronically pushed to carry overwhelming credit loads, distress is a likely outcome for many, and is yet another example of the unreasonably high expectations set for students studying music.

Pressure and stress at the higher education level occur for music teacher educators as well as undergraduate and graduate students (Bernhard, 2007b; Hamann et al., 1988; Hewitt & Thompson, 2006).[11] In a higher education focus group, Rebecca asked, "Does anyone else feel really guilty when they take time to rest?" The response from the two graduate students and three professors present was an overwhelming yes. Beauregard and Bucura (2020) called for "critical thinking in relation to cultural norms perpetuated at tertiary institutions" that fail to account for the fact that time is insufficient to manage one's responsibilities without neglecting other aspects of selfhood (p. 119). They ultimately demanded systemic evaluation and change related to work-life balance in academia. This extensive workload and "grind" culture in higher education functions to elicit feelings of guilt when considering resting. Rebecca continued, "I think the measure of success in our profession has been how close to death you work yourself." That type and extent of pressure is clearly detrimental to both emotional wellbeing and physical health.

The climate of pressure and stress in music education are not exclusive to higher education. Participants explicitly pointed to middle and high school music as sites of pressure and stress.

*Lizabeth:* The word pressure keeps coming to mind because, particularly in ensemble classes, there's a lot of pressure on students. It's not very accommodating for students who are easily overwhelmed, or who have anxiety, or who are struggling with their self-esteem. In my experience, most instrumentalists start in middle school, which is around sixth grade. That's a very precious time in your life. That's when your self-esteem is probably the lowest, because you're trying to figure out who you are. A lot of times music education pushes students when they're not ready, which can push them out of music completely or just fuel their anxiety within the space. This is especially when music is required, like when band class is required, because it's possible students aren't even choosing to be there and they have pressure applied to them to perform in a group or by themselves, and to perform at a certain standard.

Lizabeth observed the pressure beginning at the middle school level in ensemble contexts in ways that affect children's and youth's self-esteem and anxiety. In the United States, many schools begin choral and band ensembles as early as third grade, with strings ensemble instruction starting as young as fourth grade. Band, choir, and orchestra are all offered in elementary school (Give a Note Foundation, 2017). These pressures thus affect children at these developmental stages and older.[12]

*Invalidations*

A number of participants described being invalidated in music education contexts. The failure of professors to recognize Paulo's musicking skills and practices resulted in him feeling invalidated in the institutional context, and this lack of recognition constituted the majority of his negative experiences.

Paulo: While that's happening [writing music to express depression and preparing to audition for music school], and I'm having a really active life, I'm improvising a lot. I had been in an improv blues band as a middle schooler. I was a bass player in this band with my cousin, and… I fell in love with improvising, so improvising became a huge aspect of like, I just need to play. I need to express. I just need to do stuff. Then I finally got into school music, and I had what I finally wanted. I wanted to get in the school of music, and I was the biggest outsider of outsiders. I was an outsider because I had a weird sense of humor, had a little tinge of darkness, I was a pop musician, I could play anything by ear. Well, that got trained out of me. … Really early on I started to have questions about, should I be a music teacher? It was all I ever wanted, but these people don't like music.

As an active and capable musician and an avid songwriter and improviser, the Western classically-based curriculum Paulo encountered in music school made him feel that people there did not like music. His ability to play by ear was "trained out of him"; the wealth of skills he brought to music school were not only dismissed, but eradicated, invalidating his personal musicking experiences.

While experiencing profound depression in high school, Emma's school choir sang "You Will Be Found" from *Dear Evan Hansen*—a song meant to communicate that a person feeling isolated is not alone.

*Emma:* I even tried out for a solo that was that very first line ... "Have you ever felt like you were so alone" or something like that. I didn't even get that, someone else got it. ... It just felt like I was giving out my heart and telling people how I felt, but then they're like, "No, be quiet. No." Then we had a conversation because we were doing that particular song in class. "If you ever feel alone, you can always reach out to someone. This is a safe place." Yet I was feeling so alone. Yet I didn't feel like I could. If it was one of the [teacher's] favorite people, when they were feeling sad and depressed like this all of them would be swarming them. They would be swarmed and just given so much support. I felt like if I did, no one would care. Days of not feeling like you belong and that you're so alone, and then you're singing "You will be found." It's so messed up. ... As the days went by, I remember just was looking at my watch or at the time almost every five minutes. Almost like I couldn't wait to get out.

Songs that teachers intend to soothe distress may end up exacerbating it, and keeping that possibility in mind is important to programming decisions. While her choral classroom sang "You Will Be Found" from *Dear Evan Hansen* and the teacher encouraged students to "reach out" if they were struggling, Emma's experience did not match the optimistic representation and related classroom discourse. She felt explicitly that she could *not* speak up and found that nobody noticed her distress or reached out to her, all of which led to an even greater sense of isolation. Emma's teacher missed an important opportunity to contextualize the topic of the song (feeling isolated) as a pervasive issue in society, but also in schools and within this specific class of students. To Emma, singing the song felt performative, as did classroom discussions around its lyrical content. With proper contextualization, singing "You Will Be Found" could have been made meaningful and provoked important discussion and support for Emma and her peers. As it was, it invalidated Emma's experience.

Several participants offered examples of experiences they had of music being prioritized over the people involved in making the music. This privileging resulted in invalidation, and sometimes outright exclusion. Musicking is fundamentally about relationships—both sonic and social (Small, 1998). When the social relationships become subsumed by the kinds of perfectionist tendencies and push toward sonic and technical "excellence" described previously, the socioemotional environment can become toxic.

*Blaine:* [My mentor teacher] only cared about having a good band program [when I was student teaching]. He wanted them to make the [name removed] marching state competition every year. He didn't care what he had to do to get there and intentionally excluded students with disabilities or with mental health problems. He would weed them out in middle school so that they were not a part of his program in high school.

In this case, the needs of students with disabilities were considered irrelevant in light of program goals; the students themselves became a liability and were summarily dismissed. The exclusion of students with disabilities and mental health differences is alarmingly common, and also illegal in the U.S. under the guidance set by the Individuals with Disabilities Education Act (IDEA).[13] Further discouraging but in keeping with their mentor teacher's investment in the toxically competitive culture of music education, Blaine received negative feedback on their teaching when they took time to support these students.

Another participant described a time during applied lessons at the collegiate level when disability was similarly not met with compassion.[14] They experienced physical health issues during their undergraduate degree that made playing their instrument painful. Practice time had to be limited to 30-minute sessions because of the pain, but in explaining this to their primary teacher, the teacher did not offer understanding, instead prioritizing performance benchmarks and musical achievement. The teacher's lack of compassion resulted in the invalidation of this participant's physical pain and added to distress. Participants noted that priorities skewed in favor of musical "excellence" and away from compassion in ensemble settings as well as private instruction, a consistent theme in data and persistent problem among participants.

### *Abusive Teachers*

Significantly, eight participants had studied with at least one abusive music teacher between elementary school and higher education. Reported abuses included: yelling at students including those under the age of 10 for minor performance errors, making ensemble members cry, singling people out for public ridicule, discounting student capabilities, and belittling students in both private lesson and ensemble contexts. These abuses produced a climate of fear and a toxic environment for musicking, and created collective and individual trauma and distress. For the purposes of discussion, I offer a few specific examples of abusive behavior but detach the names of participants from the events they recounted to protect confidentiality. I use *they* pronouns for all participants throughout.

One participant named the issue in which a conductor prioritized the music over the people involved and their musicking experience.

Anon.: It's the people in charge of the groups. ... I had this high school orchestra that made me want to quit music, forgot about that. There was the conductor ... It was a high school group, there was this one kid. He was 9 or 10 and he was playing the bass. It wasn't youth orchestra, but he was definitely the youngest. One day, his older counterpart—the older bassist who did most of the work, and he would just fall in line—wasn't there. [The conductor] lit into him for not being able to play. Multiple kids would be crying every week. When it becomes not about the people and the experience, when it's solely on the music. That's no good.

This participant's experience reflected the kinds of abusive dynamics that Bull (2019) identified in youth ensembles in the U.K. The conductor, in this context, took an autocratic and dictatorial approach that held children to the same standards as high school students. When the music is prioritized over the people involved, abusive behavior is fostered and people doing the musicking can end up in tears. As Brown (2021) noted, perfectionism does not lead to healthy striving, and moreover, often fails to motivate.

Another participant's experience in elementary school fostered a similar fear of being yelled at.

Anon.: I did not have a great first experience with music in elementary school [because of] this teacher. She yelled a lot. She wasn't very patient. If a kid was too scared of singing or if we weren't singing loud enough, she would yell that we're mumbling. All I remember is that she yelled a lot. I was very scared of music, honestly, because I was scared of getting yelled at, simply if I sang or if I played a wrong note or something. I was literally scared of being yelled at. That was awful.

They did not experience any joyful musicking at school as a child because the teacher targeted individual students for errors. This pedagogical approach is antithetical to what Brown (2021) explained about errors constituting opportunities for learning (p. 142), and therefore as essential to growth.

Another participant described a negative experience in a community Suzuki program outside of school.

*Anon.:* I was maybe seven years old, and in my second or third year at Suzuki school. The kids in my group class on Saturday mornings, they start using vibrato, shaking their little hands. Nobody had taught me how to do vibrato in my own lessons so I wanted to keep up, so I started just kind of doing whatever vibrato note, and nobody taught it to me or anything. Then we had a moment in class once and the teacher pointed to one of the other kids like, "Oh Jeffrey, show us your vibrato" and he does it. Then the teacher says, "[Name removed], do your vibrato," and I'm doing some of whatever I did. Then she says to the class, "Don't do that."

The Suzuki teacher singled out this student in front of the others for the explicit purpose of criticism and humiliation. Shame, however, never proves motivational, nor should it ever be used as a pedagogical strategy.

Another participant shared a terrible experience they had with their primary instrument studio professor during their undergraduate music education degree.

*Anon.:* I really struggled in music school because my [instrument redacted] professor kind of gave up on me. I didn't really openly talk about it to anybody. I considered transferring schools ... I wasn't able to get myself to practice a lot [because of trauma related to practicing (details redacted)]. My professor just didn't understand why I couldn't get myself to practice. I was obviously good enough to be in the program, I was fine, but our professor was very known as being probably one of the hardest professors for any instrument in the entire [music school]. It was very common for you to leave your lessons crying ... My professor decided to label me as lazy and unmotivated. She liked to try to diagnose her students, and try to tell me that I should just take some vitamins and I would not be depressed anymore. After my first semester of sophomore year, she gave up on me and decided that I would no longer be taught by her and that I would only be taught by grad students.

This professor made the participant cry, made them feel "less than," and eventually refused to provide instruction at all, which broke an integral musicking relationship for this participant early in their undergraduate study. The professor also offered medical advice, which is highly discouraged in education and represents a line educators should not cross. This participant was traumatized by their studio experiences. Subsequently, they experienced a failure at an advancement jury and were not well supported toward remediation. They noted a major decline in their mental health as a result of these and other similar experiences with the same professor.

Anon.: [My grad student instructor] told me that I was going to flunk out. He told me to prepare that I was not going to pass, he told me that I was not good enough. He told me that I should prepare to not be a music student anymore.

The participant filed a complaint against the graduate student instructor, but harm had already been experienced because of his comments that built on the negativity of the studio professor. They identified a lack of support and experienced people actively working against them, which they found traumatizing.

I have pages of data recounting experiences of abuse from teachers. The examples shared here are merely representative. That participants recalled these specific experiences years later indicates the long-term damage incurred. There is a need for K-12 music teachers, studio teachers, and academic faculty to receive specific education on trauma-informed approaches to pedagogy, and to actively engage in guided discussion on the different ways abuse manifests in music education. Working against the cycle of abuse in ensemble contexts (Bull, 2019) and private studios[15] is a major way in which the field of music education can reduce systemic harms caused in classrooms, rehearsal halls, and music studios. These efforts will work toward reducing toxic music teaching and learning environments so that people in roles of authority will no longer cause or exacerbate distress through harmful pedagogical practices.

## Musicking

Music educators in this research study described how their participation in certain musicking practices—including Western classical ensemble-based instruction and solo performing—caused emotional distress and negatively impacted wellbeing. Notably, ensemble participation and solo playing and singing (not necessarily performing) comprised practices that participants also found supportive (see Chapter 7). Recognizing that the same musicking experiences may facilitate help or harm reminds music educators that what constitutes supportive practices can be widely variable. Additionally, while participants found music listening supportive, substantial literature shows that it can also be harmful (Alluri et al., 2022; Garrido & Schubert, 2013; Silverman, 2020; ter Bogt et al., 2021). Given the possible range of student reactions to musicking practices, remaining mindful of students' responses in the classroom is essential for educators working to foster positive musicking experiences.

*Western Classical Ensemble-Based Music Instruction*

Several participants described Western classical, director-centric, ensemble-based music instruction as detrimental to their emotional wellbeing. Paulo noted: "I don't think that ensemble-based education addresses [mental health] at all. … And I won't even say just ensembles, but like performance-based things. If it does, it addresses it through expressing the emotion of someone else." The ensemble model of music education is one of replication in which students play or sing music created by someone else. One can still emote during this process, but doing so differs vastly from playing or singing something original about one's personal experience.

Jillian commented on the replication model and problematized the synchrony required by ensembles as an erasure of individuality.

Jillian: How do you play in a traditional ensemble without conformity? … You can't. You don't. The definition of it is things happening at the same time in the same way, right? How do you embrace individuality in a setting that is built on conformity, genuinely? I've been thinking about this a lot. Reimagining the ensemble is imperative to making music education better going forward. … I think traditional ensembles can exist for the people who want them, … but I think there should be more. Why haven't we updated that? It's been a long time. Why haven't we figured out a way to make that more accessible and fun and creative? We're playing what some dead guy wrote. Even if we're playing what some alive woman wrote. If you want kids to stay, they have to be doing it, they have to be creating it.

Jillian urged the inclusion of mechanisms within music education that elicit expression of musical individuality without necessarily having to conform to uniform expressions in synchrony with others.

Ensembles may also be overwhelming, particularly for beginner students.

*Lizabeth:* Beginning band classes tend to be a big culprit of overwhelming student's cognitive load. For non-disabled students or neurotypical students, beginning band is overwhelming, let alone for students with disabilities or other struggles. Not only are you trying to produce a sound on an instrument, you are engaging yourself physically with many muscles in your body, with your air, all while remembering fingerings, note names, and probably reading music for the first time as well. I don't think it is reasonable for anyone of any age to learn how to do that many new things all at once.

Learning to play an instrument in an ensemble requires simultaneously learning and implementation of multiple skills, potentially overwhelming students. Ensembles, while supportive at times, can also present challenges in relation to self-expression, conformity, and cognitive load. Providing multiple options for ways to participate in music education may aid students in finding musicking experiences that support their emotional wellbeing and do not cause or exacerbate distress. These options, moreover, must be equally valued, and must not result in prioritizing students who choose a "traditional" path of engagement.

### *Alternatives to High-Stakes Performing*

Notably, all of the failure experiences described in this chapter were solo performance experiences, with the additional characteristic of being high-stakes. High-stakes performances involve singular opportunities that supposedly represent the sum of a person's skill or knowledge. Participants defined high-stakes experiences as assessments that determine progression or advancement—such as auditions, juries, and examinations—as well as other performances in competitive climates. Performance requirements that were not mediated with compassion and left no room for creativity or error caused emotional distress and resulted in setbacks to progress across various situations. While participants sometimes found playing and singing supportive (see Chapter 7), performance experiences that were high-stakes almost exclusively caused distress. Notably, Meghan recounted that virtual experiences during the COVID-19 pandemic changed the nature of high-stakes performance. During the 2020-21 academic year, her institution asked students to submit a recording as their jury—the final performance evaluation for the year. The fact that this high-stakes performance occurred via recording allowed Meghan to submit her twentieth take for evaluation.

*Meghan:* The 19th and the 20th [takes] I was like, I feel good. I do know this music. I do know how to play my instrument. I do know what this scale sounds like. And I played it, and it was the best I've ever played. Because I gave myself that time to remember, "Okay, I do know what I'm doing. This does sound good." I understand that that's not always practical or feasible, but I'm sure that that semester where all juries were virtual was probably the best the juries ever sounded.

The quality that made all of the failure experiences previously discussed in this chapter so traumatic was their high-stakes nature and the concomitant anxiety and distress they induced. Meghan offered a glimpse of another possible way to evaluate performances so that students have an opportunity to present their best. While recording can also be highly stressful, the opportunity for repetition can be extremely valuable.

Rebecca noted that the songwriting class she taught was the only music education context in which students were not told they were wrong. In contrast to the rest of the ensemble-based program, songwriting provided a respite from perfectionist tendencies and a mandate for uniform "excellence." Perhaps rethinking excellence (Bucura, 2020) or resisting excellence (Saunders, 2015) requires including and even centering activities such as songwriting, jamming, and similarly casual, informal, and exploratory opportunities. Classes like songwriting offer an opportunity to express one's own emotions and ideas rather than someone else's (Hess, 2019). Songwriting may also provide a way to work through emotional issues, including those rooted in grief, trauma, and other difficulties (Baker, 2013, 2015; Baker & Krout, 2012; Dalton & Krout, 2006; Riley, 2012). Classes on songwriting, improvisation, and other creativity-based forms of novel musicking make space for, and actually require, self-expression and experimenting with ideas that may not be excellent or refined at first.

*Music Listening*

Participants unequivocally described music listening as a supportive musicking practice that soothed distress (see Chapter 7). I note, however, that substantial literature within music therapy makes the case that music listening can also be harmful (see for example Alluri et al., 2022; Silverman, 2020, 2021).[16] Music may worsen a person's depressive or emotional state (Alluri et al., 2022; McFerran et al., 2013; Miranda & Claes, 2009; Silverman, 2021) or increase rumination (Alluri et al., 2022; Garrido & Schubert, 2013; Silverman, 2020), although rumination is not inherently harmful. It also may lead to avoidance (Miranda & Claes, 2009; Silverman, 2020) or social isolation (Silverman, 2020). People may believe that musicking helps them to feel better when it may, in fact, be causing harm (McFerran & Saarikallio, 2014a).

In my own experience, for example, I have done the most musical harm to myself through listening. When I am depressed, I often choose music that matches my mood. Listening repeatedly often leads me further and deeper into depression rather than helping me to resist it. Moreover, when I am in that place, I crave music that will worsen my emotional state. In music therapy, Saarikallio et al. (2015) developed a measure called the Healthy-Unhealthy Music Scale (HUMS). "Healthy" music use relates to experiences of positive emotions, relaxation, and social connection, while "unhealthy" music use may lead to rumination, avoidance, and worsening of mood. My own experience corresponds with "unhealthy" music use. A number of researchers have drawn on this scale to consider "healthy" and "unhealthy" or "adaptive" and "maladaptive" music listening practices (Alluri et al., 2022; Silverman, 2020, 2021).[17]

Music listeners often seek to match their mood (Chen et al., 2007; Hunter et al., 2011; Kahn et al., 2022; Larwood & Dingle, 2022; Taylor & Friedman, 2015; Thoma et al., 2012), leading people who are experiencing depression to be drawn to sad music (Garrido & Schubert, 2015; Kahn et al., 2022; Kerkova, 2020; Van Den Tol & Edwards, 2014). Listening to emotionally congruent music, however, may help with emotional regulation (Dingle et al., 2019). Listening to sad music may increase sadness (Garrido & Schubert, 2013, 2015; McFerran & Saarikallio, 2014b), though at times also helps people feel better (Eerola et al., 2015; Eerola et al., 2018; Garrido & Schubert, 2013; Larwood & Dingle, 2022; Sachs et al., 2015; ter Bogt et al., 2021). A number of scholars have observed that people who experience negative emotions and/or high levels of stress are more likely to use music to regulate their moods (Lonsdale, 2019; Thoma et al., 2012). Doing so can potentially worsen their moods (Garrido et al., 2017; Silverman, 2021; ter Bogt et al., 2021). Importantly, no particular genre of music is implicated in harm (Blagov et al., 2019; Silverman, 2020, 2021). Although links have been made between rock and rap music and self-harm and suicidality, this connection may have precipitating factors (North & Hargreaves, 2012).[18] Rather, context and an individual's relationship to the music bears more on the outcome. Silverman (2020) argued that a genre of music is not inherently helpful or harmful, but rather a person's music preference determines any resultant affect regulation (pp. 943–944).

Music therapy scholar Murakami (2021) theorized a model for recognizing harm in music listening, one that has implications for music education. Her Music Therapy and Harm Model identifies six potential sites of harm within music therapy: "(1) the music presented, (2) the music therapist, (3) the therapeutic application of music, (4) the therapeutic relationship, (5) client-music associations, and (6) ecological factors" (p. 10). Within a music education setting, many of these facets also operate, as I have discussed in prior sections of this chapter. While the application of music in the classroom is pedagogical and not meant to be therapeutic, misalignment of pedagogical intentions with students' individual experiences may cause harm. The music presented and the teacher can be a source of harm at times. The relationship between teacher and students may also be a site of harm, and students will all have associations with music that they bring into the classroom space. Finally, overarching ecological and contextual factors may cause harm within the classroom, such as the ideology of competition (Powell, 2023). Recognizing the potential for harm helps a teacher to be sensitive to this possibility, and to respond to any visible/audible distress that emerges among students; remembering to remain within the bounds of the role of music educator, not music therapist, is essential. As music education occurs predominantly in group settings where many individual responses from different experiences may occur at once, and music educators are not typically equipped with music therapy training or knowledge, Murakami's (2021) model is complicated in music education.

The majority of research cited here draws on quantitative methodologies. While it revealed that musicking practices, and listening in particular, may serve to either help or harm individuals, these large-scale studies do not necessarily capture the nuances of individuals' experiences. Moreover, words like "healthy" and "unhealthy" or "adaptive" and "maladaptive" reveal a medicalized and deficit paradigm that requires consideration of the ways people engage in musicking practices, particularly in relation to emotional regulation. These models may not allow for other paradigms that consider and perhaps more fully frame experiences of Madness and distress as related to musicking.

## Conclusion and Implications

Aspects of the culture of music education across K-12 and higher education, as well as particular musicking practices, provoked emotional distress among participants. Pervasive competition, cultivation of perfectionism, failure to meet expectations and standards of "excellence," pressure and stress, invalidations, and outright abuse created a toxic and traumatic culture that exacerbated or created distress. High-stakes performances and Western classical ensemble-based music education also troubled most participants. While participants found music listening helpful, literature shows that it sometimes causes harm. As Ansdell (2014) reminded readers, music is not a "straightforward panacea for personal and social problems" (p. xvii). Constructing music education spaces that support and help emotional wellbeing more often than they cause harm requires careful consideration and attentiveness to people with experiences of Madness and/or distress.

Participants' experiences shared in this chapter offer implications for practice and policy. Observations about toxicity in music education point to a need for a cultural shift away from an emphasis on competition, high-stakes performance models, perfectionism, invalidations, and abuse. Instead, we must create and foster spaces where students feel validated, in which we encourage collaboration, creativity, and the cultivation of growth and support, both individually and collectively. Such pedagogy would decenter the teacher and cultivate autonomy and agency among students. At the policy level, administrators and school boards must refuse the standardization and accountability regime that valorizes competition, perfectionism, and high-stakes tasks. These neoliberal values currently permeate all disciplines. The shift thus needs to occur in the overarching educational culture as well as in music. Fostering emotional wellbeing requires moving away from high-stakes evaluations and giving students opportunities to be more musically autonomous and in control of their own musical learning. Educators, administrators, and school districts would do well to rethink the rigidity of "excellence," leaning instead into cultivating student curiosity and musical exploration, setting positive expectations, and collaborative goal-setting, each of which serves to decouple self-worth from productivity and performance outcomes. A rethinking of these core elements of current music education praxis would likely minimize the kind of harm participants and others have experienced in music education contexts. Participants' experiences provide a powerful counterpoint to dominant music education discourse of music as an inherent good, instead framing our discipline as worthy of scrutiny and pedagogical reform for the betterment of students at all levels of musical study.

### Notes

1 I use the term "music (education)" in this chapter title and in Chapter 7 to signal that the considerations I discuss sometimes relate to music and musicking and other times to music education.
2 Organizations such as the National Association for Music Education (NAfME) in the United States and the Coalition for Music Education in Canada spend significant time asserting the value of music education. See https://nafme.org and https://coalitioncanada.ca/en/ respectively.
3 See https://nafme.org/advocacy/. Retrieved on July 13, 2023.
4 I include myself among musickers and thus use the term "we."
5 Participants were divided on using the words "crazy" or "insane" to describe practices, contexts, approaches, etc. This language did show up more frequently, however, when participants discussed the harms embedded in musicking contexts as opposed to any other topic of discussion in this research.

6 The contrast between Cheryl, who received most of their music education in Western Europe, and participants who received their music education in the U.S. speaks to the competitive climate in the U.S. that Powell (2021) elucidated.
7 At the undergraduate audition level, failure typically results in the decision to admit/not admit.
8 Stephenson and Quarrier (2005) observed: "It might also be that musicians have a facility to dissociate, because musical performance is a type of dissociative activity and, as such, musicians find it easier to dissociate or enter trancelike states where other stimuli are blocked from consciousness and performance is the sole focus of awareness. This works well if the trancelike state is a zone where one becomes 'one with the music' but not so if the dissociative zone is one where the performer feels surreal, frozen, and mentally blank. Control over these altered states of consciousness, both positive and negative, is at best only partly conscious" (p. 123).
9 This culture shift needs to occur top-down via modeling. Students require their professors and educators to be authentic in order to feel comfortable doing so. Professors and educators likely also will not feel safe without the support of administrators, who must also model vulnerability. Brown (2018) advocated vulnerability in leadership.
10 See Maas et al. (2023) for discussion of reconciling credit hours.
11 While this research on burnout among music teacher educators is older, the climate in music education has intensified since the decade of the 2000s, given increased neoliberalism, the climate of competition, and the COVID-19 pandemic.
12 See for example Austin (1990) for an argument against placing competitive pressure on students in favor of leaving room for personal growth.
13 See https://sites.ed.gov/idea/.
14 I have omitted the participant's name to avoid identifying the teacher.
15 See Rakena (2022) for an example of a trauma-informed private studio that makes flourishing the objective.
16 Music has also been used in warfare and torture (see for example Pieslak, 2009).
17 The binaries embedded in this language from music therapy implies a right and a wrong way. I prefer more complexity in language.
18 North and Hargreaves (2012) observed that the link between rap music and suicidality does not account for factors such as family dysfunction. Their overarching perspective positioned the connection between rap music and suicidality as one of correlation, not causation. Moreover, tying rap music to suicidality has racist and classist underpinnings.

## References

Abramo, J. M. (2017). The phantasmagoria of competition in school ensembles. *Philosophy of Music Education Review*, *25*(2), 150–170. https://doi.org/10.2979/philmusieducrevi.25.2.04

Allsup, R. E. (2012). The moral ends of band. *Theory into Practice*, *51*(3), 179–187. https://doi.org/10.1080/00405841.2012.690288

Alluri, V., Mittal, A., SC, A., Vuoskoski, J. K., & Saarikallio, S. (2022). Maladaptive music listening strategies are modulated by individual traits. *Psychology of Music*, 50(6), 1779–1800. https://doi.org/10.1177/03057356211065061

Ansdell, G. (2014). *How music helps in music therapy and everyday life*. Ashgate.

Austin, J. R. (1990). Competition: Is music education the loser? *Music Educators Journal*, 76(6), 21–25.

Baker, F. (2013). Music therapists' perceptions of the impact of group factors on the therapeutic songwriting process. *Music Therapy Perspectives*, 31, 138–143.

Baker, F. (2015). What about the music? Music therapists' perspectives on the role of music in the therapeutic songwriting process. *Psychology of Music*, 43(1), 122–139. https://doi.org/10.1177/0305735613498919

Baker, F., & Krout, R. E. (2012). Turning experience into learning: Educational contributions of collaborative peer songwriting during music therapy training. *International Journal of Music Education*, 30(2), 133–147. https://doi.org/10.1177/0255761411427103

Beauregard, J., & Bucura, E. (2020). To thine own self be true": One music educator's transition from higher education faculty member to high school teacher In T. D. Smith & K. S. Hendricks (Eds.), *Narratives and reflections in music education: Listening to voices seldom heard* (pp. 105–121). Springer.

Bernhard, H. C. (2005). Burnout and the college music education major. *Journal of Music Teacher Education (JTME)*, 15(1), 43–51. https://doi.org/10.1177/10570837050150010107

Bernhard, H. C. (2007a). A survey of burnout among college music majors. *College Student Journal*, 41(2), 392–401.

Bernhard, H. C. (2007b). A survey of burnout among university music faculty. *College Music Symposium*, 47, 117–126. www.jstor.org/stable/40374508

Bernhard, H. C. (2010). A survey of burnout among college music majors: A replication. *Music Performance Research*, 3(1), 31–41.

Bernhard, H. C. (2021). *Managing stress in music education*. Routledge.

Blagov, P. S., Von Handorf, K., Pugh, A. T., & Walker, M. G. (2019). Maladaptive personality and psychopathy dimensions as predictors of music and movie preferences in US adults. *Psychology of Music*, 47(6), 821–833. https://doi.org/10.1177/0305735619864630

Bradley, D., & Hess, J. (Eds.). (2022). *Trauma and resilience in music education: Haunted melodies*. Routledge.

Brown, B. (2018). *Dare to lead: Brave work. Tough conversations. Whole hearts* (iBooks ed.). Random House.

Brown, B. (2021). *Atlas of the heart: Mapping meaningful connection and the language of human experience*. Random House.

Bucura, E. (2020). Rethinking excellence in music education. *Visions of Research in Music Education*, 36, 1–29. www-usr.rider.edu/%7Evrme/v36n1/visions/3607_Bucura.pdf

Bull, A. (2019). *Class, control, and classical music*. Oxford University Press.

Chen, L., Zhou, S., & Bryant, J. (2007). Temporal changes in mood repair through music consumption: Effects of mood, mood salience, and individual differences. *Media Psychology*, 9(3), 695–713. https://doi.org/10.1080/15213260701283293

Conway, C. M., Eros, J., Pellegrino, K., & West, C. (2010). Instrumental music education students' perceptions of tensions experienced during their undergraduate degree. *Journal of Research in Music Education, 58*(3), 260–275. https://doi.org/10.1177/0022429410377114

Dalton, T. A., & Krout, R. E. (2006). The grief song-writing process with bereaved adolescents: An integrated grief model and music therapy protocol. *Music Therapy Perspectives, 24*(2), 94–107.

De Quadros, A., & Amrein, E. (2023). *Empowering song: Music education from the margins.* Routledge.

Demirbatir, E., Bayram, N., & Bilgel, N. (2012). Is the healing force of music far away from the undergraduate music education students? *International Journal of Academic Research in Business and Social Sciences, 2*(1), 341–354.

Dews, C. L. B., & Williams, M. S. (1989). Student musicians' personality styles, stresses, and coping patterns. *Psychology of Music, 17*(1), 37–47. https://doi.org/10.1177/0305735689171004

Dingle, G. A., Sharman, L. S., & Larwood, J. L. (2019). Young people's use of music for emotional immersion. In K. McFerran, P. Derrington, & S. Saarikallio (Eds.), *Handbook of music and adolescence* (pp. 25–38). Oxford University Press.

Eerola, T., Peltola, H.-R., & Vuoskoski, J. K. (2015). Attitudes toward sad music are related to both preferential and contextual strategies. *Psychomusicology, 25*(2), 116–123. https://doi.org/10.1037/pmu0000096

Eerola, T., Vuoskoski, J. K., Peltola, H.-R., Putkinen, V., & Schäfer, K. (2018). An integrative review of the enjoyment of sadness associated with music. *Physics of Life Reviews, 25*, 100–121. https://doi.org/10.1016/j.plrev.2017.11.016

Garrido, S., Eerola, T., & McFerran, K. (2017). Group rumination: Social interactions around music in people with depression. *Frontiers in Psychology, 8*, 1–10. https://doi.org/10.3389/fpsyg.2017.00490

Garrido, S., & Schubert, E. (2013). Adaptive and maladaptive attraction to negative emotion in music. *Musicae Scientiae, 17*(2), 147–166. https://doi.org/10.1177/1029864913478305

Garrido, S., & Schubert, E. (2015). Music and people with tendencies to depression. *Music Perception, 32*(4), 313–321. https://doi.org/10.1525/mp.2015.32.4.313

Give a Note Foundation. (2017). *The status of music education in United States public schools – 2017.* CMA Foundation. www.giveanote.org/media/2017/09/The-Status-of-Music-Education-in-US-Public-Schools-2017_reduced.pdf

Hamann, D. L., Daugherty, E., & Sherbon, J. (1988). Burnout and the college music professor: An investigation of possible indicators of burnout among college music faculty members. *Bulletin of the Council for Research in Music Education, 98*, 1–21.

Hendricks, K. S. (2018). *Compassionate music teaching: A framework for motivation and engagement in the 21st century.* Rowman & Littlefield.

Hess, J. (2019). *Music education for social change: Constructing an activist music education.* Routledge.

Hewitt, M. P., & Thompson, L. K. (2006). A survey of music teacher educators' professional backgrounds, responsibilities and demographics. *Bulletin of the Council for Research in Music Education, 170*, 47–61. www.jstor.org/stable/40319348

Hunter, P. G., Schellenberg, E. G., & Griffith, A. T. (2011). Misery loves company: Mood-congruent emotional responding to music. *Emotion, 11*(5), 1068–1072. https://doi.org/10.1037/a0023749

Kahn, J. H., Ladd, K., Feltner-Williams, D. A., Martin, A. M., & White, B. L. (2022). Regulating sadness: Response-independent and response-dependent benefits of listening to music. *Psychology of Music, 50*(4), 1348–1361. https://doi.org/10.1177/03057356211048545

Kerkova, B. (2020). Perception and experience of musical emotions in schizophrenia. *Psychology of Music, 48*(2), 199–214. https://doi.org/10.1177/0305735618792427

Kohn, A. (1986/1992). *No contest: The case against compeition [Why we lose in our race to win]* (Twentieth-Anniversary ed.). Houghton Mifflin Company.

Kuebel, C. R. (2019). Health and wellness for in-service and future music teachers. *Music Educators Journal, 105*(4), 52–58. https://doi.org/10.1177/0027432119846950

Larwood, J. L., & Dingle, G. A. (2022). The effects of emotionally congruent sad music listening in young adults high in rumination. *Psychology of Music, 50*(1), 218–229. https://doi.org/10.1177/0305735620988793

Lonsdale, A. J. (2019). Emotional intelligence, alexithymia, stress, and people's reasons for listening to music. *Psychology of Music, 47*(5), 680–693. https://doi.org/10.1177/0305735618778126

Maas, A., Wacker, A. T., & Allen, A. D. (2023). The push to 120: Reconciling credit hours in undergraduate music education. *Journal of Music teacher Education, 33*(1), 86–102. https://doi.org/10.1177/10570837231189822

McFerran, K., Garrido, S., & Saarikallio, S. (2013). A critical interpretive synthesis of the relationship between music and adolescent mental health. *Youth and Society, 48*(4), 521–538. https://doi.org/10.1177/0044118X13501343

McFerran, K., & Saarikallio, S. (2014a). Depending on music to feel better: Being conscious of responsibility when appropriating the power of music. *The Arts in Psychotherapy, 41*(1), 89–97. https://doi.org/10.1016/j.aip.2013.11.007

McFerran, K., & Saarikallio, S. (2014b). Depending on music to feel better: Being conscious of responsibility when appropriating the power of music. *The Arts in Psychotherapy, 41*, 89–97. https://doi.org/10.1016/j.aip.2013.11.007

McGrath, C., Hendricks, K. S., & Smith, T. D. (2017). *Performance anxiety strategies: A musician's guide to managing stage fright*. Rowman & Littlefield.

Miranda, D., & Claes, M. (2009). Music listening, coping, peer affiliation and depression in adolescence. *Psychology of Music, 37*(2), 215–233. https://doi.org/10.1177/0305735608097245

Murakami, B. (2021). The music therapy and harm model (MTHM): Conceptualizing harm within music therapy practice. *ECOS – Revista Científica de Musicoterapia y Disciplinas Afines, 6*(1), 1–16. https://doi.org/10.24215/27186199e003

North, A. C., & Hargreaves, D. J. (2012). Pop music subcultures and wellbeing. In R. A. R. MacDonald, G. Kreutz, & L. Mitchell (Eds.), *Music, health, and wellbeing* (pp. 502–512). Oxford University Press.

Payne, P. D., Lewis, W., & McCaskill, F. (2020). Looking within: An investigation of music education majors and mental health. *Journal of Music Teacher Education (JMTE)*, 29(3), 50–61. https://doi.org/10.1177/1057083720927748

Pieslak, J. (2009). *Sound targets: American soldiers and music in the Iraq War.* Indiana University Press.

Powell, S. R. (2021). Competition, ideology, and the one-dimensional music program. *Action, Criticism, & Theory for Music Education*, 20(3), 19–43. https://doi.org/10.22176/act20.3.19

Powell, S. R. (2023). *The ideology of competition in school music.* Oxford University Press.

Rakena, T. O. (2022). The objective is to flourish: Reimagining the one-to-one music teaching studio. In D. Bradley & J. Hess (Eds.), *Trauma and resilience in music education: Haunted melodies* (pp. 186–198). Routledge.

Riley, P. E. (2012). Exploration of student development through songwriting. *Visions of Research in Music Education*, 22, 1–21. www-usr.rider.edu/~vrme/v22n1/visions/Riley_Student_Development_Through_Songwriting.pdf

Saarikallio, S., Gold, C., & McFerran, K. (2015). Development and validation of the Healthy-Unhealthy Music Scale. *Child and Adolescent Mental Health*, 20(4), 210–217. https://doi.org/10.1111/camh.12109

Sachs, M. E., Damasio, A., & Habibi, A. (2015). The pleasures of sad music: A systematic review. *Frontiers in Human Neuroscience*, 9, 1–12. https://doi.org/10.3389/fnhum.2015.00404

Saunders, D. B. (2015). Resisting excellence: Challenging neoliberal ideology in postsecondary education. *Journal for Critical Education Policy Studies*, 13(2), 391–413. www.jceps.com/archives/2653

Silverman, M. J. (2020). Music-based affect regulation and unhealthy music use explain coping strategies in adults with mental health conditions. *Community Mental Health Journal*, 56, 939–946. https://doi.org/10.1007/s10597-020-00560-4

Silverman, M. J. (2021). Music-based emotion regulation and healthy and unhealthy music use predict coping strategies in adults with substance use disorder: A cross-sectional study. *Psychology of Music*, 49(3), 333–350. https://doi.org/10.1177/0305735619854529

Small, C. (1998). *Musicking: The meanings of performing and listening.* Wesleyan University Press, University Press of New England.

Stephenson, H., & Quarrier, N. F. (2005). Anxiety sensitivity and performance anxiety in college music students. *Medical Problems of Performing Artists*, 20(3), 119–125. https://doi.org/10.21091/mppa.2005.3024

Sternbach, D. J. (2008). Stress in the lives of music students. *Music Educators Journal*, 94(3), 42–48. https://doi.org/https://www.jstor.org/stable/4623690

Stoeber, J., & Eismann, U. (2007). Perfectionism in young musicians: Relations with motivation, effort, achievement, and distress. *Personality and Individual Differences*, 43(8), 2183–2192. https://doi.org/10.1016/j.paid.2007.06.036

Taylor, C. L., & Friedman, R. S. (2015). Sad mood and music choice: Does the self-relevance of the mood-eliciting stimulus moderate song preference? *Media Psychology*, 18(1), 24–27. https://doi.org/10.1080/1521326 9.2013.826589 ter Bogt, T., Canale, N., Lenzi, M., Vieno, A., & van den Eijnden, R. (2021). Sad music depresses sad adolescents: A listener's profile. *Psychology of Music, 49*(2), 257–272. https://doi.org/10.1177/0305735619849622

Thoma, M. V., Ryf, S., Mohiyeddini, C., Ehlert, U., & Nater, U. M. (2012). Emotion regulation through listening to music in everyday situations. *Cognition & Emotion, 26*(3), 550–560. https://doi.org/10.1080/02699931.2011.595390

Tucker, O. G. (2020). *"Everybody is good enough": Band teacher agency in a highly competitive environment* [Unpublished doctoral dissertation, University of North Texas]. Denton, TX.

Van Den Tol, A. J. M., & Edwards, J. (2014). Listening to sad music in adverse situations: How music selection strategies relate to self-regulatory goals, listening effects, and mood enhancement. *Psychology of Music, 43*(4), 473–494. https://doi.org/10.1177/0305735613517410

Van der Kolk, B. A., & Van der Hart, O. (1995). The intrusive past: The flexibility of memory and the engraving of trauma. In C. Caruth (Ed.), *Trauma: Explorations in memory* (pp. 158–182). Johns Hopkins University Press.

Wristen, B. G. (2013). Depression and anxiety in university music students. *Update: Applications of Research in Music Education, 31*(2), 20–27. https://doi.org/10.1177/8755123312473613

# 7 How Music (Education) Might Help

*QingYu:* Listening to music has always been at the top of my safety plans. If I was sad or angry, grieving, or dealing with trauma, music was always there for me and I always had the perfect song or playlist to listen to. Music has always helped me heal. I also find that music is a form of deep connection to others for me. If I make a playlist for someone, it means that I really care for you. It's as if sharing music is a love language. I really like making playlists for my friends, especially in times of grief and sadness.

*Chris:* Playing and listening to music is very much part of my daily personal medicine toolkit, whether I'm singing, playing violin, or enjoying my wild and wacky group of tin whistles, pennywhistles, Swanee whistles, flutes, and drums.

Participants identified several musical and social practices that supported their own emotional wellbeing. Community music therapy literature recognizes how music helps across diverse contexts and needs (Ansdell, 2014; Stige et al., 2010), and participants similarly noticed multiple practices that provided help. First, participants described the importance of creating connection—of fostering community, building relationships, and being seen and validated in music education contexts. Most participants also identified various musicking practices as supportive. These included playing or singing, ensemble experiences, jamming, songwriting, and listening strategically. Pedagogical practices also emerged as important—particularly those that supported students across a range of needs and experiences. These music educators pointed to the Universal Design for Learning, fostering student autonomy, trauma-informed praxis, and affirming pedagogies as crucial to an assets-focused music classroom. Finally, participants identified music education spaces as places where music educators might engage experiences of Madness and distress explicitly, and also provide tools for students to process emotions. Participants

DOI: 10.4324/9781032662817-8

identified these social, musical, and pedagogical practices as supportive for their own mental and emotional wellbeing, and that of their students. Music education, when carefully facilitated, may then serve to alleviate distress and soothe Madness.

## Creating Connection: Community, Relationships, and Feeling Seen

Small (1998) argued that musicking is relational. Indeed, musicking makes possible an ideal set of relations: "we bring into existence a set of relationships that model the relationships of our world, not as they are but as we would wish them to be" (p. 50). Many practices participants identified as supportive were described as including a set of ideal relationships and engaging in what I have called a *pedagogy of community* (Hess, 2019). These practices included regular fostering of community through musicking and building relationships, which ultimately resulted in participants feeling seen and validated. While these practices may seem more social than musical, Small (1998) clarified the relational nature of musicking and centered relationships in musicking. Indeed, education and music education require an ethic of care in a relational context (Hendricks, 2018, 2023a, 2023b; Hendricks et al., 2021; Noddings, 2013; O'Brien, 2011).

### *Fostering Community*

Asian American hip-hop artist Taiyo Na identified a "practice of community"—the give-and-take required when musicking in a group (Hess, 2019, p. 44). Musicking provides opportunities to honor different contributions (Lashbrook & Mantie, 2009) and come together in social synchrony (Turino, 2008). Musicking, as inherently relational (Small, 1998), offers profound ways to foster community and bring people together (Hess, 2019).

*Cheryl:* I always loved how playing music with people helped me connect to them. You're a part of something, you're part of a group.

*Chris:* I love acapella singing; that's been really good for my mental health, and is a good way to connect with people. I sing with our local hospice a cappella singing group. I think the practice of playing with any musical group of instrumentalists, finding ways to tune yourself and listen is an art of connection. It's not a verbal art, but it's very much a part of joining in belonging and resonating together, at the time you get together.

Chris talked about the give-and-take of community—the necessity of attunement to others and the way such attunement might lead to feelings of belonging. I defined attunement in Chapter 4 following Erskine (1998) as a "kinesthetic and emotional sensing of others" that offers connectedness, reciprocity, and resonance (p. 236). While I have identified challenges in perspective-taking (Hess, 2021, 2023; Hess & Bradley, 2022),[1] both Cheryl and Chris emphasized attunement with others—what Chris called "the art of connection."

For Emma, music allowed her to connect with others and build relationships.

*Emma:* Sharing music is even more fun. You can really start a conversation through music, and get to know someone. And it's just a great, great way to relax, but then also to bond with people. There's so many purposes for music, mental health-wise. It's great for when you want to be by yourself, but also when you want to be with people.

Milner (2006) observed that music, among other media, allowed youth to establish connections and solidarity with other social groups during high school. Social groups are often formed based on shared musical preferences.

Meena outlined a classroom environment that might help to cultivate community. As a social worker and studio teacher, Meena had experience with Intentional Peer Support (IPS).[2] She suggested fostering a culture of peer support in the classroom to encourage growth and community.

*Meena:* I think when the focus is only on music performance and proficiency, you're really losing the spirit of the person. I feel like encouraging students to really view music making as a way of self-improvement or somehow involving the soul. Not simply the proficiency, the musical skills, but also the person who ultimately is expressing themselves through the music, and encouraging each other to grow as people. ... Generating a dynamic of peer support among students, so that there's really a supportive vibe, like even if somebody is less proficient than another person, they're growing and focusing on nurturing growth, as opposed to competitiveness.

Peer support relies on principles of "respect, shared responsibility, and mutual agreement of what is helpful" (Mead, n.d., p. 1). In peer support, it is culture and relationships that bring forth creation of meaning and perception. Cultivating peer support in the music classroom may facilitate the "supportive vibe" Meena described and offers an alternative to the competitive culture described in Chapter 6. Fostering community could thus occur through group musicking, individual connections, and through nurturing peer support.[3]

*Building Relationships*

Most of these music educators saw musicking and music teaching as ways to build relationships, which occurs individually or within groups and is rooted in shared humanity. Fostering community involves considering what musicking does on an individual and a group level. Blaine noted: "I feel like [music] also helps me relate to students a little bit better. I love that music is an easy way to connect to kids, instead of core subjects." Musicking allowed Blaine to build relationships with their students and nurture human connection. Mary founded the Oakdale Choir[4] in Iowa to provide the opportunity for connection between men incarcerated in the Oakdale Prison and people from the surrounding community.

*Mary:* The whole Oakdale choir is the function of bringing people together to notice our common humanity. ... Then of course, reading Christopher Small and doing my dissertation research, and really delving into what that means to have that experience of music-making to build relationships, to explore, affirm, and celebrate our sense of ideal relationships, and bring that social component alongside the same value as the sonic component.

For Small (1998),

> When we perform, we bring into existence, for the duration of the performance, a set of relationships, between the sounds and between the participants, that model ideal relationships as we imagine them to be and allow us to learn about them by experiencing them.
>
> (p. 218)

Meaning is thus derived relationally. Small (1998) argued that musicking allows people to explore, affirm, and celebrate our concepts of ideal relationships (p. 106). Paulo also looked to the humanity potentially fostered by musicking:

*Paulo:* What if instead of compose, respond, connect, it was all built off of our collective humanity, and using music to be human instead of using music to be excellent? But how do you convince people that it's okay to take that turn—that we'll still have good music?

Paulo cited the U.S. National Core Arts Standards[5]—create, perform, respond, connect—and moved toward a relational approach to musicking that cultivates shared humanity. As Ansdell (2014) reminded readers:

> A participatory perspective is by nature more interested in "good musicking" than in "good music". That is to say, the goodness of a musical event is defined in terms of the quality of the relational experiences of participants and the overall social enhancement achieved.
> (p. 213)

Taking the turn toward participatory musicking does not diminish the musicking in any capacity, and moreover works to center the humanity of all musickers.

### *Feeling Seen and Validated*

Brown (2021) explicated: "I define connection as the energy that exists between people when they feel seen, heard, and valued; when they can give and receive without judgment; and when they derive sustenance and strength from the relationship" (p. 169). Conversely, when someone experiences invisibility, they are not seen, known, and valued. Invisibility is "a function of disconnection and dehumanization, where an individual or group's humanity and relevance are unacknowledged, ignored, and/or diminished in value or importance" (p. 175). Participants identified feeling seen and validated as important for students, from both a student and teacher perspective. Emma noted: "It's not like I wanted anything special. I just wanted my efforts to be acknowledged." Jillian noted:

*Jillian:* [Someone I am close to] has ADHD. And one thing that's very important for him is authentic interest. ...Which is important for anybody. If you just don't have authentic interest, you're not going to do it. And so the biggest thing for me in creating a meaningful musical experience in high school, which was my most meaningful musical experience, there was something for everybody. There was a role everybody needed to play. There was authentic interest the whole time.

Embodying authentic interest in education relationships may allow children and youth to be their full selves in music class. These music educators valued this kind of approach.

*Nicholas:* I make sure every student feels seen. I use their name with intention and I look them in the eye. I make a point to work with proximity so I'm close to them as I facilitate the lesson. I explore how they learn and what they do musically, so I'm really very aware of who each student is, as a musician. Above all, I am their relentless cheerleader.

Knowing what each individual brings to the learning space is crucial to students feeling seen and validated. Nicholas purposefully strove to emphasize such a facilitation process in their teaching. Like Meena, Chris believed a peer support structure may be helpful: "When we're able to see one another and feel nurtured and known; and to grow through peer support, then I think that creates a really different positive and co-creative dynamic." Chris wanted both teachers and students to feel safe to be their authentic selves—even in regard to identities or experiences that felt shameful.

*Chris:* One of the things I just love doing is going into MSW classes, or nursing classes, or classes of medical students, and talking about our personal lived experiences, what's brought them into this profession. Because we have our own lived experience, whether it's our mental health challenges or our families, it's something that's one of your greatest gifts and one of our greatest assets. I encourage the students not to hide it because there's so much shame around it. To me that's the essence of peer support. That is our greatest connector. That can give us the ability to be able to see, to relate, to honor, to acknowledge somebody. The more we try to hide it, the more toxic it gets. I think we should be encouraging social workers, psychiatrists, music educators to see their personal lived experiences of distress, trauma, extreme states as a qualification! Sometimes I say I think people should get paid more for it! Really, it's about finding ways to acknowledge and honor those experiences we bring with us, because I think they provide a powerful tool of connection—wonderful qualities. In my opinion, part of what makes really good music educators or clinicians is the ability to be able to acknowledge that.

Chris felt that vulnerability about identities and experiences served as the "greatest connector" between people. Indeed, participants felt that their neurodivergences helped them build relationships and empathize with others (see Chapter 4). Brown (2021) wrote that vulnerability "is the emotion that we experience during times of uncertainty, risk, and emotional exposure" (p. 13). She argued that vulnerability "is not weakness; it's our greatest measure of courage" (p. 14). Showing up authentically like Chris suggested is a measure of courage that helps people to feel seen and validated, and further inspires the kind of visibility and disclosure discussed in Chapter 5.

Being seen also requires the recognition and honoring of identities.

QingYu: There's a lot of discussion about schools being more inclusive of students' gender identities and which vocal types they want to sing in, like soprano, alto, tenor, bass. ... If I were [a] full-time teacher for my students and I were working in a choral setting, I would absolutely be like, "If you want to sing in this voice range, you can. We are going to call it soprano, alto, tenor, bass, because that's what it's called." But I would never ask my students, "You have to identify this way, and you have to sing in this way."

QingYu identified the importance of allowing youth and adults to sing the voice part that feels congruent with their gender identity. Part of what Chris described as being "nurtured and known" requires respecting and honoring all facets of students' identities.

One of Mary's goals for music education drew together the interwoven elements of fostering community, building relationships, and being seen and validated.

Mary: I think more with improvisation, with songwriting, creative music making, which is really one of my passions in music education is creating spaces for people to express themselves courageously. And in creating a space in the classroom, to teach everybody in the classroom to be hospitable, be honoring each person's ability to express themself courageously.

Expressing oneself courageously requires the kind of community participants described in this chapter's previous section on fostering community. Mary identified such a community as hospitable to individual and collective expression. For Ansdell (2014), musical hospitality "involves the generosity of welcoming in, and then the challenge of entertaining—of coping creatively and respectfully with what can happen next" (p. 205). It embodies principles of "inclusion, participation, equality, generosity, answerability and unconditional acceptance" (p. 206)—important facets of both music therapy and community music. For people to "express themselves courageously," a supportive community must be in place that nurtures peer support, relationships must be established, and participants must feel seen. Taken together, these elements form a strong social and relational foundation for musicking that supports the full range of human experiences.

## Musicking

Musicking itself positively impacted experiences of distress. These music educators identified playing or singing, participation in ensembles, jamming, songwriting, and listening strategically as supportive practices. Musicking can help people navigate our everyday lives (DeNora, 2000) and provide help and solace. As Ansdell (2014) noted:

> Music helps in many ways. It seldom just soothes: it also enlivens and motivates; calls forth emotions and movements; joins people together, but also sometimes gives them a haven away from others, or helps them transcend both their situation and themselves.
>
> (p. xii)

Musicking in these different capacities provided means through which participants could address and soothe their distress.

### *Playing and Singing*

Playing and singing proved supportive in several ways. Blaine observed: "Playing music, playing French horn just helps. ... There's just something that it makes things better for the time that I'm playing. So anytime that I get to play French horn is just a good time." Blaine's primary instrument felt supportive to them and helped bolster their mood when they took time to play.

*Cheryl:* Sometimes playing music is a nice thing to do. Especially when I was younger, it really helped me when I wasn't feeling well or something had happened. I would just go sit at the piano and play and everything felt better in that moment, basically. So that's a really beautiful experience and probably a part of why I wanted to keep working—making music my profession in this way.

Musicking offers a powerful mechanism to explore emotions (Campbell et al., 2007; Davis, 2007; DeNora, 2000; Lundqvist et al., 2009; Meyer, 1956; North et al., 2000) and also potentially offers emotional support to process grief and trauma (Bradley, 2012, 2020, 2022; Bradley & Hess, 2022; DeNora, 2013; Hill, 2009; Kinney, 2012; Rhodes & Schechter, 2014).

*Nicholas:* Playing Trad[6] music is what really makes me feel better. It has some extra emotional components. I usually play the recorder for Trad music. So if I'm like, "Oh, what do I do? I feel bored," that is a sign that I need support. Sometimes people are busy, or I just don't want to talk to that person in particular. What can I do? If I'm stuck at home by myself … I'll get out the recorder. I have a nice collection of books and music. I'll try to play some tunes, which is funny because more of the songs are fast, because I almost exclusively play dance music. There's lots of recordings of things. So I'll try to play it as fast as the recording. I'm actually a whole different musician in this genre. As a result of playing Trad music, I've learned to let go. I don't suffer from the same performance anxiety that I would with bassoon playing a difficult passage. Before, it would be like a black-and-white thing. I played it right or played it wrong. And now while playing Trad I'm like, "Oh no, I got 60% of it right that time. Alright, I got these two extra notes that time, or I got all four notes in this 16th note figure or whatever." It got me out of my own head, and toward feeling that feeling of success. The pride in achievement can actually get inside me now. It is what supports me when I'm feeling bad, or I'm feeling fine. It'll augment me either way!

Nicholas described an approach to musicking that moved away from the perfectionist mindset often pervasive in Western classical music (see for example Stoeber & Eismann, 2007). Participants identified perfectionism as a harmful practice in music education (see Chapter 6). Not only did playing Trad music make Nicholas feel better, it also allowed them to let go of perfectionism and instead experience joyful musicking.

For August, musicking allowed them to keep pace with their thinking and express their ideas more effectively and consistently.

*August:* It's a lot easier for me to talk with music than it is for me to talk with words. Of course that doesn't always happen. Sometimes you go to do a performance and you just play the stuff that's on the page the best you can and notes happen and you call it good, but like I feel much more eloquent playing music than I do talking. I do have my moments of feeling eloquent with words. I also have non-verbal periods and a whole range of experiences of verbal communication that fall somewhere in between. I think my experience of language is part of what having a positive experience with music stems from. I always feel like I very rarely have moments where I can just spit out all the words fast enough to keep up with my thoughts and feelings. When I'm playing music, I can keep pace between what I'm saying and what I'm externalizing much better, as opposed to my brain running 20 miles ahead of my mouth and not being able to say 10 different things in counterpoint with each other at the same time.

Musicking allows musickers to communicate ideas and express emotions (Berger, 2000; Cross, 2014; Davis, 2007; Hess, 2019; Lundqvist et al., 2009) and also offers a vehicle for self-expression (Baker, 2015; Hess, 2019). August was able to harness musicking toward expression.

*Ensembles*

Almost two-thirds of participants found ensemble experiences supportive to their mental health.

*Jillian:* One experience that weirdly still sticks out to me is conducting my first marching band show when I was 16 or something. I was like, "Oh, yeah, this is fun. I'm doing this." ... I was a drum major for two years in high school. That whole experience was extremely transformative for me. We drafted a leadership book for the program and completely blew up the meetings. ... We had student-led meetings and student-run leadership. And it was very musical. I think music mostly facilitates more important experiences. So the experience, yes, was the music. Music was very powerful and moving, but it's also everything that led up to that.

Jillian's analysis of their marching band experience encapsulates Small's (1998) definition of musicking. For Small, "[t]o music is to take part, in any capacity in a musical performance, whether by performing, by listening, by rehearsing or practicing, by providing material for performance (what is called composition), or by dancing" (p. 9). In other words, anything that contributes to a musical experience is part of musicking. For Jillian, participating in marching band offered them more than simply the musical component. The leadership opportunities and student direction made the experience significant. Many participants described such experiences.

*Jamming*

Participants also found jamming—informal musicking practices in collaboration with others—to be supportive of their mental health.

*Paulo:* I had jam band that met for 6 to 8 hours a week to play, so that was a quite a large amount of my way of processing stuff. It was only when I didn't have that that things became substantially harder.

As noted, musicking may provide a mechanism to explore, express, and process emotions, and jamming filled that function for Paulo. Rebecca similarly enjoyed more informal musicking opportunities: "I play keys with a rock band at church. I've had a couple of really good, really powerful musical experiences there. That feeling of flow." Elliott and Silverman (2015) took up Csikszentmihalyi's (1990) concept of flow in the context of musicking.[7] For Elliott and Silverman, an experience of flow—where a person is utterly absorbed in their musicking to the point where they might lose track of time—occurs when the musical challenge matches the level of musicianship. When the musical challenge is greater than the level of musicianship, frustration may ensue; conversely, when the level of musicianship far exceeds the musical challenge, a person may become bored. People might find themselves in a flow state when the challenge and musicianship align, and Rebecca had such experiences in her church band. The absorption of a flow experience may allow a person to temporarily put aside feelings of distress.

Mary found her experiences with the organization Music for People[8] to be freeing from the restrictions of her classical music training. Music for People facilitated free improvisation events, and Mary attended her first event during university study.

*Mary:* They believe this idea that there are no wrong notes and have a beautiful Bill of Musical Rights that you can find on their website about how every music should be celebrated. And everyone should have the opportunity to be a musician. So many of those ideas align with Small's concepts of musicking. Anyway, went out to that first one, I was like, "Oh my god, this is heaven." Because I grew up paper-trained, there are right ways or wrong ways to play music.

She went on to describe an event called *Listeners' Choice* where attendees join together in trios or quartets and listen carefully to each other in order to respond musically. Mary remembered having to be "completely in the moment responding immediately to the sounds in your ensemble." Participating in Music for People events allowed Mary to move away from "paper training" toward a liberating experience where there were "no wrong notes" and people listened attentively and responded collaboratively to others.

Jillian described an experience they had during substitute teaching that perhaps brings insight to jamming in school contexts.

*Jillian:* [Students] were making a beat and rapping. And we were doing that as a class, we were freestyling and trying to make a beat together. That was really fun. They all got to create, but we were still doing things at the same time. But you didn't have to participate for it to work. You could just listen, you could participate, you could rap, you can do a number of things. I don't see why we don't include more examples like that either on instruments or off. I don't think instruments are that important, but whatever, people seem to like them.

Jillian wanted such activities to be a regular part of school practice and valued listening alongside performing, freestyling, and rapping. Opportunities for informal musicking[9] may facilitate processing emotions as Paulo suggested above, flow experiences as Rebecca described, and relief from the more perfectionist mindset of right and wrong notes and sheet music as evident in Mary's and Jillian's comments. Such activities also make room for students to bring their lived experiences into school musicking, making musicking an important vehicle for expression (see Hess, 2019).

*Songwriting*

These music educators also identified songwriting as a helpful practice. Songwriting potentially offers a vehicle for storytelling and sharing experiences (Baker, 2015; Baker et al., 2008; DeNora, 2000; Hess, 2018, 2019; Williams, 2012), as well as expressing and processing them (Hess, 2019). It further offers an opportunity to shift from director-centered musicking to student-centered and -led experiences (see for example Green, 2008). August observed: "Writing music has been a lot better for me than the kind of traditional, learn this piece by Bach, practicing sort of thing." In a focus group, Rebecca described student responses to her songwriting course, which opened a fruitful dialogue.

*Rebecca:* I teach a [songwriting][10] class that used to be an improvising and composing class. The rest of our program is quite ensemble-focused in terms of the pedagogies that students get to experience. And again and again, the comment that comes up on the course evaluations is, "this is the only time I wasn't told that I was wrong."
*Mary:* When they took your class?

*Rebecca:* "It was so great to be in a class where I wasn't told I was wrong."

*Mary:* So in other words, percentage-wise, 80 to 90% of the students experiences they're being told, "my way or the highway." This narrow way of expressing yourself musically. Then in the 10 to 20% experience of being in your class, that was the opposite. So that's what music education is doing wrong. We need to flip that or at least get it more 50/50. I think it's a human rights issue that if we are not allowing our students to express themselves courageously. We're just squelching their humanity.

Mary pointed out the distinction between a didactic and director-centered approach to musicking, and the kind of experience students had in Rebecca's class where they could "express themselves courageously." Both teacher educators found these experiences valuable, as they provided a vehicle for students to share their experiences and tell stories. Songwriting facilitates the expression of emotions and experiences, as well as opportunities to move away from the perfectionist mindset and director-centered orientation of Western classical music traditions in music education praxis (see Chapter 6).

*Listening Strategically*

Participants described music listening as a practice that supported their emotional wellbeing. Indeed, listening to music may serve multiple functions. In 2012, Saarikallio (2012) developed and validated a scale to describe the role of music in mood self-regulation with seven subscales:

- Entertainment: Creating nice atmosphere and happy feeling to maintain or enhance current positive mood;
- Revival: Personal renewal, relaxing, and getting new energy from music when stressed or tired;
- Strong sensation: Inducing and strengthening intense emotional experiences;
- Diversion: Forgetting unwanted thoughts and feelings with the help of pleasant music;
- Discharge: Release of negative emotions through music that expresses these emotions;
- Mental work: Using music as a framework for mental contemplation and clarification of emotional preoccupations;
- Solace: Searching for comfort, acceptance, and understanding when feeling sad and troubled. (Saarikallio, 2012, pp. 97–98)

Her work explains ways in which individuals use music in multiple ways that help them regulate mood. Saarikallio's subscales are useful in considering the function of music listening.

In music therapy, researchers notice that music listening helps in several ways. Music can increase positive moods (Lonsdale & North, 2011), improve depressive states, and help to manage negative moods (Lonsdale & North, 2011; Thayer et al., 1994). Kahn et al. (2022) observed that music was their sample group's number-one choice for regulating sadness. Music may also serve as consolation (ter Bogt et al., 2017). Garrido et al. (2015) affirmed that benefits of musical activities include "mood improvement, self expression, catharsis, facilitating grieving, relaxation, reflection, socialization, community building, stress reduction, and more" (p. 2). Engaging in musicking may also facilitate relationship-building and social connection (Lonsdale & North, 2011; McFerran & Saarikallio, 2014; Papinczak et al., 2015; Schäfer et al., 2013). Kahn et al. (2022) observed that listening to music offers interpersonal benefits:

> Listening to music did not provide any less of a shared experience than talking to a friend or asking someone for advice. These findings suggest that listening to music shares much in common with interpersonal emotion-regulation strategies such as talking with other people when sad.
>
> (p. 1348)

Moreover, they argued that people may feel as accepted and understood by listening to music as they feel after talking with a friend (p. 1349).

Predictably, listening to music can also offer enjoyment (Lonsdale & North, 2011). It may additionally help individuals achieve self-awareness (Schäfer et al., 2013) or clarify one's feelings (Kahn et al., 2022). Music also potentially provides an opportunity to reminisce about the past or engage in feelings of nostalgia (Eerola et al., 2018; Lonsdale, 2019; Lonsdale & North, 2011; Vuoskoski et al., 2012), and provides a conduit through which individuals can experience their emotions more fully (Lyvers et al., 2020). Music listening can present a strategic diversion from negative experiences (Lonsdale & North, 2011), and assist listeners in managing stress and promoting wellbeing (Silverman, 2021).

A significant number of researchers have observed how individuals engage in music listening to self-regulate their mood (Allen et al., 2009; Baltazar & Saarikallio, 2016; Chang et al., 2020; Cook et al., 2019; Dingle & Fay, 2017; Dingle et al., 2016; Groarke & Hogan, 2018; Kahn et al., 2022; Larwood & Dingle, 2022; Lonsdale, 2019; Lonsdale & North, 2011; Papinczak et al., 2015; Schäfer et al., 2013; Silverman, 2021; ter Bogt et al., 2017; Thayer et al., 1994; Thoma et al., 2012; Van Den Tol

& Edwards, 2014; Vuoskoski et al., 2012; Zoteyeva et al., 2015). Self-regulation might include positive mood management (e.g. brightening the day) (Lonsdale, 2019) and negative mood management (e.g. improving one's mood) (Lonsdale, 2019; Lyvers et al., 2020).

Participants identified listening as a practice that supported them. They advocated, however, for strategic listening to promote positive emotional effects. Cheryl found solace in music listening (Saarikallio, 2012).

*Cheryl:* I find a lot of comfort in listening to music. As opposed to playing music. I have a lot of internalized, I don't know if it's perfectionism or insecurities. But I listen to music a lot, and … that's a huge support.

Emma tactically avoided songs that she listened to during a terrible year of high school when she experienced depression and profound isolation.

*Emma:* I like listening too. … Like when I'm feeling in a depressive phase. I have a depression playlist. Help get that out. But I avoid specific songs because some songs are triggers. Then I have a whole other playlist that's devoted to another mood.
*Juliet:* Some songs are triggers because they're too dark, or…?
*Emma:* Because I listened to them in my high school year when I started to listen to some specific songs more than I should.
*Juliet:* It brings you back?
*Emma:* I just avoid those because they're a little bit too close to…

She was drawn to songs that helped her "get that out" when she was in a depressive state—Saarikallio's (2012) "discharge" function. QingYu drew on music for both discharge and solace.

*QingYu:* I could definitely say if I am sad, sometimes I do listen to more sad music so I can actually feel my sadness, to let myself feel feelings. I can say that's not a bad thing, because sometimes it's important to let us feel our emotions. Because sometimes you shouldn't invalidate your feelings, which is something I'm definitely learning. That our feelings are very valid. … allowing myself to feel my feelings. So if I'm very sad, I will listen to sad music. If I'm angry, I'll listen to angry music. … I will use music to allow myself to validate my own feelings, and then soothe my own feelings.

Using music listening to validate and then process and soothe feelings points to music listening as a vehicle to address challenging emotions.

While much of the music therapy literature uses words like "adaptive" and "maladaptive" or "healthy" and "unhealthy" (Alluri et al., 2022; Garrido & Schubert, 2013; Miranda et al., 2012; Silverman, 2020, 2021) to describe listening practices and preferences, these music educators use much more nuance regarding their engagement with music that aligns with Saarikallio's (2012) scale in ways that may have both personal and classroom relevance.

This full range of musicking practices—playing and singing, ensemble experiences, jamming, songwriting, and listening strategically—all supported participants' emotional wellbeing and, to some extent, helped to alleviate distress. Importantly, what might serve one person may not serve another. Multiple participants, however, found these practices supportive, which the literature also bolsters. In Chapter 6, participants noted that high-stakes musicking and evaluations caused or exacerbated distress. The musicking experiences they described in this chapter notably do not include any high-stakes elements, instead emphasizing relational and intrapersonal aspects of musicking.

**Supporting Students with a Range of Needs**

Participants overwhelmingly wanted to construct a music education that supports students across the full spectrum of needs. This pedagogical move included different approaches to pedagogy such as the Universal Design for Learning, fostering student autonomy, trauma-informed praxis, and affirming pedagogies. As people who identified as having mental health differences, participants were interested in a variety of ways to honor students' identities, lived experiences, and perspectives. Chris described the importance of honoring a range of learning modalities in music education.

*Chris:* I think it's really vitally important that music education needs to include that kind of breadth of catering to different learning styles including how we respond and interact with music. And I know so many people who had their passion for music snuffed, because they didn't have a very accurate sense of pitch, or they couldn't recreate it vocally. Nonetheless, they were very good musicians, had a wonderful rhythmic sense. Some are folks with that auditory gift that means that they're possibly never going to read music because their ear is so good they don't need to. Many of these folks were crushed by somebody who had a very narrow sense of what makes a good musician. I think a good music education needs to broaden people's perspective and acknowledge all these different learning, processing, playing, and performing styles.

She further clarified that enacting this type of music education requires educator self-knowledge.

*Chris:* You as an educator need to know your zone: what sort of students do you teach really well? What sort of music do you teach really well? Can you teach students to listen, and to improvise, and chordal basis and harmony and that sort of thing, or are you are you an educator who was going to teach technique and music reading? How can you refer students to places where they're going to be nurtured and encouraged, rather than the kind of the shame base? Because if there's one thing that is toxic, it's the shame that I'm sure all of us who have had music as a part of our career know. Particularly if we've orbited in classical music realms, it's like this giant elephant. Some people can dance with that elephant, and other people it just crushes.

Attending to the full range of students' learning modalities potentially enables educators to move away from shaming practices that so readily occur in Western classical music training (see Chapter 6). Several participants noted that they had experienced such shame and found it troubled their emotional state. As such, attending to a range of needs is important when making pedagogical decisions.

*The Universal Design for Learning*

Several participants identified the Universal Design for Learning (UDL) as a possible pedagogical approach that helps music educators support a range of students' learning modalities, communication styles, and interests. UDL emerged from Universal Design in architecture—an approach that aims to make public spaces accessible—and promotes practices such as curb cuts. Significantly, while curb cuts were intended to provide access for wheelchair users, they additionally support people with strollers, shopping carts, suitcases or bags on wheels, and others. A design adjustment thus serves a rather large segment of the population (Guffey & Williamson, 2020; Williamson, 2019). UDL functions similarly in education. It requires teachers to plan their lessons with allowances for robust access to material. The underlying premises encourage teachers to represent knowledge in a variety of ways and to provide multiple paths to student engagement with that knowledge. It subsequently facilitates students' expression and communication of their comprehension in multiple ways, ideally the ways in which they feel best equipped (Glass et al., 2013; Rose & Meyer, 2006).[11]

Participants either named UDL explicitly or advocated for practices that align with its main ideas.

*Nicholas:* The goal is that more people are able to communicate in their mode, whatever mode that might be. There's some people who have to verbally process, and who shine in the discussion and question space. But there's also students who never want to talk to the teacher, and they only want to talk to their friends or peers. The turn-and-talk is good for that group. The verbalized learning from them is what I overhear them saying to their friend, or what their friend shares out. And maybe they're just somebody who doesn't want to be told when to communicate, and I can come up to them during group time. I can just ask casually, "Hey, what are you doing? What's your progress? How much more time do you need?" Then that's the way they'll communicate. I continue to seek ways to communicate so that I can connect verbally and otherwise with the students so there's the opportunity to celebrate a lot of different communication styles in my classroom. If I can make space for as many communication styles as possible, I feel like each person can feel supported, and like they're part of the music education classroom space.

Nicholas facilitated a diverse range of communication options for students, as UDL provides ways for students to draw on their strengths across learning, expression, and engagement.

While Chris did not explicitly mention UDL, her ideas for classroom pedagogy align with its principles.

*Chris:* What is it that's helped and encouraged and nurtured you? And what have other people tried? Let's not see that label or that diagnosis as a disability, let's see it as a superpower as well. [Let's] think about how we support one another rather than how we put people in boxes. Accommodations are great, and I'm very much in support of accommodations. However, they also remind people that they have a deficit and that they're somehow different—that they need special help. Ideally, that could be broadened and generalized to everybody, particularly in music education.

Theoretically, UDL makes accommodations unnecessary. Rather than making an individual accommodation, with UDL, teachers make that accommodation available to all students. In doing so, pedagogy becomes broadly accessible to all. For example, if a student prefers to express themself verbally rather than through writing, instead of making a communication accommodation solely for that student, verbal expression becomes an option for all students. That eliminates Chris' worry about accommodations making a person feel that they have a deficit and instead "broadens and generalizes" possibilities for representation, expression, and engagement, as she suggested.

Jillian specifically named UDL as useful and also identified some unlearning that might be necessary when employing this pedagogical approach.

*Jillian:* That's something I really like about UDL is the more you look at UDL you're just like, "yeah, just don't be a dick." Pretty much. It's just like, "Be nice, and stop assuming everybody acts like you." That's literally what it is. Then it turns out you catch yourself having these thoughts that have just been programmed in your brain like: "Kid does thing that stands out, I think, 'Wow, weird kid.'" That's something that needs to change. You have to recognize it first. So it's just catching yourself in those patterns and knowing that behavior is on a spectrum. It doesn't exist one way. We will see it in plenty of ways. And if you act different, that's okay. Let me know so I know how to support you best. But this is about you, not about my classroom. It should be about the students.

Here Jillian highlighted the necessity for teachers to recognize that students may think, learn, and express themselves in ways that are distinct from the teacher. UDL requires honoring these differences and making room for them in pedagogy. Jillian further recognized that we all hold biases that privilege our own ways of knowing and doing things and that unlearning these biases is important to supporting all students in the classroom. UDL offers a path for this approach, alongside the educator practice of critical reflection.

*Student Autonomy*

Most of these music educators also identified student choice as important to students' wellbeing.

*Lizabeth:* The first thing I'm thinking of is giving students more autonomy, not just like within guidelines, but just over their own learning in general. Because you don't know unless you ask. You don't know what your students are interested in or what's going to spark their musical interest unless you ask and maybe give them that autonomy.

Lizabeth's suggestion about student autonomy aligns well with UDL, which facilitates student control over how they encounter information, express their learning, and engage with classroom pedagogy. They also spoke to the importance of getting to know students' interests and affinities. Congruently, Chris offered that students might conduct a self-inventory.

*Chris:* I think a very powerful tool is allowing for students to do a self-inventory. To just reflect on what makes my heart sing. What do I love? What do I want to do? What do I do over and over again if I'm feeling sad or tired? What is it that I automatically go to? What is my learning modality and what's the kind of music I like to listen to? So many of us just don't get the chance to do that. We just amble along and try and fit into whatever happens to be in front of us at the time.

This type of self-reflective practice creates an opportunity for students to consider what brings them joy and what supports their wellbeing. The insights generated have great potential to inform student autonomy, as self-knowledge increases.

Drawing on her experience as a social worker and peer support worker, Meena suggested that person-centered planning may be useful in music teachers' consideration of student autonomy. Person-centered planning promotes individuals' articulation of their own goals for themselves. Meena mused about a balance wherein the teacher offers assignments based on knowledge of student's interests, while also encouraging skill development in alignment with student-articulated desires for growth. She argued that by using music that students enjoy while focusing on their current interests in skill development, the speed of progress may increase. Meena felt this approach to teaching would foster independence in students.

Beyond student choice, conducting a self-inventory, or prioritizing student-directed goal-setting, several participants also mentioned the importance of being able to rest in relation to student autonomy.

*Meghan:* I think one thing is encouraging myself to take breaks. This is music specifically. Being classically trained musicians, we constantly are telling ourselves work, work, work, practice, practice, practice. If you have free time, you need to be in a practice room. And that is hard on your mental health. Because then you're sitting in a practice room for eight hours a day and your mouth is gonna stop working, your fingers are gonna lock up and you're gonna be telling yourself it's because you're not good enough. The reality is, you are just pushing your body past its limits.

Meghan recognized some of the challenges attending music school involves, including the physical and mental fatigue that can result from constant musicking, as well as the extreme demands placed on undergraduate music students and the stress that results (Conway et al., 2010). Music educators do not always honor the limits of individual students, requiring students to monitor their stress and fatigue for themselves. Meghan deliberately chose to rest when needed to support her wellbeing. Participants expressed that having at least some degree of autonomy over one's education through a self-inventory, goal-setting, and choices about taking breaks or resting bolstered their wellbeing.

*Trauma-Informed Praxis*

These music educators also advocated for a trauma-informed approach to music education to support children and youth experiencing emotional distress rooted in trauma.

*Lizabeth:* Music can be healing, but harm can be caused through any medium, including music, and it's important for teachers to remember that. Trauma-informed pedagogy would support teachers who want to ensure they are not further harming or traumatizing students.

While I discussed some harms music can cause in Chapter 6, Lizabeth saw trauma-informed pedagogy as a specific approach through which teachers can support students who have experienced trauma. Trauma-informed pedagogy enables teachers to recognize that some student behaviors may actually be trauma responses, and respond accordingly (Hess, 2022). Caruth (1996) described trauma as "an overwhelming experience of sudden or catastrophic events in which the response to the event occurs in the often delayed, uncontrolled repetitive appearance of hallucinations and other intrusive phenomena" (p. 11). Importantly, the trauma is rooted in the event, but long-lasting effects of trauma lie in a person's response. Two people, for example, may be in the same car accident, but experience the event entirely differently. One person may be left to deal with the "intrusive phenomena" Caruth identified while the other person is able to leave the event behind without residual effects.

Nicholas had an opportunity to take an intensive training on trauma-informed teaching practice, which cultivated new understandings.

*Nicholas:* I thought to myself, "I'm now realizing that an external event can traumatize somebody, can trigger old trauma, traumatize someone the first time, but also, they can become triggered internally. And it might not have anything to do with what the external environment is. Once I realized that, I was like, "Oh, this can come out of nowhere." Now I understand that it's not out of nowhere, but it felt like out of nowhere before. Now I'm like, "Oh, students could be trauma triggered by breathing in a smell. They can see a color or design on someone's T-shirt." They get a bad surprise that seems trivial on the surface. They become hungry and they didn't expect to be hungry. Really, really small stuff. Somebody's body language or facial expression reminds them of something. We're failing to address mental health issues on a trauma level (and in other ways, too). If people implemented trauma-informed practice in music class, I would have been much more supported. Especially in high school.

Nicholas pointed to the wide range of possibilities that students might find triggering. Trauma responses may lead students to resist instruction, appear defensive, defiant, or withdrawn, or potentially experience anxiety or depression. They may not enjoy things they typically enjoyed in the past or be able to express their feelings (Hess, 2022, p. 20). Many participants identified personal trauma histories. They further acknowledged how trauma may influence a person's sense of wellbeing, and that obligates educators to utilize an approach that recognizes the potential for trauma across different situations, as well as the diversity of possible trauma responses and triggers. Trauma-informed pedagogy centers such recognitions.

*Cultivating Affirming Pedagogies*

At their core, culturally relevant pedagogy (Ladson-Billings, 1995, 2009, 2014), culturally responsive teaching (Gay, 2018; McKoy & Lind, 2023), and culturally sustaining pedagogy (Paris & Alim, 2014, 2017) are all affirming pedagogies. They affirm and celebrate the diversity students bring to the classroom with a focus on culture and race. Like UDL and trauma-informed pedagogy, culturally affirming teaching allows teachers to consider multiple facets of student identity. Nicholas wanted teachers to honor the full range of student identities, including culture, disability, and LGBTQ+ identities.

*Nicholas:* The people whose work I'm interested in see and understand how we can make the experience more humanistic within the lessons for whatever time we are directly teaching before students go and do activities. Some questions I ask myself regarding other people's work are: "Is it culturally responsive? What is a good way to reach students with disabilities? How is it differentiated?" I have my own differentiations with communication. So, if someone's work isn't differentiated on multiple levels like that, I don't feel seen by it and I'm concerned that students (both youth and adult) won't feel seen by it, either. I personally feel like I'm going to feel ignored or erased in the learning space. The queer and transgender erasure is a part of that, too. I've been afraid to show up as queer and trans in general music education workshop spaces. It seems okay to be a gay guy. All the cisgender heterosexual women who seem to be the dominant voice in those spaces love that. That stereotype is allowed, but only their lens. There's no space for other queerness. So, I figure if somebody is working to address the needs of all students, there's a chance that queerness could get addressed, too.

Nicholas insisted on pedagogy that is affirming across the full range of identities and notes the importance of this recognition for both students and educators. Affirming pedagogies must then affirm culture, race, disability, sexual and gender identities, religion, and trauma histories, as they intersect with the full range of different spectrums of identity.

Participants recognized the importance of attending to the full range of student needs and identities and drew on several pedagogical approaches to do so. These approaches also contributed to music educators' efforts to foster community, build relationships, and have students and teachers feel seen and cared for. When educators attend to students' needs and their full spectrums of identities through affirming pedagogies, children and youth are likely to feel seen as a result. Practicing affirmation of students' needs and identities in this way makes room for the affirmation of educators as well. Watts-Taffe (2022) conducted a self-study with the goal of supporting herself and her students in feeling seen and known, as well as "sitting in relationship with challenging ideas without needing to judge, fix, or dispel them" (p. 41) in the context of culturally relevant pedagogy. Affirming pedagogies not only affirm both teacher and student but also aid in grappling with difficult content including discussions of identities and emotional distress.

## An Explicit Focus on Wellbeing

Given the diverse ways that musicking can support wellbeing, participants argued that music education may constitute an appropriate place to explicitly focus on and directly discuss mental health, while also potentially offering a place to process emotions. Both of these practices center wellbeing in music education.

### A Place to Discuss Mental Health

Participants believed that music education provides an important context for direct discussion of mental health and wellbeing. Cheryl felt that music education might "be a way to talk about taking care of yourself and being present." They pointed to music's connection to society and thus its role as a potential vehicle for conversation about mental health or performance anxiety, though also offered an important caveat.

*Cheryl:* I think teachers need to have an awareness of how they talk about mental health issues—being careful not to reinscribe negative stereotypes about mental health struggles and illnesses, find ways to provide a safe environment to openly discuss mental health, be willing to accommodate students' individual needs, and make sure to equip themselves with knowledge about reliable resources to refer their students to.

While discussing mental health openly becomes important to teacher and student wellbeing in this pedagogical model, teachers must ensure that doing so does not reinscribe unhelpful stereotypes.

*Paulo:* As a profession, I think we're very behind the times in treating our art like a lived art, rather than like a museum art. I think if we could address what we do as a living thing, then ... I actually think this is one of those times when we would inherently start talking more about mental health and disability. If you could treat it as a living thing.

When considering where mental health and disability might be addressed in collegiate music study, Paulo wondered whether a class on supporting mental health might be useful, since, in his view, classes on disability have not filled that need. In his own teaching praxis, Paulo was explicit about his own experience and readily communicated that "we all have these kinds of differences." Making time for caring conversations about emotional wellbeing and providing support to alleviate student distress were consistent aspects of Paulo's teaching. His approach modeled what might be possible at the individual level, though I argue that a systemic tactic needs to accompany individual care so both the collective and each student are supported.

Meena has written several pedagogical articles for a music magazine examining topics of emotional support for distress in the string studio teaching context. In an upcoming commissioned piece, Meena planned to address how teachers can engage students who are depressed or feeling suicidal in conversation, following an Alternatives to Suicide training she attended in Massachusetts. Participants argued that explicit conversation about mental health and wellbeing should occur at all levels of music education.

*Processing Emotions*

Most participants found musicking to be a powerful way to process emotions—a possibility the literature supports (see for example Ansdell, 2014; DeNora, 2000; Kennedy-Moore & Watson, 2001; Silverman, 2021).

*Jillian:* I think because music is inherently emotional, it's definitely one of the more open contexts for things like mental health, especially as so many musicians use it as a coping mechanism. Everybody's pretty ill. What I found, a lot of people are pretty messed up about one thing or the other, and music is the way that we connect with each other and try to get through it.

Jillian wove together the idea of processing emotion with the earlier discussion of connection. For Jillian, emotional responses to music potentially serve to connect us with others.

In a focus group, Chris identified the potential catharsis of musicking as a means of expression.

*Chris:* I think one of the things that a lot of music education does get right, is it does give that voice that is a mode of expression. For example, Meena, you're talking about times when you just cry. Perhaps that was your portal to letting out what was in there. There's many ways of interpreting what that might have meant for you and only you can translate that. But for many of us, this is a really important voice. It's a language that just will not be silenced.

Music as a way to "let out what was in there" positions musicking as a powerful conduit for expression and release, what Saarikallio (2012) called "discharge."

*Emma:* Music is where I like to express my emotions, particularly. I love singing a sad song, I do not like singing happy songs. Whatever I have to sing with my voice teacher, I'm like, "Oh, this is too happy. I don't know how to do a happy song." Because the sad songs are where I really feel it and I get into the mood. Music has been a great avenue for me, especially when I'm not feeling so good. I'm singing a sad song to release that emotion in a way that's healthy. And singing a song that I really like. It really has helped a lot.

Emma also drew on musicking for discharge. Jillian, Chris, and Emma all identified musicking as a means to process emotions as well as a vehicle for expression, and a potential source of connection with others.

Meena also viewed musicking as a way to release grief and cope with high levels of stress.

*Meena:* I play music for managing stress and grief. The vibrations are very soothing. Also, it helps me process thoughts. If I feel mentally stuck with challenges or tasks, or I feel a sense of powerlessness, playing music helps me think more clearly, my mind organizes itself, and solutions to problems will spontaneously come to me.

She noted that she practiced most when she was busy, stressed, and exhausted, as it provided solace and discharge (Saarikallio, 2012). Laura likewise found that playing the clarinet in undergrad helped her through "some tough times because I could kind of work on my feelings to what I was playing." She considered how music education might support emotional wellbeing.

*Laura:* Maybe just someone [an educator could] talk about emotions and how we can exude our emotions through playing or singing. Because I was just kind of doing that for myself, not knowing how helpful that could be. But no one really came to me and told me, you know, "Hey, when you're having a tough time, these things are here for you."

Here Laura wove together the potential of musicking to help process emotions and discharge them (Saarikallio, 2012), and the need for music educators to explicitly discuss emotional wellbeing and offer strategies to support students' alleviation of distress.

## Conclusion and Implications

In this chapter, I drew on participants' ideas about how musicking might support emotional wellbeing. They revealed the importance of connection with others through fostering community, building relationships, and ensuring that students and teachers felt seen and cared for. Musicking also assisted with wellbeing. Playing, singing, ensemble participation, opportunities for jamming and songwriting, as well as listening strategically also served to support participants. Additionally, these music educators identified pedagogical strategies and approaches that may be helpful to wellbeing under the overarching idea of supporting the full range of students' needs and identities; these included the Universal Design for Learning (UDL), fostering student autonomy, trauma-informed praxis, and affirming pedagogies. Finally, participants believed that mental health and emotional wellbeing should be discussed explicitly in music education and that musicking also meaningfully helps people process their emotions. At the beginning of the chapter, QingYu and Chris described music as part of their "safety plan" and "daily personal medicine kit," respectively. These ideas resonated as participants described the ways musicking supported their wellbeing, alongside other social and pedagogical possibilities. Importantly, as noted in the introduction, music educators are not music therapists. The ideas explored in this chapter all firmly fall under the purview of music education.

Participants' insights described in this chapter have implications for educators, administrators, and policymakers. In the music classroom, music educators can purposefully foster the relational and communal, centering connection in our teaching. Participants also promoted the importance of student autonomy, which included conducting self-inventories to gauge personal needs, strengths, and interests in music learning. Moreover, educators can choose pedagogical approaches that facilitate access and affirm identities for all students. Participants identified the music classroom as a place to have explicit discussion about emotional wellbeing and to process emotions through musicking. Music educators can thus purposefully center such discussions and opportunities in classrooms. To facilitate such discussions and practices ethically, music educators require focused and expert professional development and administrative and community support. In the current climate of divisive concept laws in the U.S. that attempt to restrict teaching related to race, gender, queerness, critical race theory, and privilege (see Salvador et al., 2023 for discussion in music education), some states have also prohibited discussion about social and emotional wellbeing. Implementing participants' ideas requires repealing this punitive and restrictive legislation in order to foster the relationships, self-awareness, and explicit discussions they encourage without fear of retaliation against music teachers for emphasizing the social alongside the musical to cultivate emotional wellbeing.

These 15 music educators also shared a wide range of musicking experiences that supported their own and their students' emotional wellbeing. While some activities overlap with the kinds of experiences participants recognized as harmful in Chapter 6, they differ in an important way. Musicking practices identified as helpful were all relatively low-stakes, a stark difference from those identified as harmful. The low-stakes quality of helpful musicking opportunities requires administrators to refuse the seductive quality of highly competitive, perfectionist, and evaluative experiences and instead recognize and support the value of low-stakes musicking. Rather than seeking prestige, administrators can prioritize "good musicking" experiences over "good music" following Ansdell (2014, p. 213), and better serve their students and music educators by reducing the pressure and stress that accompany high-stakes and competition-driven experiences. What Ansdell emphasized is process over product. Good musicking may lead to good music; it is not a dichotomy and they are not mutually exclusive. Privileging "good musicking" over "good music" offers a powerful counterpoint to dominant music education practices.

## Notes

1 Works cited challenge the power dynamics embedded in perspective-taking as a facet of empathy and the potential for what bell hooks (1992) called "eating the other."
2 See www.intentionalpeersupport.org/ for more information on Intentional Peer Support.
3 Meena noted that she used the term "peer" in her work as a mental health professional. She differentiated between this usage and how El Sistema takes up the term. In the music education context, I use "peer" as understood in mental health contexts.
4 See https://oakdalechoir.lib.uiowa.edu for more information on the Oakdale Choir.
5 See www.nationalartsstandards.org.
6 Irish traditional music.
7 They spell the term "musicing." I use "musicking" to stay consistent with Small's (1998) use of the term, which I utilize throughout the book.
8 See www.musicforpeople.org/wp/.
9 Green (2008) described a comprehensive approach to facilitating informal musicking in schools.

10  Name deleted to preserve confidentiality.
11  See www.cast.org for more detail on this approach.

## References

Allen, R., Hill, E., & Heaton, P. (2009). 'Hath charms to soothe …': An exploratory study of how high-functioning adults with ASD experience music. *Autism*, *13*(1), 21–41. https://doi.org/10.1177/1362361307098511

Alluri, V., Mittal, A., SC, A., Vuoskoski, J. K., & Saarikallio, S. (2022). Maladaptive music listening strategies are modulated by individual traits. *Psychology of Music*, *50*(6), 1779–1800. https://doi.org/10.1177/03057356211065061

Ansdell, G. (2014). *How music helps in music therapy and everyday life*. Ashgate.

Baker, F. (2015). What about the music? Music therapists' perspectives on the role of music in the therapeutic songwriting process. *Psychology of Music*, *43*(1), 122–139. https://doi.org/10.1177/0305735613498919

Baker, F., Wigram, T., Stott, D., & McFerran, K. (2008). Therapeutic songwriting in music therapy. *Nordic Journal of Music Therapy*, *17*(2), 105–123. https://doi.org/10.1080/08098130809478203

Baltazar, M., & Saarikallio, S. (2016). Toward a better understanding and conceptualization of affect self-regulation through music: A critical, integrative literature review. *Psychology of Music*, *44*(6), 1500–1521. https://doi.org/10.1177%2F0305735616663313

Berger, L. M. (2000). The emotional and intellectual aspects of protest music. *Journal of Teaching in Social Work*, *20*(1), 57–76. https://doi.org/10.1300/J067v20n01_05

Bradley, D. (2012). Living with ghosts: Trauma theory and pedagogy. *2nd Symposium on LGBT Studies & Music Education*. University of Illinois—Urbana Champaign. www.researchgate.net/publication/326881478_Living_with_Ghosts_Trauma_Theory_and_Pedagogy

Bradley, D. (2020). We are all haunted: Cultural understanding and the paradox of trauma. *Philosophy of Music Education Review*, *28*(2), 4–23. https://doi.org/10.2979/philmusieducrevi.28.1.02

Bradley, D. (2022). When music haunts memory: Effects of trauma on music learning. In D. Bradley & J. Hess (Eds.), *Trauma and resilience in music education: Haunted melodies* (pp. 64–78). Routledge.

Bradley, D., & Hess, J. (Eds.). (2022). *Trauma and resilience in music education: Haunted melodies*. Routledge.

Brown, B. (2021). *Atlas of the heart: Mapping meaningful connection and the language of human experience*. Random House.

Campbell, P. S., Connell, C., & Beegle, A. (2007). Adolescents' expressed meanings of music in and out of school. *Journal of Research in Music Education*, *55*(3), 220–236.

Caruth, C. (1996). *Unclaimed experience: Trauma, narrative, and history*. The Johns Hopkins University Press.

Chang, J., Lin, P., & Hoffman, E. (2020). Music major, affects, and positive music listening experience. *Psychology of Music*, *49*(4), 841–854. https://doi.org/10.1177/0305735619901151

Conway, C. M., Eros, J., Pellegrino, K., & West, C. (2010). Instrumental music education students' perceptions of tensions experienced during their undergraduate degree. *Journal of Research in Music Education, 58*(3), 260–275. https://doi.org/10.1177/0022429410377114

Cook, T., Roy, A. R. K., & Welker, K. M. (2019). Music as an emotion regulation strategy: An examination of genres of music and their roles in emotion regulation. *Psychology of Music, 47*(1), 144–154. https://doi.org/10.1177/0305735617734627

Cross, I. (2014). Music and communication in music psychology. *Psychology of Music, 42*(6), 809–819. https://doi.org/10.1177/0305735614543968

Csikszentmihalyi, M. (1990). *Flow: The psychology of optimal experience.* Harper and Row.

Davis, J. H. (2007). *Why our schools need the arts.* Teachers College Press.

DeNora, T. (2000). *Music in everyday life.* Cambridge University Press.

DeNora, T. (2013). "Time after time": A Quali-T method for assessing music's impact on well-being. *International Journal of Qualitative Studies on Health and Well-Being, 8*(1), 1–13. https://doi.org/10.3402/qhw.v8i0.20611

Dingle, G. A., & Fay, C. (2017) Tuned In: The effectiveness for young adults of a group emotion regulation program using music listening. *Psychology of Music, 45*(4), 513–529. https://doi.org/10.1177/0305735616668586

Dingle, G. A., Hodges, J., & Kunde, A. (2016). Tuned in emotion regulation program using music listening: Effectiveness for adolescents in educational settings. *Frontiers in Psychology, 7*, 1–10. https://doi.org/10.3389/fpsyg.2016.00859

Eerola, T., Vuoskoski, J. K., Peltola, H.-R., Putkinen, V., & Schäfer, K. (2018). An integrative review of the enjoyment of sadness associated with music. *Physics of Life Reviews, 25*, 100–121. https://doi.org/10.1016/j.plrev.2017.11.016

Elliott, D. J., & Silverman, M. (2015). *Music matters: A philosophy of music education* (2nd ed.). Oxford University Press.

Erskine, R. G. (1998). Attunement and involvement: Therapeutic responses to relational needs. *International Journal of Psychotherapy, 3*(3), 235–244.

Garrido, S., Baker, F., Davidson, J. W., Moore, G., & Wasserman, S. (2015). Music and trauma: the relationship between music, personality, and coping style. *Frontiers in Psychology, 6*, 1–3. https://doi.org/10.3389/fpsyg.2015.00977

Garrido, S., & Schubert, E. (2013). Adaptive and maladaptive attraction to negative emotion in music. *Musicae Scientiae, 17*(2), 147–166. https://doi.org/10.1177/1029864913478305

Gay, G. (2018). *Culturally responsive teaching: Theory, research, and practice* (3rd ed.). Teachers College Press.

Glass, D., Meyer, A., & Rose, D. H. (2013). Universal design for learning and the arts. *Harvard Educational Review, 83*(1), 98–119.

Green, L. (2008). *Music, informal learning and the school: A new classroom pedagogy.* Ashgate.

Groarke, J. M., & Hogan, M. J. (2018). Development and psychometric evaluation of the adaptive functions of music listening scale. *Frontiers in Psychology, 9*, 1–19. https://doi.org/10.3389/fpsyg.2018.00516

Guffey, E., & Williamson, B. (Eds.). (2020). *Making disability modern: Design histories*. Bloomsbury Visual Arts.

Hendricks, K. S. (2018). *Compassionate music teaching: A framework for motivation and engagement in the 21st century*. Rowman & Littlefield.

Hendricks, K. S. (2023a). A call for care and compassion in music education. In K. S. Hendricks (Ed.), *The Oxford Handbook of Care in Music Education* (pp. 6–21). Oxford University Press.

Hendricks, K. S. (Ed.). (2023b). *The Oxford handbook of care in music education*. Oxford University Press.

Hendricks, K. S., Einarson, K. M., Mitchell, N., Guerriero, E. M., & D'Ercole, P. (2021). Caring for, about, and with: Exploring musical meaningfulness among Suzuki students and parents. *Frontiers in Education*, 6, 1–12. https://doi.org/10.3389/feduc.2021.648776

Hess, J. (2018). Detroit youth speak back: Rewriting deficit perspectives through songwriting. *Bulletin of the Council for Research in Music Education*, 216, 7–30.

Hess, J. (2019). *Music education for social change: Constructing an activist music education*. Routledge.

Hess, J. (2021). When narrative is impossible: Difficult knowledge, storytelling, and ethical practice in narrative research and pedagogy in music education. *Action, Criticism & Theory for Music Education*, 20(4), 79–113. http://act.maydaygroup.org/when-narrative-is-impossible-difficult-knowledge-storytelling-and-ethical-practice-in-narrative-research-and-pedagogy-in-music-education/

Hess, J. (2022). Rethinking "bad behavior": A compassionate response to "acting out" in music education. In D. Bradley & J. Hess (Eds.), *Trauma and resilience in music education: Haunted melodies* (pp. 19–34). Routledge.

Hess, J. (2023). When the project is not understanding: Music education for the incomprehensible. *Studies in Philosophy and Education*, 42(3), 261–282. https://doi.org/10.1007/s11217-022-09861-5

Hess, J., & Bradley, D. (2022). Conclusion: On resilience. In D. Bradley & J. Hess (Eds.), *Trauma and resilience in music education: Haunted melodies* (pp. 199–213). Routledge.

Hill, M. L. (2009). Wounded healing: Forming a storytelling community in Hip-Hop Lit. *Teachers College Record*, 111(1), 248–293.

hooks, b. (1992). *Black looks: Race and representation*. South End Press.

Kahn, J. H., Ladd, K., Feltner-Williams, D. A., Martin, A. M., & White, B. L. (2022). Regulating sadness: Response-independent and response-dependent benefits of listening to music. *Psychology of Music*, 50(4), 1348–1361. https://doi.org/10.1177/03057356211048545

Kennedy-Moore, E., & Watson, J. C. (2001). How and when does emotional expression help? *Review of General Psychology*, 5(3), 187–212.

Kinney, A. (2012). Loops, lyrics, and literacy: Songwriting as a site of resilience for an urban adolescent. *Journal of Adolescent & Adult Literacy*, 55(5), 395–404.

Ladson-Billings, G. (1995). Toward a theory of culturally relevant pedagogy. *American Education Research Journal*, 32(3), 465–491. https://doi.org/10.3102/00028312032003465

Ladson-Billings, G. (2009). *The dream keepers: Successful teachers of African American children* (2nd ed.). Jossey-Bass.

Ladson-Billings, G. (2014). Culturally relevant pedagogy 2.0: A.k.a. the remix. *Harvard Educational Review, 84*(1), 74–84. https://doi.org/10.17763/haer.84.1.p2rj131485484751

Larwood, J. L., & Dingle, G. A. (2022). The effects of emotionally congruent sad music listening in young adults high in rumination. *Psychology of Music, 50*(1), 218–229. https://doi.org/10.1177/0305735620988793

Lashbrook, S., & Mantie, R. (2009). Valuing subjugated experience: The One World Youth Arts Project. In E. Gould, J. Countryman, C. Morton, & L. Stewart Rose (Eds.), *Exploring social justice: How music education might matter* (pp. 292–303). Canadian Music Educators' Association/L'Association canadienne des musiciens éducateurs.

Lonsdale, A. J. (2019). Emotional intelligence, alexithymia, stress, and people's reasons for listening to music. *Psychology of Music, 47*(5), 680–693. https://doi.org/10.1177/0305735618778126

Lonsdale, A. J., & North, A. C. (2011). Why do we listen to music? A uses and gratifications analysis. *British Journal of Psychology, 102*(1), 108–134. https://doi.org/10.1348/000712610x506831

Lundqvist, L.-O., Carlsson, F., Hilmersson, P., & Juslin, P. N. (2009). Emotional responses to music: Experience, expression, and physiology. *Psychology of Music, 37*(1), 61–90. https://doi.org/10.1177/0305735607086048

Lyvers, M., Cotterell, S., & Thorberg, F. A. (2020). "Music is my drug": Alexithymia, empathy, and emotional responding to music. *Psychology of Music, 48*(5), 626–641. https://doi.org/10/1177/0305735618816166

McFerran, K., & Saarikallio, S. (2014). Depending on music to feel better: Being conscious of responsibility when appropriating the power of music. *The Arts in Psychotherapy, 41*, 89–97. https://doi.org/10.1016/j.aip.2013.11.007

McKoy, C. L., & Lind, V. L. (2023). *Culturally responsive teaching in music education: From understanding to application*. Routledge.

Mead, S. (n.d.). Defining peer support. Intentional Peer Support. Retrieved January 30 from https://docs.google.com/document/d/1WG3ulnF6vthAwFZpJxE9rkx6lJzYSX7VX4HprV5EkfY/edit

Meyer, L. B. (1956). *Emotion and meaning in music*. University of Chicago Press.

Milner, M. J. (2006). *Freaks, geeks and cool kids: American teenagers, schools and the culture of consumption*. Routledge.

Miranda, D., Gaudreau, P., Debrosse, R., Morizot, J., & Kirmayer, L. J. (2012). Music listening and mental health: Variations on internalizing psychopathology. In R. A. R. MacDonald, G. Kreutz, & L. Mitchell (Eds.), *Music, health, and wellbeing* (pp. 513–529). Oxford University Press.

Noddings, N. (2013). *Caring: A relational approach to ethics and moral education* (2nd ed.). University of California Press.

North, A. C., Hargreaves, D. J., & O'Neill, S. A. (2000). The importance of music for adolescents. *British Journal of Educational Psychology, 70*, 255–272.

O'Brien, M. (2011). Towards a pedagogy of care and well-being: Restoring the vocation of becoming human through dialogue and relationality. In A. O'Shea

& M. O'Brien (Eds.), *Pedagogy, oppression and transformation in a 'post-critical' climate: The return to Freirian thinking* (pp. 14–35). Continuum.

Papinczak, Z. E., Dingle, G. A., Stoyanov, S. R., Hides, L., & Zelenko, O. (2015). Young people's uses of music for well-being. *Journal of Youth Studies, 18*(9), 1119–1134. https://doi.org/10.1080/13676261.2015.1020935

Paris, D., & Alim, H. S. (2014). What are we seeking to sustain through culturally sustaining pedagogy? A loving critique forward. *Harvard Educational Review, 84*(1), 85–100. https://doi.org/10.17763/haer.84.1.982l873k2ht16m77

Paris, D., & Alim, H. S. (Eds.). (2017). *Culturally sustaining pedagogies: Teaching and learning for justice in a changing world*. Teachers College Press.

Rhodes, A. M., & Schechter, R. (2014). Fostering resilience among youth in inner city community arts centers: The case of the artists collective. *Education and Urban Society, 46*(7), 826–848. https://doi.org/10.1177/0013124512469816

Rose, D. H., & Meyer, A. (Eds.). (2006). *A practical reader in Universal Design for Learning*. Harvard Education Press.

Saarikallio, S. (2012). Development and validation of the brief music in mood regulation scale. *Music Perception, 30*(1), 97–105. https://doi.org/10.1525/mp.2012.30.1.97

Salvador, K., Abramo, J. M., Bernard, C. F., Bohn, A., Confredo, D. A., Cuthbertson, A., Deemer, R., Dilworth, R., Hall, S. N., Helton, B. C., Martin, A., McBride, N. R., McKoy, C. L., Menon, S., Sánchez-Gatt, L., Sauerland, W. R., Shaw, R. D., & Weigand, S. (2023). *Divisive concept laws and music education: A report for the National Association for Music Education*. National Association for Music Education. https://nafme.org/wp-content/uploads/2023/05/NAfME-Divisive-Concepts-Laws-and-Music-Education-Report-2023.pdf

Schäfer, T., Sedlmeier, P., Städtler, C., & Huron, D. (2013). The psychological functions of music listening. *Frontiers in Psychology, 4*, 1–33. https://doi.org/10.3389/fpsyg.2013.00511

Silverman, M. J. (2020). Music-based affect regulation and unhealthy music use explain coping strategies in adults with mental health conditions. *Community Mental Health Journal, 56*, 939–946. https://doi.org/10.1007/s10597-020-00560-4

Silverman, M. J. (2021). Music-based emotion regulation and healthy and unhealthy music use predict coping strategies in adults with substance use disorder: A cross-sectional study. *Psychology of Music, 49*(3), 333–350. https://doi.org/10.1177/0305735619854529

Small, C. (1998). *Musicking: The meanings of performing and listening*. Wesleyan University Press, University Press of New England.

Stige, B., Ansdell, G., Elefant, C., & Pavlicevic, M. (2010). *Where music helps: Community music therapy in action and reflection*. Ashgate.

Stoeber, J., & Eismann, U. (2007). Perfectionism in young musicians: Relations with motivation, effort, achievement, and distress. *Personality and Individual Differences, 43*(8), 2183–2192. https://doi.org/10.1016/j.paid.2007.06.036

ter Bogt, T., Vieno, A., Doornwaard, S. M., Pastore, M., & Van den Eijnden, R. J. J. M. (2017). "You're not alone": Music as a source of consolation among adolescents and young adults. *Psychology of Music*, 45(2), 155–171. https://doi.org/10.1177/0305735616650029

Thayer, R. E., Newman, J. R., & McClain, T. M. (1994). Self-regulation of mood: Strategies for changing a bad mood, raising energy, and reducing tension. *Journal of Personality and Social Psychology*, 67(5), 910–925. https://doi.org/10.1037/0022-3514.67.5.910

Thoma, M. V., Ryf, S., Mohiyeddini, C., Ehlert, U., & Nater, U. M. (2012). Emotion regulation through listening to music in everyday situations. *Cognition & Emotion*, 26(3), 550–560. https://doi.org/10.1080/02699931.2011.595390

Turino, T. (2008). *Music as social life: The politics of participation*. The University of Chicago Press.

Van Den Tol, A. J. M., & Edwards, J. (2014). Listening to sad music in adverse situations: How music selection strategies relate to self-regulatory goals, listening effects, and mood enhancement. *Psychology of Music*, 43(4), 473–494. https://doi.org/10.1177/0305735613517410

Vuoskoski, J. K., Thompson, W. F., McIlwain, D., & Eerola, T. (2012). Who enjoys listening to sad music and why? *Music Perception*, 29(3), 311–317. https://doi.org/10.1525/mp.2012.29.3.311

Watts-Taffe, S. (2022). Creating relational space to support explorations of culturally relevant pedagogy with prospective teachers. *Journal for Research and Practice in College Teaching*, 7(2), 41–56. https://journals.uc.edu/index.php/jrpct/article/view/5971/4836

Williams, W. R. (2012). "Untold stories to tell": Making space for the voices of youth songwriters. *Journal of Adolescent & Adult Literacy*, 56(5), 369–379.

Williamson, B. (2019). *Accessible America: A history of disability and design*. New York University Press. https://doi.org/10.18574/nyu/9781479855582.001.0001

Zoteyeva, V., Forbes, D., & Rickard, N. S. (2015). Military veterans' use of music-based emotion regulation for managing mental health issues. *Psychology of Music*, 44(3), 307–323. https://doi.org/10.1177/0305735614566841

# 8   Abolition and Distress

In April 2022, the parents of Herman Whitfield III called the police for help because their son was experiencing a mental breakdown. Whitfield was a Black classical pianist and composer, soon to be 40 years old (Andrea, 2022). Originally from Indianapolis, he attended Oberlin Conservatory, had had his music performed by the Indianapolis Symphony (Andrea, 2022), and won the Detroit Symphony Orchestra's "emerging African-American composers" competition twice (Kennett, 2023). The police arrived that April night, and Herman died 15 minutes later in police custody. He was tased, handcuffed, and restrained in the prone position until he could no longer breathe.[1] His parents released the unedited body camera footage in seeking justice for their son.[2] In April 2023, two officers, Steven Sanchez and Adam Ahmad, were indicted for their roles in Whitfield's death. They were charged with involuntary manslaughter, reckless homicide, battery resulting in serious bodily injury, and battery resulting in moderate injury and battery (Kennett, 2023). The six officers involved that night were still on paid administrative leave in April 2023, and the other four officers had not faced any charges at the time of Kennett's (2023) publication.

Policing plays a significant role in how society manages, controls, and coerces people with experiences of Madness and/or distress. In this chapter, I address the relationship between abolition and distress and consider two forms of policing. I explore participants' responses to the policing of distress and then consider other ways they believe various (music)[3] education institutions surveil and regulate experiences of Madness and distress. My interrogation of policing involves both police responses to people experiencing distress and practices related to distress that ultimately play a policing role in the lives of music educators and music students who have experiences of Madness and/or distress. Following participants, I take an abolitionist stance on policing of both kinds—literal policing, and the surveillance and regulation of Madness and distress via widespread policies

DOI: 10.4324/9781032662817-9

and practices. Like Jacobs (2021), I seek an anti-carceral response to distress that is life-affirming and community-based.

**The Police and Distress**

The police currently play a significant role in distress intervention. Attending to the thoughts that people with experiences of distress have about the police is critical to implementing anti-carceral responses to distress (Jacobs et al., 2021). Police are often first responders to situations in which a person is experiencing extreme emotional distress (Karanikolas, 2022; Lamb et al., 2002; White & Weisburd, 2018). People experiencing distress are also more likely to be subject to violence at the hands of police, including fatal violence (Butler & Sheriff, 2020; Fuller et al., 2015; Kamin et al., 2022; Karanikolas, 2022; Laniyonu & Goff, 2021; Scott et al., 2023), and are overrepresented among people who are incarcerated (Bailey et al., 2018; Fuller et al., 2015). People who experience severe emotional distress without adequate private care are three times more likely to be in prison than in a hospital (Taheri, 2016). Analysis of police responses to people experiencing severe emotional distress must furthermore be intersectional. Black people who experience an emotional crisis and encounter the police are more likely to be subject to arrest, violence, and lethal force than white people (Jacobs et al., 2021; Laniyonu & Goff, 2021; Saleh et al., 2018; Thomas et al., 2021; Watson et al., 2021). Being Black and Mad is far more dangerous than being white and Mad. Being disabled, including via neurocognitive disabilities, also increases possibilities of harm (Butler & Sheriff, 2020).[4]

Despite the frequency of distress calls, police officers often lack training to respond to extreme emotional crises (Butler & Sheriff, 2020; Cummins, 2022; Lamanna et al., 2018; Lamb et al., 2002; Martin & Thomas, 2016; Scott et al., 2023), although training has improved over the last 20 years (Fiske et al., 2021; Koziarski et al., 2021). In recent decades, many police forces have paired with social service providers in an attempt to divert people experiencing severe distress away from the criminal justice system toward social services (Lamb et al., 2002; Shapiro et al., 2014; White & Weisburd, 2018). These collaborations predominantly involve Crisis Intervention Teams (CITs), which originated in Memphis, Tennessee in the late 1980s following the death of a person experiencing distress at the hands of the police (Kirst et al., 2015; Koziarski et al., 2021; Shapiro et al., 2014; White & Weisburd, 2018), and the co-responder model developed in Los Angeles and San Diego, California (Kirst et al., 2015; Koziarski et al., 2021; Shapiro et al., 2014; White & Weisburd, 2018). CITs involve 40 hours of specialized police training in responding to people experiencing extreme emotional distress (White & Weisburd, 2018), while co-responder models pair social workers or mental health nurses with police officers to respond to distress calls. Social workers also sometimes serve as embedded staff in contact control rooms to advise call handlers about the situations in question (Kane et al., 2018; Shapiro et al., 2014). Research suggests that these interventions are moderately effective in diverting people experiencing extreme emotional distress away from the criminal justice system (Kane et al., 2018; Kirst et al., 2015; Koziarski et al., 2022; Koziarski et al., 2021; Lamb et al., 2002; Shapiro et al., 2014). Significantly, most police departments already employ one of these programs (Fiske et al., 2021; Koziarski et al., 2021).

Despite the prevalence of collaborations between police and social workers, police involvement with people experiencing extreme distress has nonetheless proven fatal (Butler & Sheriff, 2020; Fuller et al., 2015; Kamin et al., 2022; Karanikolas, 2022; Laniyonu & Goff, 2021; Scott et al., 2023), particularly for Black people (Jacobs et al., 2021; Laniyonu & Goff, 2021; Saleh et al., 2018; Thomas et al., 2021; Watson et al., 2021). Jacobs et al. (2021) urged social workers away from carceral social work toward anti-carceral responses to distress. Carceral social work follows logics of social control and white supremacy and employs coercive and punitive tactics in collaboration with the police, prosecutors, jails, prisons, juvenile and criminal courts (p. 39). Anti-carceral social work, conversely, is "life-affirming and supports the health, self-determination, and sustainability of all communities, particularly Black, Indigenous and other people of color (BIPOC), and others most oppressed and impacted by state violence" (p. 38). Citing multiple examples of anti-carceral social work, Jacobs et al. (2021) identified three themes among them. Anti-carceral social work projects decenter the social worker, instead elevating community voices, practices, and problem solving. They also engage transformative justice, restorative justice, and/or abolitionist approaches to social problems. Moreover, these projects employ mutual aid that refuses to seek solutions from oppressive structures and instead works to build something new collectively (pp. 53–54). Jacobs et al. (2021) made five suggestions toward anti-carceral social work to address social problems:

1. Learn about alternatives to policing.
2. Share and build alternatives with those most impacted.
3. Adopt internal agency policies and external policies that move away from required police involvement toward more liberatory options.
4. Strengthen community organizing and mutual aid traditions within social work.
5. Shift from individualized to collective practices. (pp. 54–55)

Community-based and life-affirming alternatives to carceral social work clearly exist. Anti-carceral social work refuses the logics of white supremacy and social control and prioritizes the lives of the minoritized and multiply minoritized.

Participants had various responses to, and experiences with, the police. They discussed the influence of privilege on encounters with the police, the need for a social work, non-police response to distress, and defunding the police. If police were to be involved in distress calls, participants felt they needed specific training beyond current offerings. They also raised ideas of police internal debriefing of critical incidents and documenting success. Participants took a community-based approach that foregrounded the collective and being preventative or proactive.

### *The Question of Privilege*

Participants noted throughout interviews the difference that privilege—particularly white privilege—made in how others perceived their Madness and distress. Jillian and Meena described the role of privilege in their police encounters.

*Jillian:* It was scary. I think I was 15 and never had talked to my parents about anything related to mental health. Then the police showed up. I was fine but I had a worried friend ... and they called the police. That person, I understand she was afraid. ... but I was fine. The police were called and they came and didn't do anything. They were just like, "So you're fine. Okay, cool. This was weird. We're gonna leave." And then we never talked about it again. There was no "Hey, are you okay?" No follow up. Two men, right? Two men in my room. It's tough because that's not what you want. That's not helpful. That is just scary. And luckily, I am documented. I'm a citizen. I am white. I was. I'm a woman, that helps.

Jillian understood that being documented, having citizenship, and being white and a woman influenced their encounter with the police. Meena noticed similar dynamics.

*Meena:* As a person who's mixed race also living in [large city name removed], I present very intelligently and so forth. So when emergency services have been called on me, I'm treated very kindly, and I know how to navigate these situations so that I don't freak out at all. It's just like, "Okay, here we go again."

> The freaking out and the fear response is what causes more problems.

Meena was aware of the privilege she held, particularly in presenting "intelligently"—likely appearing rational and calm. Doing so allowed her to navigate police encounters without physical harm. She also maintained an awareness of privilege in her clinical practice. Given the disproportionate and sometimes fatal amount of force Black people experiencing distress face in police encounters (Jacobs et al., 2021; Laniyonu & Goff, 2021; Saleh et al., 2018; Thomas et al., 2021; Watson et al., 2021), an intersectional analysis of police encounters must account for privilege.

### Resisting Policies that Make Police First Responders

Most participants did not want police to respond to people experiencing extreme distress. They mostly preferred some kind of social worker response without police involvement. Discussions included alternatives to police response and possibilities of defunding the police. Mirroring the literature, these music educators felt strongly that calling the police in response to a person experiencing distress would not ameliorate the situation and might, in fact, exacerbate it.

*Blaine:* Not calling the police is key, and having community aid established that can help with those things. I don't know what the answer is. I just know that it shouldn't be police. I don't know if it should be just a mental health professional that can be called. I don't know if it's just a doctor in general. I don't know what the answer is. ... I wish that there were other options for someone that is in a crisis.

Blaine sought community aid or other non-police options but was frustrated in not having a specific idea or answer to an acknowledged problem. August described a community-based program in Portland, Oregon, but expressed concern that therapists may report distress to police even within that program.

*August:* We do have Project Respond here in Portland, which sends out social workers or therapists to do those kinds of calls, but they can choose to work with the police at their own discretion. That's the group my therapist would have called. They weren't willing to guarantee that the police wouldn't show up at my door while I'm having a crisis because…

*Juliet:* "Discretion."

*August:* Yeah. ... If you need the police to feel safe doing your job, maybe you aren't the right person to do that job? I don't have an answer to it. Just, not the police.

August felt strongly that the police should not be a part of a response to distress; rather, mental health professionals are most appropriately equipped to provide aid in a crisis.

Paulo articulated a justice issue worthy of consideration on both sides of a distress call encounter. While a police response to distress is not just to the distressed individual, asking police to respond to a person experiencing distress also fails the police.

*Paulo:* Don't send someone with a gun. Send someone who's trained. ... I've got numerous police officers in my family, and though we have a very big difference of opinion about their role they will also agree that they're not trained for that shit. It breaks my heart. ... To send someone who's been trained to be violent, right? I mean, to be violent to enforce things, to send them out when someone is not thinking in a rational, standard sense and incapable of responding to orders is unfair ... Not only unfair and unjust to the person who needs the help, but it's also unfair to the person who's asked to go and confront them.

The violence embedded in the coercive elements of policing makes a police response to distress inappropriate. Sending someone with expertise in supporting distress improves the possibility of a positive outcome.

Nicholas and Meghan took specific issue with the role 911 plays as a resource for those experiencing distress.

*Nicholas:* I think people greatly underestimate how hard it is to access mental health care, even when you're not in a crisis. Every psychiatrist's voicemail message is "if this is an emergency, call 911." That's really putting people in harm's way, that's bad advice.

This practice of directing patients to call 911 if they are in severe distress when they hear their psychiatrist's voicemail serves to protect psychiatrists legally if harm occurs, but does not, as Nicholas suggested, serve the patient or resolve distress. Meghan wanted the person in a position to call to access a mental health provider for the person experiencing distress, by taking them to a hospital or calling a help line instead of calling 911.

*Meghan:* Stop sending the police, number one. I think the first thing we need to do when we're addressing mental health crises is to send the proper people. I know that seems like a no-brainer, it seems like a no-duh, but that's not what's happening. ... When you are experiencing that, helping the person by getting the correct people to the place or taking them to the right place [matters]. An officer who has had a 12-hour training on this is not going to be able to help, versus taking them to a hospital where they have doctors who are trained specifically in mental health. Or calling suicide hotlines and just putting it on speaker next to them. It seems aggressive, but that is a better option. Understanding what the right thing to do is when you come across this, because I don't think enough people know what their options are when a friend is going through a mental health crisis, they don't know what they're supposed to do. So by default they call 911.

Problematically, psy- professionals in hospitals can also be coercive and carceral (Karanikolas, 2022), particularly when they subject people experiencing distress to involuntary treatment. Departing from the practice of using police as first responders to mental health distress calls requires an anti-carceral social work response (see Jacobs et al., 2021).

Nicholas suggested an alternative to police intervention and hospitalization.

*Nicholas:* If someone's having a real mental health crisis, they need a psychiatrist or a therapist to show up, especially if there is no physical health crisis. The psychiatric first responder team could and probably should be trained in basic life support. Honestly, it feels like the bulk of these issues are solved by a licensed therapist. That's who I need when I'm having a crisis. I would love to just call or see my, or an emergency, therapist. I'd be like, "I feel like shit right now, it's really bad." Then the person would be like, "what are you experiencing right now, Nicholas?" Then I would be like, "this happened. That happened." The person would listen and do what they normally do during a regular therapy session, except it's an emergency therapy session. Emergency might not be the right word, a critical session or mental health crisis session.

Nicholas further imagined having access to a psychiatrist to facilitate immediate medication changes if needed. Mad Studies scholars often resist the psy- professions, a stance at odds with some participants' views.

Menzies et al. (2013) described "the critique and transcendence of psy-centred ways of thinking, behaving, relating, and being" (p. 13) as a goal of Mad Studies. Participants had a range of views on medications and psy- professionals. Certainly having access to someone with knowledge of medications could be important and urgent in the case of detrimental effects from medication. Recognizing that this possibility may not serve some remains crucial to acknowledging the wide range of relationships that people with experiences of Madness and/or distress have to psy- systems.

Participants also supported "defunding the police"—a rallying cry of Black Lives Matter protestors following the 2020 murders of George Floyd and Breonna Taylor by police (Cobbina-Dungy et al., 2022). Cobbina-Dungy et al. (2022) outlined different definitions of what "defunding" the police can involve—reform, reallocation, disbanding, and abolishing. Reform requires fundamental changes to the existing system of policing. Reallocation involves divesting funds from policing and instead investing in social services. Disbanding compels the dissolution of a police unit and rebuilding it anew, as Ferguson protestors called for following the murder of Michael Brown by police officer Darren Wilson. Abolition involves removing policing as an institution in society. Abolitionists view reform as an inadequate response to the systemic racism embedded in police departments (pp. 151–154). In Cobbina-Dungy et al.'s (2022) study, most participants aligned with the model of reallocating funds away from police budgets toward social services. Participants in this study felt similarly.

Cheryl called for "providing different resources. The classic—defunding the police—and using that money for different resources that are less violent." Paulo and Jillian wanted to see funds reallocated for a dedicated mental health unit or department to respond to cases of extreme distress.

*Paulo:* This is one of those things where when you say the word "defund," or the phrase "defund the police," [and] people don't understand [what] you're talking about. I would rather us talk about, I'm fine with saying "defund the police." … but maybe what we should also be making clear is what we want the other funds to get people who can care for other situations. The police officers—if we believe that police officers are necessary, and that's a debate—then I think they should be focused on what they need to do and not on everything else that doesn't need [to be] enforced. Like the fact that we have fire departments and police departments, and they do two different things, suggests that we would need a mental health department or something like [that].

*Jillian:* People get so afraid of the word defunding, because it's "de-." It seems negative when it's really just, police shouldn't be doing that stuff. We just want them to not be responding to literally everything. There should be a call center where you can call and then they can find what people, right? There should be one line. It doesn't have to be the police. ... Instead of having eight numbers to call, just call one place, and they can direct you.

Divesting funds from police budgets allows for the funding of much-needed social services including a specialized response team of people educated to respond to people experiencing distress while deescalating charged situations. Echoing Paulo's earlier note about injustice toward both the person experiencing distress and the police officers responding, ensuring the correct people respond to a crisis improves the chances of a positive outcome.

*Police Reform*

Participants overwhelmingly called for a move away from police responding to distress. Acknowledging that police abolition likely is not imminent, these music educators also had ideas for more immediate police reforms that could mitigate problematic and harmful distress responses. They called for specialized police trainings on responding to crises, cultural competence, and anti-bias. Additionally, participants felt that debriefing critical incidents and documenting successes as reflective internal follow-up practices might help to improve responses to distress.

Some participants saw a clear need for police training about distress and neurodivergence.[5] Police forces with a Crisis Intervention Team (CIT) provide officers with 40 hours of training on responding to distress calls (White & Weisburd, 2018), which perhaps provides a foundation on which to build further.

*Emma:* I don't think it's sheer malice or, even if it is discrimination, a lot of it is based on ignorance and lack of information. I think the best way especially with police [is to] educate people in specific ways to help people with disabilities. There have been some really disturbing videos out there, and they're following protocol, what they've been taught for neurotypical people. But this is a whole other realm and they're just resorting to what they know. That's kind of like what we do now, is we resort to what we know and that's put the person with disabilities in the back because we don't know what to do.

Emma believed current police training focused on responses to "neurotypical" people and deemed that insufficient. If police "resort to what they know" and have been trained for violence, as Paulo noted earlier, encountering someone who is neurodivergent and/or someone experiencing distress may result in violence including fatalities (Butler & Sheriff, 2020; Fuller et al., 2015; Kamin et al., 2022; Karanikolas, 2022; Laniyonu & Goff, 2021; Scott et al., 2023). These odds increase for Black people experiencing distress (Jacobs et al., 2021; Laniyonu & Goff, 2021; Saleh et al., 2018; Thomas et al., 2021; Watson et al., 2021).

While other participants alluded to bias, Meena spoke directly to the need for culturally competent service to facilitate acting in ways that preserve people's dignity.

*Meena:* I think something [that's] so important is culturally competent service. ... I feel safest when I'm working with mental health professionals, or even emergency responders, who I feel culturally can look at me and correctly assess where I've been, or my cultural background or my way of thinking and being, and then responding in a culturally empathetic way. That doesn't mean that they have to know where I'm from, but that they look at me, and then they're going to treat me with dignity and not make judgments based on the texture of my hair or something.

In the teaching context, cultural competence

entails developing certain personal and interpersonal awarenesses and sensitivities, learning specific bodies of cultural knowledge, and mastering a set of skills that, taken together, underlie effective cross-cultural teaching. Individuals begin this journey with specific lived experiences and biases, and working to accept multiple worldviews is a difficult choice and task.

(Moule, 2012, p. 5)

Cultural competence is a valid starting point, but has limitations. Culturally competent practitioners may essentialize others (Hollinsworth, 2013; Jenks, 2011; Kirmayer, 2012; Kleinman & Benson, 2006), fail to directly address inequity (Gorski, 2016; Laird, 2008), and reinscribe the whiteness of the dominant group (Danso, 2018; Fisher-Borne et al., 2015). Rather than cultural competence, then, engaging cultural humility in cultural education and anti-bias work may elicit better responses to minoritized individuals experiencing distress. Physicians Tervalon and Murray-García (1998) put forward cultural humility to address power dynamics in doctor-patient relations. Three core elements of cultural humility include: "institutional and individual accountability; lifelong learning and critical reflection;

and mitigating power imbalances" (Fisher-Borne et al., 2015, p. 174). In police-public relations, these tenets may provide the kind of respect Meena sought in her interactions with professionals. Accountability, continued learning, critical reflection, and mitigating power imbalances constitute an approach to policing that may better serve individuals experiencing distress.

Along similar lines, the critical reflection element of cultural humility requires attending to, and working against, internalized and externalized biases. Lizabeth considered a situation in their neighborhood in which someone called the police on a group of young Black siblings crossing the street.

*Lizabeth:* We all need to understand our biases, and start seeing everyone as human. I don't want to say we're all the same, because that's not true. But there's a lot of implicit bias there, because maybe whoever called the police would have helped if it was white children in the middle of the street, instead of calling the police. That's another thing we can do, is all learn to care for each other and address any biases we have.

Attending to biases such as those evidenced in Lizabeth's example is a need within the general public and particularly for the police and other helping professionals. Recognizing the racism and white supremacy embedded in policing (Jacobs et al., 2021) requires a refusal to call the police on racialized people, particularly Black people.

Some participants argued that education and competence in mental health literacy for all would ameliorate support for people experiencing distress.

*Chris:* I think firstly, we need to provide some more education for the general public on how to support people who are in distress or in extreme states. For me that includes actually de-pathologizing, which means rather than thinking of a person as someone who's got a particular diagnosis, thinking instead, "How can I be present? How can I connect?" Focusing on building some of those skills. This also involves communities being willing to become literate in mental health issues. Likewise, police also clearly need some education and some skills, and they need support.

Chris felt that encouraging people to be present with someone experiencing distress and working intentionally to find ways to connect would improve responses to distress, possibly reducing the need to involve

224  *Abolition and Distress*

outsiders via distress calls. She also advocated for education and support for the police to help them better respond to crises.

*QingYu:* I have heard that there is some kind of sensitivity training with police, but there's not enough. There have been many times where police show up to scenario scenes where an individual is dealing with a mental health crisis and it typically does not end well because they are not trained the right way. … Mental health needs to be taught to everyone. I think mental health education is most crucial to those working with other people. So the police, doctors, whatever. If you're going to work with the people and try to save their life, being trained the right way how to deal with these situations, is crucial. I think that for society, those that aren't working in life-threatening scenarios, it's really hard to end stereotyping and stigmas around certain things.

QingYu wanted everyone to learn about mental health, particularly those who serve others. Learning about mental health involves anti-bias education alongside considering the pervasiveness of stereotypes and stigmas. Such education should also include possible responses to distress. QingYu argued that education about distress would produce a better response to people experiencing it. This call for education echoes Chris' call for mental health literacy.

Participants also had specific ideas about police reform.

*Chris:* One of the keys to de-escalating the culture of an intense workplace, whether it be police or an inpatient ward, or EMTs, is to make sure that when there is a critical incident, that there's really good debriefing and support for the workers and people involved. … I think police need to build that intentionally into their culture. Otherwise, they're going to be reacting from fear.

Debriefing critical incidents may aid police in identifying other, less reactionary, response options that may inform future encounters.

*Chris:* I would like to see critical incident reports after every coercive intervention. I'm not going to change that system particularly quickly. But often there are critical takedowns of people; they're restrained or tased, or shot or killed when there were so many other possibilities. I think that every coercive act should have a critical incident process attached to it to reflect on what happened, what the learnings are, what remediation or restoration might be needed, whether there's any disciplinary or legal measures that need to be taken, and, most importantly, what needs to be put in place to ensure it doesn't happen again.

Debriefings and "critical incident reports" also facilitate opportunities for critical reflection and accountability—key tenets of cultural humility (Fisher-Borne et al., 2015). Chris also wanted to focus attention and build on successes to contribute to a more positive culture.

*Chris:* I would like to see a more intentional culture, for example, with police. A process of noticing, acknowledging and even recording or documenting the moments where there is an intervention that is really successful. The times when somebody is not locked up or restrained or killed, but might have been if another person or set of circumstances had been present. The intent is to build a culture where we notice what goes well because right now, we're so focused on everything that goes wrong that we can't see the wood for the trees. Socially and culturally, we're replicating what we're looking at, which is all of the things that haven't gone well.

Just as critically reflecting on poor police responses may allow for different responses in the future, noticing various facets of successes may facilitate similar successes in the future. Making intentional time and processes through which to notice how an encounter has gone well would allow police to recognize similar circumstances and respond accordingly, and this shift could be accomplished through simple structural changes.

### Community-Based Approaches to Distress

In alignment with Jacobs et al.'s (2021) call for anti-carceral social work that elevates community voices, practices, and problem solving (p. 53), participants privileged community-based approaches to distress.

*Lizabeth:* I think we're very individualized, we think of ourselves as individuals. I wonder how thinking of ourselves as a community, and even our mental health as *our* mental health instead of *my* mental health or *your* mental health could be helpful, too. Because then maybe your first instinct isn't to call the police. It's to help that person.

Individualism, as a mainstay of neoliberalism, places people in competition with each other and positions society as a meritocracy, whereby success emerges from simply trying hard enough (Dei & Calliste, 2000). Individualism positions each person as a separate entity rather than as an essential part of the collective social whole, and does not account for the differing degrees of privilege to which people across the full range of identities have access. The myth of the meritocracy—that anyone can succeed if they try hard enough—does not account for race, gender, class, disability, sexual identity, national status, etc. (Dei & Calliste, 2000; Goldberg, 2009). Castagno (2014) noted "[w]hen meritocracy is assumed, our focus is directed away from systemic inequities and toward individual success and failure" (p. 105). Lizabeth suggested a move away from individualism toward collectivity in a way aligned with the discussion of competition in Chapter 6. Instead of pitting people against each other, communities can learn to work collectively. Lizabeth felt doing so would produce better responses to distress.

*Abolition and Excarceration*

In her work against the prison industrial complex, Davis (1998) took an abolitionist stance that criticized how prison resembles the violence of enslavement. She emphasized the alternative precepts of excarceration:

> Prison needs to be abolished as the dominant mode of addressing social problems that are better solved by other institutions and other means. The call for prison abolition urges us to imagine and strive for a very different social landscape.
>
> (Davis & Rodríguez, 2000, p. 215)

Abolishing the prison industrial complex "imagines a world where social, political, economic, and cultural problems are not solved using prisons and hyper surveillance" (Washington et al., 2021, p. 2). It calls for community-based solutions to distress rather than policing and incarceration.

Excarceration requires considering ways to prevent people from becoming system-involved (Washington et al., 2021, p. 4), something for which Mary explicitly advocated.

Mary: We need more centers or places for people to go and know where they can go. One of the terms that I discovered in research for my book is called excarceration, which are places like community mediation centers. So many abolitionist thinkers are encouraging that we have better ways to address people in severe mental health situations. It's so complicated, every situation is going to be different. Sometimes it's related to addictions, and other times its related to a particular life situation. … But definitely we need to do something completely different. I think there are some communities across the country that have done a lot more since George Floyd was murdered on May 25, 2020.

In cases of distress, prevention requires community spaces that become viable alternatives to carceral responses to distress. Lizabeth spoke to a proactive approach that would meet every person's basic needs in ways that might prevent some distress.

*Lizabeth:* I think we need to be preventative in the first place. I understand we can't prevent everything, but to start, we need to be preventative and honestly, that starts with having everyone's basic needs met. I would identify basic needs as being your food, housing, clothes, your safety, your security, and access to medical care of health care and mental health care, and education. Because that would eliminate a lot of mental health issues to begin with, if we all had access to things preventatively.

Their ideas align with a community-based, anti-carceral and excarceration approach to social work that attends to community needs. This preventative approach resists the logics of white supremacy and social control that shape carceral social work (Jacobs et al., 2021).

## Policing in (Music) Education: How Distress is Surveilled and Regulated

Having explored the complexities of the role of policing in cases of distress, I now turn to a second form of policing. Participants identified multiple policies and practices in (music) education that they felt policed their distress as music educators and students. They described the bureaucracy required to register with a disability and receive accommodations, and the mandatory reporting by school and healthcare personnel triggered by expressions of distress. Participants also felt surveilled socially and conveyed concerns with annual reports and reviews, professional standards in music teaching, and attendance, as well as self-surveillance. Writing powerfully about surveillance across different facets of society, Foucault explained:

> A "political anatomy", which was also a "mechanics of power" was being born; it defined how one may have a hold over others' bodies not only so that they may do what one wishes, but so that they may operate as one wishes, with the techniques, the speed and the efficiency that one determines.
>
> (Foucault, 1977, p. 138)

Foucault described the processes of surveillance culture, in which bodies are compelled to operate in a particular way in accordance with a larger power structure. Considering the different facets and levels of education—particularly music education, the "rhythm" is often frenetic, characterized by intense "control of activity" and the "exhaustive use" of time (Foucault, 1977, p. 154). These 15 music educators with experiences of Madness and/or distress felt surveilled or policed in ways consistent with the control Foucault described.

*Bureaucracy to Register with a Disability and Receive Accommodations*

Half of participants felt the amount of bureaucracy required to register a disability and receive accommodations in educational contexts served as a surveilling mechanism. This bureaucracy exists for students and educators across K-12, undergraduate, and graduate education. Lester et al. (2013) described different approaches universities take to disability and accommodations, with some aiming to provide accommodations *with* and *for* students, while others only do what they deem "reasonable" or "appropriate" (p. 64)—the legal bare minimum.[6] They identified how the university is positioned as the arbiter of disability and requires extensive, and typically expensive, testing and documentation to grant accommodations (pp. 63–64). Students rarely have the authority to identify their own disability in this system (p. 63). QingYu described one such difficult and traumatic process.

QingYu: Every U.S. university has their own accommodations system ... I did receive that the last year of my schooling for some other things. It just requires so much documentation. The process [is] very difficult. The process can be also traumatizing for students. You could just link it to just how much more oppressing it can be for students to try to even seek that kind of accommodation. Trying to receive that support is already difficult as it is. Linking it with the social work aspect is a lot. People are trying to get the help they need, but there's always barriers to getting the help we need. I feel like students don't always reach out to teachers for the support they need. ... Then we try to go after the accommodation and reach all these barriers. It's like the world doesn't want us to actually receive the help.

To register with a disability, the burden of proof rests with the student,[7] but disability centers do not typically trust students without documentation, typically from a doctor or via pscyho-educational testing. Lester et al.

(2013) called this process "policing neurodiversity." Cheryl felt that part of the rationale for the degree of bureaucracy comes from the concern that people will "take advantage."

*Cheryl:* I think people are afraid that people will take advantage of saying that they have a mental condition, so that they can work less or get benefits, sort of abuse it. I guess that's the reason maybe why people want so much documentation. I don't know what ideal is, but more ideally, there will be more trust in people saying, "I am struggling with this, I need support." Ideally you would receive that support without being second guessed. I feel like struggling with ... mental health is hard enough. Also having to advocate for yourself and prove what's wrong with you is not what people need to be doing, how people should be spending their energy.

Samuels (2003) observed: "Suspicions of fraud often greet declarations of nonvisible identity. As Amanda Hamilton writes, people with nonvisible disabilities 'are in a sense forced to pass, and the same time assumed to be liars'" (p. 242).[8] Cheryl suggested that trusting a person with a disability to know what they need rather than insisting on testing and doctors' evaluations may constitute a better system for offering accommodations.

Meghan recounted an "invasive" process in high school during which her teachers were surveyed about her performance, generating documentation for her doctor to determine whether or to what degree she needed support. Meghan recalled: "Then my depression got a lot worse, because I had these teachers who knew that I had something wrong with me. And it wasn't necessary. So that was high school. I graduated on a low note." Receiving accommodations in K-12 schooling in the U.S., while protected by the Individuals with Disabilities Education Act (IDEA),[9] remains an onerous bureaucratic process that requires extensive documentation. For people like Meghan, the information gathering felt invasive and unnecessary, compounding her level of distress.

As a university faculty member, I faced a similar process when I registered with a disability. I needed documentation from my doctor and was compelled to attend several meetings to put accommodations in place. Taking people with experiences of Madness and distress at their word about what they find supportive would greatly improve the invasiveness and infantilization embedded in the process of registering a disability to receive accommodations.

Cheryl elucidated the sanism encountered by people with experiences of Madness and/or distress. They pointed to the mistrust surrounding accommodations and the deficit view held of people trying to access them.

*Cheryl:* I think there's so much distrust around what if people "abuse" or use their mental health or health as an excuse to just not have to do things. This, of course, is ridiculous, we probably all know that. It was just so harmful. That narrative, I guess, exists still, in many places. ... It's such a deficit view, whereas I don't think it has to be the case at all. How wonderful would it be if people could get the support that they need to thrive as they are. Instead of being treated as, "you're just saying that you feel depressed so that you don't have to do this work." That's even the narrative that I have within myself. I'm like, "Oh, am I using this as an excuse to just not have to do this work?" If I'm already telling myself that, I don't need anyone else to put that distrust on me on top of that. That is not going to do me any good. That is not gonna make me more productive. I guess this goes back to what people were talking about earlier about how we get these resources for working on our mental health ... so that we can be more productive. ... Like the goal of us feeling better is not just so that we just have better well-being now, it is so that we can be more productive and do more things. That is backwards and wild.

Indeed, many people choose to conceal their impairment out of concern that they will be accused of "faking it" (Cureton, 2018; Olney & Brockelman, 2003; Samuels, 2003; Sierra-Zarella, 2005). Moreover, Cheryl observed how they have internalized sanism, second-guessing whether or not they use their distress as an "excuse." In literature on race, racism, and colonization, scholars discuss internalized oppression frequently (see for example Fanon, 1967). Understanding internalized oppression in the context of sanism requires further attention in research.[10] Cheryl also recognized that the "help" people with experiences of Madness and/or distress receive from an institution occurs in service of increasing productivity rather than of the person's wellbeing. Neoliberalism thus pervades discourse about disability and accommodations for the sake of productivity (see Dolmage, 2017 for discussion of higher education contexts) and not genuine care for people.

Leaves from work due to disability are also highly policed.

*Rebecca:* The times I've had periods off from work, I have felt that the occupational health people who've been in touch with me, I haven't completely felt they're on my side. I haven't felt that they're there supporting me. I've felt that they're there to protect the university's interests. ... Maybe it's unrealistic for them to do anything different financially, but the fact that you're allowed so many weeks off with pay, and then there's a sliding scale of a decrease in the amount you get paid the longer you're off. Which is surveillance and pressure to get back to work.

Dolmage noted:

> It is 'neoliberalism' that Wendy Brown (2015) is defining in Undoing the Demos when she suggests that humanist values have been overtaken by a focus on human capital—or the economic value that might be gained or taken from human bodies and their work.
>
> (p. 28)

Rebecca's university acted on their economic interests, employing financial pressure to force her back to work. Following the lead of the person on leave and facilitating self-determination would make the process of taking leave and receiving accommodations more humane.

*Mandatory Reporting*

Participants also felt surveilled by the looming threat of mandatory reporting laws. In the U.S. context, many states have laws compelling medical and educational professionals to report a person who they believe might pose a danger to self or others.

*Rebecca:* We're [professors] told that if we meet with a student and they're suicidal, we have to call campus police and they're taken away in handcuffs. It's appalling, absolutely appalling. ... There was a period when I was first at the university, where a young man had been diagnosed with schizophrenia. The way it was dealt with in the faculty was to warn administration secretaries to be careful if he was around.

As noted in Chapter 1, "dangerousness" sticks to some bodies more than others (Daley & Van Katwyk, 2022). Stereotypes of Madness and dangerousness were certainly at play in the university response to this individual. This stereotype was prioritized over this person's wellbeing and integration into the community. Rebecca was also forced to report any suicidal ideation she noticed in others.

The potential threat of being reported, however, may prevent people experiencing suicidal ideation from disclosing it (Blanchard & Farber, 2020).

*August:* I left my last therapist because they were mandated by the state to report if I had a plan for ending my own life. I don't filter well; if I talk to somebody, I will be very, very open about stuff. My way of filtering is to avoid talking to people who are not safe to talk to, or only talk to them for very short periods of time. The form of therapy that I find the most helpful for me is the one where a relationship is created that allows the client to feel safe and to express themselves openly. ... I really value my own autonomy, and do not like the idea of somebody controlling me or choosing my actions for me, and I do not like the idea of incarceration (via forced mental health treatment in a hospital or outpatient program) for a non-crime.

Blanchard and Farber (2020) found that people will avoid disclosing suicidal ideation for fear of involuntary hospitalization, which August identified as "incarceration for a non-crime." At Rebecca's university, people experiencing distress were met with violence and a carceral response.

Mandatory reporting greatly diminishes the opportunity for a compassionate response to the person making a disclosure, since medical and educational professionals have legal steps to follow in order to maintain their job. Jillian identified mandatory reporting of suicidal ideation as problematic and harmful but had also experienced some compassion.

*Juliet:* So are there other ways that you feel mental health gets surveilled?

*Jillian:* It's hard. The idea that you have to report suicidal thoughts. ... That's never gonna make anything better. Luckily a lot of places I've seen or been have been like, "As long as we can guarantee your safety, we don't have to... We understand that suicidal thoughts happen." That's a direction a lot of people have moved in. But yeah, it's surveilled.

Mandatory reporting constitutes a literal form of surveillance that typically involves a carceral approach to distress. Medicalized responses to distress further dehumanization when they lack the compassion Jillian described and often result in (involuntary) engagement in the psy- system.

### Social Surveillance

Participants also observed some degree of social surveillance—among friends, in workplaces, in communities, and in families. They felt pressure to behave in particular ways to avoid being stigmatized in social and professional situations.

*August:* When I'm having a hard time with stuff, I feel this social current telling me not to dump on people. Like a collective voice is saying "don't be too negative." I don't know if it's regional or national or international or whatever. But it seems to be increasing here. Not that it was ever that open. It's always felt like, to one degree or another, you really shouldn't talk about your problems. And if you do, you should keep it very brief and light and well-processed. I'm frustrated with this current because it makes no room for people who can't follow this cultural mandate because we don't have good filtering or impulse control around that kind of stuff. When I hang out with most people I'm really, really on edge about like, "Oh my god, if I say how I'm doing, are they going to tell me I'm a terrible person for expressing how I feel?"

August felt they had to censor themself and that friends would not respond well to an authentic expression of a hard time.[11] This kind of self-censoring becomes exhausting; it involves continual assessment of the communication climate (Hayes et al., 2005) before and while voicing one's experience.

Nicholas expressed concern about being ostracized if their colleagues discovered their distress.

*Nicholas:* Mental health is socially surveilled, that seems like the main thing. If somebody identifies you as a little cuckoo, they tell all their friends. In the K-12 school setting, you become a pariah. It depends on your major, depends on school. For job stuff, it is a hot hellish mess. I feel like mental health is heavily surveilled at work. Everybody is like, "Hey, how ya doing?" And you are supposed to say, "Okay, fine." If you look even a little bit withdrawn, they ask you "what's wrong?" If you tell them, you can become a pariah. They can tell the boss, they tell their work friends. This also applies to social pressure between students.

Self-censoring at work can lead to burnout (Kelly et al., 2022). While Kelly et al. did not explore self-censoring in relation to distress, their findings related to burnout certainly apply to self-censoring of distress. Nicholas believed that not self-censoring could have grave consequences in their school, making honest social interactions with colleagues nearly impossible.

Participants also remarked on social surveillance in communities.

*Paulo:* I think communities police mental health as well. There's only so much deviation from the norm that people will allow for.

If someone is consistently outside of that, they can engage the wrath of a group of people.

August described "the sense of people just scanning each other for danger and being very shut off." Paulo's use of the word "wrath" combined with August's use of "danger" recalls the discussion in Chapter 1 about the strong public association between Madness and dangerousness (see for example Daley & Van Katwyk, 2022). Communities police people who are experiencing Madness and distress, and this kind of surveillance exerts pressure to "pass" or conform with what Paulo called the "norm."

*Chris:* I think there's so many unacknowledged ways that [policing/surveillance] happens. It happens in housing, it happens in employment, it happens in school. There's kids who were kicked out of school, there's doctors who are kicked out of med school, or nurses who are kicked out and deregistered. Whatever your occupation, actually. If you have a ton of distress, you're often negatively impacted and there's a punitive element. ... I think in the community, for example, [if] you want to be on a board and someone says, "Oh, you know, she's (name a diagnosis)," or "She was in a psych hospital." It happens socially, and I think it happens in so many areas of our lives.

Chris noticed multiple settings situated in institutional structures and in the community that fostered discrimination against people with experiences of Madness and distress, naming education as one potential site for policing these differences.

Families, too, may participate in policing family members experiencing distress, stripping people with Madness or distress of relational trust and their own sovereignty. Jillian noted: "A lot of young kids or teenagers and such, their parents go through their stuff all the time. So yeah. There's not a lot of privacy."

*Paulo:* I get parents being super protective of their kids, I can completely get it. But they can misplace that protectiveness to being anti-difference. That's where things change. I think the policing of it. I also think families can be major policing.

Instead of policing distress or calling the police, family members might benefit from posing the questions Chris asked in relation to educating people for crises: "How can I be present? How can I connect?" Connecting to a family member experiencing distress may allow them to feel supported.

Posing these questions could ease the social surveillance that occurs in friendships, at work, in communities, and in families.

*Institutions*

In addition to social surveillance, participants observed how institutions police people with experiences of Madness and distress both within and beyond music education contexts. They discussed the role that annual reports and reviews, professional standards, and attendance policies play in policing distress.

Annual reports and reviews may act as policing measures for (music) educators with experiences of Madness and/or distress. At the higher education level, faculties, schools, and/or colleges typically require an annual accounting of work submitted at a specified time. Rebecca experienced extreme stress due to this evaluation in relation to her productivity. These evaluations often directly affect pay raises and thus have economic implications.

*Rebecca:* I think that that's the vehicle for my pressure is having to do this annual performance evaluation and submit a report every year, showing how productive I've been in the various areas of my job, and worrying that I don't have enough numbers in one column.

At K-12 levels, administrations evaluate teachers one or more times a year, often using the Danielson Framework in the U.S.[12] A person with experiences of Madness and/or distress may worry intensely about such evaluations and feel pressure to perform in a way that capitulates to the surveillance they feel through these processes. These worries extend beyond people with experiences of Madness and/or distress to the entire educator population. Teacher/faculty evaluations, as facets of neoliberal, corporate education reform policies, cause mass distress among the educator population. In a study of high-stakes evaluations among K-12 music teachers, participants described "lack of sleep, weight gain, less time for spouses, partners, children, and a need for therapy" (Robinson, 2017, p. 51). To deal with the stress, these music teachers requested anxiety medication, sought therapy, and "vented" to family members and colleagues (p. 51). This level of distress makes it clear that high-stakes teacher/faculty evaluation policies require significant reform or abolition.

Professional standards may also contribute to feeling surveilled in music education.[13] As a music teacher educator, Paulo critiqued the ableism embedded in professional standards documents, particularly the requirement to be of "sound mind."[14]

*Paulo:* I think standards, professional standards in general. Right now [we're] going through this revision of our [university's] professional teaching standards, and I had to go [through it] with a fine tooth comb because it was really ableist. Unintentionally so. But there's this notion of, what does it mean to be a professional? Sometimes those professional standards talk about being sound of mind. Who the fuck is sound of mind? Especially who the fuck is sound of mind *all the time*? I think that and professional expectations, I refuse to have this conversation with students. I have colleagues who have no problem with it. But if a student is consistently depressed, there are other teachers who will be fine with saying, "how are you going to function as a music teacher if you're always depressed?" I just refuse to have that kind of conversation. My conversation is "Okay. So depression is part of your life. How can we develop some strategies for dealing with that and the stressfulness of being a teacher?" That to me is different. One of them is dismissive. The other one is proactive.

He took a different approach with students and helped them find ways to navigate experiences of Madness and/or distress while also being an educator. Paulo's response to ableist discourse, however, is not embedded in standard (music) teacher preparation. Most future teachers therefore do not necessarily receive these kinds of insights from professors, potentially leading them to believe they do not belong in the program and/or the profession. The ableism embedded in professional standards and evaluations may thus negatively impact teachers who experience Madness and/or distress.

The pressure of these standards was also felt by participants in the K-12 music teaching context.

*Nicholas:* My previous psychiatrist, my mom, and many others have cautioned me about being open with [my mental health] at work, because they thought that's all people would see me as if they knew. The worst part is, it was probably sound advice. But at this point, I have enough of a command of my illness, and also my disability, that I can frame a narrative of it for people (which I shouldn't have to do). Overall, I'm happy to do it because I want people to know about this and other disabilities because the kids and families are disabled in many ways.

Nicholas understood the risks of visibility and had those risks impressed upon them by their psychiatrist and family. They prioritized, however, being visible and framing their experiences for others to destigmatize experiences of Madness and distress. They also inferred that schools heavily surveilled students' and teachers' mental health. While both Paulo and Nicholas recognized the pressure exerted by professional standards, they defied them in different ways, making interventions that allowed them to frame these experiences on their own terms.

Discourse about disability and education frequently acknowledges the ableism embedded in mandatory attendance policies (Birdwell & Bayley, 2022; Nicolas, 2017; Sapir & Banai, 2023). Such attendance policies demonstrate a prioritization of the musical product over the people involved in making it (see also Chapter 6).

*Jillian:* Especially the way that they police attendance at [ensembles]. Here at [institution], it's bad. I've heard horror stories and it's like, God forbid you take anything for your mental health. That's not even an option. If you have a surgery, maybe you can miss rehearsal, but you should have scheduled it on a different day because you had the schedule. That's just extremely unfair.

Stringent attendance expectations in ensembles, like the one Jillian observed in an undergraduate context, pervade multiple levels of education. Birdwell and Bayley (2022) found that attendance policies "disproportionately harm students who are already marginalized and struggling, preventing them from succeeding" (p. 228). While their work examined writing education, the pressure of music education (Bernhard, 2021; Conway et al., 2010) likely intensifies how these policies affect students and may exacerbate distress. Institutions thus participate in the policing of (music) students and educators, using annual reports and reviews, professional standards, and attendance as tools of surveillance. Participants were aware of these forms of policing across educational levels and also resisted it in various ways.

*Self-Surveillance*

Self-surveillance among those with experiences of Madness and/or distress constitutes a crucial part of discussing policing. A number of participants alluded to self-censoring in some form—policing themselves or self-surveilling to avoid a range of consequences. Laura named such policing explicitly.

*Juliet:* How have issues with mental health impacted your journey in music education?

*Laura:* I think mostly ... kind of setting up barriers for myself, and not to share with people and not necessarily have them see some of what might be considered ugly parts of the disorder. Disorders.
*Juliet:* I get that.
*Laura:* Kind of policing myself.

The overarching structures of sanism and ableism can compel people to mask their distress as discussed in Chapter 5. As noted, participants in Blanchard and Farber's (2020) study mostly avoided discussing their suicidality in therapeutic contexts due to fear of mandatory reporting. Policing oneself may be deemed necessary in professional settings and even in personal ones.

Foucault (1977) provided a model pertinent to this discussion: Bentham's Panopticon. He offered it as an example of a self-regulatory model in a prison system. In the Panopticon, the prison architecture is structured in a circle around a tall tower that emits a strong light. Inside the tower, a guard is theoretically present, monitoring all cells clearly visible from the tower. The light, however, is bright, making it impossible for anyone imprisoned to be sure of whether, or when, they are being observed. The result is a "state of self-conscious and permanent visibility that assured the automatic functioning of power" (Foucault, 1977, p. 201). Permanently unsure of whether the guard was observing, individuals self-regulated according to the prison code of behavior. Laura articulated how she kept the "ugly parts of the disorder" to herself to avoid stigma or other consequences, as other participants described in Chapter 5 about their decisions to mask or conceal their experience. Schools, among other institutions and social relationships, can thus be framed as functioning akin to Bentham's Panopticon, wherein the perception of constant observation forces extreme self-regulation.

## Conclusion and Implications

Policing distress has become a widespread practice, both through literal policing and through other forms of surveillance that impact (music) educators and students with experiences of Madness and/or distress. Most participants opposed involving the police in distress calls, preferring anti-carceral approaches to social work (Jacobs et al., 2021). If the police do get involved with a person experiencing extreme distress, these music educators identified a need for specialized training, debriefing critical incidents, and documenting successes with two goals: (1) to bring aid rather than danger to already difficult situations; and (2) to continually improve on police intervention tactics through accountability, transparency, and reflective practices. They also looked to community-based responses that might reduce distress and provide compassion, consistent with Jacobs et al.'s (2021) findings, and strategized abolitionist and excarceration possibilities.

While participants did not comment on School Resource Officers (SROs)—law enforcement officers placed in schools—it is notable that SROs far exceed the number of nurses, school counselors, social workers, and psychologists (Love, 2023, p. 144). The budget for police in schools in the U.S. far exceeds the budget for mental health resources. The conversation about policing and mental health therefore must include a rethinking of the place of SROs in schools and a redistribution of public funding to increase the number of nurses, school counselors, social workers, and pyschologists. Love (2023) noted that in Florida during the 2018/2019 school year, not a single school in the state met the industry standards for the recommended ratio of school counselor to students (p. 144). Even though participants did not comment on SROs, a call for anti-carceral resources requires the removal of SROs from schools and a drastic increase of mental health resources.

Beyond police involvement, participants felt their distress was surveilled in other ways in (music) education. These included the bureaucracy required of students and educators to register a disability and receive accommodations, the duty of mandatory reporting from certain professionals, and the social surveillance that occurred in friendships, communities, families, and among colleagues. They also described troubling surveillance mechanisms used in/by (music) education institutions including annual reports and reviews, professional standards, and attendance policies. Lastly, they noticed how they policed themselves in accordance with perceived sanist norms, enacted through the policing and surveillance mechanisms just listed. Participants took an abolitionist approach to policing, as well as to the other ways in which they felt surveilled. They wanted anti-carceral resources to be available in cases of distress and wished to be trusted in cases involving institutional support.

Police are often first responders to distress calls within current systems (Karanikolas, 2022; Lamb et al., 2002; White & Weisburd, 2018). Making abolition part of the conversation surrounding people experiencing Madness and/or distress makes room for anti-carceral responses and excarceration strategies that may alleviate distress and deescalate difficult situations. The prevalence of so many other mechanisms of policing distress, Madness, and disability in (music) education specifically means (music) educators must also attend to these other forms of surveillance and work toward better ways of supporting people experiencing distress.

Participants' tendencies toward abolition have implications both for literal policing and the surveillance that occurs in (music) education. An abolitionist approach offers a powerful counterpoint to the often carceral tactics of policing including in schools and surveillance of Madness and distress. The ongoing record of police violence against people experiencing distress alongside the continual, and often lethal, brutality against Black people in particular make clear that the institution of policing requires an overhaul, if not complete abolition. Participants leaned toward abolition but also suggested possible reform strategies. Changes to policing structures at the macro level occur through legislation and budget allocations (see for example Neumann, 2021). Such changes require consistent advocacy and activism from the people and their representative policymakers. Participants' observations of police responses to distress and suggestions toward abolition or reform provide additional perspectives for abolitionists and activists.

Accounting for participants' perspectives on surveillance of distress in (music) education also requires changes to policy and practice. Participants objected to the level of bureaucracy involved in registering a disability and receiving accommodations. This process remains invasive and requires extreme levels of disclosure that do not honor individuals' rights to privacy. Participants preferred a process that placed more trust in the person with a disability—including those with experiences of Madness and/or distress—to know what they need in terms of accommodations. Changing this process must occur at both the level of legislation and in local administrative processes for school districts. Doing so would reflect a larger change in the perceptions of people with experiences of Madness and distress, eschewing the stigmas and stereotypes discussed in Chapter 1 in particular, and refusing any narrative that the person wishing to acquire accommodations is "faking it" (Cureton, 2018; Olney & Brockelman, 2003; Samuels, 2003; Sierra-Zarella, 2005). In the U.S. context, the pertinent legislation is the Individuals with Disabilities Education Act (IDEA)[15] for students, and the Americans with Disabilities Act (ADA)[16] for all ages, including educators at all levels. Changes to the overdisclosure required and the lack of trust demonstrated in disabled and Mad people themselves will require activism and advocacy, and a willingness on the part of all involved to engage in a shift of mindset away from sanist and oppressive stereotypes, stigmas, prejudice, discrimination, and bias.

Mandatory reporting remains a problematic legal requirement. If a person is in imminent danger, professionals must act to ensure they receive care and support. Currently, care and support often take the form of hospitalization (sometimes via police intervention) including involuntary hospitalization and treatment. While some participants cited positive experiences with voluntary hospitalization, involuntary hospitalization and policies such as community treatment orders can involve forced treatment and coercion that often cause great harm (Fabris, 2011). As a society, we would do well to reconfigure care and support systems toward a focus on community care and creative ways of supporting safety. Peer support spaces such as *Hearing Voices Network*[17] provide anti-carceral alternatives that work to facilitate safety. Such macro changes also involve significant changes in policy and the very nature of mandatory reporting laws.

In (music) education, participants problematized the ableism and sanism embedded in annual reports and reviews, professional standards, and attendance policies. Changes to these types of policies must occur within institutions and governing bodies such as teacher accreditation groups. Administrators and leaders can carefully review policies and processes currently in place for educators and students, identifying issues of ableism and sanism, and then work to eradicate them. In some cases, hiring a consultant with expertise in ableism and sanism to create genuinely inclusive policies and processes may be important to implementing meaningful, lasting change. Examining these policies and processes must also involve accounting for other identity-based oppressions. Understanding the ways in which ableist and sanist policies disproportionately and negatively impact racialized students and teachers, for example, requires careful consideration followed by action. Policies in music education can be disability- and Mad-affirming. Careful attention to and revision of ableist and sanist policing of disabled and Mad students and educators can facilitate genuinely inclusive policies and practices that benefit (music) education and all those involved in it.

## Notes

1 Prone restraint has been shown to alter respiratory and cardiac physiology (Steinberg, 2021).
2 See www.youtube.com/results?search_query=herman+whitfield+iii for body camera footage. Please be advised that this content is graphic.
3 I use the term *(music) education* in this chapter to signal that the considerations I discuss apply to both general education and music education contexts.
4 Butler and Sheriff (2020) pointed to the killing of a 13-year-old boy with autism in Utah.
5 Butler and Sheriff (2020) concurred.
6 Lester et al. (2013) studied accommodations for students. This work could be extended to include faculty, staff, administrators, etc.
7 Registering as a professional is a similar process.
8 Hamilton's letter to the editor can be found here: https://web.archive.org/web/20020208202529/www.ragged-edge-mag.com:80/archive/look.htm.
9 See https://sites.ed.gov/idea/.
10 Walker (2021) did engage with internalized oppression in this context.
11 Since the time of the interview, this dynamic shifted for August. They noted: "I want to point out as a separate note that since the initial interview I've rediscovered old friends and made new friends who also prioritize open

expression of feelings and I have a few people I know I can trust to support me without involving police if I want to avoid ending my life. Having friends like this has made a huge difference in my overall mental health and quality of life, in combination with cherry picking evidence-based strategies that I've learned from therapy."

12  See https://danielsongroup.org/the-framework-for-teaching/.
13  Organizations such as the Association for Advancing Quality in Educator Preparation (AAQEP) and the Council for the Accreditation of Educator Preparation (CAEP) in the U.S. heavily emphasize the role of dispositions in educator preparation. See https://aaqep.org/standard-1 and www.caepnet.org/~/media/Files/caep/standards/2022-initial-standards-1-pager-final.pdf?la=en respectively.
14  At the time of the interview, the university where Paulo taught was in the process of developing a set of expected teacher dispositions and skills that relied heavily on ableist assumptions including "stability of mind and emotion" and "assumptions about hearing, seeing, and moving that would outright exclude numerous disabled educators." These are the types of professional standards to which he referred.
15  See https://sites.ed.gov/idea/.
16  See www.ada.gov.
17  See www.hearing-voices.org/hearing-voices-groups/.

## References

Andrea, L. (2022). 'Phenomenally talented': Oberlin grad Herman Whitfield III remembered as genius pianist. *Indianapolis Star*. www.indystar.com/story/news/crime/2022/04/27/herman-whitfield-pianist-indianapolis-police-taser-death-mental-health-services/9554930002/

Bailey, K., Rising Paquet, S., Ray, B. R., Grommon, E., Lowder, E. M., & Sightes, E. (2018). Barriers and facilitators to implementing an urban co-responding police-mental health team. *Health and Justice*, 6, 1–12. https://doi.org/10.1186/s40352-018-0079-0

Bernhard, H. C. (2021). *Managing stress in music education*. Routledge.

Birdwell, M. L. N., & Bayley, K. (2022). When the syllabus is ableist: Understanding how class policies fail disabled students. *Teaching English in the Two Year College*, 49(3), 220–237. www.proquest.com/scholarly-journals/when-syllabus-is-ableist-understanding-how-class/docview/2664104753/se-2

Blanchard, M., & Farber, B. A. (2020). "It is never okay to talk about suicide": Patients' reasons for concealing suicidal ideation in psychotherapy. *Psychotherapy Research*, 30(1), 124–136. https://doi.org/10.1080/10503307.2018.1543977

Brown, W. (2015). *Undoing the demos: Neoliberalism's stealth revolution*. Zone Books.

Butler, S. M., & Sheriff, N. (2020). *Innovative solutions to address the mental health crisis: Shifting away from police as first responders*. Brookings. www.brookings.edu/research/innovative-solutions-to-address-the-mental-health-crisis-shifting-away-from-police-as-first-responders/

Castagno, A. E. (2014). *Educated in whiteness: Good intentions and diversity in schools*. University of Minnesota Press.

Cobbina-Dungy, J., Chaudhuri, S., LaCourse, A., & DeJong, C. (2022). "Defund the police:" Perceptions among protesters in the 2020 March on Washington. *Criminology & Public Policy*, 21(1), 147–174. https://doi.org/10.1111/1745-9133.12571

Conway, C. M., Eros, J., Pellegrino, K., & West, C. (2010). Instrumental music education students' perceptions of tensions experienced during their undergraduate degree. *Journal of Research in Music Education*, 58(3), 260–275. https://doi.org/10.1177/0022429410377114

Cummins, I. (2022). 'Defunding the police': A consideration of the implications for the police role in mental health work. *Police Journal: Theory, Practice and Principles*, 96(2), 230–244. https://doi.org/10.1177/0032258X211047795

Cureton, A. (2018). Hiding a disability and passing as non-disabled. In A. Cureton & T. E. Hill Jr. (Eds.), *Disability in practice: Attitudes, policies, and relationships* (pp. 15–32). Oxford University Press.

Daley, A., & Van Katwyk, T. (2022). De-coupling and re-coupling violence. In P. Beresford & J. Russo (Eds.), *The Routledge international handbook of Mad Studies* (pp. 253–265). Routledge.

Danso, R. (2018). Cultural competence and cultural humility: A critical reflection on key cultural diversity concepts. *Journal of Social Work*, 18(4), 410–430. https://doi.org/10.1177/1468017316654341

Davis, A. Y. (1998). From the prison of slavery to the slavery of prison: Frederick Douglass and the convict lease system. In J. James & A. Y. Davis (Eds.), *The Angela Y. Davis reader* (pp. 74–95). Blackwell.

Davis, A. Y., & Rodríguez, D. (2000). The challenge of prison abolition: A conversation. *Radical Philosophy Review*, 27(3), 212–218. www.jstor.org/stable/29767244

Dei, G. J. S., & Calliste, A. (Eds.). (2000). *Power, knowledge and anti-racism education*. Fernwood Publishing.

Dolmage, J. T. (2017). *Academic ableism: Disability and higher education*. University of Michigan Press.

Fabris, E. (2011). *Tranquil prisons: Chemical incarceration under community treatment orders*. University of Toronto Press.

Fanon, F. (1967). *Black skin, white masks*. Grove Press.

Fisher-Borne, M., Cain, J. M., & Martin, S. L. (2015). From mastery to accountability: Cultural humility as an alternative to cultural competence. *Social Work Education*, 34(2), 165–181. https://doi.org/10.1080/02615479.2014.977244

Fiske, Z. R., Songer, D. M., & Schriver, J. L. (2021). A national survey of police mental health training. *Journal of Police and Criminal Psychology*, 36, 236–242. https://doi.org/10.1007/s11896-020-09402-1

Foucault, M. (1977). *Discipline and punish: The birth of the prison* (A. Sheridan, Trans.). Vintage Books.

Fuller, D. A., Lamb, H. R., Biasotti, M., & Snook, J. (2015). *Overlooked in the undercounted: The role of mental illness in fatal law enforcement encounters*.

Treatment Advocacy Center. www.researchgate.net/publication/291331905_Overlooked_in_the_Undercounted_The_Role_of_Mental_Illness_in_Fatal_Law_Enforcement_Encounters?channel=doi&linkId=569fb6ca08ae21a564271318&showFulltext=true

Goldberg, D. T. (2009). *The threat of race: Reflections on racial neoliberalism*. Wiley-Blackwell.

Gorski, P. (2016). Rethinking the role of "culture" in educational equity: From cultural competence to equity literacy. *Multicultural Perspectives*, 18(4), 221–226. https://doi.org/10.1080/15210960.2016.1228344

Hayes, A. F., Glynn, C. J., & Shanahan, J. (2005). Validating the willingness to self-censor scale: Individual differences in the effect of the climate of opinion on opinion expression. *International Journal of Public Opinion Research*, 17(4), 443–455. https://doi.org/10.1093/ijpor/edh072

Hollinsworth, D. (2013). Forget cultural competence: Ask for an autobiography. *Social Work Education*, 32, 1048–1060. https://doi.org/10.1080/02615479.2012.730513

Jacobs, L. A., Kim, M. E., Whitfield, D. L., Gartner, R. E., Panichelli, M., Kattari, S. K., Downey, M. M., McQueen, S. S., & Mountz, S. E. (2021). Defund the police: Moving towards an anti-carceral social work. *Journal of Progressive Human Services*, 32(1), 37–62. https://doi.org/10.1080/10428232.2020.1852865

Jenks, A. C. (2011). From "lists of traits" to "open-mindedness": Emerging issues in cultural competence education. *Culture, Medicine, and Psychiatry*, 35(2), 209–235. https://doi.org/10.1007/s11013-011-9212-4

Kamin, D., Weisman, R. L., & Lamberti, J. S. (2022). Promoting mental health and criminal justice collaboration through system-level partnerships. *Frontiers in Psychiatry*, 13, 1–8. https://doi.org/10.3389/fpsyt.2022.805649

Kane, E., Evans, E., & Shokraneh, F. (2018). Effectiveness of current policing-related mental health interventions: A systematic review. *Criminal Behaviour and Mental Health*, 28(2), 108–119. https://doi.org/10.1002/cbm.2058

Karanikolas, P. (2022). Imagining non-carceral futures with(in) Mad Studies. In P. Beresford & J. Russo (Eds.), *The Routledge international handbook of Mad Studies* (pp. 217–222). Routledge.

Kelly, S., Brown, W. S., & Drye, S. (2022). Do we burn ourselves trying to save face? Face concerns as a predictor of subordinate willingness to self-censor and burnout. *International Journal of Business Communication*, OnlineFirst, 1–19. https://doi.org/10.1177/23294884221118896

Kennett, J. (2023, April 27). One year after Herman Whitfield's death; One step closer to a fully funded mental health crisis response team. *Indianapolis Recorder*. https://indianapolisrecorder.com/one-year-after-herman-whitfields-death-one-step-closer-to-a-fully-funded-mental-health-crisis-response-team/

Kirmayer, L. J. (2012). Rethinking cultural competence. *Transcultural Psychiatry*, 49(2), 149–164. https://doi.org/10.1177/1363461512444673

Kirst, M., Pridham, K. F., Narrandes, R., Matheson, F., Young, L., Niedra, K., & Stergiopoulos, V. (2015). Examining implementation of mobile, police-mental health crisis intervention teams in a large urban center. *Journal of Mental Health*, 24(6), 369–374. https://doi.org/10.3109/09638237.2015.1036970

Kleinman, A., & Benson, P. (2006). Anthropology in the clinic: The problem of cultural competency and how to fix it. *PLoS Medicine*, *3*(10), 1673–1676.

Koziarski, J., Ferguson, L., & Huey, L. (2022). Shedding light on the dark figure of police mental health calls for service. *Policing: A Journal of Policy and Practice*, *16*(4), 696–706. https://doi.org/10.1093/police/paac006

Koziarski, J., O'Connor, C., & Frederick, T. (2021). Policing mental health: The composition and perceived challenges of Co-response Teams and Crisis Intervention Teams in the Canadian context. *Police Practice and Research: An International Journal*, *22*(1), 977–995. https://doi.org/10.1080/15614263.2020.1786689

Laird, S. E. (2008). *Anti-oppressive social work: A guide for developing cultural competence*. SAGE Publications Inc.

Lamanna, D., Shapiro, G. K., Kirst, M., Matheson, F. I., Nakhost, A., & Stergiopoulos, V. (2018). Co-responding police–mental health programmes: Service user experiences and outcomes in a large urban centre. *International Journal of Mental Health Nursing*, *27*(2), 891–900. https://doi.org/10.1111/inm.12384

Lamb, R. H., Weinberger, L. E., & DeCuir Jr., W. J. (2002). The police and mental health. *Psychiatric Services*, *53*(10), 1266–1271. https://doi.org/10.1176/appi.ps.53.10.1266

Laniyonu, A., & Goff, P. A. (2021). Measuring disparities in police use of force and injury among persons with serious mental illness. *BMC Psychiatry*, *21*, 1–8. https://doi.org/10.1186/s12888-021-03510-w

Lester, J. N., Dostal, H., & Gabriel, R. (2013). Policing neurodiversity in higher education: A discourse analysis of the talk surrounding accommodations for university students. In C. D. Herrera & A. Perry (Eds.), *Ethics and neurodiversity* (pp. 52–66). Cambridge Scholars Publishing.

Love, B. L. (2023). *Punished for dreaming: How school reform harms Black children and how we heal*. St. Martin's Press.

Martin, T., & Thomas, S. (2016). Police officers' views of their encounters with people with personality disorder. *Journal of Psychiatric and Mental Health Nursing*, *22*(2), 125–132. https://doi.org/10.1111/jpm.12099

Menzies, R., LeFrançois, B. A., & Reaume, G. (2013). Introducing Mad Studies. In B. A. LeFrançois, R. Menzies, & G. Reaume (Eds.), *Mad matters: A critical reader in Canadian Mad Studies* (pp. 1–22). Canadian Scholars' Press, Inc.

Moule, J. (2012). *Cultural competence: A primer for educators* (2nd ed.). Wadsworth, Cengage Learning.

Neumann, E. (2021, February 12). Oregon Legislature considers bill to create local crisis intervention teams. OPB. www.opb.org/article/2021/02/12/oregon-legislature-cahoots-crisis-intervention-health/

Nicolas, M. (2017). Ma(r)king a difference: Challenging ableist assumptions in writing program policies. *WPA: Writing Program Administration*, *40*(3), 10–22.

Olney, M. F., & Brockelman, K. F. (2003). Out of the disability closet: Strategic use of perception management by select university students with disabilities. *Disability & Society*, *18*(1), 35–50. https://doi.org/10.1080/713662200

Robinson, M. (2017). Music teachers' perceptions of high stakes teacher evaluation. *Arts Education Policy Review*, *120*(1), 45–56. https://doi.org/10.1080/10632913.2017.1373380

Saleh, A. Z., Appelbaum, P. S., Liu, X., Stroup, T. S., & Wall, M. (2018). Deaths of people with mental illness during interactions with law enforcement. *International Journal of Law and Psychiatry*, *58*, 110–116. https://doi.org/10.1016/j.ijlp.2018.03.003

Samuels, E. J. (2003). My body, my closet: Invisible disability and the limits of coming-out discourse. *GLQ: A Journal of Lesbian and Gay Studies*, *9*(1-2), 233–255. www.muse.jhu.edu/article/40803

Sapir, A., & Banai, A. (2023). Balancing attendance and disclosure: Identity work of students with invisible disabilities. *Disability & Society*, *OnlineFirst*, 1–21. https://doi.org/10.1080/09687599.2023.2181765

Scott, M., Sabatini, S., & Mama, R. (2023). Defund the police? or reimagine the police? Leaders in law enforcement's perspective on the role of social workers in law enforcement. *Journal of Evidence-Based Social Work*, *20*(2), 241–257. https://doi.org/10.1080/26408066.2022.2156831

Shapiro, G. K., Cusi, A., Kirst, M., O'Campo, P., Nakhost, A., & Stergiopoulos, V. (2014). Co-responding police-mental health programs: A review. *Administration and Policy in Mental Health and Mental Health Services Research*, *42*, 606–620. https://doi.org/10.1007/s10488-014-0594-9

Sierra-Zarella, E. (2005). Adapting and "passing": My experiences as a graduate student with multiple invisible disabilities. In L. Ben-Moshe, R. C. Cory, M. Feldbaum, & K. Sagendorf (Eds.), *Building pedagogical curb cuts: Incorporating disability in the university classroom and curriculum* (pp. 139–146). The Graduate School, Syracuse University.

Steinberg, A. (2021). Prone restraint cardiac arrest: A comprehensive review of the scientific literature and an explanation of the physiology. *Medicine Science and Law*, *61*(3), 215–226. https://doi.org/10.1177/0025802420988370

Taheri, S. A. (2016). Do crisis intervention teams reduce arrests and improve officer safety? A systematic review and meta-analysis. *Criminal Justice Policy Review*, *27*(1), 76–96. https://doi.org/10.1177/0887403414556289

Tervalon, M., & Murray-García, J. (1998). Cultural humility versus cultural competence: A critical distinction in defining physician training outcomes in multicultural education. *Journal of Health Care for the Poor and Underserved*, *9*(2), 117–125.

Thomas, M. D., Jewell, N. P., & Allen, A. M. (2021). Black and unarmed: Statistical interaction between age, perceived mental illness, and geographic region among males fatally shot by police using case-only design. *Annals of Epidemiology*, *53*, 42–49. https://doi.org/10.1016/j.annepidem.2020.08.014

Walker, N. (2021). *Neuroqueer heresies: Notes on the neurodiversity paradigm, autistic empowerment, and postnormal possibilities* (ePub ed.). Autonomous Press.

Washington, D. M., Harper, T., Hill, A. B., & Kern, L. J. (2021). Achieving juvenile justice through abolition: A critical review of social work's role in shaping the juvenile legal system and steps toward achieving an antiracist future *Social Sciences*, *10*(6), 1–17. https://doi.org/10.3390/socsci10060211

Watson, A. C., Pope, L. G., & Compton, M. T. (2021). Police reform from the perspective of mental health services and professionals: Our role in social change. *Psychiatric Services*, *72*(9), 1085–1087. https://doi.org/10.1176/appi.ps.202000572

White, C., & Weisburd, D. (2018). A co-responder model for policing mental health problems at crime hot spots: Findings from a pilot project. *Policing: A Journal of Policy and Practice*, *12*(2), 194–209. https://doi.org/10.1093/police/pax010

# Conclusion
## A Mad-Affirming Music Education

Literature indicates the importance of listening to people with lived experiences of mental health struggles when making decisions about support and policy (see for example Sweeney, 2016). In this conclusion, I consider what music education can learn from attending to the voices of the 15 music educators with lived experiences of Madness and distress who participated in this research. Importantly, they revealed many elements of music education that supported them individually. Following Andrzejewski (2023) who observed that people who experienced Madness and/or distress in academia succeeded because of support and understanding from individuals in power, I wish to make these individual considerations structural. Given the current context of collective trauma from the COVID-19 pandemic, wars and conflicts across the globe, ongoing police brutality, the continued oppression of minoritized and multiply minoritized individuals and groups, and the historical and present-day effects of colonialism and enslavement, in tandem with individual experiences of Madness and/or distress, music educators must learn to account for these realities and provide support. Madness and distress are widespread, although severity and presentation vary. As noted in the introduction, suicide rates in the U.S. are sharply rising (Singh, 2023); from April to June of 2020, 40.9% of people in the U.S. reported at least one adverse symptom of mental health (Czeisler et al., 2020). These statistics indicate a full-blown mental health crisis in the U.S. Music educators thus have a duty to attend to Mad voices in seeking to address distress in the field and in classrooms. In this conclusion, I describe what music educators can learn from listening. I ultimately work to construct a Mad-affirming music education for students, teachers, and scholars.

Crucially, Mad Studies is a praxis discipline (Morgan, 2022), and therefore must have practical implications that are rooted in theory. Sanism, as explicated in Mad Studies, leads to epistemic injustice in which people with experiences of Madness and/or distress are wronged in their/our capacities as knowers (Fricker, 2007). In this book, I aimed to address the hermeneutical injustice that music educators and music students with experiences of Madness and/or distress face. This group experiences what Fricker (2013) described as hermeneutical marginalization in that it is a "group which does not have access to equal participation in the generation of social meanings" (p. 1319). Medina (2017) explained: "[N]on-dominantly situated people often find their meanings and communicative contributions not taken seriously, improperly heard, deemed deficient, reinterpreted, distorted, and too quickly dismissed, and in these ways they are hermeneutically disrespected and wronged" (44). Historically and presently, society dismisses and fails to value the contributions of people with experiences of Madness and/or distress to the hermeneutical resources that would otherwise allow music educators and students with such experiences to make sense of them.[1] Participants in this research made a unique contribution to the hermeneutical resources in music education in ways that may support similarly situated others in understanding their own experiences. Listening to participants' voices offers a profound contribution to both music education and to Mad Studies, and further facilitates hermeneutical justice.

In this conclusion, I address topics thematically rather than summarizing chapter by chapter. I begin by considering how disability studies models can serve people with experiences of Madness and distress, and how teachers could mobilize these models through their pedagogy. Then I explore how music educators might benefit from understanding the broad range of conceptualizations these 15 music educators held about experiences of Madness and distress and explicate how the Universal Design for Learning may support different conceptualizations. I turn subsequently to visibility (being "out") in music education, examining the complexities and value of such decisions for people experiencing Madness and distress. I further consider and explore the complicated intersections of visibility with shame and empathy. In alignment with an anti-carceral approach to surveillance of mental health, I advocate for an abolitionist approach to mental health in music education. Next, I explore the help/harm dichotomy of musicking. This exploration leads to an offering of implications for music education and explication of approaches to pedagogy that may prove useful. I then consider the importance of recognizing assets as contextual and reflect upon participants' views of the benefits of (their) neurodivergence. I explicate Walker's (2021) concept of neurocosmopolitanism as a way forward, then conclude by returning to the contrapuntal methodology presented in this book's introduction. I center pedagogy throughout.

## Considering Disability Studies

I explored several models of thinking about disability from disability studies in Chapter 2. Participants expressed ideas that either aligned directly or indirectly with specific existing models. I thus argue that disability studies models can be useful in helping music educators with experiences of Madness and/or distress apply language and conceptual frameworks to their/our experiences. In Chapter 2, I explicated the social model (Oliver & Sapey, 1999; Shakespeare, 2017), complex embodiment (Siebers, 2008, 2017), the cultural model (Snyder & Mitchell, 2006), DisCrit (Annamma et al., 2022; Connor et al., 2016), a critical realist approach (Shakespeare, 2014), and the social confluence model (Lubet, 2013) for what they might offer people with experiences of Madness and/or distress. Following participants and in alignment with Mad Studies (LeFrançois et al., 2013; Menzies et al., 2013), I resist an exclusively psy-based paradigm (the medical model) (Dobbs, 2012; Linton, 1998).

Models from disability studies offer some explanatory power for experiences of Madness and/or distress and may help music educators with such experiences theorize them in a way that allows for meaning- and sense-making. Participants, however, were divided about whether they considered their mental health differences a disability. This tension brings complexity to using disability studies models to consider experiences of Madness and/or distress. While participants differed in their perspectives on (their) neurodivergence as disability, most found disability studies models to be helpful to their framing and conceptualization of experiences. I therefore argue that disability studies models are of use to music educators looking for ways to think about experiences of Madness and distress, both personally and for the students they teach. Elsewhere I have argued that having a critical, anti-oppressive theoretical orientation helps music educators better serve students in ways that align with their values (Hess, 2020, 2022b). Love (2019) asserted that theory is the "North Star" that guides pedagogical actions.[2] Being well-versed in different models from disability studies enables music educators to enact pedagogy in ways that support disability in alignment with their/our values.

The social model distinguishes between *impairment* and *disability*, asserting that an impairment only becomes a disability when the environment is disabling (Oliver & Sapey, 1999; Shakespeare, 2017). The social model allows for explicit focus on disabling barriers. In my own thinking about pedagogy, I often turn first to the social model explicitly because of its attention to barriers. While much agency has been wrested away from teachers in many places, music educators do still have at least some degree of agency and control in their classrooms. The social model urges teachers to examine barriers and remove them. Employing such a model may help music educators consider ways to make classrooms and pedagogy *en*abling rather than *dis*abling and create an environment that serves students across the full spectrum of dis/ability.

DisCrit—the blending of disability studies with critical race theory (CRT)—helps educators understand the ways that racism and ableism are co-constituted, and recognize dynamics such as the racialization of special education (Annamma et al., 2022; Connor et al., 2016; Erevelles et al., 2006). DisCrit facilitates acknowledgement of intersectionality in music education, particularly as it relates to disability, inclusive of people who experience Madness and/or distress. Considerations of privilege pervaded this study's data. Most participants were white and noticed how their whiteness protected them from experiencing sanism to the same degree that their BIPOC colleagues and peers do when disclosing experiences of Madness and/or distress. QingYu noted that they "experienced so much intersectionality being a person of color, being someone that experiences mental health problem[s], being a person that's disabled, being a person that is gay, I'm not cisgender," and were more prone to experiencing oppression as a result of these intersecting, embodied identities. Employing DisCrit as an orienting framework in the classroom aids music educators in recognizing the ways in which students might be multiply minoritized, and the intersecting systems of oppression that interlock to shape their lives.

As noted in Chapter 2, complex embodiment (Siebers, 2008, 2017), the cultural model (Snyder & Mitchell, 2006), a critical realist approach (Shakespeare, 2014), and the social confluence model (Lubet, 2013) each offer more complex ways to consider disability than the dichotomous medical and social models. They account for the messiness and nuance of disability, and consider the effects of disabling environments on individuals' lived experiences; they also emphasize factors that derive from the body (Siebers, 2008) and further acknowledge that impairments are not neutral; rather, they significantly impact the experience of disability (Shakespeare, 2014). Using these models to orient classroom praxis furthers music educators' means of critically examining representations of disability with students (Snyder & Mitchell, 2006). Lubet's (2013) social confluence model helps teachers notice the fluidity of disability—that a disability may impact a person in disparate ways from moment to moment dependent on context. Drawing on models of disability as frames to inform classroom praxis encourages teachers to acknowledge and respond to the diverse ways that disabilities, inclusive of experiences of Madness and/or distress, occur in the classroom.

### Accounting for Conceptual and Experiential Variety and the Universal Design for Learning

Participants conceptualized mental health differences in a wide variety of ways. They described a spectrum of differences, refused binary thinking, referenced the neurodiversity paradigm, and identified an "ability profile." Understanding that there are many ways to think about Madness and distress brings diversity to thinking about these experiences among students, educators, and scholars.

Participants demonstrated a strong proclivity for the idea of neurodiversity as a spectrum or range of human neurocognitive diversity, as explored in Chapter 3. Indeed, this was the most common conception, which I assert has significant pedagogical implications. As explicated in Chapter 7, the Universal Design for Learning (UDL) aims to provide robust access to learning; this access occurs by inviting educators to vary the ways they represent knowledge and engage students, and offer students choices of how they express their learning (CAST, n.d.; Rose & Meyer, 2006). UDL facilitates acknowledgement that such adjustments likely benefit not only students with disabilities but all students. In conceptualizing neurodiversity as a spectrum, educators can recognize the broad variety of ways that people access materials and demonstrate learning. UDL facilitates educators' use of this conceptualization.

Using the neurodiversity paradigm, educators can recognize the variations across all people in terms of neurocognitive functioning and unsettle notions of "normative functioning." Through its acknowledgment of the wide variation of human neurodiversity, this paradigm works to destigmatize difference, as difference is simply variation. Similarly, the refusal of binary thinking makes room for a spectrum of neurocognitive difference and resists normative conceptions. Conceptualizing an ability profile that is spiky[3] encourages teachers to recognize strengths and weaknesses in themselves and in students, and further notice the ways that individuals' characteristics are contextual.[4] Employing UDL helps students cater to their strengths in how they demonstrate their learning. UDL thus becomes useful across a range of different conceptualizations of experiences of Madness and distress.

### The Importance of Visibility and Representation

Most participants chose to be "out" about their experiences of Madness and distress, with 9 of 15 choosing to be identified in this book. Other participants preferred not to disclose. All, however, worked to normalize such experiences across various settings. Participants considered representations of Madness and/or distress and noticed when and how they saw themselves reflected or erased in the public sphere. They identified people they viewed as significant influences and encouraged a practice of centering artists with experiences of Madness and/or distress—including historical and contemporary composers and performers—in music education.

Highlighting the importance of visibility and representation of people with experiences of Madness and/or distress revealed the crucial work of normalizing and destigmatizing such experiences in Chapter 5. Hiding and concealing an aspect of identity may lead to that aspect becoming pathologized (Weller, 2015),[5] as well as potentially some degree of internalized shame (Brown, 2021) and subsequent worsening of these experiences. Participants in music education at all levels—students, teachers, music teacher educators, scholars—need models of people who experience Madness and/or distress. For educators, that may mean disclosing if conditions feel supportive enough to do so. Being "out" actively refuses the pathologization of mental health differences and works toward normalizing and destigmatizing experiences of Madness and distress. Employment precarity, however, may make being "out" difficult. Stigma—or the marking of so-called "spoiled identities" (Goffman, 1963)—affects people with experiences of Madness and distress, and can lead to discrimination in ways that particularly impact employment (Elraz, 2018; Glover et al., 2010; Lettieri et al., 2021; Martin et al., 2000; Østerud, 2022; Russinovaa et al., 2011; Stuart, 2006). In cases where music educators at any level feel the need to "pass" as "neurotypical" rather than disclose,[6] they can reference musical artists with experiences of Madness and/or distress as models, and have explicit discussions about this facet of identity as participants suggested in Chapter 5.

The COVID-19 pandemic pushed dialogue about mental health to the surface, as evidenced by President Biden's discussion of the topic in his 2022 State of the Union address (Jacobson, 2022). Madness and distress are more visible at present, with topical conversations more prevalent than in the past. As Emma noted, however, mental health discourse that occurs in the popular sphere because it is currently "trendy" fails to capture more severe and negative experiences of Madness and distress. People who struggle with experiences of Madness and/or distress need realistic representations in the same way people across the full range of minoritized identities appreciate seeing their identities accurately represented in the public sphere. Such representation remains vital even as discourse has become more inclusive, as participants shared that misrecognition or erasure of their other identities—including their gender and racial identities—negatively impacted their emotional wellbeing. Children and youth involved in K-12 music education, collegiate music education students, and music educators at all levels would benefit from seeing themselves represented among musickers across gender, race, disability, sexual identity, socioeconomic class, religion, age, national status, as well as other identities including mental health differences. Representation, however, often remains stereotypical. Working against stereotypes of all minoritized identities becomes part of striving toward visibility.

"Stereotype threat," which makes the visibility of realistic models essential, describes

> a social-psychological predicament that can arise from widely known negative stereotypes about one's group ... The existence of such a stereotype means that anything one does or any of one's features that conform to it to make the stereotypes more plausible as a self-characterization in the eyes of others, and perhaps even in one's own eyes. We call this predicament stereotype threat and argue that it is experienced, essentially, as a self-evaluative threat.
> (Steele & Aronson, 1995, p. 797)

Solórzano et al. (2001) noted that stereotype threat becomes a self-fulfilling prophecy (p. 62). Stereotypes currently dominate discourse, practice, and representations about "mental illness" and Madness (Bueter, 2019; Carver et al., 2017; Corrigan et al., 2010; Crichton et al., 2017; LeBlanc & Kinsella, 2016; Lee, 2021; Scrutton, 2017; Sullivan, 2019; Williams, 2014; Wolframe, 2013). There is great potential that stereotype threat deeply affects people with experiences of Madness and distress. Working against these stereotypes requires more people to be "out" about their experiences in ways that represent the full range of experiences on the spectrum of neurodiversity, Madness, and distress.

Privilege plays a significant role in the question of disclosure. As mentioned, the mostly white participants in this study felt they did not experience sanist discrimination in the same way as their BIPOC colleagues, peers, and students. Privilege potentially provides a shield[7] to do work in ways that might make being "out" about experiences of Madness and/or distress easier for people who are minoritized and multiply minoritized. Privilege thus comes with responsibility. People with the most privilege across the identities they occupy are likely to experience less stigma, stereotyping, and sanist discrimination, and thus have some obligation to do normalizing, destigmatizing, and depathologizing work when possible. When that is not possible due to imminent discrimination, music educators can engage in smaller acts of normalization through inclusion of musical artists who are "out"[8] in curricular materials.

### Visibility, Shame, and Empathy

When considering whether one can be out about experiences of Madness and/or distress, shame may be a factor. This consideration is especially true given the ongoing stigmatization and stereotyping of such experiences. While stigma is a form of discrimination (Carver et al., 2017; Corrigan et al., 2010), making shame unwarranted, pervasive sanism often makes it a factor when considering whether and in what context(s) to share one's experiences openly. As I explicated in Chapter 5, Brown indicated silence, secrecy, and judgment as the three essential components that set the conditions for shame (Brown, 2021, p. 137). Because of stigma, people with experiences of Madness and/or distress may feel bound to secrecy or silence for fear of societal judgment. Empathy serves as the antidote to shame (Brown, 2021, p. 138). Because shame acts to isolate a person, empathy becomes a "hostile environment for shame" (p. 138) in offering connection rather than isolation. Brown argued that shame is a social emotion. "Shame happens between people and it heals between people. Even if I feel it alone, shame is the way I see myself through someone else's eyes" (p. 138).

Significantly, participants felt they had increased levels of empathy due to their experiences of Madness and/or distress. The idea that empathy can dissolve feelings of shame perhaps has further implications for the question of visibility. When people with experiences of Madness and/or distress feel that they can be "out" about these experiences, they potentially have empathy to offer others who are similarly situated. Empathy can act as a social relief of any shame they have about their experiences. Participants spoke candidly about the increased relationality and potential for connection that they attributed to their experiences of Madness and/or distress. If, as Brown suggested, empathy and connection heal shame, people with experiences of Madness and/or distress may be uniquely positioned to help others with similar experiences release any shame they hold. Teaching is inherently relational. If shame heals and dissipates when met with empathy and connection, the teaching relationship has the capacity to provide an antidote to shame. When educators offer kindness instead of judgment, silence, and/or secrecy about experiences of Madness and/or distress, shame becomes unnecessary. The increased senses of relationality and empathy participants experienced have potential implications for the destigmatization of experiences of Madness and/or distress and the increased visibility that may result.

## Anti-Carceral Approaches to Madness and Distress

In Chapter 8, I advocated for an abolitionist and anti-carceral approach to Madness and distress. Participants felt surveilled in society, in educational institutions, and specifically in music education contexts. They scrutinized annual reports and reviews, professional standards in music teaching, and attendance, as well as issues surrounding self-surveillance. They challenged both the bureaucracy required to register with a disability and the policy of mandatory reporting. Taking these concerns into account, it is also imperative to understand carceral responses to Madness and/or distress through intersectional analysis.

In considering policing and surveillance, leadership in institutions must prioritize listening to people with experiences of Madness and/or distress and acknowledging the needs we articulate. Mad Studies centers Mad voices in the discourse, and abolition requires taking people at their word. First and foremost, an anti-carceral approach in education would remove the requirement to disclose a detailed medical history to receive accommodations. That level of surveillance is unnecessary when people with experiences of Madness and/or distress often know which accommodations might offer the support we need. Likewise, providing a detailed medical history constitutes a financial restriction to receiving accommodations.[9] Rather than a medical model approach that focuses on deficits, institutions can take a social model approach to accommodations for both students and educators. This change would forefront consideration of how the school/workplace disables the person in question, then work to remove those barriers. Removing barriers does not require a medical history, but instead listening to the student or educator at the center of the experience as they recount their lived reality.

Carceral education work—the practice of mandatory reporting of suicidality which involves the police—also necessitates a different solution. Educators, institutions, and policymakers might look to the intentional peer support model as a possibility. As noted in Chapter 7, peer support relies on principles of "respect, shared responsibility, and mutual agreement of what is helpful" (Mead, n.d., p. 1). Peer support would likely require a reimagining of care in schools, as well as institutional reconsideration of interpretation of existing laws, but would better serve educators and students experiencing distress than the current carceral approach.

Participants also described being surveilled socially. In such cases, normalizing and destigmatizing experiences of Madness and distress will work against social stigma and potentially lessen this dynamic. As noted in Chapter 5, visibility and representation assist with normalizing such experiences. Participants further problematized annual reports and reviews, professional standards, and attendance as mechanisms by which they felt policed in educational spaces. Policies regarding these practices must be evaluated for ableism and sanism and reworked in a way that is Mad-affirming. Mandatory attendance policies, for example, receive frequent mention in discourse about ableism and education (Birdwell & Bayley, 2022; Nicolas, 2017; Sapir & Banai, 2023), and were a concern shared by this study's participants. Such policies can easily be revised to be Mad-affirming and more flexible for everyone, as can other policies and practices. Participants felt specifically surveilled in music education in multiple ways, in their roles as both students and educators. Attending to the policies and practices they identified and addressing the embedded sanism and ableism will facilitate a more Mad-affirming, inclusive music education.

## Understanding the Help/Harm Dichotomy

In Chapters 6 and 7, participants elucidated ways that music education can both help and harm people with experiences of Madness and/or distress. Understanding this dichotomy in all its complexities is essential to supporting such people. These 15 participants generally agreed that certain practices in music education have been helpful to them. These practices were social, musical, and pedagogical. They noted the broad importance of connections, which included fostering community, building relationships, and feeling seen and validated in music education contexts. Participants also appreciated the benefits of some musicking practices, most notably ensemble experiences, playing or singing, jamming, songwriting, and strategic listening. Importantly, participants experienced these practices as low-stakes, although at times ensemble and solo performance experiences could be high-stakes and harmful. They also identified several pedagogical practices such as the Universal Design for Learning, trauma-informed praxis, culturally responsive teaching, LGBTQ+ affirming pedagogy, and fostering student autonomy as helpful in ameliorating distress. These music educators felt that explicitly addressing experiences of Madness and distress in the classroom may be supportive. Participants found these social, musical, and pedagogical practices helpful to their own mental and emotional wellbeing as well as that of students.

Various aspects of music education also harmed participants, each of which related to toxic elements in the culture of music education and specific musicking practices. They identified the competitive nature of music education, the culture of perfectionism, experiences of failure to meet expectations, a high degree of pressure and stress, experiences of invalidation, and relationships with abusive teachers as toxic elements of music education culture that proved injurious to their emotional (and sometimes physical) wellbeing. Certain musicking practices, particularly those that were high-stakes, also negatively impacted wellbeing for participants. Whereas they found ensemble participation, playing, and singing helpful in some contexts, at times Western classical ensemble-based music instruction and solo performing also caused emotional distress; this dynamic was most pronounced in respect to graded performances, competitions, and auditions. In addition, the literature established the potential harm of music listening (see for example Alluri et al., 2022; Silverman, 2021), even though participants identified music listening as unequivocally helpful.

Music education has the potential to help and/or harm people's emotional wellbeing, and this dichotomy is complex. Participants' descriptions of playing and singing, as well as participating in Western classical ensemble-based instruction, as both helpful and harmful makes clear that what may be good for one person may be terrible for another. Context and individual needs must be taken into account to understand these experiential variations. The high-stakes quality of certain musicking activities tended to exacerbate distress. How can music educators navigate this quagmire to support students experiencing Madness and/or distress? Music educators might first acknowledge the ways in which music education can be harmful instead of focusing solely on the advocacy platform of music as an unequivocal good. Almost all study participants identified ways they had been harmed by their experiences in K-12 and postsecondary music education. With this dynamic in mind, music educators would be wise to acknowledge that music education is not always congruous with emotional wellbeing and that children and youth, as well as young adults, may be negatively impacted by music. Most particularly, participants all agreed that the competitive and perfectionist culture cultivated in Western classical music study proved harmful to their emotional (and often physical) wellbeing.[10] Making changes to this culture appears crucial to constructing a music education supportive of wellbeing. Indeed, Powell (2023) called for alternatives to the current ideology of competition that pervades music education:

> Once the impossible—a way of music learning and teaching not accounted for by the current system—enters the frame, a transformation of the status quo is possible. The impossible makes change possible. This does not always mean a new genre of music. It can mean the same tradition of music seen from a new perspective—valued, assessed, practiced, conceptualized and validated in a new way that does not involve standardized, quantified measurement through competition. We must change the very coordinates by which we view, comprehend, and evaluate what "good" music education is.
>
> (p. 106)

Powell called for "student welfare" to serve as the limit for music education and described this limit as incompatible with the current hegemonic system of competition (p. 123).[11] His demand for the consideration of student welfare is compatible with prioritizing students' and teachers' emotional and physical wellbeing.

Participants in higher education also found the culture's focus on productivity and competition harmful. This culture, too, requires a paradigm shift. While the helpful/harmful dichotomy is complicated by some people feeling motivated and excited by competition,[12] the fact that all participants in this study found the competitive, perfectionist, and productivity-driven aspects of music education culture toxic is deeply problematic. It indicates that our discipline must make some significant changes in order to render a music education more supportive of students' and educators' emotional and physical wellbeing. These changes will benefit musickers with experiences of Madness and/or distress, while undoubtedly also preventing new experiences of distress, benefitting all involved. Music educators can instead embrace the kind of relational practices participants identified as helpful—fostering community, building relationships, and facilitating feeling seen and validated in music education contexts. De Quadros and Amrein (2023) theorized an approach they called *Empowering Song*, rooted in their choral praxis in carceral spaces. Their approach is liberatory, deeply relational, abolitionist, embodied, and centered on reciprocity and responsibility. Empowering Song stands in stark contrast to the competition- and product-oriented model that participants identified as harmful to their wellbeing and offers an alternative model of music education that cultivates many of the aspects participants identified as helpful.

A Mad-affirming music education acknowledges that musicking can be both helpful and harmful across K-12, undergraduate, and higher education contexts. Music educators can acknowledge the help/harm dichotomy and explicitly lean into the ways that musicking and music education helps, while avoiding the harms as much as possible. Participants identified both individual and school-based musicking practices they found helpful or harmful. Recognizing the individualized nature of what might feel helpful or harmful, music educators can make this concept explicit to students and guide them to identify the musicking practices and social elements of musicking that feel helpful to them. These practices may differ widely across student populations at all levels and across geographies. Identifying helpful practices enables students to compile musicking resources that may be helpful to them when they experience distress. Individuals experiencing distress may not always be able to think of a helpful practice in the moment, so creating resources in advance could constitute a meaningful aid. Music educators can also help students identify practices that feel harmful in order to consciously avoid them during times of distress in particular. Music educators can similarly compile resources for themselves to assist with distress, moving through the same process through which they have guided students. A Mad-affirming music education therefore supports students and educators in identifying ways in which musicking may support their distress. Such an education calls upon educators to explicitly teach students at all levels how to discern whether a practice feels helpful or harmful, which differs widely from person to person and potentially varies with time. Doing this kind of individualized work with students also enables teachers to amass a collection of practices that a significant number of students find helpful, centering those in their praxis with increasing intentionality and skill over time. In all types of music-learning settings, students also require repercussion-free options for opting out if something feels harmful. This right of refusal aligns with the UDL principle of providing options for engagement. Acknowledging how musicking may both help and harm enables both educators and students at all levels to identify with specificity what might be helpful or harmful to themselves and others in moments or periods of distress, but also preventatively. Becoming more mindful of distress triggers facilitates educators and students to lean into the helpful practices they/we have identified when triggers occur.

### Recognizing Assets as Contextual

In Chapter 3, Chris and August argued that personal characteristics and qualities of neurodivergence are not inherently strengths or weaknesses, rather encouraging the view that these can be assets or liabilities depending on context. Additionally, this conceptualization frames characteristics as fluid rather than static. Recognizing the contextual and fluid nature of characteristics allows educators and students to conceptualize them as value-neutral. This defies common conceptions of asset pedagogies which typically include culturally relevant pedagogy (Ladson-Billings, 1995, 2009, 2014, 2015), culturally responsive teaching (Gay, 2018; McKoy & Lind, 2023), and culturally sustaining pedagogy (Paris & Alim, 2014, 2017). These pedagogical approaches focus on the value of what students bring to their education as opposed to taking a deficit view.

Asset pedagogies nonetheless remain helpful in acknowledging that individual characteristics can act as assets. The idea that they can change from a perceived liability to an asset with a change of context broadens the discussion of culturally relevant pedagogy, culturally responsive teaching, and culturally sustaining pedagogy, and encourages music educators to create contexts in which these positive changes occur. UDL caters particularly well to this idea; it allows students to control the context for their learning in ways that utilize their characteristics as assets. I argue that UDL is also an asset pedagogy. The way it varies action and expression, representation, and engagement provides students means to draw on the characteristics they feel are assets in the classroom and offers them agency in how they access material and demonstrate learning.[13] An assets-based approach to pedagogy recognizes the presence of diverse characteristics in music education and views diversity as *community cultural wealth* (Yosso, 2005). A Mad-affirming music education recognizes diverse characteristics and frames them as assets in given contexts.

An approach to pedagogy that views characteristics as assets depending on context may help students to cultivate self-compassion. When students and educators understand that characteristics may serve as liabilities in some contexts but assets in other contexts, this understanding may foster increased self-compassion among students and educators about themselves. Neff (2003, 2011) identified three primary tenets of self-compassion: self-kindness, a sense of common humanity, and mindfulness. Recognizing the context-specific nature of characteristics as assets, Neff's first two tenets apply in particular. When students and educators recognize that their characteristics are value-neutral, fluid, and contextual, they may be kinder to themselves in contexts where certain characteristics do not serve them well. Neff's second tenet of "common humanity" asks individuals to recognize their experience as common to the human experience in moments of suffering, helping people bridge the gap between self and others. In the case of common humanity, understanding that all people have characteristics which act as assets or liabilities and vary by context may allow increased self-compassion.

Approaches beyond this rethinking of asset pedagogies can also be helpful to constructing a Mad-affirming music education. Trauma-informed pedagogy, for example, accounts for trauma responses and teaches in a way that supports distress (Hess, 2022a). In the context of trauma-informed teaching, music educators can offer students agency over their responses to instruction in ways that also grant them some degree of control over the experiences themselves (Hess, 2022a). Following the recognition that music can harm as well as help, teachers can guide students to use music carefully in order not to further exacerbate distress or cause distress where it did not previously exist (Hess, 2022a). Given its direct attention to distress, trauma-informed pedagogy potentially offers a powerful contribution to a Mad-affirming pedagogy that includes ways to soothe distress.[14]

### Benefits of Neurodivergence

Participants described several characteristics of neurodivergence they viewed as assets (see Chapter 4). These included increased empathy and compassion, a focus on cultivating relationality, overinclusiveness, curiosity, and an awareness of other's needs. They further identified some of these characteristics as specifically useful to teaching. The characteristics they identified are deeply interpersonal and highly conducive to teaching and learning effectiveness. Music educators might aim to cultivate these and similar characteristics and value them when they show up in students and teachers with experiences of Madness and/or distress.

Hendricks (2018) put forward an approach to compassionate music teaching that centers empathy. Her work aligned in many ways with the increased sense of empathy, compassion, and relationality participants in this study described. She distinguished between cognitive empathy and affective empathy: "*cognitive empathy*, or the ability to consider in our minds what someone else might be experiencing, and *affective empathy*, or the ability to actually feel in our bodies and emotions what others are feeling" (56). Participants generally indicated experiencing affective empathy, having a felt sense of emotional states both they and their students have experienced. Hendricks extended these ideas toward what she called *compassionate* or *motivational* empathy "in which a person not only understands and feels for (and with) others but also feels compelled to make things better for people in need" (p. 57). She described this as a "caring for" rather than a "caring about" (p. 57). She later extended "teachers caring *for* and *about* students, to an experience of learners and teachers caring *with* one another in music-learning settings" (Hendricks, 2023, p. 12, emphasis in original).[15] While I have extensively challenged the power relations potentially embedded in empathetic encounters (Hess, 2019, 2023), participants centered empathy and its value in relational teaching. Following the lead of these 15 music educators, I suggest a compassionate music teaching that also attends to embedded power relations. Hendricks (2018) provided several suggestions for fostering compassionate empathy in music teaching:

1. Model empathy and action.
2. Provide artistic experiences for perspective taking.
3. Be sensitive to the nonverbal messages that students may be giving.
4. Engage students in dialogue with one another.
5. Minimize the focus on competitiveness and increase a sense of community.
6. Provide a safe learning space where mutual caring and concern is the norm.
7. Stay attuned to your own emotional and physical needs. (see pp. 69–71 for full descriptions)

Participants described their tendencies toward empathy as particularly sensitive to nonverbal messages they received from others and further opposed a climate of competition in favor of community. They observed their care and concern for others rooted in their own challenging experiences of Madness and/or distress and described examples of modeling "mutual caring and concern." Moreover, participants were deeply attuned to their own emotional and physical needs. Embracing all tenets of Hendricks' compassionate approach to music teaching enables educators with experiences of Madness and/or distress to put their increased sense of empathy, compassion, and relationality to use in the classroom.[16]

Accounting for power, as I discuss in the next section, facilitates a compassionate Mad-affirming music education that attends to the full range of oppressive structures that target identity.

## Neurocosmopolitanism and Music Education

In considering her work on neurodiversity, Walker (2021) noted: "When working to bring about transformation on any scale from the personal to the global, it's vital to ask oneself what it might look like if one's work were to someday succeed in the fullest way possible" (pp. 85–86). She went on to elaborate a dream of neurocosmopolitanism:

> Neurocosmopolitanism consists of approaching neurodiversity in the same spirit in which the cosmopolite approaches cultural diversity. To embrace the neurodiversity paradigm is to refuse to pathologize neurocognitive styles and experiences that differ from our own, and to accept neurodiversity as a natural, healthy, and important form of human biodiversity—a fundamental and vital characteristic of the human species, a crucial source of evolutionary and creative potential. Neurocosmopolitanism goes beyond this baseline of acceptance, though, just as cosmopolitanism goes beyond mere tolerance of cultural differences. The neurocosmopolitan seeks to actively engage with and preserve human neurodiversity, and to honor, explore, and cultivate its creative potentials, in a spirit of humility, respect, and continual openness to learning and transformation.
>
> (p. 87)

Walker envisioned a world in which neurodiversity is honored, explored, and cultivated. In this conceptualization, no bodymind is privileged as more "normal" or "correct" (p. 88), and neurodiversity in all of its variations is appreciated. In neurocosmopolitanism, variations in "perception, cognition, embodiment, experience, needs, and styles of communication and interaction" (p. 88) are embraced wholeheartedly.

While openmindedness and an open orientation is certainly one aspect of cosmopolitanism (Delanty, 2019; Delanty & Harris, 2019), cosmopolitanism has also been sharply criticized for its embeddedness in coloniality and capitalism (Beck, 2002; Delanty & Harris, 2019; Dhawan, 2013; Mignolo, 2002; Rao, 2013). Scholars therefore call for a critical cosmopolitanism (Beck, 2002; Delanty & Harris, 2019; Mignolo, 2002; Rabinow, 1986) theorized from the perspective of the subaltern, or the "exteriority of modernity (this is, coloniality)" (Mignolo, 2002, p. 160). Dhawan (2013) argued that progressive activists and intellectuals who intervene on behalf of subaltern groups often reinscribe the "power relations that they seek to demolish" (p. 145).[17] In theorizing a neurocosmopolitanism, I assert that it must prioritize attention to power and subalternity. Indeed, to attend to power and subalternity in the context of neurocosmopolitanism, a DisCrit analysis focuses attention on the co-construction of racism and ableism, and centers voices of the racialized and disabled population (Annamma et al., 2022; Connor et al., 2016). In attending to the coloniality inherent in cosmopolitanism, DisCrit refuses to allow dominant voices to subsume the voices of the minoritized and multiply minoritized. Neurocosmopolitanism must be theorized at the grassroots level, centering the voices of the multiply minoritized.

I theorize neurocosmopolitanism drawing on literature that conceptualizes a critical cosmopolitanism. Delanty and Harris (2019) explained several of its characteristics: "the centrality of openness and overcoming of divisions, the interaction, the logic of exchange, the encounter and dialogue, deliberative communication, self and societal transformation (transformational) and critical evaluation" (p. 94). The encounter between Self and Other thus remains central to cosmopolitanism. Rabinow (1986) proposed a critical cosmopolitanism deeply rooted in ethics. For Rabinow, critical cosmopolitanism "is an oppositional position, one suspicious of sovereign powers, universal truths, overly relativized preciousness, local authenticity, moralisms high and low" (p. 258). It is deeply "suspicious of its own imperial tendencies" (p. 258) and is "highly attentive to (and respectful of) difference, but is also wary of the tendency to essentialize difference" (p. 258). Understanding the convergence of these perspectives, neurocosmopolitanism centers the encounter within an ethical disposition of openness that is attentive to power and wary of essentialism.

Beck (2002) theorized *cosmopolitanization from within* that considers the intrapersonal or internal response to the globalized encounter (pp. 25–26). For Beck, the "central defining characteristic of a cosmopolitan perspective is the '*dialogic* imagination'. By this I mean the clash of cultures and rationalities within one's own life, the '*internalized* other'" (p. 18, emphasis in original). Delanty and Harris (2019) concurred that cosmopolitanism is dialogic:

> One of the features of cosmopolitanism as a process of self-transformation is its communicative dimension. As a dialogic condition cosmopolitanism can be understood in terms of critical dialogue or deliberation. A deliberative conception of culture and politics captures the cosmopolitan spirit of engaging with the perspective of the Other as opposed to rejecting it.
>
> (p. 95)

The dialogic encounter leads to transformation. Delanty and Harris described a self and societal transformation in response to the encounter with the other, involving a pluralization and the possibility of deliberation (p. 95). A critical cosmopolitanism opens up new horizons in which

> cultures undergo transformation in light of the encounter with the Other. It can take different forms [r]anging from the soft forms of multiculturalism to major re-orientations in self-understanding in light of global principles or re-evaluations of cultural heritage and identity as a result of inter-cultural encounters.
>
> (pp. 95–96)

Transformation is therefore a central goal of a critical cosmopolitanism, and such transformation is rooted in ethics and is attentive to power relations and subalternity.

Neurocosmopolitanism involves an openness to neurodivergence and prioritizes the relational encounter. Mignolo (2002) observed that most stories of modernity[18] have been told from the perspective *of* modernity, necessitating a need to reconceptualize cosmopolitanism from the perspective of coloniality (p. 159). Following Mignolo, neurocosmopolitanism must occur on the terms of the neurodivergent. It attends to power differentials across different sites of identity including, but not limited to: race, gender, social class, disability, sexuality, religion, age, national status, and size. Neurocosmopolitanism values multidimensional identities and recognizes how dominant identities hold social, cultural, and economic capital (Annamma et al., 2016; Bourdieu, 1986). Walker (2021) identified neurocosmopolitanism as what might happen if neurodiversity work would someday radically succeed (pp. 85–86). In order to arrive at such a possibility, significant destigmatizing and normalizing work is required. Privileging the relational encounter may enable such work to occur. Perhaps most importantly, neurocosmopolitanism centers the encounter with an endgame of transformation. The hesitancy that some participants had about being "out" about their experiences of Madness and/or distress reveals the urgent need for transformation.

In music education, neurocosmopolitanism involves an openness to the full range of neurodiversity, alongside acknowledgement and analysis of its intersections with other sites of identity. It recognizes embedded power relations and normalizes a wide range of cognitive, experiential, emotional, embodied, communicative, and dispositional diversity. Neurocosmopolitanism values the different inclinations people hold toward musicking and the myriad ways that musicking can prove helpful or harmful to individuals diverging widely from person to person and moment to moment. For music educators, neurocosmopolitanism entails creating a space that welcomes a full range of human diversity through approaches such as UDL (CAST, n.d.) or culturally responsive teaching (Gay, 2018; McKoy & Lind, 2023); it makes room for students and educators to discover the contexts in which their characteristics act as assets, as well as recognizing situations in which those same characteristics may be liabilities. For Walker (2021),

> A neurocosmopolitan perspective, by contrast, privileges no bodymind as the "natural" default way of being, nor as more "normal" or intrinsically correct than any other, just as a hallmark of cosmopolitanism is the recognition that no one culture is more intrinsically correct, natural, or "normal" than any other. The neurocosmopolite welcomes and appreciates the differences among bodyminds—all the manifold variations in perception, cognition, embodiment, experience, needs, and styles of communication and interaction—in the same open-minded and profoundly egalitarian spirit with which the true cosmopolite greets cultural differences.
>
> (p. 88)

A Mad-affirming music education that aims toward neurocosmopolitanism encourages students and educators alike to: (1) appreciate the differences across perception, cognition, embodiment, experience, needs, and styles of communication and interaction that they/we bring to the learning encounter; and (2) to value each individual for the qualities and characteristics they possess. Following a DisCrit approach to analysis, such a music education recognizes the roles of systems of power, systemic discrimination across identities, and the interdependence and co-constitution of these systems (Annamma et al., 2016). A Mad-affirming education takes transformation as its goal toward a world in which neurodiversity is normalized, valued, and appreciated, and where the voices of the multiply minoritized are especially prioritized.

### Returning to the Contrapuntal Methodology

In this book's introduction, I noted that within a contrapuntal methodology (Said, 1993), the responsibility to engage with dissident voices and the ability to respond means that the voices can be perceived as "transforming each other continuously" (de Groot, 2005, p. 223). In this book, I facilitated relational encounters with 15 insightful music educators who have experiences of Madness and/or distress. In attending to their voices, I aimed to make clear the imperative of transforming sanism in music education as it intersects with other oppressions; the result is a neurocosmopolitanism that recognizes the wisdom these music educators offer alongside all music students and music educators with experiences of Madness and/or distress. Following Said (1993), participants made the "voyage in" to resist dominant music education practices and their embedded sanism and ableism. DisCrit demands the privileging of "voices of marginalized populations, traditionally not acknowledged within research" (Annamma et al., 2016, p. 19). Mad Studies similarly centers the voices of people with experiences of Madness and/or distress (Beresford & Russo, 2022; LeFrançois et al., 2013; Russo & Sweeney, 2016). It also centers resistance. A Mad-affirming music education accordingly prioritizes the voices of students and educators with experiences of Madness and/or distress. In attending to these valuable perspectives, the resulting music education will be better equipped and positioned to serve music educators, music students, and scholars with experiences of Madness and/or distress in ways that honor all that they/we bring to every teaching, learning, and musicking encounter.

# Notes

1 I note here that society certainly values the *musical* contributions of people with experiences of Madness and/or distress, but does not necessarily enable their contributions to the generation of *social meanings* that allow people to make sense of their experiences. This dynamic perpetuates the "struggling artist/genius" stereotype I discussed in the introduction.
2 See in particular Chapter 6.
3 August used the term "spiky" in Chapter 3: "Neurodiversity tends to be described in terms of deficiencies, but because it is a spiky profile, it often pairs with areas where someone is above average. It could be a spiky profile, where a lot of things are average and then there are some deficits. But very, very commonly, it's a spiky profile where there are really strong areas."
4 I discussed this idea in Chapter 3 and return to it later in this chapter.
5 This idea was articulated by Lisa Laughman, who drew on Weller's (2015) work.
6 I note here that neurodiversity is a spectrum. Rather than considering neurotypical as a type of person, Walker (2021) defined someone who is neurotypical as someone who is not harmed by neuronormativity.
7 Cornel West articulated the idea of using privilege as a shield during the opening plenary of the American Educational Research Association (AERA) Annual Meeting in April 2023.
8 In the case of historical figures who were not neccesarily "out" because such visibility operated differently in decades and centuries past, educators might introduce artists whose neurodivergence has been studied and named by scholars such as Redfield Jamison (1993).

9 In the U.S., neurocognitive testing to receive a diagnosis, healthcare visits, and paperwork from a medical professional all typically come at a financial cost that can be substantial, depending on insurance coverage.
10 Bernhard (2021) offered elements of physical and emotional wellbeing to help music educators navigate stress. These elements include sleep, exercise, nutrition, gratitude, happiness, and mindfulness. Participants in this study discussed sleep, exercise, and mindfulness in particular as supportive of their wellbeing. The competitive climate and ideology of competition in music education proved harmful to all participants' wellbeing.
11 Powell clarified: "I'm thinking of 'limit' in two ways: First, in the Hegelian sense of freedom in that 'true' freedom isn't just a lawless terrain in which individuals can do whatever they want (the libertarian view of freedom), but is instead a structured society with certain laws and customs in (what Hegel calls 'the state' in the Philosophy of Right) which allow us to express our freedom as a community. For a contemporary example, libertarians might see laws which restrict gun ownership as a state suppression of freedom but, taking my view, we can see gun laws as providing the social structure for our freedom *from* gun violence, which allows us to develop our life. So, this limit (on individual action) is necessary for the true freedom. The secondary way I'm conceptualizing the limit is a self-imposed limitation that paradoxically (dialectically) allows our creative freedom to propagate, like Dogme 95 or the White Stripes—limiting their material helps their creativity flourish. So, in music education, I'm saying we need to institute a limit (student welfare, which is contextual) in order to (1) have the true freedom *from* an oppressive, standardized competitive structure and (2) to allow music educators and their students' creativities and potentialities to flourish because it's not a laissez-faire, do whatever you want scenario that paralyzes us with (the illusion of) infinite freedom (à la Kant)" (Powell, personal correspondence, September 17, 2023, emphasis in original).
12 As noted in Chapter 6, Brown (2021) eschewed the external motivation of perfectionism in favor of healthy, internally-motivated striving (p. 142).
13 See Kieran and Anderson (2018) for an extended discussion of culturally responsive teaching and UDL.
14 Some might see my omission of social emotional learning (SEL) as a significant gap in a book about emotional wellbeing in music education. While I find some elements of the CASEL framework helpful in relation to emotional regulation, I have a longstanding concern that emotional regulation is about compliance rather than wellbeing. Richerme (2022) has critiqued the neoliberalism embedded in the framework. Simmons (2019) wrote against the white-washing of this pedagogical approach. Indeed, Simmons (2021) noted that SEL "done poorly faces the risk of becoming 'white supremacy with a hug.'" Given these important critiques, I do not include it here as a possibility, but note that an equity-conscious version of SEL that works against white supremacy and neoliberalism might be constructive in music educators' work toward emotional wellbeing. Simmons (2021), for example, offers an anti-racist approach to SEL.

15 Hendricks cited her previous work (Hendricks, 2021).
16 These 15 participants observed an increased sense of empathy, compassion, and relationality as a result of their experiences of Madness and/or distress. I do not generalize this finding to the larger population of people who have such experiences.
17 I do, however, think that there are occasions when a person with privilege across various identities can use their privilege as a shield in ways that might benefit the cause, as noted in endnote 7.
18 Modernity typically describes norms and practices associated with the Enlightenment such as egalitarianism, equality, fraternity, universalism, individualism, and meliorism. Goldberg (1993) clearly traced the ways that such values are implicated in racist culture and are not inclusive of minoritized groups.

## References

Alluri, V., Mittal, A., SC, A., Vuoskoski, J. K., & Saarikallio, S. (2022). Maladaptive music listening strategies are modulated by individual traits. *Psychology of Music*, 50(6), 1779–1800. https://doi.org/10.1177/03057356211065061

Andrzejewski, A. (2023, July 5). Academics don't talk about our mental ilnesses. We should. *The Chronicle of Higher Education*. www.chronicle.com/article/academics-dont-talk-about-our-mental-illnesses-we-should?cid=gen_sign_in&sra=true

Annamma, S. A., Connor, D. J., & Ferri, B. A. (2016). Touchstone text—Dis/ability Critical Race Studies (DisCrit): Theorizing at the intersections of race and dis/ability. In D. J. Connor, B. A. Ferri, & S. A. Annamma (Eds.), *DisCrit: Disability studies and critical race theory in education* (pp. 9–32). Teachers College Press.

Annamma, S. A., Ferri, B. A., & Connor, D. J. (Eds.). (2022). *DisCrit expanded: Reverberations, ruptures, and inquiries*. Teachers College Press.

Beck, U. (2002). The cosmopolitan society and its enemies. *Theory, Culture & Society*, 19(12), 17–44. https://doi.org/10.1177/026327640201900101

Beresford, P., & Russo, J. (Eds.). (2022). *The Routledge international handbook of Mad Studies*. Routledge.

Bernhard, H. C. (2021). *Managing stress in music education*. Routledge.

Birdwell, M. L. N., & Bayley, K. (2022). When the syllabus is ableist: Understanding how class policies fail disabled students. *Teaching English in the Two Year College*, 49(3), 220–237. www.proquest.com/scholarly-journals/when-syllabus-is-ableist-understanding-how-class/docview/2664104753/se-2

Bourdieu, P. (1986). The forms of capital. In J. G. Richardson (Ed.), *Handbook of Theory and research for the sociology of education* (pp. 241–258). Greenwood.

Brown, B. (2021). *Atlas of the heart: Mapping meaningful connection and the language of human experience*. Random House.

Bueter, A. (2019). Epistemic injustice and psychiatric classification. *Philosophy of Science*, 86, 1064–1074.

Carver, L., Morley, S., & Taylor, P. (2017). Voices of deficit: Mental health, criminal victimization, and epistemic injustice. *Illness, Crisis, & Loss, 25*(1), 43–62. https://doi.org/10.1177/1054137316675715

CAST. (n.d.). *CAST*. Retrieved March 6, 2023 from www.cast.org

Connor, D. J., Ferri, B. A., & Annamma, S. A. (Eds.). (2016). *DisCrit: Disability studies and critical race theory in education*. Teachers College Press.

Corrigan, P. W., Morris, S., Larson, J., Rafacz, J., Wassel, A., Michaels, P., Wilkniss, S., Batia, K., & Rüsch, N. (2010). Self-stigma and coming out about one's mental illness. *Journal of Community Psychology, 38*(3), 259–275. https://doi.org/10.1002/jcop.20363

Crichton, P., Carel, H., & Kidd, I. J. (2017). Epistemic injustice in psychiatry. *BJPscych Bulletin, 41*(2), 65–70. https://doi.org/10.1192/pb.bp.115.050682

Czeisler, M. É., Lane, R. I., Petrosky, E., Wiley, J. F., Christensen, A., Njai, R., Weaver, M. D., Robbins, R., Facer-Childs, E. R., Barger, L. K., Czeisler, C. A., Howard, M. E., & Rajaratnam, S. M. W. (2020). Mental health, substance use, and suicidal ideation during the COVID-19 pandemic—United States, June 24–30, 2020. *Centers for Disease Control and Prevention*. www.cdc.gov/mmwr/volumes/69/wr/mm6932a1.htm?s_cid=mm6932a1_w

de Groot, R. (2005). Perspectives of the polyphony in Edward Said's writings. *Journal of Comparative Poetics, 25*, 219–240.

De Quadros, A., & Amrein, E. (2023). *Empowering song: Music education from the margins*. Routledge.

Delanty, G. (2019). Introduction: The field of cosmopolitanism studies. In G. Delanty (Ed.), *Routledge international handbook of cosmopolitanism studies* (pp. 1–8). Routledge.

Delanty, G., & Harris, N. (2019). The idea of critical cosmopolitanism. In G. Delanty (Ed.), *Routledge international handbook of cosmopolitanism studies* (pp. 91–100). Routledge.

Dhawan, N. (2013). Coercive cosmopolitanism and impossible solidarities. *Qui Parle: Critical Humanities and Social Sciences, 22*(1), 139–166. www.jstor.org/stable/10.5250/quiparle.22.1.0139

Dobbs, T. L. (2012). A critical analysis of disabilities discourse in the *Journal of Research in Music Education*, 1990–2011. *Bulletin of the Council for Research in Music Education, 194*, 7–30. https://doi.org/10.5406/bulcouresmusedu.194.0007

Elraz, H. (2018). Identity, mental health and work: How employees with mental health conditions recount stigma and the pejorative discourse of mental illness. *Human Relations, 71*(5), 722–741. https://doi.org/10.1177/0018726717716752

Erevelles, N., Kanga, A., & Middleton, R. (2006). How does it feel to be a problem?: Race, disability, and exclusion in educational policy. In E. A. Brantlinger (Ed.), *Who benefits from special education?: Remediating (fixing) other people's children* (pp. 77–99). Lawrence Erlbaum Associates.

Fricker, M. (2007). *Epistemic injustice: Power and the ethics of knowing*. Oxford University Press.

Fricker, M. (2013). Epistemic injustice as a condition of political freedom? *Synthese, 190*(7), 1317–1332.

Gay, G. (2018). *Culturally responsive teaching: Theory, research, and practice* (3rd ed.). Teachers College Press.

Glover, C. M., Corrigan, P. W., & Wilkniss, S. (2010). The effects of multiple categorization on perceptions of discrimination, life domains, and stress for individuals with severe mental illness. *Journal of Vocational Rehabilitation, 33*(2), 113–121. https://doi.org/10.3233/JVR-2010-0520

Goffman, E. (1963). *Stigma: Notes on the management of spoiled identity.* Prentice-Hall, Inc.

Goldberg, D. T. (1993). *Racist culture: Philosophy and the politics of meaning.* Blackwell.

Hendricks, K. S. (2018). *Compassionate music teaching: A framework for motivation and engagement in the 21st century.* Rowman & Littlefield.

Hendricks, K. S. (2021). Authentic connection in music education: A chiastic essay. In K. S. Hendricks & J. Boyce-Tillman (Eds.), *Authentic connection: Music, spirituality, and wellbeing* (pp. 237–253). Peter Lang.

Hendricks, K. S. (2023). A call for care and compassion in music education. In K. S. Hendricks (Ed.), *The Oxford Handbook of Care in Music Education* (pp. 6–21). Oxford University Press.

Hess, J. (2019). *Music education for social change: Constructing an activist music education.* Routledge.

Hess, J. (2020). Teaching back: Navigating oppressive encounters in music teacher education. *Visions of Research in Music Education, 34*, 1–31. www-usr.rider.edu/%7Evrme/v34n1/visions/Hess_Teaching_Back.pdf

Hess, J. (2022a). Rethinking "bad behavior": A compassionate response to "acting out" in music education. In D. Bradley & J. Hess (Eds.), *Trauma and resilience in music education: Haunted melodies* (pp. 19–34). Routledge.

Hess, J. (2022b). Theory as the "north star": An introduction to race theories for music education. *Music Educators Journal, 109*(2), 47–55. https://doi.org/10.1177/00274321221138547

Hess, J. (2023). When the project is not understanding: Music education for the incomprehensible. *Studies in Philosophy and Education, 42*(3), 261–282. https://doi.org/10.1007/s11217-022-09861-5

Jacobson, L. (2022). State of the Union: Biden addresses student mental health, saying their "lives and education have been turned upside-down." *The 74 Million.* www.the74million.org/article/biden-to-declare-unprecedented-student-mental-health-crisis-during-tonights-state-of-the-union/

Kieran, L., & Anderson, C. (2018). Connecting Universal Design for Learning with Culturally Responsive Teaching. *Education and Urban Society, 51*(9), 1202–1216. https://doi.org/10.1177/0013124518785012

Ladson-Billings, G. (1995). Toward a theory of culturally relevant pedagogy. *American Education Research Journal, 32*(3), 465–491. https://doi.org/10.3102/00028312032003465

Ladson-Billings, G. (2009). *The dream keepers: Successful teachers of African American children* (2nd ed.). Jossey-Bass.

Ladson-Billings, G. (2014). Culturally relevant pedagogy 2.0: A.k.a. the remix. *Harvard Educational Review, 84*(1), 74–84. https://doi.org/10.17763/haer.84.1.p2rj131485484751

Ladson-Billings, G. (2015). You gotta fight the power: The place of music in social justice education. In C. Benedict, P. K. Schmidt, G. Spruce, & P. G. Woodford (Eds.), *The Oxford handbook of social justice in music education* (pp. 406–419). Oxford University Press.

LeBlanc, S., & Kinsella, E. A. (2016). Toward epistemic justice: A critically reflexive examination of "sanism" and implications for knowledge generation. *Studies in Social Justice, 10*(1), 59–78.

Lee, J. Y. (2021). Anticipatory epistemic injustice. *Social Epistemology*, Online First, 1–13. https://doi.org/10.1080/02691728.2021.1924306

LeFrançois, B. A., Menzies, R., & Reaume, G. (Eds.). (2013). *Mad matters: A critical reader in Canadian Mad Studies*. Canadian Scholars' Press, Inc.

Lettieri, A., Soto-Pérez, F., Franco-Martín, M. A., de Urríes, F. d. B. J., Shiells, K. R., & D'íez, E. (2021). Employability with mental illness: The perspectives of employers and mental health workers. *Rehabilitation Counseling Bulletin, 64*(4), 195–207. https://doi.org/10.1177/0034355220922607

Linton, S. (1998). *Claiming disability: Knowledge and identity*. New York University Press.

Love, B. L. (2019). *We want to do more than survive: Abolitionist teaching and the pursuit of educational freedom*. Beacon Press.

Lubet, A. (2013). *Music, disability, and society*. Temple University Press.

Martin, J. K., Pescosolido, B. A., & Tuch, S. (2000). Of fear and loathing: The role of "disturbing behavior," labels, and casual attributions in shaping public attitudes toward people with mental illness. *Journal of Health and Social Behavior, 41*(2), 208–223. https://doi.org/10.2307/2676306

McKoy, C. L., & Lind, V. L. (2023). *Culturally responsive teaching in music education: From understanding to application*. Routledge.

Mead, S. (n.d.). *Defining peer support*. Intentional Peer Support. Retrieved January 30 from https://docs.google.com/document/d/1WG3ulnF6vthAwFZpJxE9rkx6lJzYSX7VX4HprV5EkfY/edit

Medina, J. (2017). Varieties of hermeneutical injustice. In I. J. Kidd, J. Medina, & G. Pohlhaus Jr. (Eds.), *The Routledge handbook of epistemic injustice* (pp. 41–52). Routledge.

Menzies, R., LeFrançois, B. A., & Reaume, G. (2013). Introducing Mad Studies. In B. A. LeFrançois, R. Menzies, & G. Reaume (Eds.), *Mad matters: A critical reader in Canadian Mad Studies* (pp. 1–22). Canadian Scholars' Press, Inc.

Mignolo, W. D. (2002). The many faces of cosmo-polis: Border thinking and critical cosmopolitanism. In C. A. Breckenridge, S. Pollock, H. K. Bhabha, & D. Chakrabarty (Eds.), *Cosmopolitanism* (pp. 157–187). Duke University Press.

Morgan, H. (2022). Mad Studies and disability studies. In P. Beresford & J. Russo (Eds.), *The Routledge international handbook of Mad Studies* (pp. 108–118). Routledge.

Neff, K. (2003). Self-compassion: An alternative conceptualization of a healthy attitude toward oneself. *Self and Identity, 2*, 85–101.

Neff, K. (2011). *Self-compassion: The proven power of being kind to yourself*. HarperCollins.

Nicolas, M. (2017). Ma(r)king a difference: Challenging ableist assumptions in writing program policies. *WPA: Writing Program Administration*, *40*(3), 10–22.

Oliver, M., & Sapey, B. (1999). *Social work with disabled people* (2nd ed.). Palgrave MacMillan.

Østerud, K. L. (2022). Mental illness stigma and employer evaluation in hiring: Stereotypes, discrimination and the role of experience. *Sociology of Health & Illness*, *45*(1), 90–108. https://doi.org/10.1111/1467-9566.13544

Paris, D., & Alim, H. S. (2014). What are we seeking to sustain through culturally sustaining pedagogy? A loving critique forward. *Harvard Educational Review*, *84*(1), 85–100. https://doi.org/10.17763/haer.84.1.982l873k2ht16m77

Paris, D., & Alim, H. S. (Eds.). (2017). *Culturally sustaining pedagogies: Teaching and learning for justice in a changing world*. Teachers College Press.

Powell, S. R. (2023). *The ideology of competition in school music*. Oxford University Press.

Rabinow, P. (1986). Representations are social facts: Modernity and postmodernity in anthropology. In J. Clifford & G. E. Marcus (Eds.), *Writing cultures: The poetics and politics of ethnology*. University of California Press.

Rao, R. (2013). Postcolonial cosmopolitanism: Making place for nationalism In J. Tripathy & S. Padmanabhan (Eds.), *The democratic predicament: Cultural diversity in Europe and India* (iBooks ed., pp. 328–371). Routledge.

Redfield Jamison, K. (1993). *Touched with fire: Manic-depressive illness and the artistic temperament*. Simon & Schuster.

Richerme, L. K. (2022). The hidden neoliberalism of CASEL's social emotional learning framework: Concerns for equity. *Bulletin of the Council for Research in Music Education*, *232*, 7–25. https://doi.org/10.5406/21627223.232.01

Rose, D. H., & Meyer, A. (Eds.). (2006). *A practical reader in universal design for learning*. Harvard Education Press.

Russinovaa, Z., Griffinb, S., Blocha, P., Wewiorskic, N. J., & Rosoklijad, I. (2011). Workplace prejudice and discrimination toward individuals with mental illnesses. *Journal of Vocational Rehabilitation*, *35*(3), 227–241. https://doi.org/10.3233/JVR-2011-0574

Russo, J., & Sweeney, A. (Eds.). (2016). *Searching for a rose garden: Challenging psychiatry, fostering Mad Studies*. PCCS Books Ltd.

Said, E. W. (1993). *Culture and imperialism*. Vintage Books.

Sapir, A., & Banai, A. (2023). Balancing attendance and disclosure: identity work of students with invisible disabilities. *Disability & Society*, OnlineFirst, 1–21. https://doi.org/10.1080/09687599.2023.2181765

Scrutton, A. P. (2017). Epistemic injustice and mental illness. In I. J. Kidd, J. Medina, & G. Pohlhaus Jr. (Eds.), *The Routledge handbook of epistemic injustice* (pp. 347–355). Routledge.

Shakespeare, T. (2014). *Disability rights and wrongs revisited* (2nd ed.). Routledge.

Shakespeare, T. (2017). The social model of disability. In L. J. Davis (Ed.), *The disability studies reader* (5th ed., pp. 190–199). Routledge.

Siebers, T. (2008). *Disability theory*. The University of Michigan Press.

Siebers, T. (2017). Disability and the theory of complex embodiment: For identity politics in a new register. In L. J. Davis (Ed.), *The disability studies reader* (5th ed., pp. 310–329). Routledge.

Silverman, M. J. (2021). Music-based emotion regulation and healthy and unhealthy music use predict coping strategies in adults with substance use disorder: A cross-sectional study. *Psychology of Music, 49*(3), 333–350. https://doi.org/10.1177/0305735619854529

Simmons, D. (2019). Why we can't afford whitewashed social-emotional learning. *ASCD Education Update, 61*(4), 2–3. www.ascd.org/el/articles/why-we-cant-afford-whitewashed-social-emotional-learning

Simmons, D. (2021). Why SEL alone isn't enough. *ASCD, 78*(6). www.ascd.org/el/articles/why-sel-alone-isnt-enough

Singh, K. (2023, August 10). US suicide deaths reached record high in 2022, CDC data shows. Reuters. www.reuters.com/world/us/us-suicide-deaths-reached-record-high-2022-cdc-data-shows-2023-08-11/

Snyder, S. L., & Mitchell, D. T. (2006). *Cultural locations of disability*. The University of Chicago Press.

Solórzano, D. G., Ceja, M., & Yosso, T. J. (2001). Critical Race Theory, racial microaggressions, and campus racial climate: The experiences of African American college students. *Journal of Negro Education, 69*(1/2), 60–73.

Steele, C. M., & Aronson, J. (1995). Stereotype threat and the intellectual test performance of African Americans. *Journal of Personality and Social Psychology, 69*(5), 797–811. https://doi.org/10.1037//0022-3514.69.5.797

Stuart, H. (2006). Mental illness and employment discrimination. *Current Opinion in Psychiatry, 19*(5), 522–526. https://doi.org/10.1097/01.yco.0000238482.27270.5d

Sullivan, P. J. (2019). Epistemic injustice and self-injury: A concept with clinical implications. *Philosophy, Psychiatry, & Psychology, 26*(4), 349–362. https://doi.org/10.1353/ppp.2019.0049

Sweeney, A. (2016). The transformative potential of survivor research. In J. Russo & A. Sweeney (Eds.), *Searching for a rose garden: Challenging psychiatry, fostering Mad Studies* (pp. 49–58). PCCS Books Ltd.

Walker, N. (2021). *Neuroqueer heresies: Notes on the neurodiversity paradigm, autistic empowerment, and postnormal possibilities* (ePub ed.). Autonomous Press.

Weller, F. (2015). *The wild edge of sorrow: Rituals of renewal and the sacred work of grief*. North Atlantic Books.

Williams, V. (2014). *"Sanism," a socially acceptable prejudice: Addressing the prejudice associated with mental illness in the legal system* [Unpublished Doctoral Dissertation, University of Tasmania]. Australia.

Wolframe, P. M. (2013). The madwoman in the academy, or, revealing the invisible straightjacket: Theorizing and teaching saneism and sane privilege. *Disability Studies Quarterly, 33*(1). https://dsq-sds.org/article/view/3425/3200

Yosso, T. J. (2005). Whose culture has capital? A critical race theory discussion of community cultural wealth. *Race Ethnicity and Education, 8*(1), 69–91. https://doi.org/10.1080/1361332052000341006

# Afterword

"It's been so long since I needed my suicidality playlist, I forgot I had it."

I made this comment to a friend when my proposal for this book was under review. Three terrible things had happened over a two-week period: (1) I received a major professional rejection that felt extremely personal; (2) an allegation I had made against a medical professional who harmed me was dismissed; and (3) my health insurance company notified me that they were cutting off access to my bipolar meds in a month-and-a-half's time because they wanted me to take something cheaper. This awful confluence triggered a bipolar depression, putting me in a dangerous place.

The threat of losing my medication terrified me. While I do not believe that medication is the only or best way to address being bipolar, it is how I choose to handle it for myself. Until four years ago I had never found a medication that quieted my suicidality. Until 2019, I had been suicidal for at least part of every month, and up to 13 solid months at a time, since I was 16 years old. In 2019, I started a new medication that made that voice abate. Until that fall, I did not know it was possible for me to live without relatively constant suicidality. The relief was significant. Now, four years later, my insurance company wished to stop paying for the medication despite it being the only one I have ever had success with among dozens tried. During this two-week period I spent 6 hours on hold with the insurance company only to ultimately learn I had to wait until the deadline passed to appeal their coverage determination. It felt ironic and cruel that this threat to my stability, in combination with the other factors, was wrecking the very stability that medication supports.

On the day I made that remark to a friend, I had been listening to my full music collection on shuffle when a song came on. When I heard it, it occurred to me that the song was on my grief playlist. Surely at least some of what I was experiencing was grief, so it felt like a good idea to listen to it. On that playlist, one of the songs was a cover of a song that was on my suicidality playlist. It had been so long since I needed my suicidality playlist, I forgot it existed. I found the playlist and began to listen.

I learned a long time ago that I need to be very careful with music when I'm in a dangerous place. When I feel suicidal, I crave listening to artists and songs that feed my darkness and plummet me further into it. Knowing this about myself, I have a list of artists and songs that I need to explicitly avoid when I am in severe distress. My suicidality playlist, therefore, is a collection of affirming songs that communicate hope through struggle. They are positive, but not in a way that feels like toxic positivity. These songs are not what I *crave* when I am suicidal; they are what I *need*. So I listened to nothing but that playlist for days on end. I added a few songs since it had been four years since I had listened to it last, and I have encountered many "new-to-me" albums, songs, and artists since then.

After four years with no threat to my stability, I found myself in the throes of despair and distress. Experiencing Madness and distress requires an ever-present vigilance. Even in periods of stability, the threat of instability is always there. People with experiences of Madness and/or distress are familiar with this precarity. We are never healed. An unexpected confluence of circumstances can take away stability in an instant. A trigger does not even have to be present to provoke distress, moods can simply shift. Given the sometimes fleeting nature of stability and the constant threat of instability, all people who experience Madness and distress can do is equip ourselves with resources to access in times of struggle, and hope that they will be enough when those times come. Despite our best plans and intentions, there is never certainty that they will be sufficient. Every time I come out the other side of the darkness, it feels like I barely made it, and also like I have survived a traumatic event, which I have. In my personal experience, and as I write this afterword, I know that musicking can be a part of the resources people with Madness and/or distress can use for survival. The music educators in this study agreed. I thus offer this book as a means of considering ways that musicking might help in times of distress, and how music educators and policymakers can positively contribute to that effort. Survival is never guaranteed, but resources increase the odds and musicking can be a part of that. As music educators, we can help people find ways that musicking might help them personally during periods of struggle. That is my greatest intent in putting forward a Mad-affirming music education.

# Appendix 1
## A Note on Methods

Having elaborated Said's (1993) contrapuntal methodology in the introduction, I offer this appendix to share insights into my choices regarding research methods. I begin by explicating my response to Patel's (2016) move from ownership to answerability in educational research. I then explain my approach to participant selection and share information about participants. Then I describe interviewing and focus groups, followed by a discussion of data analysis. I return to Patel in conclusion to account for reciprocity, accountability, and answerability.

### From Ownership to Answerability

Consistent with Said's anti-colonial contrapuntal methodology, I drew on Patel's (2016) work on decolonizing educational research to inform this project. Patel made an important shift in educational research from ownership to answerability—that is, from the colonial mindset of research akin to property acquisition, to answerability to research participants. She called on researchers to answer three important questions when undertaking a project: "Why This? Why Me? Why Now?" (p. 57). Answering these questions provided the foundation for this book. I briefly describe my motivations.

Why this? Music has great potential to soothe distress (Bradley & Hess, 2022) or otherwise regulate it (Saarikallio, 2012), but music education rarely focuses on that potential in classrooms and scholarship. Purposefully considering how music education might better serve students, teachers, and scholars with experiences of Madness and/or distress is likely to improve the experience for everyone. The Universal Design for Learning (UDL) approach to pedagogy draws on Universal Design in architecture, which aimed to make buildings and public spaces accessible by creating designs that make it possible for people with the full range of human differences to access any facility (Guffey & Williamson, 2020; Williamson, 2019). Design strategies such as curb cuts allow wheelchair users to navigate sidewalks, but this access extends to people with strollers, suitcases, or shopping carts. Design changes that center disability thereby benefit many people. The same logic applies to this book project. Designing music education pedagogy with Madness and distress in mind may better serve students, educators, and scholars in music education.

Why me? I am a member of this community. Stigma and fear of reprisal led me to suppress my bipolar identity before I received tenure, passing as neurotypical. I made this decision in light of the prevalence of workplace discrimination and fears about employability discussed in Chapter 5. Indeed, when a person does disclose, they might feel significant pressure to pass as neurotypical (Wolframe, 2013). Now that I feel I can be "out" about this aspect of my identity, I believe I have a responsibility to make it safer for others to express their identities, particularly as someone who personally holds multiple dominant identities. I wish for this safety to extend to people across all identities and all facets of music education—students and educators at all levels, as well as scholars. The question of whether or not to disclose remains a serious concern for people with experiences of Madness and distress. Being visible alongside participants may help destigmatize experiences of Madness and distress and generate informed conversation on the subject.

Why now? In 2023, we are in the process of recovering from the global COVID-19 pandemic, now determined to be endemic. People have struggled immeasurably with distress during this time (Czeisler et al., 2020), including those who previously had not. Struggles with experiences of Madness and/or distress have intensified, or perhaps just come to the surface. Students, educators, and scholars at all levels need tools to soothe distress more now than ever before. Music offers one such tool, and we can teach toward that potential in music education. Beyond the individual level, music educators must implement changes to pedagogy, praxis, and policy to better support both students and educators with experiences of Madness and/or distress. I offer implications at the end of each chapter, and throughout the conclusion chapter.

**Participant Selection**

I employed several purposive sampling strategies to select participants, including maximum variation sampling, selecting key informants, and snowball sampling (Patton, 2015). My dominant strategy, maximum variation sampling (Patton, 2015, p. 405), targeted a wide range of identities in relation to music education. I looked for people in preservice teacher education, practicing teachers, graduate students, music teacher educators, scholars, and studio teachers. I wanted to include participants with a range of different experiences in music education, while ensuring some commonalities. The 15 participants I selected varied in their music education experiences as sought; all participants had some formal music education, almost all had attended an undergraduate music program, and almost all had classroom teaching experience. I also selected key informants when possible (Patton, 2015, p. 406). Because of the sensitive and personal nature of the subject matter, I mostly selected participants either known to me or known to people who know me well. Participants I selected had elaborated on this topic in my presence, and I knew they would be engaged and insightful. I did not put out an open call at any stage because I valued the importance of relationship in this research. My third approach to participant selection involved snowball sampling (Patton, 2015, p. 408), and I found two participants using that strategy. As noted in the introduction, I do not claim that this participant group is broadly representative; the group is skewed particularly in relation to race and gender. My approach to participant selection allowed me to be in conversation with a group of thoughtful individuals who have deeply considered the intersection of Madness and/or distress with music education. What each person brought to the project was immensely valuable. My specific criteria were relatively open: (1) had experience in music education both as a student and a teacher (including preservice teachers); and (2) identified an issue with their own mental health. I include participants' demographic descriptions in their own words below.

### A Feminist Approach to Interviewing

In developing the interview protocol, I used a semi-structured approach in which I prepared a series of open-ended questions but also had the freedom to follow up for additional detail as relevant (Roulston, 2010, p. 15). I drew on Castillo-Montoya's (2016) Interview Protocol Refinement (IPR) framework to refine my interview questions. Castillo-Montoya suggested four phases: "(1) ensuring interview questions align with research questions, (2) constructing an inquiry-based conversation, (3) receiving feedback on interview protocols, and (4) piloting the interview protocol" (p. 811). I aligned my interview questions with my research questions, ensured they were inquiry-based but also felt conversational, and then sought feedback on the protocol from a scholar of disability studies. I incorporated the suggestions I received, piloted the protocol, then refined further afterwards.

In the interviewing process I took a feminist approach (DeVault & Gross, 2007; Oakley, 1981; Roulston, 2010). While typically applied to interviewing women, this approach attends dynamically to self-disclosure, ethics, relationships, and power, all of which appealed to me and aligned with goals of this project. Feminist interviewing focuses on meaning-making of both the personal and the political (DeVault & Gross, 2007).

*Table A1* Participant Descriptions

All participant descriptions in this table describe social locations, sites of identity, and teaching details at the time of the interview.

| Name | Pronouns | Age | Country | Music Teaching Experience | Self-Described Demographics |
|---|---|---|---|---|---|
| Blaine Banghart-Broussard | they/them | 20s | U.S. | Former elementary general music teacher, currently teaching high school brass lessons | "I am white. I'm in my 20s. I am non-binary, my pronouns are they/them and I also identify as trans. I'm bipolar with some depression and anxiety sprinkled in for zest. I live in the south, middle-class." |
| Meghan Barrett | she/her | 20s | U.S. | Completed student teaching in middle school band | "I am a white woman raised probably lower middle-class. Learning disability-wise, I have pretty severe ADHD. I have an ... unnamed chronic illness." |
| Jillian Bowe | they/them | 20s | U.S. | Fifth year undergraduate student in music education degree, student teaching | "I am white, upper middle-class. Queer and non-binary." |
| Cheryl** | they/them | 20s | From Western Europe, now in the U.S. | Upper elementary and middle school general and choral music teacher, completing a master's degree in music education | "White queer. Financially stable. Able-bodied. Non-binary." |
| Mary Cohen | she/her | 50s | U.S. | Previously taught elementary music for 10 years, currently an Associate Professor at the University of Iowa | "I self-identify as female, she/her pronouns. White, my ethnic background is Russian and German. A second generation as far as that goes. Married, heterosexual." |

Appendix 1 281

| | | | | |
|---|---|---|---|---|
| Lizabeth Desmet | they/them | 20s | U.S. | Completed student teaching in elementary general music | "I identify as white. My gender, I identify as a non-binary woman. I know that those terms are contrasting, but that's where I'm at. We can also call that gender non-conforming. … I was raised upper class, upper middle-class. That's had a lot of impact on my life. I have ADHD. I have depression. I have anxiety. … I'm queer." |
| Chris Hansen | she/her | 60s | From New Zealand, now in the U.S. | Preschool music teacher, pre-instrumental teacher (which involved beginning music literacy, "making instruments, and introducing students to a range of instruments, musics, and sound-making"), private violin teacher, and itinerant music teacher, currently running an international peer support education business | "I identify as a white, lesbian, married person with five kids and a grandchild. I am also an educator, an activist, and a business owner, as well as a user and survivor of psychiatry. I'm a new New Zealand citizen [currently living in the U.S.]." |
| August Knight* | he/they | 30s | U.S. | Violin, viola, music theory, and composition studio teacher | "Race, I'm white. Gender? Yes, probably. When I have to use words for it, I usually do stuff in the masculine-ish direction. I am autistic and I would consider that a disability using the social model. I was raised middle-class. I'm a broke musician in a large city. I don't know what class that is. I think private music teachers end up being like very high-paid service class." |

(Continued)

Table A1 (Continued)

| Name | Pronouns | Age | Country | Music Teaching Experience | Self-Described Demographics |
|---|---|---|---|---|---|
| Laura* | she/her | 40s | U.S. | Previously taught elementary music and beginning band, previously taught university classes through a graduate assistantship and as a Visiting Professor, doctoral student in music education | "I'm a white female. I'm middle-class. And I have several disabilities, mood disabilities. I am Bipolar 2 with severe depression. I have borderline personality disorder. I also have anxiety." |
| QingYu Zhong | they/them | 20s | U.S. | Substitute music teacher, working on year 1 of a master's degree in social work | "I identify as non-binary. I prefer they/them pronouns. I am Chinese, so I'm Asian. I'm Jewish. I identify as gay. I identify as a disabled person with a mobility disability and I am part of the neurodivergent community. I have ADHD." |
| Meena* | she/her | 30s | U.S. | Strings studio teacher, former elementary music teacher at a Waldorf school, working as a social worker | "I identify as cis female, heterosexual. I am mixed race. I'm half white, Caucasian, and [my] other half is East Indian, so Desi. My mother has heritage of Italy, Hungary and Slovakia. My father is from Nepal. My beliefs are Buddhist, and Eastern spiritual values and Buddhist Psychology inform my overall worldview." |

| | | | | | |
|---|---|---|---|---|---|
| Paulo* | he/him | 40s | U.S. | Former elementary general music teacher, currently Assistant Professor at a university | "You know on different days, it's different. … I would say bipolar is my first thing I would say right now. Especially having been sick, I've watched the fluctuation go a little bit more wobbly than normal, you know. … White, hetero, cis man, father now. … Kind of upper middle-class. Musician. Teacher. Stuff like that." |
| Emma Pilmer | she/her | 20s | U.S. | Senior year undergraduate student in choral music education degree, student teaching | "I am a proud Asian American who has been adopted. Female, she/her, and I identify as autistic. I've recently been diagnosed as autistic." |
| Nicholas Prosini | they/them | 40s | U.S. | Previously taught middle school band and orchestra, teaching K-5 general music for the last 5–6 years | "White, trans non-binary, middle-class, disabled, 40 years old, queer, and Jewish." |
| Rebecca* | she/her | 60s | Canada | Previously taught high school music, currently Full Professor at a university | "White, Caucasian, female. I identify as female and I prefer she/her pronouns. I do identify as somebody with mental health problems in a number of areas." |

Notes:
*Pseudonyms
**First name only

Researchers typically employ feminist interviews in doing feminist work, and to advance women's interests in the context of patriarchy (Roulston, 2010, p. 23). I did not intend to appropriate this approach for a completely different context; I argue that the refusal to acknowledge experiences of Madness and distress and the common decision to hide or mask an integral facet of one's true identity is at least partially rooted in patriarchy. Indeed, many men do not admit to these experiences or seek help due to stigma and toxic masculinity (Harris, 2021). It thus makes sense that participants, with one exception, identified as women, non-binary, or trans. The influence of patriarchy and toxic masculinity on the willingness to share experiences of Madness and distress made feminist interviewing an appropriate approach. Furthermore, feminist interviewing is intersectional in the way it accounts for power differentials and the vastly different and complex positions and identities that people hold.

A feminist approach to interviewing also takes the stance that self-disclosure is appropriate, as there is "no intimacy without reciprocity" (Oakley, 1981, p. 49). I disclosed my bipolar identity to all participants who did not already know, as well as acknowledging the ways in which my social location differed from theirs (Edwards, 1990, as cited in DeVault & Gross, 2007, p. 181). This process aided us in recognizing the ways in which finding common ground may be far more complex than simply assuming that one shared identity is enough (DeVault & Gross, 2007, pp. 179–180). Feminist interviewing aims to build relationships—an encounter and knowledge-sharing between people with common interests or experiences (DeVault & Gross, 2007, p. 178). It furthermore promotes equitable and reciprocal research relationships (Roulston, 2010, p. 21). Evidencing this and in keeping with Oakley (1981), relationships participants developed with each other and with me have continued beyond the conclusion of the study. Most importantly, I chose this approach in the interest of creating knowledge *for* rather than *about* participants (DeVault & Gross, 2007, p. 184). Because individuals with experiences of Madness and distress often suppress their experiences publicly and professionally, such experiences have become invisibilized. My hope is that knowing how others navigate and think about such experiences may ultimately be helpful to others with similar experiences. In writing about my conversations with participants, taking a feminist approach facilitated my work toward relationships that are ethical, non-exploitative, sincere, and involve genuine interest through free and open dialogue (Roulston, 2010, p. 23). Feminist interviewing attends to power; as such, I did not aim to erase any of the complex power differentials embedded in researcher-participant relationships (Harding, 2007).

Consistent with feminist interviewing, I made confidentiality optional in this project, noting that confidentiality sometimes fails to serve feminist goals (DeVault & Gross, 2007, p. 187). Patton (2015) acknowledged changes in confidentiality norms in qualitative research in the interest of ensuring participants have the capacity to "own their story" if they wish. Ultimately, nine of this study's participants chose to be identified, while five selected a pseudonym and one went by their first name only. The insights participants offered were consistently brilliant and I sought a way for them to receive credit for their ideas. While my ideas shaped the questions I asked in interviews, the chapters of this book emerged entirely from participants' insights.

I acknowledge, however, that intent differs from impact. In this section, I outlined my intentions. I am unsure, however, how participants received this intent. Roulston (2010) argued that feminist interviewers must: (1) acknowledge the way social science research heightens ethical issues; (2) believe participants; and (3) work to establish trust (p. 22). I intended this research to be useful to participants as well as to readers. I have and will continue to urge participants to let me know if my intent and impact are incongruent.

## Focus Groups

Focus groups are typically homogenous (Patton, 2015, p. 429). I originally intended to hold focus groups for participants at different levels of music education, but as the project proceeded it seemed that identity-based focus groups may be both more comfortable and of greater use to participants. I gave participants options of what could be possible, then planned focus groups according to their responses. All but one participant took part in a focus group and two participants contributed to two. In relation to identity, I held a focus group for non-binary and trans music educators. In relation to music education, I held a focus group for preservice music educators, a group for those involved in higher education music education (graduate students and professors), and a group for studio teachers. I also facilitated a focus group for music educators who now do peer support or social work.

Attending to the ethos of feminist interviewing (DeVault & Gross, 2007; Oakley, 1981; Roulston, 2010), I wanted these groups to be useful to participants—to provide opportunities to learn how others with experiences of Madness and/or distress navigate music education. I prepared open-ended questions for focus groups, all of which were conducted on Zoom. At the beginning of each I offered a reminder of confidentiality, noting the challenges of confidentiality in focus groups (Roulston, 2010, p. 40). I then put my questions in the chat and invited participants to attend to the questions if they found them useful, but otherwise prompted them to take the discussion in whatever direction would serve them. In all focus groups, participants attended to some of my questions and also steered toward other topics for discussion. Kleiber (2004) acknowledged that minimal literature attends to the meaning of the focus group experience from the participant's perspective (p. 96). I intended these groups to serve participants, with a secondary interest in how/whether they might be useful to the research. Following Roulston (2010), I wished to unsettle the asymmetrical power relations embedded in researcher-participant relationships (p. 39) to the degree possible. As such, I also shared my experiences when relevant to the discussion and was frank throughout about my bipolar identity and other facets of my positionality.

## Data Analysis

Throughout the process of conducting interviews (May through December of 2022) and holding focus groups (January and February of 2023), I kept regular analytic memos (Saldaña, 2016) to attend to my thoughts about these conversations. I continued memoing throughout my coding and analysis processes to note, trouble, confound, and challenge what I thought I knew about the data. I also engaged in a workshop on mandala drawing as data analysis with Kakali Bhattarcharya in the fall of 2022 that allowed me to artistically reflect on what I knew about the data thus far and spend several hours considering the emergent themes through art. In both the memoing and mandala-drawing processes, I attended particularly to reflexivity and power relations.

I used two phases in coding of the data. In the first phase, I employed elemental methods including structural coding, in vivo coding, and affective methods including emotion coding and values coding, which were each pertinent given the subject matter (Saldaña, 2016). I also utilized attribute coding to track demographics (Saldaña, 2016). I went through each conversation line-by-line and coded using the CAQDAS software NVivo, which tracks codes with coding stripes and incorporates simultaneous coding. Throughout this first coding phase, I paused to reflect on codes following each interview and focus group, then rearranged and subsumed codes as appropriate (Saldaña, 2016, p. 79).

In the second coding phase, I employed axial coding to reorganize the codes, subsume codes when appropriate, and recognize which codes were dominant or of less consequence (Saldaña, 2016, p. 244). I removed redundant codes and prioritized those that were most representative (Boeije, 2010, p. 109, as cited in Saldaña, 2016, p. 244). Axial coding accounts for the consideration of relationships between categories and subcategories, and ascertainment of the properties and dimensions of a category (Saldaña, 2016, p. 244). I continued to memo throughout both phases of the coding process, recording my observations and questions about codes and categories.

When I had a complete rough draft, I sent all the chapters with data generated from our conversations—both interviews and focus groups—to participants for feedback. I received substantial commentary on the whole document from six participants, and comments suggesting specific changes and revisions to individual contributions from the other nine. I spent the next few months attending to their feedback and suggestions, leading to significant alterations to the document.

## Returning to Ownership vs. Answerability

In this project I worked to incorporate Patel's (2016) anti-colonial shift from ownership to answerability in research. I hope to continue to be in relationship with participants, and that this book will be of use to them and to others similarly situated. I sent all transcripts to participants to verify and edit as they saw fit and also sent writing in progress for their valuable feedback. The degree of participant vulnerability in this study required me to be highly accountable for my writing. Power dynamics in research are fraught with injury (Smith, 2012). In holding myself as answerable to participants, I attend to the potential for injury and work against it. I feel immensely privileged to have been privy to the stories of these 15 music educators and am grateful to have spent significant time with their journeys and ideas. In the larger context of Said's (1993) contrapuntal methodology, it is my wish that participants' voices offer an impetus toward the transformation of music education to better support all people with experiences of Madness and distress.

## References

Boeije, H. R. (2010). *Analysis in qualitative research*. London, U.K.: SAGE.

Bradley, D., & Hess, J. (Eds.). (2022). *Trauma and resilience in music education: Haunted melodies*. New York, NY: Routledge.

Castillo-Montoya, M. (2016). Preparing for interview research: The interview protocol refinement framework. *The Qualitative Report, 21*(5), 811–831. Retrieved from https://nsuworks.nova.edu/tqr/vol21/iss5/2

Czeisler, M. É., Lane, R. I., Petrosky, E., Wiley, J. F., Christensen, A., Njai, R., . . . Rajaratnam, S. M. W. (2020). Mental health, substance use, and suicidal ideation during the COVID-19 pandemic — United States, June 24–30, 2020. *Centers for Disease Control and Prevention*. Retrieved from www.cdc.gov/mmwr/volumes/69/wr/mm6932a1.htm?s_cid=mm6932a1_w

DeVault, M. L., & Gross, G. (2007). Feminist interviewing: Experience, talk, and knowledge. In S. N. Hesse-Biber (Ed.), *Handbook of feminist research: Theory and praxis* (pp. 173–197). Thousand Oaks, CA: SAGE.

Edwards, R. (1990). Connecting method and epistemology: A white woman interviewing black women. *Women's Studies International Forum, 13*(5), 477–490. doi:10.1016/0277-5395(90)90100-C

Guffey, E., & Williamson, B. (Eds.). (2020). *Making disability modern: Design histories*. New York, NY: Bloomsbury Visual Arts.

Harding, S. (2007). Feminist standpoints. In S. N. Hesse-Biber (Ed.), *Handbook of feminist research: Theory and praxis* (pp. 45–790). Thousand Oaks, CA: SAGE.

Harris, B. (2021). *Toxic masculinity: An exploration of traditional masculine norms in relation to mental health outcomes and help-seeking behaviors in college-aged males*. (Senior Theses. 431). University of South Carolina—Columbia, Columbia, SC. Retrieved from https://scholarcommons.sc.edu/senior_theses/431

Kleiber, P. B. (2004). Focus groups: More than a method of qualitative inquiry. In K. deMarrais & S. D. Lapan (Eds.), *Foundations for research: Methods of inquiry in education and the social sciences* (pp. 87–102). Mahwah, NJ: Lawrence Erlbaum Associates, Inc.

Oakley, A. (1981). Interviewing women: A contradiction in terms. In H. Roberts (Ed.), *Doing feminist research* (pp. 30–61). London: Routledge & Kegan Paul.

Patel, L. (2016). *Decolonizing educational research: From ownership to answerability*. New York: Routledge.

Patton, M. Q. (2015). *Qualitative research and evaluation methods* (4th ed.). Los Angeles, CA: SAGE.

Roulston, K. (2010). *Reflective interviewing: A guide to theory and practice*. Los Angeles, CA: SAGE.

Saarikallio, S. (2012). Development and validation of the brief music in mood regulation scale. *Music Perception, 30*(1), 97–105. doi:10.1525/mp.2012.30.1.97

Said, E. W. (1993). *Culture and imperialism*. New York, NY: Vintage Books.

Saldaña, J. (2016). *The coding manual for qualitative researchers* (3rd ed.). Los Angeles, CA: SAGE Publications.

Smith, L. T. (2012). *Decolonizing methodologies: Research and indigenous peoples* (2nd ed.). London: Zed Books.

Williamson, B. (2019). *Accessible America: A history of disability and design*. New York, NY: New York University Press.

Wolframe, P. M. (2013). The madwoman in the academy, or, revealing the invisible straightjacket: Theorizing and teaching saneism and sane privilege. *Disability Studies Quarterly, 33*(1). Retrieved from https://dsq-sds.org/article/view/3425/3200

# Appendix 2
# A Call for Activism

In the U.S., the majority of states have passed or are considering legislation that restricts teaching related to race, gender, queerness, critical race theory, and/or privilege (see Salvador et al., 2023 for discussion in music education). Some states have also prohibited discussion about social emotional learning (SEL), which aims to facilitate emotional regulation.[1] While this book does not align with SEL practices, it nonetheless prioritizes emotional wellbeing, and the pedagogical approaches suggested may be targeted by the aforementioned legislation.

In 2022, the number of people who completed suicide in the U.S. reached a record of 49,000 people, an increase of 2.6% from 2021 (Singh, 2023). Experiencing Madness and distress can be fatal. People need access to tools that can help address and mediate distress and soothe Madness, and this book demonstrates ways that music education may contribute to that effort. Talking about these issues openly is crucial. Bans on processing and discussing distress in some states are potentially life-threatening. Moreover, the elements of these laws that limit discussions related to race, gender, and sexuality also target the most vulnerable. The prohibition of these topics constitutes an erasure of history, privilege, and identity, which causes harm to minoritized people's emotional wellbeing. These laws outlaw the ability to name and discuss experiences of oppression, or to place such experiences in sociohistorical and sociopolitical contexts.

Other countries have similarly prohibited or limited education about racial, ethnic, and LGBTQ+ identities. Countries with ongoing colonial projects, for example, such as Canada, the U.S., Australia, and New Zealand often fail to acknowledge Indigeneity including language and culture in schools and settler implication in colonialism, impacting the success of Indigenous students (see Blackwell, 2021; Brown, 2019; Skerrett, 2019; Thunig, 2019 for further context).[2] Following the U.S. example, government officials in the U.K. and Australia have spoken against teaching critical race theory (Trilling, 2020; Wilson, 2021). Russia and Hungary have targeted teaching about LGBTQ+ identities in schools (see for example Associated Press, 2013; Nicholson, 2021; Sverdlov, 2020). Approximately 100 towns or regions across Poland have declared themselves "LGBT-free zones" that are "free of LGBT ideology" (Ash, 2020), limiting possibilities for education. In countries such as Oman, Kuwait, United Arab Emirates, Malaysia, Papua New Guinea, Pakistan, Jamaica, Guyana, Sudan, Egypt, and Kenya[3] where LGBTQ+ identities are criminalized, LGBTQ+-affirming discussions cannot occur in schools (see for example Rédaction Africanews with Agencies, 2023). In addition, "Memory laws" or "government actions designed to guide public interpretation of the past" (Snyder, 2021) are in place in Russia and Poland. Under Putin, Russia controls the interpretation of historical events in a way that justifies the current distribution of power and privileges the feelings of the powerful over the experiences of the vulnerable (Snyder, 2021). In Poland, the far right Law and Justice Party limit discussions of Polish Christians' complicity in the Holocaust for fear of such discussions' impact on national identity (Dekel, 2021; Donadio, 2018). These kinds of erasures rooted in law are certainly detrimental to the emotional wellbeing of people in targeted minoritized groups and sanction stigma, bias, and discrimination by the general population.

In offering this book as a way to consider how best to support students and educators who experience Madness and/or distress, I am alarmed by the laws that prohibit discussions of emotional regulation. Discourse in music education regarding these laws urges music educators to consider their context and respond with a pedagogical approach appropriate to the current local political climate. Such micro acts of resistance and subversion are vital, but larger-scale activism, organizing, and resistance is necessary to move toward genuine liberation for all. Participants in this book suggested powerful ways to support people experiencing Madness and/or distress in music education, with full acknowledgment of the impact of oppression and other contextual factors. I call for the wholesale repeal of punitive legislation. Robust teaching about issues of race, privilege, and LGBTQ+ identities as well as explicit education about the full range of structurally oppressive systems that target minoritized groups is imperative for all populations, and particularly for those who are minoritized and multiply minoritized. This teaching must occur alongside ways to support emotional wellbeing across all intersectional identities. To prohibit doing so at minimum exacerbates or creates distress among people who are minoritized across the full range of identity spectrums, and at worst becomes life-threatening. Repealing such legislation is thus imperative to cultivating emotional wellbeing informed by history, power relations, and an intersectional understanding.

## Notes

1 See https://casel.org.
2 Canada released Calls to Action from the Truth and Reconciliation Commission in 2015. Indigenous history is now taught in schools including the history of residential schools. Notably, in Ontario, Doug Ford cancelled the creation of Indigenous curriculum at the beginning of his term in office as premier of the province (Crawley, 2018).
3 See https://features.hrw.org/features/features/lgbt_laws/ and www.equaldex.com.

## References

Ash, L. (2020, September 21). Inside Poland's 'LGBT-free zones'. BBC News. www.bbc.com/news/stories-54191344

Associated Press. (2013, June 30). Russia passes anti-gay-law. The Guardian. www.theguardian.com/world/2013/jun/30/russia-passes-anti-gay-law

Blackwell, T. (2021, July 31). Why residential schools in U.S. have remained part of the country's buried past. National Post. https://nationalpost.com/news/why-residential-schools-in-u-s-have-remained-part-of-the-countrys-buried-past

Brown, L. (2019). Indigenous young people, disadvantage and the violence of settler colonial education policy and curriculum. *Journal of Sociology*, 55(1), 54–71. https://doi.org/10.1177/1440783318794295

Crawley, M. (2018, July 9). Ontario cancels curriculum rewrite that would boost Indigenous content. CBC News. www.cbc.ca/news/canada/toronto/ontario-education-truth-and-reconciliation-commission-trc-1.4739297

Dekel, M. (2021, June 1). Poland's current memory politics are rewriting history. Boston Review. www.bostonreview.net/articles/polands-current-memory-politics-are-rewriting-history/

Donadio, R. (2018, February 8). The dark consequences of Poland's new Holocaust law. The Atlantic. www.theatlantic.com/international/archive/2018/02/poland-holocaust-law/552842/

Nicholson, E. (2021, July 9). Hungary bans LGBTQ content from schools, but some teachers say they will defy it. *National Public Radio (NPR)*. www.npr.org/2021/07/09/1014744317/anti-lgbtq-law-in-hungary-will-hurt-the-people-it-claims-to-protect-critics-say

Rédaction Africanews with Agencies. (2023, March 10). Kenyan launches LGBTQ crackdown in schools. Africa News. www.africanews.com/2023/03/10/kenyan-launches-lgbtq-crackdown-in-schools/

Salvador, K., Abramo, J. M., Bernard, C. F., Bohn, A., Confredo, D. A., Cuthbertson, A., Deemer, R., Dilworth, R., Hall, S. N., Helton, B. C., Martin, A., McBride, N. R., McKoy, C. L., Menon, S., Sánchez-Gatt, L., Sauerland, W. R., Shaw, R. D., & Weigand, S. (2023). *Divisive concept laws and music education: A report for the National Association for Music Education*. National Association for Music Education. https://nafme.org/wp-content/uploads/2023/05/NAfME-Divisive-Concepts-Laws-and-Music-Education-Report-2023.pdf

Singh, K. (2023, August 10). US suicide deaths reached record high in 2022, CDC data shows. Reuters. https://www.reuters.com/world/us/us-suicide-deaths-reached-record-high-2022-cdc-data-shows-2023-08-11/

Skerrett, M. (2019). Colonialism, Māori early childhood, language, and the curriculum. In E. A. McKinley & L. T. Smith (Eds.), *Handbook of Indigenous education* (pp. 483–504). Springer.

Snyder, T. (2021, June 29). The war on history is a war on democracy. *The New York Times Magazine*. www.nytimes.com/2021/06/29/magazine/memory-laws.html

Sverdlov, L. (2020, September 15). Russian teachers ordered to track, report LGBTQ students to gov't – report. The Jerusalem Post. www.jpost.com/international/russian-teachers-ordered-to-track-report-lgbtq-students-to-govt-report-642332

Thunig, a. (2019, July 4). Even education has been used as a weapon of white supremacy in Australia. The Guardian. www.theguardian.com/commentisfree/2019/jul/05/even-education-has-been-used-as-a-weapon-of-white-supremacy-in-australia

Trilling, D. (2020, October 23). Why is the UK government suddenly targeting 'critical race theory'? The Guardian. www.theguardian.com/commentisfree/2020/oct/23/uk-critical-race-theory-trump-conservatives-structural-inequality

Truth and Reconciliation Commission of Canada. (2015). *Truth and reconciliation commission of canada: Calls to action*. https://ehprnh2mwo3.exactdn.com/wp-content/uploads/2021/01/Calls_to_Action_English2.pdf

Wilson, J. (2021, July 9). Australia's absurd moral panic around critical race theory aims to silence demands for justice. The Guardian. www.theguardian.com/commentisfree/2021/jul/10/australias-absurd-moral-panic-around-critical-race-theory-aims-to-silence-demands-for-justice

# Notes on Sources

I gratefully acknowledge the *Bulletin of the Council for Research in Music Education* for granting permission to reprint the three vignettes on pp. 24–25 from the following article:

Hess, J. (2022). Sanism and narrative research: Making room for Mad stories. *Bulletin of the Council for Research in Music Education, 234,* 24–44. https://doi.org/10.5406/21627223.234.02

# Index

*Note:* Page numbers in **bold** denote tables, end of chapter notes are denoted by a letter n between page number and note number.

ability: ideology of 57, 58, 59; as property 64
ability profiles 78–81
ableism *see* sanism and ableism
abusive teachers 163–166
affective empathy 102, 103, 104, 262
affirmation approaches 66
affirming pedagogies 200–202
Agamben, G. 37
Ahluwalia, P. 15
Ahmed, S. 17
Americans with Disabilities Act (ADA) 90, 239
ampersand problem 62
Amrein, E. 149, 259
Andrzejewski, A. 7, 248
Annamma, S. A. 61–62
annual reports and reviews 235, 241, 256
Ansdell, G. 145–146, 171, 183, 185, 186, 206
anti-psychiatry movement 35–36
Aronson, J. 254
Ashcroft, B. 15
asset pedagogies 80–81, 94, 260–261
attendance policies 237, 241, 256
attunement 50, 104–105, 106, 181
August (participant) **281**; conceptualizing mental health differences 78–80, 81; disclosure decisions 118; harmful experiences 151, 153–154; policing of distress 217–218; supportive practices 187–188, 190; surveillance in music education 231–232, 233, 234
autonomy, student 197–199
awareness 103–104

Banghart-Broussard, Blaine *see* Blaine (participant)
Barrett, Meghan *see* Meghan (participant)
Bayley, K. 237
Beaupert, F. 37
Beauregard, J. 160
Beck, U. 264
Bentham's Panopticon 238
Beresford, P. 29–30, 35
Bernhard, H. C. 160, 268n10
Biden, Joe 3, 253
Bilge, S. 58
binary thinking, resisting 83–84
bio-medical psychiatric models 30, 35–36, 37–38; *see also* medical model of disability
Birdwell, M. L. N. 237
Black, E. R. 8
Black Lives Matter 220
Blaine (participant) **280**; benefits of neurodivergence 104; conceptualizing mental health differences 76; disability studies models 48, 59; disclosure decisions 124–126; harmful experiences 150, 163; policing of distress 217; supportive practices 182, 186

Blanchard, M. 232, 238
bodyminds concept 47, 49–51, 56, 85
Boulez, P. 14
Bowe, Jillian *see* Jillian (participant)
Brockelman, K. F. 121
Brosnan, L. 37
Brown, B. 5, 83, 102, 117, 150, 152, 153, 154, 164, 165, 183, 184–185, 255
Brune, J. A. 84
Buber, M. 131
Bucura, E. 152, 160
Bull, A. 164
Burstow, B. 36

Campbell, P. 30
Cantón, M. I. 38
Carstairs, G. M. 15
Caruth, C. 199
Castagno, A. E. 226
Castillo-Montoya, M. 279
Cavar, S. 4
Chandler, S. J. 8
Chapman, R. 75, 77
Chatmon, B. N. 138n6
Cheryl (participant) **280**; benefits of neurodivergence 101, 105; conceptualizing mental health differences 82; disability studies models 48–49; disclosure decisions 122; harmful experiences 153, 155; policing of distress 220; representation 133, 134, 136; supportive practices 180–181, 186, 193, 202; surveillance in music education 229–230
Chew, K. 77
Chris (participant) **281**; benefits of neurodivergence 100; conceptualizing mental health differences 76, 80, 86; disability studies models 54; disclosure decisions 117–118; harmful experiences 145, 151, 153; language use 90–92, 94; policing of distress 223–225; supportive practices 179, 180–181, 184, 185, 194–195, 196, 198, 202; surveillance in music education 234
classical ensemble-based music instruction 167–168

Cobbina-Dungy, J. 220
cognitive empathy 102, 104, 262
Cohen, Mary *see* Mary (participant)
Collaborative for Academic, Social, and Emotional Learning (CASEL) framework 39
Collins, P. H. 58
colonial psychiatry 15–16
common humanity perspective 127, 261
communities, social surveillance in 233–234
community, fostering 180–182, 185
community treatment orders 37, 240
community-based approaches to distress 225–226
compassion 101–103, 107–109, 261–262
compassionate empathy 262
competitive culture 147–150, 258–259
complex embodiment model 57–60, 251
composers, with mental health struggles 134–135
contextual factors 37–38, 81–83
contrapuntal methodology 13–17, 266–267, 277
Convention on the Rights of Persons with Disabilities (CRPD) 37, 54
Corrigan, P. W. 29
cosmopolitanism, critical 263–265
Costa, L. 30
course loads 159–160
COVID-19 pandemic 3, 14, 128, 129, 168–169, 253, 278
Cox, P. 124
creativity, music teaching and 109–110
credit loads 159–160
Crenshaw, K. 58
Crichton, P. 29, 32
Crisis Intervention Teams (CITs) 214–215, 221
critical cosmopolitanism 263–265
critical incident reports 224–225
critical movements 35
critical race theory 61, 205, 251, 289
critical realist approach 65–67, 251
Csikszentmihalyi, M. 189
cultural competence 222
cultural humility 222–223, 225
cultural model of disability 60–61, 251

culture of music education *see* toxic culture of music education
culture of shame 117–118
curiosity 106

Daley, A. 34–35
dangerousness 34–35, 231, 234
Davis, A. Y. 226
Davis, L. J. 57
de Groot, R. 14, 266
De Quadros, A. 149, 259
*Dear Evan Hansen* (musical) 129, 162
defunding the police 220–221
Delanty, G. 264–265
Desmet, Lizabeth *see* Lizabeth (participant)
Dhawan, N. 263–264
diagnostic language 87–90
DiGeronimo, T. F 4
disability: bodyminds concept 47, 49–51, 56, 85; mental health differences as 47–51
disability studies models 51–71, 250–251; complex embodiment 57–60, 251; critical realist approach 65–67, 251; cultural model 60–61, 251; DisCrit 61–65, 251, 264, 267; medical model 5, 51–53, 55; social confluence 67–69, 78, 251; social model 53–56, 66, 250–251
disclosure decisions 115–128, 136–138, 252–255; disclosing 125–128; intersectionality and 136, 254; masking 124–125, 159; as normalizing and destigmatizing 119–120; not disclosing 121–124; privilege and 254; shame and 116–118, 254–255; stigma and 115, 116–118, 120–121, 136, 253, 254–255
discrimination 115; *see also* stigma
DisCrit model 61–65, 251, 264, 267
discussion-based classes 158–159
dissociation 157, 173n8
distress, use of term 4–5
Dobbs, T. L. 51, 53, 55, 58–59
Dolmage, J. T. 231
DuBois, W. E. B. 5

Elliott, D. J. 189
Elraz, H. 116

Emma (participant) **283**; benefits of neurodivergence 108; conceptualizing mental health differences 86; disability studies models 56; disclosure decisions 119; harmful experiences 152–153, 159, 162; policing of distress 221; representation 129, 130, 253; supportive practices 181, 183, 193, 204
emotion processing 203–205
empathy 101–103, 255, 261–262
empowering song approach 149, 259
ensembles 167–168, 188
epistemic injustice 27–28, 248–249
epistemic justice 30–32, 249
Erevelles, N. 64
Erskine, R. G. 104, 181
Evans, H. D. 120
excarceration 226–227

Fabris, E. 31, 32, 34, 35, 37, 75, 100
failure experiences 153–157
families, social surveillance in 233–234
Farber, B. A. 232, 238
Ferguson, T. J. 83
Fernando, S. 15
fetishization of mental health differences 130–131
Fey, J.-M. 4, 29, 32, 34, 115
flow experiences 189
forced treatment 36–37, 240
Foucault, M. 227–228, 238
Fricker, M. 27–28, 249

Garrido, S. 192
Goffman, E. 71n5, 120–121, 253

Hamilton, A. 229
Hansen, Chris *see* Chris (participant)
harmful experiences 145–172, 257–260; abusive teachers 163–166; competitive culture 147–150, 258–259; failure to meet expectations 153–157; high-stakes performances 168–169; invalidations 161–163; music listening 169–171; perfectionism 150–153, 163, 164, 187; pressure and stress 157–161; Western

classical ensemble-based music instruction 167–168
Harris, C. I. 64
Harris, N. 264–265
Hearing Voices Network 241
help/harm dichotomy 257–260; *see also* harmful experiences; supportive practices
Hendricks, K. S. 81, 102, 261–262, 268n15
hermeneutical injustice 27–28, 249
high energy 110
high-stakes performances 168–169
hospitality, musical 185

identity-first language 93–94
ideology of ability 57, 58, 59
ideology of competition 147–150, 258–259
impression management 120–121
individualism 225–226
Individuals with Disabilities Education Act (IDEA) 90, 163, 229, 239
influential individuals 131–132
Ingram, R. A. 9, 24
injustice, epistemic 27–28, 248–249
internalized sanism 230
intersectionality 58, 71n7; complex embodiment and 58, 59, 60; disclosure decisions and 136, 254; DisCrit model 61–65, 251, 264, 267; in Mad Studies 33–35; policing of distress and 214, 216–217, 226; sanism and 33–34
Interview Protocol Refinement (IPR) framework 279
invalidations, in music education 161–163
invisibility 183
*I-Thou* and *I-It* relationships 131

Jacobs, L. A. 215
jamming 188–190
Jewel 8
Jillian (participant) **280**; benefits of neurodivergence 103–104; disability studies models 54–55, 68; disclosure decisions 122; harmful experiences 148–149, 157–158, 167; language use 90; policing of distress 216, 220–221; supportive practices 183, 190, 197, 202; surveillance in music education 232, 234, 237
Johnson, M. 85

Kadison, R. 4
Kahn, J. H. 105, 192
Kapur, R. L. 15
Kelly, S. 233
King, C. 33
Kinsella, E. A. 26, 28
Kleiber, P. B. 286
Knight, August *see* August (participant)

Lakoff, G. 85
language use 4–5, 24–25, 87–95; diagnostic language 87–90; empowering language choices 93–94; neutral language rooted in difference 91–92; non-diagnostic language 90–91; person-first vs. identity-first language 93–94; whole body health model 92–93
Laura (participant) **282**; benefits of neurodivergence 110; disability studies models 49, 52, 55; disclosure decisions 122, 127; supportive practices 204–205; surveillance in music education 237–238
LeBlanc, S. 26, 28
LeFrançois, B. A. 24, 32, 33
Lester, J. N. 228–229
Liegghio, M. 31
Linton, S. 51
listening to music 169–171, 191–194
Lizabeth (participant) **281**; benefits of neurodivergence 100; conceptualizing mental health differences 77–78, 81–82, 83–84; disability studies models 64–65; harmful experiences 149, 160–161, 168; language use 90; policing of distress 223, 225, 226, 227; representation 129–130, 133, 134, 136; supportive practices 197–198, 199
Love, B. L. 239, 250
Lubet, A. 67, 78, 251

McGrath, C. 151
Mad genius musician stereotype 9

*Mad Matters: A Critical Reader in Canadian Mad Studies* 24
Mad Studies 9, 24–26, 29–40; anti-psychiatry movement and 35–36; contextual factors 37–38; critical movements and 35; critiques of mental health laws 36–37; "in/discipline" of 9, 24; epistemic justice 30–32; foregrounding lived experiences 29–30; intersectionality in 33–35; Madness as a way of knowing 30–32; in music education 39–40; resisting sanism 32–33; terminology 24–25
Madness, use of term 4, 24–25
mandatory reporting 231–232, 238, 240–241, 256
Martin, J. K. 115
Mary (participant) **280**; conceptualizing mental health differences 85; disclosure decisions 122, 123, 126; harmful experiences 149; language use 92; policing of distress 226–227; supportive practices 182, 185, 189, 190–191
masculinity, toxic 135–136, 138n6, 284
masking 124–125, 159
matrix thinking 58
Mead, S. 181
medical model of disability 5, 51–53, 55, 93; *see also* bio-medical psychiatric models
Medina, J. 249
Meena (participant) **282**; benefits of neurodivergence 99, 102; conceptualizing mental health differences 87; disability studies models 53, 63; disclosure decisions 117–118, 127; language use 88; policing of distress 216–217, 222; representation 130–131; supportive practices 181–182, 198, 202, 204
Meghan (participant) **280**; benefits of neurodivergence 108–110; conceptualizing mental health differences 86–87; disability studies models 61; disclosure decisions 127; harmful experiences 151–152, 154, 155–156, 159–160, 168–169; language use 89; policing of distress 218–219; supportive practices 198–199; surveillance in music education 229
mental health differences, benefits 99–111, 261–263; awareness and attunement 103–105; compassion 101–103, 107–109, 261–262; creativity 109–110; curiosity 106; empathy 101–103, 255, 261–262; high energy 110; overinclusiveness 106–107; relationality 101–105, 107–109; self-awareness of needs 105; support of music teaching praxis 106–110
mental health differences, conceptualizing 75–87, 94, 251–252; ability profiles 78–81; asset pedagogies and 80–81, 94, 260–261; contextual factors 81–83; as disability 47–51; metaphors 85–87; neurodiversity paradigm 75, 76–77, 252; nonbinary thinking 83–84; spectrum of difference 77–78, 83–84, 252; as "superpower" 112n4; whole body health model 85
mental health differences, describing 4–5, 24–25, 87–95; diagnostic language 87–90; neutral language rooted in difference 91–92; non-diagnostic language 90–91; person-first vs. identity-first language 93–94; whole body health model 92–93
mental health differences, representation 128–136, 137–138, 252–254; composers and musicians 134–136; influential individuals 131–132; the need to feel seen 132–134; stereotype threat and 254; trendy, romanticized, and fetishized 129–131
mental health laws 36–37
Menzies, R. 24, 220
meritocracy 225–226
metaphors 85–87
Mignolo, W. D. 263, 265
Mills, C. 4, 29, 32, 34, 115
Milner, M. J. 181
Mingus, Charles 8
Mitchell, D. T. 60–61, 65

mood self-regulation 191–193
Morgan, H. 24, 32, 56
motivational empathy 262
Moule, J. 222
Murakami, B. 170, 171
Murray-García, J. 222
music education 3, 5–6; empathy and 103; explicit focus on wellbeing 202–205; Mad Studies in 39–40; neurocosmopolitanism and 265–266; representation in 133–134; *see also* musicking; pedagogical practices; project overview; surveillance and regulation in music education; toxic culture of music education
Music for People 189
music listening 169–171, 191–194
music therapy 169–171, 179, 192, 194
Music Therapy and Harm Model 170, 171
musical hospitality 185
musicians, with mental health struggles 135
musicking 6; alternatives to high-stakes performing 168–169; building relationships 182–183; emotion processing and 203–205; ensembles 167–168, 188; feeling seen and validated 183–186; fostering community 180–182, 185; harmful experiences 145–147, 166–171, 257, 259–260; jamming 188–190; music listening 169–171, 191–194; playing and singing 186–188; relationality and 105, 180–186; songwriting 169, 190–191; supportive practices 186–194, 205–206, 257, 259–260; Western classical ensemble-based music instruction 167–168

National Association for Music Education (NAfME) 145
Neff, K. 127, 261
neurocosmopolitanism 263–266
neurodivergence, benefits 99–111, 261–263; awareness and attunement 103–105; compassion 101–103, 107–109, 261–262; creativity 109–110; curiosity 106; empathy 101–103, 255, 261–262; high energy 110; overinclusiveness 106–107; relationality 101–105, 107–109; self-awareness of needs 105; support of music teaching praxis 106–110
neurodivergence, conceptualizing 75–87, 94, 251–252; ability profiles 78–81; asset pedagogies and 80–81, 94, 260–261; contextual factors 81–83; disability 47–51; metaphors 85–87; neurodiversity paradigm 75, 76–77, 252; nonbinary thinking 83–84; spectrum of difference 77–78, 83–84, 252; as "superpower" 112n4; whole body health model 85
neurodivergence, describing 4–5, 24–25, 87–95; diagnostic language 87–90; neutral language rooted in difference 91–92; non-diagnostic language 90–91; person-first vs. identity-first language 93–94; whole body health model 92–93
neurodivergence, representation 128–136, 137–138, 252–254; composers and musicians 134–136; influential individuals 131–132; the need to feel seen 132–134; stereotype threat and 254; trendy, romanticized, and fetishized 129–131
neurodiversity paradigm 75, 76–77, 252
neuronormativity 84
neutral language 91–92
Nicholas (participant) **283**; benefits of neurodivergence 104–105; conceptualizing mental health differences 82–83; disability studies models 59–60; disclosure decisions 128; language use 89–90, 93; policing of distress 218, 219; supportive practices 184, 187, 196, 200–201; surveillance in music education 233, 236–237
Nichols, J. 71n8
nonbinary thinking 83–84
non-diagnostic language 90–91
normalizing movements 116–117, 120

Oakdale Choir, Iowa 182
Oakley, A. 284

Oliver, M. 54
Olney, M. F. 121
Østerud, K. L. 115–116
overinclusiveness 106–107

Panopticon 238
Patel, L. 277, 287
patriarchy 135–136, 284
Patton, M. Q. 285
Paulo (participant) **283**; benefits of neurodivergence 106–107; disability studies models 50–51, 52–53, 56, 59, 64, 66, 68, 69; disclosure decisions 119–120, 122, 123–124, 126; harmful experiences 156, 161–162, 167; policing of distress 218, 220; representation 132–133; supportive practices 182–183, 189, 202–203; surveillance in music education 233–234, 235–236, 237
Payne, P. D. 160
pedagogical practices: affirming pedagogies 200–202; asset pedagogies 80–81, 94, 260–261; effects of neurodivergence on 106–110; student autonomy 197–199; supportive 194–202; trauma-informed praxis 199–200, 261; Universal Design for Learning (UDL) 106, 110, 195–197, 198, 252, 277–278; *see also* toxic culture of music education
pedagogy of community 180
peer support 117–118, 181–182, 184, 241, 256
perfectionism 150–153, 163, 164, 187
person-centered planning 198
person-first language 93–94
Pilmer, Emma *see* Emma (participant)
playing and singing 186–188
policing of distress 213–227, 238–241; abolition and excarceration 226–227; anti-carceral social work 215–216, 219; community-based approaches 225–226; Crisis Intervention Teams (CITs) 214–215, 221; defunding the police 220–221; intersectionality and 214, 216–217, 226; need for non-police responses 217–220; police reform 221–225; privilege and 216–217, 226; School Resource Officers (SROs) 239; *see also* surveillance and regulation in music education
polyphony 14
Poursanidou, K. D. 24, 31, 33, 35, 36
Powell, S. R. 147, 258–259, 268n11
pressure, in music education 157–161
Price, M. 48, 49–50, 85, 88
privilege 10–11, 75; competition and 148; disclosure decisions and 254; DisCrit model 62–65, 251; in Mad Studies 33–35; policing of distress and 216–217, 226
professional standards 235–237, 241, 256
project overview 6–7; confidentiality 284–285; contrapuntal methodology 13–17, 266–267, 277; data analysis 286–287; feminist approach to interviewing 279–285; focus groups 285–286; interdisciplinary approach 12–13; language use 4–5; from ownership to answerability 277–278, 287; participant selection 278–279; participants 9–12, **280–283**; positionality 7–8; systems focus 12
Prosini, Nicholas *see* Nicholas (participant)

QingYu (participant) **282**; benefits of neurodivergence 101–102, 107–108; conceptualizing mental health differences 78; disability studies models 63, 66–67, 251; disclosure decisions 120, 124; harmful experiences 155, 158–159; language use 89, 93–94; policing of distress 224; supportive practices 179, 185, 193; surveillance in music education 228
Quarrier, N. F. 173n8

Rabinow, P. 264
Radhakrishnan, L. 16
Razack, S. 103
Rebecca (participant) **283**; benefits of neurodivergence 101, 110; disability studies models 47–48; disclosure decisions 122, 126–127; harmful experiences 145, 154–155, 156–157,

Index 301

160, 169; supportive practices 189, 190–191; surveillance in music education 230–231, 235
Redfield Jamison, K. 134–135
registering a disability 228–231
relationality: as benefit of neurodivergence 101–105, 107–109; building relationships 182–183; feeling seen and validated 183–186; fostering community 180–182, 185; musicking and 105, 180–186
representation of mental health differences 128–136, 137–138, 252–254; composers and musicians 134–136; influential individuals 131–132; the need to feel seen 132–134; stereotype threat and 254; trendy, romanticized, and fetishized 129–131
research methods 277–287; data analysis 286–287; feminist approach to interviewing 279–285; focus groups 285–286; from ownership to answerability 277–278, 287; participant selection 278–279
resilience 7, 12
Richerme, L. K. 268n14
Robinson, M. 235
Rodríguez, D. 226
romanticization of mental health differences 129–130
Rosqvist, H. B. 75
Roulston, K. 285, 286
Russo, J. 4, 33, 35

Saarikallio, S. 170, 191–192, 193, 204
safe people 68, 71n8, 124–125
Said, E. W. 13–14, 15–16, 267
Samuels, E. J. 229
sanism and ableism 5, 26–29; defined 8; epistemic injustice 27–28, 248–249; internalized 230; intersectionality and 33–34; resisting 32–33; stereotypes 8–9, 28–29, 32–33; stigma 29, 32–33, 40n6, 48, 51, 55, 59–60; surveillance in music education and 229–230, 235–236, 237, 241, 256–257; *see also* DisCrit model
Sapey, B. 54
scandalizing movements 116–117

schizophrenia 118
School Resource Officers (SROs) 239
self-awareness of needs 105
self-censoring 233, 237
self-compassion 127, 261
self-inventory 198
self-kindness 261
self-naming strategy 61
self-regulation of mood 191–193
self-stigma 29, 40n6
self-surveillance 237–238
Setti, V. P. C. 118
Shakespeare, T. 61, 65–67
shame: abusive teachers and 165; disclosure decisions and 116–118, 254–255; empathy and 255; failure to meet expectations and 153–154, 157; perfectionism and 153
Shimrat, I. 31
Siebers, T. 55, 57–59
Silverman, M. 189
Silverman, M. J. 170
Simmons, D. 39, 268n14
Small, C. 146, 179, 182
Snyder, S. L. 60–61, 65
social aetiology model 34, 38
social confluence model 67–69, 78, 251
social emotional learning (SEL) 39, 268n14
social model of disability 53–56, 66, 250–251
social surveillance 232–235
Solórzano, D. G. 254
songwriting 169, 190–191
Spandler, H. 24, 31, 33, 35, 36
spectrum of difference 77–78, 83–84, 252
Speed, E. 34, 38
Spelman, E. 62
"spoiled identities" 120–121, 253
state of exception 37
Steele, C. M. 254
Steinert, H. 116–117, 120
Stephenson, H. 173n8
stereotype threat 254
stereotypes 8–9, 28–29, 32–33, 253
stigma 29, 32–33, 40n6, 48, 51, 55, 59–60; disclosure decisions and 115, 116–118, 120–121, 136, 253, 254–255

strategic music listening 191–194
stress, in music education 157–161
struggling artist stereotype 8–9
student autonomy 197–199
student welfare 258
Style, E. 132, 133
subalternity 263–264
suicidal ideation, mandatory reporting of 231–232, 238, 256
suicide 3, 135–136
"superpower" 112n4
supportive practices 179–206, 257–260; affirming pedagogies 200–202; building relationships 182–183; discussing mental health openly 202–203; emotion processing 203–205; empowering song approach 149, 259; ensembles 188; feeling seen and validated 183–186; fostering community 180–182, 185; jamming 188–190; music listening 191–194; pedagogical 194–202; peer support 117–118, 181–182, 184, 241, 256; playing and singing 186–188; songwriting 169, 190–191; student autonomy 197–199; trauma-informed pedagogy 199–200, 261; Universal Design for Learning (UDL) 106, 110, 195–197, 198, 252, 277–278
surveillance and regulation in music education 227–241, 255–257; annual reports and reviews 235, 241, 256; attendance policies 237, 241, 256; bureaucracy to register a disability and receive accommodations 228–231; mandatory reporting 231–232, 238, 240–241, 256; professional standards 235–237, 241, 256; self-surveillance 237–238; social surveillance 232–235

Taggart, D. 34, 38
teachers, abusive 163–166
Tervalon, M. 222
testimonial injustice 27
Toth, K. E. 121

toxic culture of music education 146–166, 171–172, 257–260; abusive teachers 163–166; competition 147–150, 258–259; failure to meet expectations 153–157; invalidations 161–163; perfectionism 150–153, 163, 164, 187; pressure and stress 157–161
toxic masculinity 135–136, 138n6, 284
trauma-informed pedagogy 199–200, 261
trendy, mental health differences as 129

Union of Physically Impaired Against Segregation (UPIAS) 53–54
Universal Design for Learning (UDL) 106, 110, 195–197, 198, 252, 277–278
unwanted identities 83
U.S. National Core Arts Standards 183
U.S. Patriot Act (2001) 37

Van Katwyk, T. 34–35
visibility: feeling seen and validated 183–186; *see also* disclosure decisions; representation of mental health differences
Voronka, J. 30
vulnerability 184–185

Walker, N. 5, 76–77, 78, 81, 84, 85, 93, 263, 265, 266
Washington, D. M. 226
Watts-Taffe, S. 201
White, W. L. 36
whiteness: of Mad Studies 33, 34; as property 64; *see also* privilege
Whitfield, Herman, III 213
whole body health model 85, 92–93
Wilson, D. J. 84
Wolframe, P. M. 26
Wristen, B. G. 148

Zhong, QingYu *see* QingYu (participant)

For Product Safety Concerns and Information please contact our EU representative  GPSR@taylorandfrancis.com
Taylor & Francis Verlag GmbH, Kaufingerstraße 24, 80331 München, Germany